something happened

something happened

A Political and Cultural Overview of the Seventies

Edward D. Berkowitz

COLUMBIA UNIVERSITY PRESS   NEW YORK

Columbia University Press
Publishers Since 1893
New York   Chichester, West Sussex

Library of Congress Cataloging-in-Publication Data

Berkowitz, Edward D.
    Something happened : a political and cultural overview of the seventies /
Edward D. Berkowitz.
        p. cm.
    Includes bibliographical references and index.
    ISBN 978–0–231–12494–2 (cloth : alk. paper)—ISBN 978–0–231–12495–9 (pbk. : alk. paper)—
    ISBN 978–0–231–50051–7 (electronic)
        1. United States—Politics and government—1969–1974. 2. United States—
Politics and government—1974–1977. 3. United States—Politics and government—
1977–1981. 4. United States—Social conditions—1960–1980. 5. Nineteen seventies.
6. Political culture—United States—History—20th century. 7. Popular culture—
United States—History—20th century. I. Title.

E855.B37 2006
973.924—dc22

2005050739

♾ *Columbia University Press books are printed on permanent and durable acid-free paper.*

Printed in the United States of America

c 10 9 8 7 6 5 4
p 10 9 8 7 6 5 4 3 2 1

For my Father, Monroe Berkowitz,
a source of love, support, and uncommon wisdom.

Contents

Introduction   1

1. Nixon, Watergate, and Presidential Scandal   12

2. Vietnam and Its Consequences   32

3. Running Out of Gas: The Economic Downturn and Social Change   53

4. The Frustrations of Gerald Ford   71

5. Congress and Domestic Policy in the Age of Gerald Ford   84

6. Jimmy Carter and the Great American Revival   104

7. The Rights Revolution   133

8. The Me Decade and the Turn to the Right   158

9. The Movies as Cultural Mirror   178

10. Television and the Reassurance of the Familiar   198

11. The End of the Seventies   219

Notes   235
Selected Bibliography   259
Acknowledgments   265
Index   267

something happened

Introduction

The nineteen seventies, considered as an informal era rather than as a formal decade, began during 1973 and lasted until Ronald Reagan assumed the presidency in 1981. During 1973 America's involvement in the Vietnam War ended, and the oil crisis that would usher in an economic recession started. In that same year, the vice president of the United States resigned from office, and the president faced a political crisis that would lead to his resignation in August 1974. Taken together, these events ended the self-confident period that had prevailed after the Second World War and marked the start of something new. In this new era, a wide range of Americans—Democrats and Republicans, conservatives and liberals, blacks and whites, men and women—questioned the commonly held assumptions of the postwar era.

The fact that the economy deteriorated during the seventies caused people to lose faith in the politicians and economists who were in charge of managing it. Between 1970 and 1973, the unemployment rate never rose above 6 percent, and the inflation rate peaked at 6.2 percent. Between 1974 and 1981, the unemployment rate never went below 5 percent, and the inflation rate reached 7 percent or higher in 1974, 1975, and every year between 1978 and 1981.[1] What economists called stagflation—the simultaneous appearance of high prices and high unemployment—had become a fact of American life. Professional economists, who had been summoned to Washington after the Second World War and put in charge of advising the president on the management of the economy, emerged as heroes in the sixties. Their professional tools gave them the ability to fine-tune the economy so that growth became the norm and the fear of depression receded. After 1973, however, the economy developed an immunity to the economists' medicine. The prevailing theories no longer predicted economic performance.

The oil shocks jolted the economy and impaired its functioning. Between 1967 and 1973, America's oil imports nearly tripled in volume, and the nation became more dependent on foreign oil, much of it from the Arabian gulf. In October 1973, the nations in the gulf region raised the price of their oil by 70 percent. Then they withheld oil from the United States to protest America's support for Israel in its war with Egypt.[2] In the panic that ensued, the nation's drivers waited in long lines for expensive gasoline. Americans felt themselves to be at the mercy of hostile foreign powers.

In the past, the United States might have disciplined the oil-producing countries in the Middle East through the threat of war. In 1973 and again at the end of the decade, that option lacked the force it might have had because of the nation's experience in Vietnam. The United States had intervened in that country's civil war and failed to alter the outcome. President Lyndon Johnson had widened the nation's commitment to the Vietnam War in 1965. Three years later American involvement in Vietnam reached its peak. Between 1969 and 1973, President Nixon, in a halting and often painful process, disengaged America from Vietnam. At the beginning of 1973, the last Americans left Vietnam, but the South Vietnamese carried on the battle alone. When the war finally ended in 1975, Congress refused to allow President Gerald Ford to send American soldiers back to Vietnam. The war concluded with the conquest of South Vietnam by North Vietnam and with the reversal of the interventionist policy that had prevailed a decade earlier. The result dampened the nation's confidence in its political and military leaders and made liberals and conservatives wary of military adventures abroad. The self-confidence of the postwar era that had emboldened the United States to fight the Cold War around the world ebbed. Important foreign policy initiatives of the early seventies, such as the effort to achieve detente with the Soviet Union, came under increasing attack after 1972.

In the postwar era, the nation looked to its presidents for leadership and accorded the office a great deal of respect. That situation changed in 1973 with the Watergate scandal. Reelected in a landslide in 1972, President Richard Nixon came close to impeachment and resigned in disgrace in 1974. Using funds raised for his reelection, the president conducted a private and illegal vendetta against his enemies. The president's men broke into the office of a psychiatrist to uncover damaging evidence about the author of a study of the Vietnam War. The president sanctioned the use of disruptive tactics in the 1972 election, such as bugging the headquarters of the Democratic National Committee. Nixon's taped conversations, which his political adversaries forced him to make public, caused him to seem both vindictive and petty. Through all of these actions, President Nixon violated the postwar image of the coolly competent national leader and, in so doing, undermined the institution of the presidency itself at just the moment when the nation faced unprecedented challenges at home and abroad.

The Legacy of the Sixties

The scandal that engulfed President Nixon, the oil crisis, the recession caused by the oil shock to the economy, and the loss of the Vietnam War all caused Americans to rethink the assumptions that had guided public policy in the postwar era. Legislative activity reached a peak in 1965 when Congress passed civil-rights, federal aid to education, and health-insurance laws that were among the most important pieces of domestic legislation in American history. Between 1965 and 1972, Congress built on those foundations. Then the window for the expansion of the welfare state closed. In 1972 Congress approved two major laws expanding Social Security and Medicare and initiating an ambitious new federal welfare program for the elderly and the disabled. At the time, both Republicans and Democrats believed that further expansion of the federal government's power and in particular a national health insurance program to cover people of all ages would inevitably follow. Despite frequent discussion of welfare reform and national health insurance after 1973, however, the talk never turned into action. Although social-welfare expenditures continued to grow, in part because the level of key social benefits such as Social Security was linked to the inflation rate, the federal social welfare programs created between 1973 and 1981 as often as not marked efforts to constrain the growth of the welfare state rather than to expand it.

During the sixties, the cause of black civil rights enjoyed widespread political support, particularly in the northern states. Postwar America was not free of racial tensions, even in places far removed from the Deep South, as conflicts in such places as Detroit and the South Gate community on the southern fringe of Los Angeles demonstrated.[3] Yet these subterranean conflicts failed to derail the national cause of civil-rights legislation. In 1965, in one of the epochal legislative achievements of the sixties, Congress passed the Voting Rights Act, the second of the three major civil-rights laws created in that decade. Northern liberal politicians and many of the voters who voted for them in record numbers in 1964 regarded racial segregation in the south as an anachronism in a growing national economy and as a blot on the nation's image during the Cold War. Solving the problem involved overcoming the resistance of an entrenched group of southern congress-men who, as beneficiaries of a one-party system, had accrued seniority that gave them the power to block legislation. Once that obstacle was removed, as it was after the death of President John F. Kennedy and the election of 1964, the force of law would end discrimination and allow blacks to join whites in the expanding economy.

The hopeful legacy began to sour after 1972. In a sense, the Voting Rights Act of 1965 backfired on its Democratic sponsors. By facilitating the participation of African Americans in the electoral process in the South, it hastened the growth of a two-party system in the South and strengthened the Republican party's base in presidential elections. Between 1932 and 1964, the Republicans won only two of nine presidential elections. After that, the Republicans defeated the Democrats in seven of the ten presiden-tial elections.

Key domestic legislation also produced adverse outcomes related to civil rights. The much-heralded Elementary and Secondary Education Act of 1965, which brought substantial federal funds to local school districts, seemed to do little to improve public schools in the nation's cities in the period from 1973 to 1981. Instead, violent battles broke out over busing stu-dents from one section of the city to another in order to create racial bal-ance in city schools. The result was a mass exodus of those students who could afford to leave. Predominantly white schools became black schools without ever achieving the desired goal of racial integration. Not just bus-ing, a judicial remedy to the segregation problem in education, but also affirmative action, a bureaucratic elaboration on the employment provi-sions of the 1964 Civil Rights Act, created controversy. As the economy crumbled, majority whites resented governmental efforts to come to the aid of blacks.

Hence, a decade after the widely acclaimed passage of key education, health-insurance, and civil-rights laws, the majority of America's voters—the ones who reelected Richard Nixon by a landslide in 1972—believed that the laws had made things worse rather than better and that policy-makers needed to come up with new approaches in all of these areas. If the sixties were the age of "great dreams," the seventies were a time of rude awakenings.[4]

The Historiography of the Seventies

That basic proposition framed the way in which historians initially viewed the seventies. One school of thought proclaimed the existence of a lazy, apathetic, narcissistic, self-absorbed seventies. In this version, the sixties were an era of frenetic political activity. By way of contrast, it "seemed like nothing happened" during the seventies.[5] People rejected the sense of social purpose that characterized the sixties and turned inward to create what journalist Tom Wolfe famously described as the "me decade."[6]

The nothing-happened, me-decade school of historians wrote close to the events of the era. Inevitably, revisionism set in as time passed. A later school of thought holds that the seventies reversed the great dreams of the sixties but in a positive way that led to the great American revival in the 1980s. To reach this conclusion, conservatives wrote of Ronald Reagan in the way that liberals had once written of Franklin Roosevelt. Arthur Schlesinger Jr. made the middle third of the twentieth century the age of Roosevelt; conservatives, for their part, appropriated the seventies as an important part of the age of Reagan. Schlesinger wrote about a crisis of the old order that took place in the 1920s and paved the way for the New Deal in the 1930s.[7] For some contemporary historians, the crisis of the 1970s was the crisis of liberalism that produced Reagan's conservative revival.[8] The work of these historians reflects changes in attitudes toward conservatism in the intellectual community. In the 1950s, following the lead of Richard Hofstadter, mainstream historians attributed a "paranoid style" to conservative politics and believed that liberalism, in Lionel Trilling's words, was the country's "sole intellectual tradition."[9] Those who wrote toward the end of the century, when conservative politics had once again entered the American mainstream, had to revise their opinions.

In a final transformation, yet another interpretive strain makes the seventies out to be an important era in their own right. In this view, the seventies were more than a reaction to the excesses of the sixties or a preview of the global economy that would dominate the eighties and nineties. What exactly they were remained somewhat vague, however. For the conservative David Frum, the seventies were the true sixties—the time in which America took on the trappings of informal dress and loose morals.[10] If Frum eyed these changes with regret, feminist author Ruth Rosen described the era as "arguably the most intellectually vital and exciting" for American women, producing "an amazing array of revelations and changes in social, political, and public thought and policy."[11] Thus, women had their sixties in the seventies. In these and other ways, writers on the subject transform the seventies into the period that best explained the emergence of modern America. One can learn "how we got here," in Frum's phrase, by studying the seventies. In the seventies, according to Bruce Schulman, who offers a balanced and perceptive account of the era, America got made over, and "its economic outlook, political ideology, cultural assumptions, and fundamental social arrangements changed."[12]

The Seventies and the Crisis of Competence

So how can one best characterize the seventies? The era marked the end of a postwar consensus that applied to how America was governed and how its economy was managed. At the heart of the consensus lay an optimistic faith in professional expertise as a way to solve social problems and as a catalyst for progress. Economists learned how to manage the economy to permit private markets to function but to eliminate many of the shocks and hazards inherent in private enterprise. The government successfully balanced freedom and security. A growing stock of knowledge contributed to progress. Medical researchers eradicated polio and other dangerous diseases. Engineers programmed a complex mission that enabled man to walk on the moon. These acclaimed activities by professionals peaked in the early seventies at the point where American prosperity reached a relative maximum. Beginning in 1973, people's faith in their political and professional leaders waned.

Polling data, although always slippery and contradictory, documented this loss of faith. In 1975 nearly 70 percent of the people polled by a national opinion survey agreed that "over the last ten years, this country's leaders have consistently lied to the people." According to the Harris poll, public confidence in the medical establishment dropped from 73 to 42 percent between 1966 and 1975. As Peter Carroll has written, "The faith in doctors and lawyers, the skepticism about corporate leaders, the omnipresent distrust of politicians—all produced a spreading disillusionment about the competence of the dominant institutions of society."[13]

This crisis of competence defined the seventies and produced major changes in the ways in which Americans viewed their world. The president became just another flawed individual in a society with many failings, and the presidency lost power to the legislative branch of government. That loss weakened the president's power to act as commander in chief. In the postwar era, the nation twice went to war in Asia to show its dedication to the Cold War. During the seventies, Congress prevented the president from engaging in such military adventures.

medical advancement

In the postwar era, America maintained the world's strongest economy. During the seventies, the nation's position of international preeminence weakened. A nation known for its exports began to run large trade deficits and to import oil, a critically important raw material. When the price of this foreign oil rose, it produced a crisis in the economy for which neither politicians nor economic experts had ready answers. Postwar models failed to comprehend the economic realities of the seventies.

In the seventies, as the economy deteriorated, households found it necessary to increase their supply of labor in order to maintain their standard of living. The result was a revolution in labor expectations that accelerated the mass entrance of women into the labor force. This revolution produced changes that rippled through society. More women elected to end their marriages and get divorced. Women had fewer children in the baby-bust seventies than in the baby boom that followed the war. More men and women chose not to marry.

THE RIGHTS REVOLUTION

In these and many other ways, the optimistic sixties gave way to the pessimistic seventies. Yet, for many Americans, the seventies were a time of great hope. For example, the revolution in black civil rights took place in the sixties, but a much more broad-based civil-rights movement, affecting far more people, occurred in the seventies. As part of the rights revolution of the seventies, a series of laws, judicial rulings, and executive decisions produced major changes in American life. In the sixties, people talked about women's liberation. In the seventies, the nation debated an equal-rights law for women, the Supreme Court approved abortion on demand, and the nation's schools restructured their programs to end disparities in the treatment of boys and girls. In the sixties, homosexuality remained a psychiatric disability that many people believed required therapeutic treatment. In the seventies, gay rights became a matter of public record. In the sixties, people with disabilities had little sense of themselves as members of a minority group. In the seventies, the federal government required all of its programs to be accessible to the disabled. The rights revolution, in turn, led to changes in American politics on both the right and the left. Affirmative action and busing were sixties concepts but seventies issues.

Debates over detente, abortion, disability rights, homosexuality, bilingual education, and disability rights were also defining characteristics of the seventies. As America tacked first left and then right, the debates acquired a particular urgency. Because Watergate took place in a Republican administration, it bolstered the political fortunes of the Democrats. As a consequence, the era began not with a move toward the right, as is commonly supposed, but rather with a major Democratic victory in the Congressional elections of 1974. Liberals contributed to Jimmy Carter's victory over Gerald Ford in 1976, reversing or at least amending the results of the 1972 election. As the era's second major recession engulfed Carter, the country was posed for a revival of interest in conservative ideas and ultimately for the Reagan revolution of 1981.

MEDICINE AND THE CHANGES OF THE SEVENTIES

An important strain of seventies thought involved a revolt against the postwar orthodoxy that could not be comprehended in conventional political terms. The field of medicine might serve as an example of a distinct change between the postwar era, which culminated in the sixties, and the seventies. In the sixties, a key problem of public policy was to guarantee the access of the elderly to hospitals. In the seventies, the policy discussion shifted to how to contain hospital costs. Health-maintenance organizations gained popularity in the seventies because of their perceived economic efficiency, in particular their ability to limit the number and duration of hospital stays.

The rights revolution of the seventies also affected developments in medicine. Minority groups made major efforts to gain power in their interactions with doctors. Leaders of the disability-rights movement complained, for example, that doctors treated them as patients to be cured rather than as autonomous individuals. Those in the vanguard of the movement for women's rights expressed "frustration and anger" toward doctors who were "condescending, paternalistic, and non-informative." They sought to remove the act of childbirth from the "medical maze."[14] As a consequence, more than one hundred free-standing birth centers became operational between 1974 and 1984. [15]

This feminist critique of the way in which women were forced to deliver their babies transformed the most important event in the life cycle. What had once been the realm of the professional obstetrician—with the prospective fathers imperiously removed to a distant waiting room, nervously reading magazines, fingering the cigars in their pockets, and counting out dimes to use in the pay phone down the hall—became an integrated space.

Fathers coached mothers on how to get through the process without taking any possibly deleterious medicine that might make the baby less alert and lower the test scores that measured the baby's condition at birth.

Doctors advised throughout the process but left more of the choices up to the prospective parents. Nurses, who were often women, saw themselves as the family's advocates in the complex negotiations with the doctors, who were often men.

This development coincided with repeated demands by feminists to be able to terminate their pregnancies, so that having a baby became a matter of personal choice rather than a biological inevitability. As some women pushed for abortion on demand, others insisted that the act be prosecuted as murder. Neither side saw the medical profession as an ally. Women on the left and women on the right objected to aspects of medical practice.

In general, people felt more free to challenge doctors in the seventies that they had in the postwar era. A key indicator of this trend came in the realm of medical malpractice. In the seventies, doctors became more accountable for their actions, and more people from outside the profession began to scrutinize their activities. In this setting, people learned how to sue doctors for malpractice. Juries, sensitive barometers of community grievances, transformed legal torts into financial settlements. The costs of practicing medicine thus increased because doctors needed to pay more for malpractice insurance. In the middle of the decade, the major malpractice-insurance companies tripled their rates.[16] "Clearly, the existing malpractice system has become a national problem," wrote a doctor associated with the National Academy of Sciences to a foundation executive in 1975.[17]

In the post war era, people grew accustomed to medical miracles. Richard Nixon invoked this positive tradition when he declared war on cancer in 1971. Despite the lavish attention showered upon the disease, no dramatic breakthrough, no equivalent of the polio shots, occurred in the seventies. Lewis Thomas, the popular medical writer, blamed inflated expectations. Nixon naively believed that "all, or nearly all, of the already important ideas are already in hand, and that given the right kind of administration and organization, the hard problems can be solved."[18] Thomas realized that it was not so simple.

Thomas, a medical doctor and member of the medical research establishment, joined a growing chorus of skeptics who lacked his educational pedigree. According to historian James Patterson, the seventies "witnessed an unprecedented flowering of popular doubts concerning science, professional expertise, orthodox medicine, and the priests of the Cancer church." When the popular actor Steve McQueen got cancer, he turned to the use of laetrile, a folk medicine made from the pits of apricots, rather than go through the prescribed cancer regimen. He died anyway.[19]

In a major reversal of the postwar wisdom, people looked beyond medicine to cure their cancers and other ills. Some turned to faith and folk remedies. Others emphasized prevention—taking care of oneself through diet, exercise, and salutary habits as a means of evading medical treatment. In the seventies, a nation of people in their twenties who were gathering the paunch that so often accompanied the onset of middle age discovered jogging. Jim Fixx's *Complete Book of Running* became a bestseller in 1977. Seven years later, Fixx, a man in his fifties, dropped dead of a heart attack while running. Neither laetrile nor jogging guaranteed immortality, yet in the seventies many people tried them anyway.

The trend toward self-help received the endorsement of some of the nation's most important leaders and produced great concern among many academic doctors. In 1978 Joseph Califano, who served as secretary of health, education, and welfare for Jimmy Carter, issued a major report to "help Americans fight against obesity, alcoholism, and many other costly everyday health problems." The *Washington Post* editorialized that "people can do far more to improve their health by acting themselves than they can by waiting for symptoms and then going to doctors."[20] A group of academic, research-oriented doctors charged that Califano was doing the nation a disservice by emphasizing "individual responsibility for health way out of balance with governmental and social responsibilities." The debate illustrated the negotiations over where the line between individual and social responsibility should lie. If the sixties was an era of government grants to fix social problems and regulatory laws to assure proper behavior, the seventies was a time in which people rediscovered the power of the marketplace and individual responsibility and raised questions about the effectiveness of regulation to change behavior in a desired way.

A Plan of Attack

To get at these and other changes, this book explores the political, economic, and cultural history of the period between 1973 and 1981 in detail. It contains more details about politics, political economy, and public policy than do previous accounts of this period, yet it also tries to incorporate comments on cultural developments, such as the television shows and movies of the era. In particular, the book uses culture as a means of exploring how Americans understood the changes of the time and how they reconciled the present with the past.

The first part of the book considers the triggers that launched the era: Watergate, Vietnam, the oil crisis, and recession. The second part explores how Presidents Ford and Carter tried, and largely failed, to cope with the challenges of the seventies. In the process, the conventional wisdom of the postwar decades became discredited, but no prevailing philosophy or idea arose to take its place. The third part of the book looks at the seemingly anomalous rights revolution. It examines the effects of this revolution on America and demonstrates how some Americans took steps to protect themselves from what they saw as its negative effects. The fourth part of the book turns to culture. It discusses movies that offer perceptive commentary on changes in American life in the 1970s and how the television industry reacted to these changes while trying to maintain its status as a form of mass culture accessible to everyone.

The intended audience is people for whom the seventies represents the distant past. The hope is that having lived in the seventies is not a prerequisite for understanding them, a feeling that so many books on this subject project. Instead, history can both re-create and interpret experience. If the project is successful, readers will see how the seventies altered the postwar wisdom but also arrive at their own understanding of the era's significance.

I
Nixon, Watergate, and Presidential Scandal

During the seventies, America devoured its presidents in what journalist Max Lerner described as fits of "tribal cannibalism."[1] Richard Nixon, the first of the era's presidents, sent the institution on a downward spiral. The Watergate scandal that resulted from his misuse of power became one of the era's signature events. It altered the course of electoral politics after 1973, enabled the legislative branch of government to gain power at the expense of the executive branch, increased the level of scrutiny of a president's private behavior, and made Americans more cynical about the government's ability to improve their well-being. Watergate also changed the career paths of politicians who aspired to the presidency. Beginning in 1976, governors, rather than senators, became president.

THE LIFE OF RICHARD NIXON

Richard Nixon, an intensely private man, lived one of the most public lives in American history. He was perhaps the last of the twentieth century politicians whose life spooled like a newsreel across the public imagination. Born in 1913, he spent his entire political career in the postwar, rather than the New Deal, era. The southern California of his youth resembled the pages of a John Steinbeck novel more than it reflected the glamour of nearby Hollywood. Still, Nixon found the means to attend college, a fact that set him apart from most people his age. Graduating in 1934 from Whittier College, a Quaker school located near his hometown, he earned a scholarship to the newly established Duke Law School, finishing third in his class in 1937. At

Duke he lived in such humble surroundings that he showered in the school gym. His situation reinforced his view of life as a struggle. He practiced law in Whittier before the war brought him briefly to Washington, D.C., for a job at the Office of Price Administration. In the Navy, he served as a transport officer in the South Pacific. Discharged in 1946, he returned home to run for Congress in the California district that included Whittier. Like John F. Kennedy, another Navy veteran and another distinguished postwar politician, he became a member of the Eightieth Congress, part of the insurgency that produced a Republican majority in both houses. It would happen only once more in Nixon's political career.[2]

When the Eightieth Congress convened, Nixon had just turned thirty-three. His diligence in pursuing Alger Hiss, accused of being a communist and a Russian spy, made him a household name in his first term. The case became an important touchstone for his career. As people like the president of Harvard fell back on personal ties and a sense of class solidarity to defend Harvard Law School graduate Alger Hiss, Nixon worked around the clock, often in isolation, to expose him. Nixon, it seemed, saw himself as an outsider, despite his spectacular success and important ties to influential citizens and institutions, such as the *Los Angeles Times*, in southern California. In time, he would win two presidential elections, and his daughter would marry Dwight Eisenhower's grandson. None of that sapped Nixon's sense of grievance. Characteristically, victory often made him feel let down and caused him to isolate himself rather than celebrate with others.[3]

As he smoldered, he advanced to the head of his class in the Republican Party. He climbed the steep step from the House to the Senate in 1950, a faster rise than that enjoyed by political wunderkinder John F. Kennedy and Lyndon Johnson, both of whom labored in relative obscurity in the House longer than Nixon. Nixon became an important postwar politician in part because he came from a state rich in electoral votes and, as someone newly on the scene, carried no baggage from the New Deal era in which the Republican Party had been viewed as the party of privilege, a creature of the economic royalists. When he delivered the California delegation to Eisenhower in 1952, Eisenhower and his backers thought highly enough of Nixon to put him on the national ticket.[4]

Then came another of the signature events in his career. When Nixon was accused of maintaining a secret fund to spend for political purposes, Eisenhower took his time coming to his defense. Eisenhower's emotional distance reinforced Nixon's sense that he would have to face adversity alone. Nixon saved himself by going on television and delivering a speech that appealed to the sympathy of the American people. Preparing for the speech,

Nixon sank into himself, just as he had during the Hiss case, staying up all night and seeking solitude. "Sleepless nights," he later wrote in a revealing autobiography, "to the extent that the body can take them, can stimulate creative mental activity."[5] He chose to speak in an empty auditorium, dead tired but summoning up reserves of energy that came from the challenge of the situation. The "Checkers" speech, in which Nixon mentioned a dog that his family had received as a gift, attracted a huge audience of sixty million television viewers.

The next time Nixon acquired such a large audience came in his ill-fated first presidential debate with John F. Kennedy in 1960. Forced to perform in the same room as Kennedy, with the studio warmer than Nixon would have preferred, he began to sweat, smearing the makeup he used to cover his heavy beard and making him look haggard rather than coolly in command. His appearance projected the wrong image in a contest that marked a personal choice as much as it reflected the power of his party to mobilize voters. Once again, Nixon felt betrayed by those he thought should have supported him. Eisenhower made personal appearances on Nixon's behalf only at the end of the campaign. Nor did Nixon believe that Norman Vincent Peale and other right-leaning Protestants helped him by calling attention to Kennedy's Catholicism. Once again, the establishment betrayed him.

Nixon moved to New York and went into the private law practice. Remarkably, he worked himself back into contention as a viable political candidate by 1968. He projected himself as a cooler, wiser man than had run in 1960, and this time he won. It helped that the Republicans had no obvious candidate to run since the party's previous standard bearer, Barry Goldwater, had been annihilated by Lyndon Johnson in 1964. Goldwater ran squarely into the flood of sympathy for the Democrats after JFK's assassination less than a year before the election. Democrats portrayed him as someone who would have an unsteady grip on the nuclear trigger, a dangerous man. Nixon was, by contrast, a realist and someone who might get the nation back on track after the seeming disarray of the tumultuous events of 1968.

THE ELECTION OF 1968

As befit the self-confident postwar era, both of the presidential candidates in 1968 were former senators who had served as vice presidents in previous administrations. Democrat Hubert Humphrey, Johnson's vice president since 1965 and the former Minneapolis mayor and Minnesota senator, had lost the nomination to John F. Kennedy in 1960. He received the vice-presidential nomination in 1964 in part because President Johnson could not abide Robert Kennedy and did not want to give him a leg up to the White House. Humphrey won the 1968 nomination as a replacement for Johnson after LBJ decided not to run.

In a close election, Nixon defeated Hubert Humphrey by more than 100 electoral votes, sweeping all of the states west of the Mississippi except for Minnesota, Texas, Washington, and Hawaii. With the exception of Texas, a border state and the home of Lyndon Johnson, Humphrey failed to carry a single state in the Deep South, a region that, until 1948, had stood solidly behind the Democratic Party in presidential elections. In 1968, George C. Wallace, a former governor of Alabama running on the American Independent ticket, took five of the southern states.[6]

The fact that the Democrats had replaced the Republicans as the party in the vanguard of civil rights raised significant doubts, borne out by the 1968 election, about whether the Democrats could hold on to their southern base. As political guru Kevin Phillips told journalist Garry Wills at the time, white Democrats would desert the party in droves once the party became the home of black voters in the south.[7] In the 1968 election, Nixon also made significant inroads among urban ethnics, including Catholics, who had previously been among the most Democratic of voters but who resented the ameliorative measures for blacks that Democrats were supporting.

If the Republicans could maintain such a pattern, it spelled future difficulties for the Democrats, who had been far from dominant in recent presidential elections. Between 1948 and 1968, the Democrats had lost three of the six presidential elections, and two of the others had been extremely close. The coalitions that made up the national political parties had always been tenuous, but the Democrats in modern times had featured a particularly odd marriage of conservative southerners and liberal northern ethnics. Nixon's election proved that the Republicans could break into this coalition by finding the common denominator between the two groups. Perhaps the bulk of white, middle-class voters who resided in what was coming to be called the Sun Belt could be won over to the Republican cause and united with northern blue-collar workers who were rapidly coming to think of themselves as middle class as well.[8] Such a coalition, essentially conservative in outlook, might constitute, as a popular political cliché put it, an emerging Republican majority.

PRESIDENT NIXON

A winner by some half a million votes out of the more than 73 million votes cast, Nixon followed the model that had been established for postwar presidents. He used his powers to manage the economy, even taking the unorthodox step of imposing price and wage controls in the summer of 1971. Looking to win reelection in 1972, he tried to position the economy so that it peaked at the time of the presidential campaign. He won plaudits for his skilled handling of foreign relations. To do anything else, however, such as passing social legislation, required reaching an accommodation with a Congress that remained solidly under Democratic control. Nixon, as political historians are fond of pointing out, was the first president elected to office since Zachary Taylor in 1848 whose party failed to carry either the House or the Senate. If he proposed a domestic agenda of his own, the Democrats could either vote it down outright or co-opt it. In a bidding war with Congress, Nixon would always lose. He did his best to make proposals that might divide the Democrats, who remained splintered between their southern conservative and northern liberal wings, so as to come up with legislation for which he could take credit.

Whatever he did, it seemed, was not enough to dislodge the Democrats from their hold over Congress. Furthermore, the federal bureaucracy could not be employed easily as an agent of the president's will. Everywhere there were people, plugged into the congressional committee structure, running programs that ran contrary to the president's interests. Nixon decided, to the extent that pressing events permitted time for reflection, that he would try to remedy the problem during the second term. In the meantime, he fell back on his natural tendency to hunker down and isolate himself, consciously keeping the details of his policies secret not only from the press but from members of his own cabinet.

THE ELECTION OF 1972

Whatever doubts Nixon had about his performance, he compiled what many regarded as an enviable record during his first term. The Democrats realized they would face an uphill battle if they expected to defeat him in 1972. As usual, a host of senators, such as Henry Jackson, Hubert Humphrey, and George McGovern, announced their willingness to run. So did a few congressmen, such as Wilbur Mills of Arkansas and Shirley Chisholm, a black congresswoman from New York, as well as the mayors of two key cities, John Lindsay of New York and Sam Yorty of Los Angeles. These categories reflected the Democrats' electoral hold over the Congress and their considerable strength in the big cities.

On March 14, 1972, George Wallace, the one candidate in the race who, with the possible exception of Mayor Yorty, made no claim to close ties with the federal government, beat all of his rivals in the Florida primary. The victory served as a powerful reminder that not all Democrats shared the more liberal ideology and not all Democrats came from the north or the Pacific coast. In his rhetoric, Wallace captured some of the resentments that many people felt toward experts who appeared to rule their lives without any real regard for the consequences and who were themselves quite remote from the daily struggle to earn a living and raise a family. In the campaign, Wallace talked about "the intellectual snobs who don't know the difference between smut and great literature," "the hypocrites who send your kids half-way across town while they have their chauffeur drop their children off at private schools," and "briefcase-carrying bureaucrats."[9] If an unlikely winner of the Democratic nomination, Wallace was nonetheless an important figure in the Democratic primaries, and the prospect of his running as an independent candidate threatened to derail Nixon's strategy of picking up electoral votes in the South.

The candidate who came into the election with the highest expectations was Edmund Muskie, a former governor of Maine who had won election to the Senate in 1958, 1964, and 1970.[10] In 1968 he had made an appealing vice-presidential candidate on the ticket with Hubert Humphrey, and he hoped to cash in on some of that goodwill in 1972. He won the New Hampshire primary that traditionally inaugurated the primary season, yet that showing was expected of the former governor of Maine. He then proceeded to fade in the Florida primary and in the April 4 Wisconsin primary.

The primary beneficiary of Muskie's collapse was George McGovern. McGovern came from the sparsely populated state of South Dakota and held a Ph.D. in history, putting him squarely in Wallace's class of intellectual snobs. He had even been a professor at a small, Methodist-affiliated college in South Dakota before practicing politics full-time. In 1956 he won election to the House and ran for the Senate in the Kennedy-Nixon election of 1960. After he lost, he became a minor functionary in the Kennedy administration until he won a Senate seat in 1962. His association with the Kennedys gave him a sense of glamour that he otherwise lacked. In 1968 he became a late stand-in for the assassinated Robert and in 1972, with the help of astute manager Gary Hart, he launched a full-scale campaign. When he won the Wisconsin primary, he succeeded in knocking Muskie out of the race. He was now the front-runner, although he still had to contend with George Wallace.

McGovern and Hart proved adept at leveraging primary wins. A new delegate-selection process that McGovern had helped to engineer put more emphasis on primaries (Humphrey had won in 1968 without winning the primaries) and less on the discretionary choices of political professionals and urban bosses such as Mayor Richard Daley of Chicago. In the new process, the party hoped to be more representative of the people who belonged to it and voted for its candidates. More blacks from the South and more women from across the country would attend the 1972 convention. As a consequence, the proportion of female convention delegates rose from 13 percent in 1968 to 40 percent in 1972.[11]

In such a party, George Wallace still did surprisingly well, even without the support of blacks or labor unions. By mid-May, Wallace had racked up 3.35 million votes in the primaries.[12] At just that time, Wallace made an appearance in the suburban town of Laurel, in the Maryland corridor between Washington and Baltimore. Laurel was the sort of place in which Wallace did well—a predominantly white area in a suburban county that was rapidly becoming black. The white people of Laurel felt they had fled the city and its problems only to find those problems chasing them into the suburbs. Although Wallace was not at his best that day and not able to achieve the cadences that moved audiences, he nonetheless received a sympathetic reception. After the rally, a man named Arthur Bremer approached him and asked to shake his hand. When Wallace instinctively offered his hand, Bremer shot Wallace in the abdomen, stomach, and rib cage. The incident left him paralyzed. It mattered only a little that he won the Michigan and Maryland primaries the next day.

George McGovern, the outsider in presidential politics, won the nomination. He soon ran into serious problems with his vice-presidential selection of Thomas Eagleton, a senator from Missouri. Eagleton had received electric shock as a treatment for mental illness. At the time, this form of therapy was common for patients with serious depression. Along with immersing patients in soothing warm baths, it was one of the few things that doctors could do for their acutely ill patients. Even in 1972, however, such a mark on one's medical record cast serious doubts over one's ability to lead the nation. Above all, a president, or a president in waiting, needed to appear calm and collected as he stared down the Russians and faced the uncertainties of the nuclear age. Someone who had been mentally ill might not be strong enough to do that, or so one might conjecture. In fact, the situation had never arisen before: it was a product of the medicalized, postwar age. As a good liberal, McGovern understood that suffering from depression carried no stigma, any more than one might disqualify a candidate for having had measles or polio. Still, pressure arose to do something about Eagleton and, after waffling, McGovern decided to replace him on the ticket with Sargent Shriver, President Kennedy's brother-in-law.

The incident damaged McGovern. So did the fact that the convention was managed without due regard for the sensibilities of the television audience. The open nature of the convention, designed to be appealing, ended up delaying the proceedings, so that McGovern made his acceptance speech in the small hours of the morning. A proposal that every American receive a grant of money, known as a demogrant, also hurt McGovern, as did his apparent lack of enthusiasm for Israel. According to political analyst Michael Barone, even as the Republicans held their convention, McGovern's candidacy had collapsed. In polling data, McGovern never rose above 35 percent of the vote.[13]

McGovern lost to Nixon badly. Nixon gained nearly 61 percent of the vote and won all of the states except for the District of Columbia and the Kennedy stronghold of Massachusetts. Nixon ran well with nearly all of the groups that he set out to court. White southerners who had voted for John F. Kennedy in 1960 voted for Richard Nixon in 1972. Pennsylvania gave McGovern less than 40 percent of its votes, as did Maine, New Jersey, West Virginia, Ohio, and Indiana. McGovern even failed to carry his home state of South Dakota (and indeed he would lose his Senate seat in 1980) or either of the states of his vice-presidential candidates. It looked as though a Republican majority had emerged.[14]

Even with this tremendous victory, Nixon felt a sense of disappointment. For one thing, he could not break through the Democratic stranglehold over Congress. The Republicans gained twelve seats in the House but actually lost seats in the Senate, in stark contrast to previous landslides such as Johnson's victory in 1964. Despite Nixon's overwhelming vote total, he would find it harder than ever to get his legislation through Congress.

WATERGATE

McGovern turned out to be the easiest opponent Nixon ever faced in a presidential election. That fact did not mitigate the tough approach that the president took toward the election. In his zeal to win, Nixon stepped over the bounds of propriety and became embroiled in the Watergate scandal.

Watergate began in the postwar tendency of presidents to seek their own counsel from independent and politically reliable sources rather than depending on the agencies of the permanent government. At the very beginning of the Nixon administration in 1969, for example, John Ehrlichman, one of Nixon's principal aides, hired John Caufield, a former New York City policeman, to start a White House "investigations unit" that would be accountable to the president rather than to other federal law-enforcement agencies, such as the FBI. Caufield undertook operations that fell into the realm of political intelligence, such as investigating Senator Edward Kennedy's 1969 automobile accident at Chappaquidick. The fear was that the local authorities in Massachusetts would try to cover up the senator's negligence. Through Caufield's secret operation, the White House hoped to stay abreast of the situation, which had obvious implications for the 1972 presidential election.[15] In addition, Nixon and his advisors felt the need to plug leaks. Nixon believed that he and his National Security Advisor were involved in sensitive negotiations that would suffer if they were prematurely exposed in the press. To cut down on leaks, the president ordered the creation of a special unit within the White House known as "the plumbers."

The plumbers sprang into action after the publication of the Pentagon Papers. As Watergate historian Stanley Kutler details, Nixon picked up the Sunday New York Times on June 13, 1971, to read a front page story about his daughter Tricia's White House wedding. On that same page, the president saw an excerpt from the Pentagon Papers, which were classified studies of America's involvement in the Vietnam War. The material reflected poorly on the Kennedy and Johnson administrations, not on Nixon. Still, Nixon and National Security Advisor Henry Kissinger concluded that the leak could be detrimental to the conduct of foreign relations. In public, the administration sued the New York Times over its right to publish the papers. In private, the administration contemplated more drastic actions, such as firebombing the Brookings Institution in order to steal the papers of the former National Security Council staff members who worked there. Although that plan never came off, the plumbers did break into the office of the psychiatrist of Daniel Ellsberg, the principal author of the Pentagon Papers and the person who leaked the papers to the New York Times, in an effort to find confidential information that might be damaging to him.

The plumbers, like any other bureaucratic entity, continued to seek projects that would prove their usefulness to the Nixon administration. One of their ranks suggested that they might destabilize the Democratic convention in Miami by hiring prostitutes who would service the delegates and in that manner obtain material for blackmail. In the end, the group decided upon something more modest: bugging the Democratic National Headquarters in the Watergate office complex, near the Kennedy Center in Washington. On the first try to plant a bug at the Democratic headquarters, the burglars bungled the job and ended up locked in a banquet hall at the adjoining Watergate Hotel. On the second try, they managed to place a bug on a secretary's phone and on the deputy director's phone. These actions were deemed insufficient, however, and the burglars returned to the Watergate complex on the evening of June 17, this time to bug the personal phone of the Democratic National Committee director. In this instance they again botched the job, leaving tape over the door that was noticed by the night watchman, and they ended up being arrested by the District of Columbia police.[16]

From the beginning it was obvious that these were not ordinary burglars out for items that they could convert into quick cash. For one thing, the target was an unusual one. For another thing, the men carried $2,300 in cash with the serial numbers in sequence and sophisticated equipment including a walkie-talkie, a short-wave receiver that could pick up police calls, forty rolls of unexposed film, two thirty-five-millimeter cameras and three pen-sized tear-gas guns. And one of the men identified himself in court as a former employee of the Central Intelligence Agency.[17]

White House officials tried to cover up the administration's role in the burglary. They did it well enough to get through the election without serious political damage. The national news media lacked the means to pursue the story. CBS White House correspondent Dan Rather called the Watergate break-in a local story and said he and his network colleagues did not have the local contacts necessary to break it.[18] Instead, the story became the province of young reporters on the local beat, including two reporters from the *Washington Post* who stumbled on to the assignment of a lifetime. They were a Mutt and Jeff pair: Bob Woodward was a Yale graduate and former ROTC cadet with WASP-ish good looks. Carl Bernstein, his partner, had flunked out of the University of Maryland. Although he was a quicker and surer writer than Woodward, his editors worried about the accuracy in the details of his reporting. Thrown together on the Watergate case, these two reporters on the metro beat, on a paper that more than most valued its national political reporters, began to write Watergate stories under a joint byline. Their dogged reporting would become the stuff of legend and bring them a fortune (they sold their notes on Watergate to the University of Texas for five million dollars and wrote two hugely successful Watergate books).[19]

Right after the burglary they reported that one of the Watergate burglars was also the national-security coordinator of President Nixon's reelection committee.[20] At the beginning of August they wrote that a cashier's check for $25,000, apparently a donation for the Nixon campaign, ended up in a Watergate burglar's bank account.[21] Only weeks before the election, on October 10, they revealed "a massive campaign of political spying and sabotage" directed by White House officials. This campaign had affected the outcome of the Democrat primaries, since the White House operatives targeted Edmund Muskie, the candidate whom they most feared, and caused him to lose ground in the race.[22]

Despite the best efforts of Woodward, Bernstein and a growing number of other reporters, the repeated denials of the stories by White House and Republican Party officials worked. It seemed likely in November, 1972 that Nixon would serve out the four years of his term, possibly improving upon the impressive record of his first administration.

INTERLUDE: SPIRO AGNEW

Here an unrelated story intervened in the Watergate case and affected its outcome. In 1962 Spiro Agnew, a Republican politician in Maryland, become the chief executive of Baltimore County, a sprawling and growing entity that surrounded the city of Baltimore. Four years later, Agnew benefited from a split in the Democratic Party and became the unlikely winner of the Maryland gubernatorial race (the next Republican governor of that state would not come along until 2002). His chief opponent, a chronic campaigner named George P. Mahoney, used the slogan, "Your home is your castle; protect it," as a way of calling attention to the consequences of an open-housing law that might lower property values. Mahoney's racist views alienated many of his fellow Democrats, who lent their support to Agnew in the general election. Hence, Spiro Agnew, the son of a Greek immigrant, moved to the historic city of Annapolis and became governor. He gained a reputation as a progressive governor, with a liberal record on the environment and welfare.

Agnew's image changed as a result of the riots that broke out in Baltimore and other Maryland locations after Martin Luther King's death. Agnew blamed the leaders of the black community in Baltimore for not taking a tougher stance toward the rioters and the rioters themselves for not obeying the law. The notoriety that Agnew gained for his position in favor of "law and order" was not unlike the publicity that Massachusetts governor Calvin Coolidge had earned for keeping order during the Boston police strike of 1919. In both cases, their actions led to their places on the vice-presidential ticket of the Republican Party. In Agnew, Nixon saw someone with ties to both the liberal and conservative wings of the party, who could be portrayed as an expert in urban problems, and who was a white ethnic with a political base in a border state.

In his relations with Agnew, Nixon carried the psychic baggage from his years as Dwight Eisenhower's vice president. It was the president's job to act presidential, to be above the battle, and not to stir up ugly partisan forces. The vice president's job was to act on the president's behalf and to carry out the administration's partisan agenda. It took Agnew some time to find his footing, but he soon grabbed the nation's attention with a series of speeches that impugned the integrity of those who demonstrated against the Vietnam War and who controlled the nation's media. Although Agnew had become a controversial figure, Nixon, no stranger to presidential ambivalence over whether or not to renominate a vice president, put Agnew on the 1972 ticket.

As the Watergate situation heated up in 1973, Agnew provided ballast against the unlikely prospect that Nixon would be impeached. If the Democrats somehow succeeded in removing Nixon, they would find themselves saddled with the even more objectionable Agnew, who would gain a base from which to launch a 1976 presidential run. Then fate intervened. Criminal charges arose that dated from Agnew's days as Baltimore County executive. In the go-go atmosphere of sixties suburbia and in the tradition of Maryland politics, it appeared that Agnew had taken kickbacks from construction companies. Eventually he was confronted with charges of tax evasion and bribery that forced him to resign his office on October 10, 1973. He pleaded no contest to a charge of tax evasion and received a sentence of three years' probation and a $10,000 fine.[23]

Watergate Breaks Into the Open

By the time Agnew left office in 1973, the Watergate affair had blossomed into a full-scale scandal. At the very beginning of the year, the five Watergate burglars, plus two others who had been implicated in the burglary, either pleaded guilty or, in the case of former Nixon aides G. Gordon Liddy and James W. McCord Jr., were found guilty by a jury of burglary, wiretapping, and eavesdropping on the Democratic Party headquarters. Meanwhile, the Democrats who controlled Congress itched to get in on the action. Senate majority leader Mike Mansfield wrote to the head of the Senate Judiciary Committee that a low-profile senator should be put in charge of an investigation. He had in mind Sam Ervin of North Carolina. Early in February, the Senate voted 77 to 0 to create the Select Committee on Presidential Campaign Activities and to let Ervin, a former judge who was at the end of his congressional career, chair it.[24]

Ervin's career was not untypical of a southern senator. He had worked as an attorney in North Carolina and was fond of describing himself, in a folksy manner, as a country lawyer. If so, he was one with a Harvard Law School degree and connections good enough to get elected three times to North Carolina's general assembly and to gain a seat on the North Carolina supreme court. His brother became a congressman, and when he died, Sam filled the seat. Then he went back to the court, but when Senator Clyde Hoey died in 1954, Ervin was appointed to fill the post. For the next twenty years, he held a safe Senate seat.

A few weeks after Ervin's appointment, the time came for the sentencing of the Watergate burglars. Defendant James McCord produced a letter that he gave to presiding judge John Sirica, a Republican but a stern jurist who had sensed from the beginning that the White House was covering up the details of the case. McCord indicated that the defendants had been pressured to plead guilty and to remain silent at the specific urging of the White House. He implicated Nixon staffer Jeb Magruder, counsel John Dean, and former Attorney General John Mitchell in the effort to get the burglars to commit perjury in order to deflect attention away from the White House.[25]

Nixon scrambled to maintain the cover-up. On April 30 he pleaded his case on national television. He portrayed himself as a hard-working, responsible, innocent man. He had gone off on a historic mission to Moscow and heard about the Watergate break-in while recuperating in Florida. The "senseless, illegal action" appalled him. The fact that employees of his reelection committee were involved shocked him. He ordered an investigation and received "repeated assurances" that no members of his administration were involved. Nixon pledged he would do all he could to bring the guilty to justice. He took the painful steps of accepting the resignations of Bob Haldeman and John Erlichman, whom he described as his "closest advisors," and Attorney General Richard Kleindienst. At least five other administration or reelection officials, including John Mitchell and acting FBI Director L. Patrick Gray, had already quit.[26] At this point, the *Washington Post* described Watergate as "a national scandal of historic proportions. It is an affair now being compared to such scandals as Teapot Dome in the 1920's and the Grant scandals of a century ago."[27]

Watergate shifted to new venues. On May 18, 1973, Elliot Richardson, the former secretary of both the Department of Health, Education, and Welfare and the Defense Department, who now found himself called on to fill the recently vacated post of attorney general, announced the appointment of a special prosecutor for the Watergate case. Most of the people whom Richardson had approached about the post were wary of it, fearing that White House officials would hamper their work. In the end, Richardson prevailed upon Archibald Cox, a Harvard law professor who, among other jobs, had served as the head of Kennedy's issue staff in the 1960 campaign and who had worked in the Kennedy justice department. No one could accuse Cox of favoring Nixon. On the same day as Richardson's announcement, Ervin's committee began televised hearings.

As Watergate became a daily television program, it gained a greater hold on the nation's imagination. John Dean, the former White House counsel who had turned against the president, took the role of star witness at the Ervin hearings. He offered damning information to the Senate investigators and federal prosecutors, telling them that on at least thirty-five separate occasions between January and April he had discussed the Watergate cover-up with the president or in the president's presence. On June 25, Dean, dressed in a conservative summer suit with his strikingly pretty fiancée sitting primly behind him, testified in front of Ervin and the television cameras. Speaking in an uninflected monotone, he laid out the evidence against Nixon in a lawyerly fashion. Through seven long hours of testimony, he asserted that Nixon had been involved in the cover-up from the very beginning and that the White House had engaged in illegal political espionage activities.[28] More and more of these activities were bursting into the open, as in the discovery of a memo to John Ehrlichman describing the plan to burglarize the offices of Daniel Ellsberg's psychiatrist.[29] In Dean's near-total recall of Oval Office conversations, one particular phrase stood out: "We have a cancer growing on the presidency," Dean claimed he told the president.[30]

The Watergate case took a dramatic turn only a few weeks after Dean's testimony. With the stakes so high, all the witnesses rehearsed in front of the committee staff before they went on television. That procedure allowed the politicians on the committee to script the hearings and control the pace of events. During one of these rehearsals on a Friday the thirteenth in July, White House appointments secretary Alexander Butterfield briefed the staff on the administration's office procedures. Then someone asked if, by any chance, some of the president's conversations had been recorded. "I was hoping you fellows wouldn't ask me about that," replied Butterfield, who proceeded to reveal the existence of a taping system in the White House that recorded nearly all of the president's conversations.[31] In an instant, Dean's testimony, already dramatic and damning, acquired new significance. It no longer needed to be his word against the president's. If the committee got access to the tapes, it could decide just who was telling the truth. It took little time for the Senate committee and the Watergate prosecutor to demand that the tapes be turned over to them.

The disclosure of the tapes created a new crisis for Nixon that was to have a profound effect on the presidency. His first reaction was simply to deny Watergate investigators access to the tapes. Hence, they became the object of litigation in which the courts needed to decide if the public's right to know superseded the president's executive privileges. The situation prompted a second major television address by Nixon, his most elaborate effort to explain the Watergate crisis to date. Speaking in the middle of the summer vacation season, Nixon continued to profess his innocence. He noted that, of all the witnesses to appear before the Senate committee, only John Dean had contradicted the president's version of events. He also once again declared his desire to uncover the facts of the case. Still, he refused to turn over the tapes. If he did, then "the confidentiality of the Office of the President would always be suspect," with a chilling effect on the candid conversations and political horse-trading so necessary to presidential effectiveness. Yielding the tapes "would cripple all future Presidents by inhibiting conversations between them and those they look to for advice."

The president tried to turn the tables. He emphasized that Watergate represented an abuse of the system by people who held themselves above the rules. He linked such behavior to the excesses of the sixties, when it became fashionable for individuals to assert "the right to take the law into their own hands." When the liberals acted that way, Nixon claimed, with characteristic bitterness, they were praised for their idealism. When people like Nixon insisted on the "old restraints" and "warned of the overriding importance of operating within the law and by the rules," they were ridiculed as reactionaries. Watergate was a matter for the courts. The president of the United States needed to get back to the "urgent business of the nation."[32]

Nixon's rhetorical ploy impressed none of the authorities who were investigating him. At the end of August, Sirica ordered Nixon to turn over nine tapes for the judge to review in private. On October 19, Nixon felt it necessary to offer a compromise to defuse the situation. He suggested that Senator John Stennis, a Democratic stalwart from Mississippi, another country lawyer appointed to fill a Senate seat who stayed on to win six elections of his own, listen to the tapes and prepare summaries for Archibald Cox. That way the president's concerns over confidentiality would be respected and the legal process would be served.

Cox rejected the compromise. Nixon ordered Richardson to fire Cox. Richardson refused to do so, resigning instead. The deputy attorney general also refused to carry out Nixon's order, and he was fired. It took Robert Bork, the third in command in the Justice Department, to execute the president's will. The evening ended with FBI agents sealing off Richardson's and Cox's offices. The *Washington Post* called it "the most traumatic government upheaval of the Watergate crisis," but most people called it the Saturday night massacre. "Nixon is a Cox sacker," read a popular bumper sticker.[33]

The movement to impeach the president grew in intensity. On that Monday evening's NBC news broadcast, for example, reporter Ray Scherer told of telegrams that were swamping Capitol Hill offices, most demanding Nixon's impeachment. Anchor John Chancellor summarized the unfavorable editorials that had appeared in the nation's newspapers.[34] Nixon beat a strategic retreat, turned over some of the tapes to Sirica, and named Leon Jaworski as the new Watergate special prosecutor. On November 17, in a tense press conference held near the carnival atmosphere of Disney World, Nixon tried to demonstrate that he still possessed leadership qualities. "People have got to know whether or not their President is a crook," he said. "Well, I'm not a crook. I've earned everything I've got." At the press conference, the president reassured his questioners that he would supply more Watergate evidence from tapes and presidential documents, as well as more information about his personal finances, which had also come under attack.[35]

Any momentum the president might have gained from his appearance in Orlando was lost only a few days later when reports surfaced of a gap of about eighteen and a half minutes on a tape of a conversation between Nixon and Haldeman that had taken place right after the break-in. To some it looked as though the president's men had tampered with evidence, even if Rose Mary Woods, Nixon's loyal secretary, explained how it was possible for the gap to have been created in the normal course of the transcription process.[36]

TOWARD RESIGNATION

"One year of Watergate is enough," Nixon declared in his 1974 State of the Union address to the jeers of the Democrats in the audience. For Jaworski, Sirica, and the Democrats in Congress it was not nearly enough.[37] On February 6 the House of Representatives took the fateful step of authorizing the House Judiciary Committee to investigate whether grounds existed for the president's impeachment. The grand jury that had been considering matters related to Watergate indicted all of the principals and named the president, in a phrase that soon made the rounds of smart political conversation, as an "unindicted co-conspirator." Meanwhile, Jaworski, the Senate, and the House kept asking for more tapes.

In response to a subpoena from the House Judiciary Committee, Nixon made a third major address to the nation on the subject of Watergate on the evening of April 29. He would not release the tapes, he said, but he would release edited transcripts. He appeared on television with folders piled up next to him and explained that they contained more than a thousand pages of transcripts of his private conversations related to Watergate, including all of the subpoenaed material and more besides. He intended to give the transcripts not just to the authorities but to the general public as well.[38]

Nixon realized that the papers would be damaging. If anything, he underestimated the severity of the situation. The damage lay not only in the harm the papers did to the president's efforts to stave off impeachment but also in the way they harmed Nixon's image and, by extension, the image of the presidency itself. The postwar perception of the president as a powerful, benevolent figure who acted in the nation's interest ended with the release of the tapes.

Even before the postwar era, the presidency had been a carefully staged affair. In Roosevelt's day, he spoke off the record to reporters, who could only attribute a quote to him if he gave them permission to do so. The obvious fact that Roosevelt was a paraplegic confined to a wheel chair received no mention in the press. Although Kennedy gave spontaneous press conferences on national television, reporters respected his privacy and allowed him to pursue extramarital affairs with impunity. During sensitive foreign crises, the press held back stories that Kennedy decided were not in the public interest. Johnson got fewer free passes and Nixon still fewer, with such stories as the secret bombing of Cambodia exposed in the *New York Times*. Watergate made the exposure of presidential secrets a national obsession.

The Watergate story reoriented the conduct of journalism in the seventies. The glamour beats of the war and postwar eras came on battlefronts.

Hence, CBS reporters Edward R. Murrow and Walter Cronkite became famous through their coverage of the Second World War. The big stories of the postwar era, such as Vietnam and the assassination of John F. Kennedy, produced their share of top-line print reporters, including Tom Wicker and David Halberstam of the *New York Times*. But the key television anchor spots in the next generation went to the White House reporters of the Watergate era: Dan Rather of CBS and Tom Brokaw of NBC. Television was increasingly the medium that reported breaking news. Newspapers became the domain of the dogged investigative reporters, like Woodward and Bernstein, who probed beneath the surface to uncover the "real" significance of the story. In a world in which politicians tried to cover up the truth, a world with a hidden inner meaning, such reporters gained increasing legitimacy. Newspapers began to run more and more investigative features on the front pages, taking readers behind the scenes and refusing to be content with the official version of events.

On April 30 Nixon formally released the transcripts of his conversations, "the most extraordinary documents ever to come out of the White House," according to the *Washington Post*. The papers were edited to delete extraneous material, and some profanities were excised from the transcripts and replaced with the instantly famous phrase "expletive deleted."[39] Hence, when in the middle of one conversation, an aide broke into Nixon's office with the news that the Italians had devalued the lira, Nixon replied, "I don't give a (expletive deleted) about the lira."[40] The papers showed Nixon to be a mean and petty man, lacking in presidential qualities. Presidents were not supposed to swear or make derogatory references toward Jews, and here was indisputable evidence, released by the president himself, that showed that Nixon did both. "Deplorable, disgusting, shabby, immoral," said Republican Senator Hugh Scott of Pennsylvania.[41]

As the public versions of the transcripts appeared in newspapers and in instantly available paperbacks that sold three million copies in a week, the public, which had been the audience for the formal drama of the presidency staged by the president himself and presented by the media, got to go backstage and observe the actors in their dressing rooms. The results were titillating in the manner of movie gossip magazines and extremely compelling. They also stripped the presidency of much of its dignity and ended the postwar presidential mystique. The seventies were firmly launched.

It remained only to tie up the loose ends of the Nixon presidency. The House Judiciary Committee began its impeachment hearings in May, and

Jaworski asked the Supreme Court to order the recalcitrant president to obey judicial subpoenas. Nixon returned to the pageant of the presidency, going on trips to the Middle East and to Russia and receiving warmer welcomes there than in Congress. The president lost the case in the Supreme Court, and the House Judiciary Committee adopted three articles of impeachment. On August 5, 1974, Nixon released a tape that proved to be the "smoking gun" and caused even his allies on the Judiciary Committee to abandon him. Impeachment in the House and conviction in the Senate appeared certain. Before that could happen, Nixon announced on April 8, 1974, that he would resign from office.

THE NIXON LEGACY

The next morning, speaking to the White House staff before leaving the White House, Nixon gave the last of his great public appearances. His worried and saddened family stood at his side—his wife Pat, who was there for him just as she had been during the Checkers speech, and his now grown-up daughters with their top-drawer husbands in tow. Nixon seemed to melt before the television cameras so that all of his protective layers were burned off and the very essence of his being was exposed. He talked tearfully about his father, "a common man," and his mother, a "saint" who had survived the tragedy of burying two of her children. The death of his brothers made Nixon think about Teddy Roosevelt, who had lost his wife and mother on the same fateful day yet, with the endurance and tenacity that Nixon and those of his generation had come to admire, he had pulled himself off the canvass, gotten back into the ring, and proven himself a man. Nixon concluded with the tag line for his presidency: "Always give your best, never get discouraged, never get petty; always remember, others may hate you but those who hate you don't win unless you hate them and then you destroy yourself."[42] Then, like the Wizard of Oz, he got in a flying machine and returned to civilian life.

Nixon left behind a considerable mess for others to clean up. For one thing, he disrupted the emergence of a Republican political majority that appeared to be forming in 1972. The Watergate scandal reinvigorated the Democrats and made them a potent political force during the seventies. For another thing, he reinforced the natural suspicion of Congress toward the executive branch. In the seventies, there would be congressional investigations of national-security organizations, countless oversight hearings to make sure that the president carried out the will of Congress, and myriad legislative efforts to restrict the president's war-making and budgetary powers. Finally, he gave the press a license to expand the boundaries of public life to include what were previously private activities. The information generated would change the way Americans judged the character of their president and other public officials.

- Republican party seriously disrupted
- Suspicion of executive branch by Congress
- press & media completely changed, fewer boundaries

2

Vietnam and Its Consequences

Although the Vietnam War ended in 1975 and America's defeat became the second of the signature events that launched the seventies, America's disengagement from it began at the end of the sixties. The search for peace with honor in Vietnam consumed Richard Nixon's presidency and shaped his foreign policy. As the president sought detente with the Russians and reached out to China, he always kept the effect of these initiatives on the Vietnam War in mind. The desire for secrecy in the negotiations to end the war contributed to the conditions that created Watergate.

Richard Nixon left office with a double legacy that would affect the position of the United States in the world during the seventies. The outcome of the Vietnam War made his successors wary of direct intervention in foreign wars, and the atmosphere created by Watergate caused Congress to regard key agencies entrusted with the protection of national security, such as the Central Intelligence Agency, with suspicion. The postwar consensus on foreign policy that had supported wars in Korea and Vietnam and massive American intervention into the affairs of foreign nations ended. The seventies became an era, as Walter Isaacson puts it, of "disengagement" rather than "intervention," despite the desires of many hawks to maintain the confrontational spirit of the cold war.[1]

The Beginning of the Vietnam War

America's involvement in Vietnam grew out of the nation's postwar concern for the shape of the postcolonial world. In the great nineteenth century scramble for colonies, Vietnam had come under the control of the French in the 1880s as part of the French Indochinese Union. Early in World War II, the Japanese made Vietnam part of their empire. After the Americans defeated the Japanese, the question arose of what would happen to Vietnam and the other nations of southeast Asia that had come under Japanese influence. This question acquired a greater urgency after the "fall" of China, the most populous nation in the world, to the communists in 1949. In the late forties one could detect the influence of the Soviet Union extending to the west and taking over the nations of eastern Europe and reaching to the south and east in Asia. On both theaters of the Second World War, therefore, the Soviet Union appeared to be adopting an aggressive stance. The conventional wisdom held that the Soviets needed to be contained both in Europe and in Asia.

This general guide failed to provide a definitive course of action on Vietnam. One possibility was that the United States could aid the League for the Independence of Vietnam in the first Indochina war (1946–1954) against the French and turn Vietnam into an ally of America. The British and the French opposed that solution, however, and persuaded the United States to support the reestablishment of French colonial rule in Vietnam. In 1954, the Vietnamese leader Ho Chi Minh succeeded in defeating the French, reopening the question of Vietnam. By this time the United States had already fought a war on the Korean peninsula that reinforced its desire to contain communism in this region. As a consequence, the United States acquiesced to the Geneva Peace Accords that created three independent states, Laos, Cambodia and Vietnam, but divided Vietnam into two zones, with the expectation that the country would be unified after elections were held in 1956. America came to the aid of the South Vietnamese, and the 1956 elections never took place. By the time Kennedy was in office, a civil war had erupted in South Vietnam in which the supporters of the northern regime, guerilla troops known as the Viet Cong, sought to overthrow the South Vietnamese government and unify the country under the rule of Ho Chi Minh. Eisenhower had sent the first advisors to South Vietnam. Kennedy decided to follow suit, and by the end of 1962 the Americans had more than 11,000 military advisors in the country. Whether or not Americans fully realized it at the time, the Vietnam War had begun.

During the Johnson administration, America's commitment to the war increased. Lyndon Johnson agreed in the spring of 1965 to send 82,000 troops to Vietnam in an effort to "break the will" of the North Vietnamese army and the Viet Cong. By 1966, he had committed 200,000 American soldiers to Vietnam. The North Vietnamese responded to this buildup with one of their own, sending more troops into the south and receiving ever-greater amounts of military aid from Russia and China. By the end of 1968, more than half a million Americans were in Vietnam and over 30,000 Americans had been killed in action. By this time the Americans had dropped more bombs on North Vietnam than the United States had used in the entire Korean War.[2] The object became not victory in the sense of a unified Vietnam sympathetic to American interests but rather eliminating the North Vietnamese from the South.[3]

Once it became clear that the Vietnam War would not be won easily, and in the absence of leaders who tied the war to daily concerns, the American will to fight it faded. By 1967 politicians were beginning to turn against the war. In April of that year, for example, Martin Luther King said, "This war is a blasphemy against all that America stands for."[4] The American media did not paint the same heroic picture of Vietnam as they had of the Second World War, and some of the coverage featured atrocities committed by Americans. In March 1968, for example, American soldiers killed 450 innocent civilians, raped the women in the village, and blew apart children with hand grenades in what became known as the My Lai Massacre.[5] Liberators were not supposed to act that way.

Early in 1968, the North Vietnamese launched a major military offensive against the south. The Americans and South Vietnamese managed to repulse the attack, yet the offensive reinforced the impression that the will of the North Vietnamese would never be broken, no matter how many troops we committed to the region or how many bombs we dropped on North Vietnam. Johnson and his advisors sought a way out of the conflict. As Dean Acheson, Truman's former secretary of state and an architect of the Cold War, noted, "the issue is can we do what we are trying to do in Vietnam? I do not think we can. The issue is can we, by military means, keep the North Vietnamese off the South Vietnamese. I do not think we can. They can slip around and end run them and crack them up."[6] President Johnson failed to reach an acceptable settlement before the end of his administration because neither the North nor the South Vietnamese would agree to terms. The North continued to hold on to the hope of outlasting the United States and winning the war; the South thought it might be able to make a better deal under Richard Nixon.

RICHARD NIXON AND THE VIETNAM WAR

Richard Nixon inherited the Vietnam War just as his Republican predecessor and former boss Dwight Eisenhower had inherited the Korean War.

inheriting wars

Both tried to reassure voters that they would put an end to the conflicts. In Nixon's case, he succeeded in his objectives only after four more years of fighting.

In the effort to end the Vietnam War, National Security Advisor Henry Kissinger played good cop to Nixon's bad cop. He would be the reasonable one who warned that Nixon could be restrained from a natural impulse toward violence only if he could get results from diplomacy. Nixon encouraged Kissinger in this role-playing, which emphasized the tough and decisive sides of the president's personality and drew upon his image as a veteran cold warrior. Kissinger, a German refugee whose family had fled Nazi Germany and who had become a distinguished Harvard professor of international relations, combined an ability to write fluidly with an ability to pass between the intellectual concerns of academia and the practical concerns of government. Nixon worried at first that Kissinger's thick German accent would alarm the American people, yet, as time passed, Kissinger, with his tremendous flair for publicity, emerged as a spokesman for the administration's foreign policy, eclipsing cabinet members and, at times, Nixon himself. As Nixon's reputation declined, Kissinger managed to maintain his image as the foreign-policy expert, with none of the taint that other Nixon staffers received from Watergate.

Kissinger and Nixon believed that the war in Vietnam could not just end: it had to end on honorable terms for America, however those terms were defined. As Kissinger noted in 1969, the very fact that half a million Americans had been sent to Vietnam settled the issue of whether Vietnam was important.[7] Nixon proceeded to conduct the war in what might be called a contrapuntal manner. He punctuated gestures toward peace with sharp and sudden escalations in an effort to induce an appropriate response from North Vietnam. In consultation with his military leaders, Nixon decided that one problem with America's conduct of the war was that the North Vietnamese could use Cambodia, which bulged out to the west of South Vietnam, as a sanctuary to move arms, troops, and ammunition from the North to the South. After considerable hesitation, Nixon authorized a secret bombing raid to wipe out the communist headquarters thought to be located in the Fish Hook region of Cambodia. This region bordered on South Vietnam and was so close to the capitol city of Saigon that it could have been its suburb. Although the raid failed to accomplish its objective, the lack of a public outcry emboldened Nixon to authorize more secret bombing raids on Cambodia.[8]

As Nixon escalated the war in private, he began the public removal of American troops from Vietnam. The idea was for the South Vietnamese to take over more of the fighting. At the beginning of 1970, Kissinger believed that a new round of secret Vietnam peace talks could begin. When these talks broke off, the administration contemplated a more dramatic escalation. Hence on April 30, 1970, Nixon announced a formal extension of the war into Cambodia. With a map of Cambodia and Vietnam placed on an easel beside him, Nixon said, in the syncopated style of his other Vietnam messages, that in the name of peace he had to intensify the fighting. For that reason, he had approved an American and South Vietnamese incursion into Cambodia. The president noted that the North Vietnamese did not respect the sovereignty of Cambodia and the Cambodians had put out a call for help. To do nothing was to surrender the people of the region to the tyranny of communism. Nixon linked his actions with the bold ones taken by President Roosevelt in the Second World War and President Kennedy in the Cuban Missile Crisis.[9]

If the president thought he could rally the nation to his side and earn the respect of the international community with his speech, he was wrong. Communist leaders acted predictably, yet even America's closest allies refused to support the president. Members of Congress, usually cautious about criticizing an act of war that the president had equated with the most sacred moments of America's history, questioned the unilateral nature of the president's actions. Robert Dole, a sympathetic Republican senator from Kansas, worried that the public might react adversely.

As for those who opposed the war, perhaps the president deliberately sought a confrontation with his critics, or maybe he did not factor in the coincidence of his actions and the springlike end-of-the-semester mood on college campuses. Nixon's actions caused college students to speak out against the war as they had never done before and would never do again. At Princeton, MIT, Indiana, Penn State, the University of Maryland, and many other places, students rallied against the war.[10] Those in positions of authority on the nation's campuses lent their tacit support, as in the president of Columbia University's call for a moratorium against the war.[11]

The situation became even more tense over the course of the next few days, until the fatal shooting of four Kent State University students on Monday, May 4, the third day of violence there, took the nation's attention away from the invasion of Cambodia and focused it on the war at home. That Friday an incident in lower Manhattan flickered across the nation's television screens. During a lunch break from the many construction projects then underway, a group of workers, who came to be known as "hardhats," confronted antiwar protesters who had gathered in front of the New York Stock Exchange to protest the war and the killings at Kent State.[12]

According to CBS reporter Morton Dean, the workers beat up antiwar pro-
testers, broke police lines, stormed city hall, and derided New York Mayor
John Lindsay for putting the flag at half mast in tribute to the slain Kent
State students.

That evening, as students came to Washington to protest against the
war, President Nixon called a press conference at which the reporters
asked him about the Cambodian invasion and the incident at Kent State.
Nixon repeated that he had brought back 115,000 American soldiers from
Vietnam and intended to bring another 150,000 home. "Don't judge us
too quickly," he said of his foreign policy. The president backtracked,
though only a little, on a statement he had made earlier in the week at the
Pentagon. On that occasion he compared the young soldiers fighting the
war and the students protesting the war to the detriment of the students.
"You see these bums, you know," the president had said, "blowing up the
campuses." Playing on generational sympathies, the president added, "the
boys that are on college campuses today are the luckiest people in the world
going to the greatest universities and here they are burning up the books."
At the press conference, the president said he regretted describing the
students as bums but could not resist adding, "When students on university campuses burn buildings, when they engage in violence, when they
break up furniture, when they terrorize their fellow students and terrorize the faculty, then I think 'bums' is perhaps too kind a word to apply to
that kind of people." Even as the president blustered, he urged the nation
not to lose sight of the big picture. If the United States allowed the North
Vietnamese to come into the South, they would "massacre the civilians
there by the millions" and that would mean that America would be finished
"as the peace-keeper in the Asian world."[13]

On the evening of the press conference, Richard Nixon had one of those
dark nights of the soul that made him such a fascinating character. He
stayed up late making phone calls to such people as Norman Vincent Peale,
Nelson Rockefeller, Thomas Dewey, and his friend Bebe Rebozo. He tried
to sleep but could not. At a little before four thirty in the morning he set off
for the Lincoln Memorial with his valet Manolo. There he met protesters
waiting for an antiwar rally to begin later that morning. The president tried
to make conversation but could not reach the college students. He told
them a parable of his generation. When he was a young man, he thought
that Neville Chamberlain was the greatest man living and that Winston
Churchill was a madman. Only later did he realize that Chamberlain was a
good man but that Churchill was right. The lesson was that sometimes one
needed not to be perceived as nice by appeasing the enemy but rather to

stand up against aggression. Although such a stance did not lead to instant approval, it produced the best results in the long run. The students, who saw the world in different terms, failed to absorb that lesson, although they could believe that Nixon was a madman. Ronnie Kemper of Syracuse University told CBS reporter Bob Schieffer that the president avoided the issues and rambled; Lynn Shatzkin, another Syracuse undergraduate, noted that the president babbled. Still restless, the president moved on the Capitol and got a startled janitor to let him into the House of Representatives. There he urged Manolo to go to the well of the House and make a speech. Next he went to the Mayflower Hotel and had breakfast.[14] H. R. Haldeman, Nixon's aide, called it, "the weirdest day so far."[15] Nixon appeared to be facing another in a series of monumental crises that defined his career.

The crisis soon passed, and the Vietnam War continued. In March 1972, the North Vietnamese launched yet another invasion of the South. In May, the president responded with a massive retaliation that included the mining of Haiphong Harbor and air and naval strikes against military targets in the north. "There is only one way to stop the killing," the president said, and that was to take decisive action against the enemy and win the war. The welfare of the 60,000 American soldiers still in Vietnam and the honor of the country demanded that the president respond to the provocations of the North Vietnamese. In private the president said, "The bastards have never been bombed like they're going to be bombed this time."[16]

This time no uproar followed the president's actions. To be sure, people on campuses protested, but not to the same extent they had two years earlier. There were now fewer Americans in Vietnam and less prospect that any more American soldiers would be sent there. As with the other American escalations, this one helped to halt the North Vietnamese advance and prolong the war.

At this point in the conflict, the South Vietnamese managed to field an army of some 1.2 million men who were supported by American air power. North Vietnam realized that there was no immediate way to win the war. As a consequence, the North Vietnamese leaders became more receptive to a cease-fire and instructed their negotiators in Paris—the site of talks that had lurched along since the presidency of Lyndon Johnson—to seek a negotiated settlement. The North Vietnamese negotiators implied that they might be willing to drop their demand that the Thieu government of South Vietnam be immediately replaced by a coalition government. That concession proved key to a deal in which the North Vietnamese troops would remain in position in the South and the government of South Vietnam would also stay in place. All American prisoners of war would be released, and all of the remaining 27,000 American military forces would leave Vietnam.[17]

By this time the American presidential election had once again entered the picture. Nixon felt no particular urge to settle before the election took place. He thought his support of the war helped to strengthen his hold over blue-collar Democrats. At the same time, he knew the Congress returned by the election would not be any more receptive to the war than the one that was sitting in 1972. Further complicating the situation was the recalcitrance of the South Vietnamese to agree to the terms that the North and the Americans found acceptable. Talks halted, yet again, in November. In December the president ordered the last major escalation of the war. Over the course of twelve days beginning on December 18, in a campaign that became known as the Christmas bombings, the United States dropped some 40,000 tons of bombs on North Vietnam, mostly between the capitol of Hanoi and the port of Haiphong. Then on January 23, 1973, the president announced that an agreement had been reached and the American involvement in the war would end. The terms were the same as had been reached in October.[18]

OUTREACH TO CHINA

As President Nixon scraped together the money to fight the war throughout his first term, he and National Security Advisor Henry Kissinger realized that the nation had neither the resources nor the desire to fight another war like the one in Vietnam. Nixon noted that the United States had dominated the planet since World War II, but was no longer "in the position of complete preeminence or predominance." "Our resources were no longer infinite in relation to our problems," Kissinger recalled. This stringency suggested the need "to set priorities, both intellectual and material."[19] Nixon believed that establishing a new relationship with China and achieving detente with the Russians should head the list of his foreign policy goals. He linked these projects with his overarching desire to end the Vietnam War. On April 14, 1969, for example, Henry Kissinger met with Soviet ambassador Anatoly F. Dobrynin and asked for Soviet help in negotiating with the government in Hanoi.[20]

Nixon's visit to China and Carter's subsequent diplomatic recognition of that country constituted the era's most dramatic foreign policy development. Ever since the "fall" of China in 1949, American contact with mainland China was minimal. Although China had gone over to the communist camp and was lost to us seemingly forever, those experts who followed its development realized that relations between the Chinese and Russians, as one might expect of two large nations with a common border, were fraught with difficulties. In the spring of 1969, for example, military clashes erupted on the Sino-Soviet border and lasted through the summer and into the fall. The Chinese took steps to assert their independence from Russia and did not want to be perceived by the world community as a Soviet satellite. Hence, the Soviet occupation of Czechoslovakia in August 1968 disturbed the Chinese. They worried that the Soviets might try to apply the Brezhnev Doctrine, or the right to intervene in another socialist state to preserve true socialism in the face of counterrevolutionary threats, to areas in China's sphere of influence. As for Richard Nixon, he, along with many of the postwar politicians with an international outlook, such as John F. Kennedy, had tried to capitalize on the fall of China as a sign that the nation needed to prosecute the Cold War more vigorously. Still, he recognized that the Chinese regime, unlike, say, the regime in Cuba, was in place to stay and that China needed to be pulled "back into the world community." Therefore, he made establishing contact with China one of his foreign policy objectives and thought that the Chinese disagreements with the Russians might be exploited to America's advantage.[21]

As Nixon and Kissinger pursued their plans for peace with honor in Vietnam in public, they sent out feelers to the Chinese in private. On February 1, 1969, the president asked Henry Kissinger, his personal diplomat and the person whom he trusted for sensitive missions, to use an Eastern European channel to spread the message that the administration was interested in talking with the Chinese. In the curious way of diplomacy, the Chinese absorbed this information and contemplated it. On April 6, 1971, the Chinese invited the American ping-pong team, playing at a tournament in Japan, to the World Table Tennis Championships in Beijing. The State Department gave its formal approval to the visit, saying that such an overture was consistent with the president's desire to improve relations with Communist China. The British, French, and Canadian teams also accepted invitations from the Chinese. For the United States, it was the first formal invitation from the Chinese government in twenty-one years.

When the American team arrived in China, it quickly became clear that the visit was not going to be routine. Ordinary athletes received extraordinary treatment and found themselves transformed into cultural ambassadors on the cutting edge of the cold war. On April 14, Prime Minister Zhou Enlai met with the team and announced the beginning of a new chapter in U.S.-China relations. He declared that western reporters would be allowed to visit China. Nixon made simultaneous overtures to the Chinese, such as opening direct trade and easing travel restrictions.

Private diplomacy proceeded in concert with these public gestures. In May 1971, Nixon and Kissinger sent a message to the Chinese through the Pakistanis in which they proposed a secret meeting between Kissinger and Zhou Enlai "on Chinese soil preferably at some location within convenient flying distance from Pakistan." On June 2, 1971, Zhou Enlai accepted the American proposal, and the Americans made secret preparations to send Kissinger to China in July. At the beginning of July, Henry Kissinger left for what was billed as a fact-finding tour of Asia but was in fact the cover for the trip to China.[22]

After the successful completion of this trip, Nixon went public and announced on July 15, 1971, that he would visit China himself.[23] The nightly network newscasts contained not a word about China, mentioning only that the president would address the nation later that evening. His address to the nation took nearly everyone by surprise: the network commentators, who were supposedly in the know about Washington events, the Chinese nationalists on Taiwan, the U.S. State Department, the government of South Vietnam, and the leaders of the Soviet Union. In a stroke, Nixon had reconfigured the world.

VISITING CHINA

Nixon then turned his modus operandi inside out and made a public spectacle of his February 1972 visit to China. It occurred at the beginning of an election year and at the end of a sweeps period on television, when viewer levels, bolstered by special programming and by the forbidding weather in many parts of the country, were at their height. Nixon and his aides, such as H. R. Haldeman who had a background in advertising and public relations, composed the trip as a television special—an eight-day miniseries that dominated the nation's airwaves.

When Nixon landed in Beijing on February 21, he made sure that he was the first one off the plane. He approached Zhou Enlai and shook his hand, thus erasing the slight that former Secretary of State John Foster Dulles had imparted in 1954 by refusing to make that simple gesture. Only then did the rest of the party, including Secretary of State William Rogers and Henry Kissinger, disembark. Nixon and his entourage ate lunch and then found themselves whisked off to a meeting with Chairman Mao Zedong that had not been on the original schedule. During this meeting, Nixon and Mao reassured one another that neither had territorial designs on the other, and Mao told Nixon that people on the right, like Nixon and Prime Minister Heath of England, were good for the interests of China because, unlike their colleagues on the left, they were not inclined to be pro-Soviet. Mao even told Nixon that he had read Nixon's autobiographical *Six Crises* and pronounced it "not a bad book."[24]

The fact that the meeting with the ailing Mao took place and that Mao was so affable indicated that the Chinese wanted to go all out for Nixon, rolling out their biggest attractions and finest hospitality. In a formal banquet hosted by Zhou that showed off the skills of Chinese chefs, American and Chinese leaders toasted one another. During four days of talks in Beijing, telegenic events abounded as President and Mrs. Nixon visited the Great Wall, the Ming Tombs, and the Imperial Palace. Then the presidential party set out for China's Zhejiang Province and toured the West Lake. Finally, on February 27, the Americans and their Chinese hosts arrived in the city of Shanghai, whose name at least was familiar to Americans, and there they signed a final communiqué before Nixon headed home to considerable fanfare.[25]

For Henry Kissinger and Richard Nixon, the trip could not have gone more smoothly. It seemed to confirm the wisdom of conducting diplomacy in secret and then working to mold public events to maximum advantage. Henry Kissinger captured the sense of euphoria when he wrote in his memoirs that an often error-prone White House had really delivered on the China trip: "Pictures overrode the printed word." Any criticism that might have developed of the Shanghai Communiqué was blotted out by the "spectacle of an American President welcomed in the capital of an erstwhile enemy."[26]

Mindful of the links between one diplomatic objective and the other, Nixon and Kissinger hoped that China would assist in the effort to end the Vietnam War. China did make behind-the-scenes efforts to persuade the North Vietnamese to compromise, particularly during the delicate period when negotiations were underway for Nixon's visit. In the end, they were unable to exert much influence over the North Vietnamese, just as the North Vietnamese could not convince the Chinese to call off Nixon's visit.[27]

Without a doubt Nixon's visit to China changed the geometry of the cold war, even if it did not speed up the negotiations to end the Vietnam War. The Chinese gained U.S. acquiescence for their admission to the United Nations, which meant that the government in Taiwan had to withdraw from that body. They also received a measure of protection against what they perceived as the territorial and economic threats posed by Russia and

Japan. A link to China became a permanent part of America's diplomatic baggage. When Nixon resigned, for example, Ford hastened to reassure the Chinese that "our relationships with the People's Republic of China will remain a cardinal element of American foreign policy."[28] Carter carried through on the basic design, announcing in December 1978 that full normalization and the establishment of diplomatic relations between the counties would take place at the beginning of 1979.[29]

During the meeting between Mao and Nixon, Mao mentioned the critical role that Henry Kissinger had played in bringing the two leaders together. Kissinger, who as usual was in the same room as Nixon during a critically important moment, demurred about the size of his contribution, telling Mao that "it was the president who set the direction and worked out the plan." Such modest rhetoric aside, the moment marked a crucial point along Kissinger's path to superstardom. He became one of the era's great celebrities, a figure of considerable glamour and, in some quarters, even of sex appeal. Unlike nearly everyone else in the Nixon White House—lawyer Len Garment and flamboyant domestic aide Daniel Patrick Moynihan were significant exceptions—Kissinger maintained his contacts not only in the upper reaches of academia and with such political figures as his former patron Nelson Rockefeller but also with people in the media. Barbara Walters, the rising star of the *Today Show*, was a frequent companion. Kissinger became close friends with Hollywood producer Robert Evans and attended, as a special guest of honor, the March 1972 premiere of *The Godfather*. By that time a Gallup Poll ranked him fourth on the list of the people Americans most admired, behind only Nixon, Billy Graham, and Harry Truman. The next year, as Nixon's star faded, Kissinger claimed the top spot on the list. In the Nixon White House, the glamour lay in Kissinger's realm of foreign policy and super-diplomacy rather than in the more mundane tasks related to domestic policy.[30] Nixon tried to keep his foreign policy successes to himself, yet he could not restrain the irrepressible Kissinger.

China helped to make Henry Kissinger a star, and Kissinger helped to make China a star attraction. China exerted a strong influence over American life in the seventies. In the 1930s, a trip to the Soviet Union, recently recognized by President Roosevelt, acquired a sense of exotic appeal among intellectuals and tourists with a stomach for adventure. In the 1970s, something similar happened with China. For people who had been everywhere, China became the place to go. The list of visitors included economist John Kenneth Galbraith, actress Shirley McLaine, and journalists such as Joseph Alsop and James Reston. Many of these people gushed over what they saw. As one perceptive observer noted, "The monstrous China of the Korean conflict and the Cold War which threatened its neighbors and enslaves its own people now became the China of acupuncture, ancient art treasures, delicious food, purposeful peasants sculpting the countryside."[31] Public interest in Chinese art and artifacts grew, so that one could find galleries devoted to Chinese art along fashionable thoroughfares in New York. People knew that China was somehow important, even if the pace of change was slow after 1972.

OUTREACH TO RUSSIA AND DETENTE

President Nixon cared little about China as a cultural phenomenon, except to the extent that it brought him favorable publicity in an election year. What mattered more to him was the larger mosaic of Cold War politics. Hence, as he made overtures to China, the president also concentrated on the nation's relations with the Soviet Union and worked his way toward a policy that became known as detente. As one expert puts it, "from 1969 to 1972 the two countries moved slowly and unevenly toward a conjunction of interests that would permit their improving relations. Rather suddenly the conjunction blossomed at a summit meeting in May, 1972."[32] The basic motivation for the improvement in relations was a desire to lower the costs of national security.

As in domestic policy, however, the president's opponents could play to either side of him. Those who approved of the basic idea of disarmament and who opposed the Vietnam War could argue that the president's policies did not go far enough. Those who disapproved of detente could argue that the president's policies went too far. The Democratic Party, as it turned out, held people on both sides of the spectrum, creating an opposition to detente that gained momentum as Nixon's political fortunes declined.

Early in the Nixon administration, the Soviet ambassador took Henry Kissinger aside and asked him to set up a meeting with the new president. At that meeting, Dobrynin broached the idea of a summit. It took longer to reach an agreement on a Soviet summit than it did to arrange Nixon's visit to China. In fact, the trip to China made it all the more important to the Soviets that Nixon visit Russia as well. After the same sort of secret diplomacy that marked nearly all of Nixon's foreign policy efforts, the countries agreed that Nixon would go to Moscow in May 1972—springtime of an election year and, as it turns out, another sweeps month on the television networks.[33]

Like the trip to China, Nixon's mission to Moscow contained daily media events that emphasized the theme of progress in U.S.-Soviet relations. Nearly everyday the president signed some sort of agreement with the Russians. On his first full day in Russia, for example, Nixon and Soviet President Nikolai Podgorny put their signatures on an agreement that concerned environmental protection. The next day the president and Premier Alexei Kosygin signed a space-cooperation agreement. As one agreement was followed by another, President and Mrs. Nixon went on public tours of the major sights. With reporters in tow, for example, Mrs. Nixon visited a secondary school, the Moscow Metro, the circus, and Moscow's GUM department store.[34]

The main event came late on Friday, May 26, and early the next morning when the president and General Secretary Leonid Brezhnev signed a treaty and an interim agreement on the limitation of strategic arms. The televised ceremony took place shortly after midnight in the green and gold hall of St. Vladimir in the Grand Kremlin Palace. One set of documents limited defensive anti-ballistic-missile sites and radar systems in the United States and Soviet Union. Each country was allowed to deploy two ABM systems, one to protect its capital city and the other to protect part of its offensive weapon systems. The other set of documents froze the level of land- and sea-based intercontinental ballistic missiles and nuclear warheads for a period of five years. The entire complicated set of agreements became known as the Strategic Arms Limitations Talks treaty.[35]

The agreements underscored the fact that both sides thought they could save money on their military expenditures without sacrificing their internal security, although there were people on both sides who doubted the prudence of the cuts and thought that the leaders might be endangering their followers. The entire SALT process also demonstrated how far military technology had come since the first atomic bombs had been dropped in 1945. Atomic bombs were just one part of a nuclear arsenal that also included delivery systems that worked on land and sea, detection systems that alerted the countries to incoming missiles, and defensive missiles that could, at least in theory, neutralize the other country's offensive missiles. With only a little imagination, one could perceive generation after generation of weapons as each country worked to gain the advantage over the other. The agreements that Nixon and Brezhnev signed were an attempt to begin to put some limits on this process.

Nixon used his visit to Moscow to give a televised address to the Russian people that was also broadcast in the United States. Speaking as much to his American audience as to his Russian one, the president said that the "arms control agreement is not for the purpose of giving either side an advantage over the other. Both of our nations are strong, each respects the strength of the other, each will maintain the strength necessary to defend its independence." He reassured the Russians that the United States did not "covet" anyone else's "territory" and sought only the right "to live in peace, not only for ourselves but for the people of this earth." [36] About 100 million people heard the president deliver these remarks at a time when he was at the very zenith of his power.

Throughout the trip, the president did his best to reassure Americans that he understood their apprehension about the trip. He emphasized that he would not bargain away America's vital interests to accommodate the Soviets. During the trip, he also talked up America's virtues. For example, he made a point of attending the Baptist Church on a Sunday in Moscow, giving the American press a chance to note that it was one of only forty churches in a city of 7 million people.[37]

The trip culminated in another major Kremlin ceremony in which Nixon and Brezhnev signed what was billed as a statement of the "Basic Principles of Relations" between the two countries. It was not a formal treaty that would require the approval of the Senate but rather an idealistic statement of how the relationship between the countries should precede, a sort of blueprint for the process that would become known as detente. In the statement, each side assured the other of its good intentions because "in the nuclear age there is no alternative to conducting their mutual relations on the basis of peaceful coexistence." The two countries pledged to "avoid military confrontation" in order to "prevent the outbreak of nuclear war." The two nations would "exercise restraint in their mutual relations" and always be prepared to negotiate in order "to settle differences by peaceful means."[38] For a sober and much-edited diplomatic document, the basic principles read almost like poetry.

When Nixon gave Brezhnev a Cadillac El Dorado to match the Citroen and Renault that the Soviet leader had recently received from President Georges Pompidou of France, the meeting ended on a gracious and hopeful note. Walter Cronkite, the nation's anchorman, summed up the summit with the judgment that it had exceeded expectations and marked a definite personal achievement of Nixon's diplomacy. The SALT treaty was a particular triumph. With his visits to China and Russia, Nixon, according to one expert, reinforced "America's position as the fulcrum in triangular diplomacy."[39]

WATERGATE AND THE WANING OF DETENTE

In this scheme of triangular diplomacy, much depended on the personal touches of Nixon and Kissinger. The equation of foreign policy and personal diplomacy left Nixon's geopolitical initiatives vulnerable after his reelection. His involvement in the Watergate scandal and the resulting loss of prestige made it more difficult to sustain the pace of his earlier triumphs. The return summit with Brezhnev, for example, took place in the thick of the Watergate hearings in the Senate. As Brezhnev arrived in Washington, the Senate leaders announced that John Dean's testimony before Sam Ervin's committee would be postponed for a week because, as Senator Howard Baker put it, summit meetings should not have competition.

Nixon and Brezhnev tried hard to emulate the productivity and good fellowship of the first summit but without much success. This time, Nixon gave Brezhnev a Lincoln Continental (a Chrysler Imperial might have sent the wrong signal), and on the very first day of the summit the two leaders, who according to CBS's Roger Mudd acted like "old buddies," agreed to share information in such fields as oceanography and agriculture. Nixon took Brezhnev on a boat ride on the Potomac and acted the genial host. After a trip to Camp David, the pair returned to Washington and signed what the White House hoped would be perceived as two important agreements. One contained a call for negotiations before the end of 1974 on a treaty to reduce the number of nuclear weapons. The other concerned sharing information for the peaceful use of nuclear energy.[40]

Then the summit moved from Washington to San Clemente, California, in part to match the hospitality that Brezhnev had shown Nixon in Kiev but in part to get away from the Watergate hearings. Brezhnev met some visiting astronauts and hugged movie star Chuck Connors, who presented him with a set of Colt 45s, yet not even those photogenic events could divert the nation's attention from Watergate.[41] NBC news buried the story of Brezhnev's final departure from Washington to Europe on June 25 some twenty minutes into its nightly news broadcast. John Dean's testimony dominated the news of the day.[42]

Kissinger tried to pump up the summit's importance and in particular noted that there might be a permanent agreement to limit offensive nuclear weapons within a year. The White House pointed to agreements, such as a commitment by the two countries to urgent consultation in the event of a nuclear threat and a promise not to threaten each other or each other's allies, as evidence of progress. But the reporters wanted to know whether Nixon and Brezhnev had discussed Watergate. No, replied Kissinger, Watergate was not mentioned because that was a domestic policy matter.[43]

INTERLUDE: WAR IN THE MIDDLE EAST

Watergate remained a preoccupation during the war that broke out in the Middle East between Egypt and Israel and provided the first big post-summit test of Soviet-U.S. relations. Wishing to end the Israeli occupation of the Egyptian Sinai, Egypt launched a surprise attack on Israel on October 6, 1973. As the administration formulated its response to this direct assault on an American ally, Nixon also had to contend with the resignation of Vice President Agnew on October 10 and the Saturday night massacre some ten days after that. Attempting to use the new channels that the summits had created, the United States and the Soviet Union worked to get a cease-fire resolution through the United Nations. On October 22, 1973, the United Nations Security Council adopted a jointly sponsored cease-fire resolution.

The height of the crisis came after the adoption of this resolution. The cease-fire proved difficult to maintain, with both sides sniping at the other and seeking to gain maximum advantage in the period after the war. At one point, the Israelis moved to surround the Egyptian Third Army Corps, which was trapped on the southeast bank of the Suez Canal and cut off from the rest of the country. The Soviets told the Americans that it was their obligation to get the Israelis to observe the cease-fire and threatened unilateral action against Israel, an action that Kissinger described as "one of the most serious challenges to an American president by a Soviet leader."[44] At this point, Kissinger appeared to be coordinating American foreign policy largely on his own; Brezhnev even took the unorthodox step of corresponding directly with him, rather than with the preoccupied Nixon. Kissinger decided that the United States had to stop the Soviets from taking unilateral action.

On his own initiative and without so much as informing Nixon of Brezhnev's threatening note, Kissinger convened a meeting of the National Security Council and put the military on high alert. In time a settlement favorable to the United States was reached in which Egypt and the United States reestablished diplomatic relations and the Egyptians made overtures to the Israelis that resulted in peace between the two countries.[45] Still, the crisis tested the ability of the United States to conduct its foreign relations in the midst of serious domestic distractions. In the past a Middle East war would have galvanized the nation's attention; in October 1973, it was just one story among many.

A final Nixon trip to Russia at the end of June 1974 appeared to be about his historical legacy rather than the immediate tensions of the Cold War. By this time, the impeachment process was in full swing, and the president's travels had a desperate quality to them, as if he preferred to be abroad. The country was not nearly as enchanted with the summit process as it had been earlier. Television anchors, who did not go on this trip, noted that the Russians censored the reports from their correspondents and highlighted the lack of religious freedom in the Soviet Union and the desire of many groups to leave the country.[46] This final Nixon summit produced an agreement over strategic nuclear weapons that the press judged as falling short of expectations. The president spoke about creating the structure for a permanent peace that would open the way toward joint ventures between the two nations, such as an upcoming Soviet-American space mission. He left office without being able to complete this structure.

THE END OF THE VIETNAM WAR

Instead, Nixon's immediate legacy was a humiliating defeat in Vietnam. After the formal end of American involvement in 1973, Nixon hoped that, if the destruction of South Vietnam were imminent, the United States would somehow intervene to stop it. Congress, playing upon Nixon's political vulnerability, made sure that would not happen with the passage of the Case-Church bill (named for its sponsors, Senator Clifford Case, Republican of New Jersey and Senator Frank Church, an Idaho Democrat) in June 1973. This measure guaranteed that no more federal funds would be spent for U.S. military involvement in Indochina. Then in spring 1975 Cambodia fell to the Khmer Rouge, and the North Vietnamese launched a final battle to conquer South Vietnam and reunite the country under communist rule. President Gerald Ford tried to reassure the South Vietnamese that the United States would do something, as the fortunes of the South Vietnamese army worsened. He made a personal appearance before a joint session of Congress on April 10, 1975, and appealed for a billion dollars worth of aid for South Vietnam. Some of the congressmen, amazed that Ford would seek to prolong the war, walked out on Ford, who got the message, as he later stated publicly, that "the war is finished as far as America is concerned."[47]

One final moment remained. On April 28, 1975, the president received word that the North Vietnamese had begun the last attack on Saigon. Ford ordered the embassy, the remaining piece of American ground on Vietnamese soil, to be evacuated. The next day American television viewers heard John Chancellor tell them that the evacuation of Saigon was complete, marking the end of twenty-five years of American involvement in

Vietnam. About 900 Americans and more than 5,000 South Vietnamese were evacuated. Marines had to hold back South Vietnamese who desperately wanted to get on a helicopter and leave Saigon. Many South Vietnamese citizens clawed at the top of the wall around the embassy only to have their fingers mashed by the rifles of U.S. Marines. The next day Saigon fell to the North Vietnamese, who renamed it Ho Chi Minh City and declared a final victory to the war. The sight of people clinging to the pontoons of the overloaded helicopters as they struggled to get off the roof of the embassy would be one of the indelible images of the era.

The United States and Vietnam paid a high price for the long war. More than 20,000 Americans died on Nixon's watch alone, including more than 4,000 killed during the last year of fighting. The marginal benefits of those final four years of the war under Nixon's watch were difficult to discern. In all, 58,022 American lives were lost in Vietnam, and the United States spent some $140 billion on the war. A staggering number of Vietnamese died—an estimated 924,048 soldiers loyal to the North Vietnamese and over 185,000 South Vietnamese soldiers.[48] To put the matter in the economic terms that someone like Robert McNamara, Lyndon Johnson's secretary of defense, might have favored, the nation spent a lot of money, accrued high opportunity costs, lost a great deal of human capital, and still failed to halt the takeover of South Vietnam by the North. In the end the United States either lost its will, came to its senses, or both.

THE CENTRAL INTELLIGENCE AGENCY AFTER VIETNAM AND WATERGATE

America's defeat in Vietnam and the politics of presidential scandal exercised a large influence over the era that was to follow. Vietnam became the new template for American foreign policy, and, taken together, the Vietnam defeat and Watergate affected nearly every institution concerned with the country's international relations. The fate of the Central Intelligence Agency in the seventies was a good example.

This postwar successor to the Office of Strategic Services played a key role in the Cold War. It gathered information about foreign countries ranging from the crop yields in Hungary to the state of nuclear-weapons research in Russia and engaged in secret missions designed to further United States' interests. Oversight always presented a problem. If the CIA wanted to engage in secret activities, its head could hardly appear in open congressional session and request money for, say, a coup in Iran. At the same time, its fiscal operations needed to be integrated with those of the rest of the government, and, however much latitude one granted the agency, the effectiveness and even the morality of its actions had to be reviewed by someone. At first, gentlemen trusted gentlemen to run the agency responsibly. In the postwar era, the CIA recruited many of its operatives from the same Ivy League ranks as filled the top positions in the State Department and the staffs of key congressional committees. Watergate changed the climate of acceptance for passive restraints on the CIA and created a movement that the agency be more directly accountable to Congress and the American people.

Just as in the Watergate scandal, investigative journalists led the way. On December 22, 1974, Seymour Hersh reported in the New York Times that the CIA had engaged in domestic activities with the object of disrupting the anti–Vietnam War movement. In this manner, the drive to reform the CIA became tied to recriminations over the way in which America managed the war. It fit a familiar historical pattern. The immediate aftermath of war was often a time of economic and ideological tension even after great American victories. People looked for scapegoats to explain why things were going wrong. Just as Senator Joseph McCarthy sought to expose the subversion from within that led to postwar problems, so Watergate, another type of secret conspiracy, encouraged people to dig beneath the surface of American foreign policy in order to uncover the corruption lying below. The unhappy ending to the Vietnam War reinforced this tendency. The Democratic Congress hastened to investigate how the Republicans in the White House had failed to restrain the CIA and, in so doing, had exacerbated the problems of the Vietnam era.

The CIA story broke after Nixon's departure, which meant his successor Gerald Ford was forced to deal with it. Ford created a presidential commission to investigate the activities of the CIA. He put former New York governor Nelson Rockefeller, his house liberal, in charge. Public disclosure of secret intelligence activities proved to be a continuing problem, with the result that the Rockefeller Commission could not publicize much of what it found. The Senate eagerly followed up with its own Select Committee and gave Frank Church, the Idaho Democrat, presidential candidate, and leading critic of the Vietnam War, the primary role. Leaked secrets, such as the CIA's attempts to assassinate Fidel Castro, tarnished the image of the United States. The nation's Cold War exploits no longer looked so heroic, a major difference between the seventies and the postwar era. Eventually, the head of the CIA resigned, and Congress, in an assertion of its powers that was typical of the times, created a more formal oversight structure for the agency.[49]

THE MEANING OF THE FALL OF VIETNAM

The changes in the CIA showed how Vietnam and Watergate triggered the events that followed in the seventies. They also demonstrated how the immediate reactions to these events involved moving the country left, rather than the right, and strengthening the fortunes of the Democrats rather than the Republicans. As a symbol, however, the Vietnam War remained in flux. In Vietnam the United States spent lots of money, lost lots of lives, and still could not prevent North Vietnam from taking over the South. Yet what looked like a major mistake in 1973 came to be viewed as a more noble project as the immediate rancor of the debate over the war faded. The facts were that the North Vietnamese did not conquer the south while the United States was actively involved in the war, and the U.S. showed the rest of the world that it was willing to pay a high price to resist Communist aggression.[50] The image of the Vietnam War benefited from the ultimate victory of the United States in the cold war.

In the seventies, though, the war left the country with a loss of confidence in its military that undermined its commitment to engage in a protracted struggles abroad. That negative feeling caused a renewed search for allies who would represent American interests in strategic locations around the world and who might have the means and the resources to finance their own defense against communism. American leaders felt the need to engage in a more pragmatic diplomacy, based on practical considerations, as opposed to the ideologically based diplomacy that put the Americans on the side of the "free" world in the struggle against communism. At home, in concert with these other activities, America's leaders sought ways of reducing military expenditures without, at the same time, endangering the national security. In the seventies, the world looked very different than it had only a few years before.

3

Running Out of Gas

The Economic Downturn and Social Change

Even more than Watergate and Vietnam, the economy was the factor that gave the seventies its distinctive character. After the great run of postwar prosperity, the state of the economy slid into stagnation for much of the period between 1973 and 1982. This downturn differed from other postwar recessions that had featured business slowdowns and temporary layoffs. Although those things occurred in the seventies, they happened in a more sustained and deeper way and with the added twist of inflation accompanying the slowdowns. It looked at the time as though a crucial climacteric had been reached and that the great streak of economic growth that characterized the postwar period was over for good. It became fashionable to predict that Americans would no longer be able to enjoy the luxuries to which they had become accustomed, such as fast and powerful cars fueled by inexpensive gasoline, houses heated and cooled to perfection, and diets that were heavy on beefsteak rather than macaroni and cheese.

Poor economic performance eroded the respect that Americans had for their political leaders. It was an accepted part of the post–New Deal order that the president managed the economy so that it grew without wrenching changes in the business cycle. Indeed, economic scholars who had studied the business cycle in minute detail in the thirties and forties focused their attention on governmental policy in the postwar era. In particular, economists examined the things that the president could do to adjust the economy, fine-tuning, in the idiom of the sixties, so that it continued to hum. The government's performance became more important than the activities of individual businesses.

It took well into the eighties for the economy to regain its vitality. Therefore, just as the thirties left a permanent mark in the way that Americans thought about the economy and policymakers used the federal government to stabilize the economy, so the seventies, with great inflation, worries about productivity, and the energy crisis, reoriented America's approach to economic policy.

Despite the eventual recovery in the eighties, the seventies were a time of considerable economic anxiety. Some of the effects of this anxiety produced permanent changes in the structure of the American economy. Many companies, for example, confronted by international competition and other factors that led to small returns in their core markets, such as steel, moved into new areas of economic endeavor where, in an inflationary era, the possibility for profits was greater. In this manner, Armco Steel, one of the nation's major steel producers, ended the decade of the seventies by doing some 40 percent of its business outside of the steel industry. No longer sure of the long-term health of steel manufacturing, this once-proud company turned to what it perceived as the more lucrative real estate business. The consequences for those who worked in Armco's mills were severe. They faced not only declining real wages in the face of the virulent inflation but the possibility of unemployment as Armco cut back its operations. The real estate operation, whatever its level of profitability, required fewer employees than did the manufacture of steel.

Even beyond troubled industries like steel, the corporate culture was changing in the seventies in ways that would become fully visible in the eighties. No longer was holding stock predominantly something that wealthy individuals did to maintain the value of their fortunes. New entrants into the market, distressed by the low level of returns on government-regulated bank deposits, invested in mutual funds, which were run by professional money managers. These mutual funds, along with pension funds and large financial institutions such as insurance companies, made large block trades. That phenomenon, in turn, made trading more volatile, as money managers sought stocks that promised short-term gains rather than long-term appreciation and that paid maximum dividends. Eventually, this new emphasis on stock profitability would lead to profound changes in corporations in the eighties, such as downsizing to reduce the payroll and take advantage of improvements in technology and in more extreme cases the transfer of manufacturing operations from the United States to lower-wage countries abroad. The seventies, then, were an important way station in the transformation of the strong, but largely insular postwar economy into the stronger, but less secure global economy.[1]

The Big Picture

In broad outline, the rate of growth of the gross national product, an aggregate measure of the size of the economy, fell dramatically during the seventies. In the period between 1960 and 1973, the average annual compound rate of growth for the GNP was on the order of 4 percent. In the period from 1973 to 1982 it went down to 1.8 percent. The unemployment rate, which was 4.8 percent in 1973, rose to 8.3 percent in 1975. By the end of the decade, the inflation rate reached double digits. For the entire decade, the average inflation rate was 8.8 percent, which was well above the postwar average.[2]

The era's first recession occurred between March 1973 and March 1975. It featured the initial oil shock of the decade, a sudden rise in the price of oil that forced a rise in prices more generally and increased the cost of production in nearly all industries. In October 1973, for example, oil prices rose by more than 50 percent and then doubled in January 1974. Despite a sustained recovery that began in 1975, a second recession started in 1978 and lasted for the rest of the decade and beyond. It, too, contained an oil shock that made it hard for motorists to find gas for their cars and that had a depressing effect on the entire economy.

The economic problems of the seventies affected nearly every American household and the entire world. The average worker's real after-tax pay grew rapidly from the forties through the mid-sixties and then a little more slowly after that. It hit a postwar high in 1972, the year of Nixon's overtures to Russia and China and his triumphant reelection. Then it declined, recovered only a little in middecade, and fell again. Hence, by 1979 the workers' take-home pay was 6 percent below its 1972 level. If one looked at household, rather than individual income, the results were much the same. In constant 1983 dollars, a married couple earning a median income of $26,982 in 1970 received an income of only $26,856 in 1982.[3] As American earnings stagnated, America's relative economic position in the world declined. In 1951, with much of Europe's productive capacity still affected by the war, the United States accounted for about a third of the world's trade. By 1971 that proportion had fallen to 18 percent. In that year the nation recorded its first trade deficit of the century, and conditions only grew worse as the era progressed. Although there was a reprieve in 1975, the deficits continued in 1976 and 1977.[4] Although the United States had far more total wealth than any other country, its gross domestic product per capita was no longer the highest in the world; in 1950, 1960, and 1970 the United States had stood first in the world in that category. In 1980, after the economic dislocations of the seventies, the United States fell to number eleven on the list, behind the Scandinavian countries and the Netherlands and Belgium.[5]

One did not have to be an econometrician to detect the country's problems. The long gas lines in 1974 and 1979 became the stuff of American legend, the sort of visual symbol that provided an instant reminder of bad times, much like the cartloads of money being wheeled down the street during the rampant inflation of Weimar Germany. Other troubling signs of change could be found in most American towns and cities. As the price of gasoline rose, auto dealerships found themselves stuck with costly, fuel-inefficient cars that were difficult to sell. Americans began to turn to Japanese car brands, such as Toyota, Nissan, and Honda, all of which surpassed the Volkswagen during the seventies. Japan became the country's leading seller of foreign cars, and Americans bought almost two million of them in 1977.[6] By contrast, the Japanese bought only fifteen thousand American cars.

In John Updike's fictional depiction of the decade, his hero Rabbit Angstrom sells Toyotas in the eastern Pennsylvania town of Brewer. As the novel begins, Rabbit reflects that "there isn't a piece of junk on the road gets better mileage than his Toyotas, with lower service costs." In Rabbit's world, "the people out there are getting frantic, they know the great American ride is ending." Rabbit sells them Toyotas as a means of turning their "rotten" dollars into yen.[7]

THE PRESIDENT AND MACROECONOMIC POLICY

As the seventies began, President Nixon and his advisors thought they had a good handle on how to manage the economy. For Nixon and for every other postwar president, economic experts were built into the institutional machinery of the White House. In 1946 Congress had legislated a symbolic statement that the nation should strive for full employment and created a Council of Economic Advisors to make recommendations to the president on that matter. By the time of John F. Kennedy's administration, the council, which produced an annual economic report of the president, enjoyed growing influence over the nation's economic policy.

The Kennedy-era tax cut, enacted in 1964, validated the wisdom of the economists on the Council of Economic Advisors, who pointed out that, although the federal budget was in deficit, it would generate a surplus if the economy were at full employment. The tax cut would send the nation along the path to full employment. When the tax cut produced generally salutary results, it boosted the dependence of the president on his economic experts. By 1965 the Council of Economic Advisors enjoyed unprecedented prestige, and its chairman had more access to the president than did most members of the cabinet, who were often forced by the president to do the council's bidding. Depending on the advice of the Council of Economic Advisors, Presidents Johnson and Nixon hoped to fine-tune the economy to take the shocks out of the business cycle and prevent an economic meltdown on the order of the great depression.[8]

The collaborative endeavor of economic policy extended well beyond the White House. The three main factors over which the federal government exercised influence were the tax rate, the level of federal spending, and the money supply. In the seventies, the tax rate mattered because most of the nation's workers had tax payments deducted from their regular paychecks. A reduction in the tax rate, therefore, meant a larger paycheck. Most workers would go out and buy something with the extra money, stimulating the economy. But the president could not reduce the tax rates by fiat. He needed to work with Congress, which passed legislation governing the tax code and the tax rates.

The level of federal spending affected the economy because the federal government was itself an important factor in the demand for goods and services. If the government decided to build a bomb or a bomber to fight the Vietnam War, that meant more money to companies in places like Seattle, Los Angeles, and St. Louis and a boost to the local economies. Although the president made annual suggestions as to the appropriate size of the federal government, it was, however, hard for him or for anyone else to control the budget's actual size. A budget, as political scientist Aaron Wildavsky famously put it, was only a prediction of future events.[9] A federal budget consisted of thousands and thousands of individual items, each of which was the responsibility of some congressional committee. Reaching an agreed-upon total was difficult.

The importance of the money supply stemmed from the fact that, other things being equal, prices moved with the money supply. If the size of the money supply increased and the level of the nation's goods and services remained the same, that meant that more money was chasing the same amount of goods. Because there were more dollars in the same economy, each dollar was worth less and hence it took more dollars to buy the same goods as before; the nominal price of the goods rose. In a similar sense, a contraction in the money supply implied a decline in the price rate. The government had the means of influencing the money supply through the actions of the central bank or Federal Reserve. This bank could, for example, buy or sell government securities. When it bought these securities, it put money into circulation, and when it sold securities it drew money out of circulation. The bank also had an influence over the interest rate, which was, in effect, the price of money. If money became more expensive because of rising interest rates, people hesitated to undertake new projects that required them to borrow money. Lowering interest rates had the effect of stimulating economic activity Of course, neither the president nor Congress could order the Federal Reserve Board to do anything. It was another institutional element of economic policy that needed to be coordinated with the others.

Despite the apparent abundance of economic policy tools and the favorable results that had been produced by following the advice of the Council of Economic Advisors in 1964, the economy proved very difficult for Richard Nixon and his successors to manage during the seventies. The conventional theories failed to predict the economy's course. One government official, in charge of making important economic estimates, expressed the sense of bafflement and confusion that prevailed in policymaking circles when he said that "our 1972 estimates turned out to be very wrong, very quickly. But if we had predicted what actually happened in the 1970s we would have been practicing in an asylum."[10]

THE PROBLEM OF INFLATION

The phenomenon of inflation proved particularly perplexing to understand and hence to control. One explanation for inflation was that it reflected a growth in the money supply and therefore one remedy might be a rise in the interest rate. Another explanation for inflation was that the economy was being forced to operate beyond full capacity. A generation of economics students learned that when the gross national product reached a level beyond full capacity the difference was made up through inflation. The remedies might be a rise in the tax rates or a decrease in government spending.

In both cases the implicit assumption was that high rates of inflation went with low rates of unemployment. Economists observed an explicit trade-off, known as the Phillips curve, between unemployment and inflation. Since an increase in the unemployment rate tended to be associated with a decrease in the inflation rate, experts could presumably maneuver the economy's position along the curve to produce the ideal blend of employment and prices.

Even though the Phillips curve rested on empirical observation rather than theoretical deduction, it made intuitive sense. If inflation persisted and the government decided to raise the interest rates, then the cost of a construction project would rise and the demand for such projects would fall, with the result that the construction company might decide to lay off workers. If the government decided to combat inflation by reducing its spending, then less money would reach companies making widgets for the government and the companies might be forced to let workers go. Each of these illustrations supported the idea of an inverse relationship between employment and inflation.

The trouble was that the economic tools as they had evolved in the postwar era worked better to stimulate the economy than to slow it down. This result reflected the intellectual pedigree of the tools, which arose in response to the condition of deflation. The problem during the great depression was not rising prices that put goods and services out of people's reach but falling prices that went hand-in-hand with unemployment. Workers without money in their pockets could not afford to buy things, even though the prices of those things were falling. The more that demand fell, the more prices fell, creating what might be called a deflationary spiral. So economists thought of ways that government could act to stimulate the economy. In theory, each of the tools in the economic kit could work on inflation as well as on deflation. The obverse of increasing government spending was to decrease government spending and of expanding the money supply was contracting it. Yet politically it was easier to gin up government spending then to cut it back, to lower interest rates rather than to raise them.

The nightmare of the seventies that first materialized on Nixon's watch was that the Phillips curve trade-off failed to show up. Inflation and unemployment occurred simultaneously. Deflating the economy, difficult under any circumstances, became that much harder to accomplish in the seventies because unemployment made conventional remedies particularly painful. Reducing government spending and raising interest rates would almost certainly worsen the condition of unemployment. In other words, the Phillips curve trade-off had many potentially negative but few positive effects, and the phenomenon of inflation remained something of a mystery.

New sorts of institutional factors appeared to be operating. Maybe inflation, once started, could not be controlled. A wage increase, for example, might cause a ripple to go through the entire economy until the general price level rose. That in turn might create the expectation of further inflation that would, in and of itself, exacerbate the problem. Future wage settlements in key industries would, for example, need to forecast future inflation. And the phenomenon of inflation tended to be amplified by such things as Social Security benefits that were indexed to the rate of inflation and wage rates keyed to the inflation rate in important industries such as automobiles.

NIXON AND PRICE CONTROLS

Richard Nixon, a Republican, inherited the intellectual baggage of his predecessors and the understanding that to control inflation he would have to accept some unemployment. His economic advisors endeavored to design a path that would bring prices down and set the stage for a noninflationary expansion of the economy, preferably in time for the congressional elections in 1970. What happened was not reassuring. The CEA used its statistical skills to estimate a level of growth below which the inflation rate could be expected to go down. Actual output fell below that level but without any significant decline in the stubborn inflation rate.

Democrats in Congress argued that it was necessary to clamp down on inflation by setting formal limits on how much wages and prices could rise. In a skillful political game of cat and mouse, Congress passed legislation in 1970 that gave the president authority to impose wage and price controls, should he wish to do so.[11] Nixon accepted the challenge and announced a major new economic policy in August 1971. He tried to deal with all of the nation's economic problems simultaneously. Nixon's package included an investment tax credit to stimulate the economy and respond to the fact that not all of the nation's productive capacity was being exploited. The president also proposed repealing an existing excise tax on automobiles and increasing income tax exemptions, which had already been legislated, sooner than planned. To help the ailing balance of payments, Nixon suggested the traditional political remedy of raising the price of imports by taxing them.

Then there was the tricky problem of the dollar. In the postwar economy, the dollar acted as an international currency. As the United States bought a record amount of goods and services from abroad, the sellers of those goods accepted dollars in payment. In theory, each of the dollars could be converted into gold at an officially agreed upon rate. In fact, the United States did not have enough gold as its disposal to support the volume of dollars that were in circulation. If a mass movement started to convert dollars into gold, then the United States would have to take countermeasures of some sort, which might mean going off the international gold standard. As constituted, the gold standard contained a powerful weapon against inflation. If one nation shipped gold to another to remedy a trade deficit, then the gold-backed money supply of that nation would fall and, as the money supply fell, so would prices. As prices fell, the goods and services would become more attractive to other nations and the problems that caused gold to be shipped would be eased. That was the theory. If, however, the United States went off the gold standard and suspended the convertibility of dollars into gold, then one would expect those dollars to be worth less and prices to rise. So Nixon and his economic advisors made what might be called a cross-cutting move. They took the nation off the gold standard and allowed the dollar to float in international currency markets, but they accompanied the move with price and wage controls for ninety days to restrain inflationary expectations. Similarly, the expansionary tax cuts were balanced by restraining cuts in federal spending.[12]

The problem with price and wage controls was that even if they worked in the short run, they would have to end at some point, and at that point a sudden inflationary burst might occur. In the case of the United States, the imposition of the controls occurred just before a series of untoward events put pressure on the economy and created an explosion of inflation. The events doomed the controls, making them, in the word of Nixon economic advisor Herbert Stein, "powerless." First, food prices rose as the demand for American agricultural products increased because of large purchases made by the Soviet Union and other foreign countries in 1972. Then came the first of the decade's oil shocks. Oil prices increased fourfold. With food and oil costing more, the general price level shot upward and produced the worst inflation of the postwar era. The high price of oil soon affected the general level of business activity, and by the end of 1973 the United States economy was in a recession. The consumer price index went up 12.2 percent in 1974.[13]

THE ENERGY CRISIS IN HISTORICAL PERSPECTIVE

If inflation was the major economic problem of the seventies, then the energy crisis was its proximate cause. As a consequence, economic policy needed to focus not just on the traditional concerns related to unemployment and inflation but also, for the first time, on energy policy. Because of energy's synergistic role in the economy and its identity as both a domestic- and foreign-policy issue, it became the exception to many of the decade's policy rules.

Energy prices functioned something like interest rates. Low energy prices, like low interest rates, encouraged economic expansion. The energy problem of the seventies involved tremendous rises in the price of gasoline and other fuels used to power the American economy. One solution for the energy crisis, like the solution to the inflation problem, was for energy prices to come down. Simple economic theory dictated that, if energy prices came down, then the consumption of energy would go up.

But considerations related to foreign policy and international security complicated the matter of lowering energy prices. The most obvious way to make energy prices lower was to increase the available supply of that commodity. Importing more oil from abroad turned out to be the easiest way of accomplishing this result, but depending on foreign oil created major threats to the nation's security. The nations with the most oil to sell were not sympathetic to U.S. policy objectives in the Middle East. Giving those nations the power to limit the nation's energy supply meant that unfriendly nations could affect the nation's ability to wage war. The best option appeared to be developing secure sources of domestic oil. If the country could manage to accomplish that objective, however, then the price of oil, at least in the short run, would surely rise, exacerbating the inflation problem and restricting the ability of the economy to grow.

Like many aspects of an economy with the simultaneous appearance of unemployment and inflation, the energy situation had an almost Alice-in-Wonderland quality. It was clear that oil, although a natural commodity like soy beans or pork bellies, was different from most other commodities. Soy beans and pork bellies could be replenished on a seasonal basis, but the supply of oil could not be manipulated so easily. Adding to the problem, some commodities, like oil, mattered more than others because fewer substitutes existed for them. If the nation lost its supply of bananas, people could switch to other fruits or do without. The nation simply could not do without oil without altering its lifestyle beyond recognition.

Oil, natural gas, and similar products pumped from the ground acquired great importance during the course of the twentieth century. In the nineteenth century, John D. Rockefeller made a fortune in oil at a time when its main uses were as an illuminant and a lubricant. In time, electricity replaced kerosene and natural gas as the means of lighting up cities at night and commodities like turpentine could also serve as lubricants. This substitution of one commodity by another was a natural process of change over time. In the twenties, to use a gastronomic example, aspiring middle-class couples served chicken rather than beef at dinner parties because chicken was the more expensive, fancier meat. Fried chicken was a company dish. In the seventies, dinner at a steak house implied an upscale evening. Fried chicken was food for common folks, available at fast-food joints.

Oil became a more precious commodity over time, just as beefsteaks did. The advent of the automobile made oil the fuel that powered America's most important product. Americans also used gas as their fuel of choice for cooking, and many heated their houses with home heating oil. In older homes, during the seventies, one could still see external chutes through which merchants had kept houses supplied with coal for their furnaces. New homes were built without coal chutes because people used different sources of energy to keep their homes warm. New England, in particular, depended on home heating oil to get through the cold winters.

Although important, oil was both plentiful and homegrown in the postwar period. Rockefeller's Standard Oil Company started as the result of an oil boom not in Saudi Arabia and other areas now associated with oil but rather in a region near the border of Pennsylvania and Ohio. In time, Texas, Oklahoma, Louisiana, and California became major oil-producing states. In 1913, at the dawn of the automobile age, the United States produced something like two-thirds of the world's supply of oil. Then discoveries in other parts of the world, often by American, British, or Dutch companies, changed the picture. In the postwar period, a major glut of oil developed in an international market that was controlled by American and European refiners who sold their products under names like Esso (for Standard Oil), BP (for British Petroleum), and Shell (for Royal Dutch Shell). According to expert Daniel Yergin, the production of oil went from 8.7 million barrels per day in 1948 to 42 million barrels per day in 1972. At the same time, America's share (if not the share of American companies) of the total world production fell by almost two-thirds, from 64 to 22 percent. As fast as the world burned oil, it discovered new reserves of oil, but most of the newly discovered oil was in the Middle East, not in the United States. By 1973 more than a third of the oil that America consumed came from abroad.[14]

American oil production peaked at the very beginning of the seventies, but the demand for oil continued to grow in America's factories, power plants, homes, and motor vehicles. The Middle Eastern countries, gaining political autonomy and independence both from their former colonial masters and from the oil companies, began to have more of an influence over the price of oil. Using their newfound leverage, the petroleum-exporting nations raised the share of revenues that they expected from the oil companies in 1971 and raised the price of oil as well.

NIXON AND ENERGY

When President Nixon imposed price and wage controls in August 1971, he had in mind oil as a major source of rising prices. Under Nixon's system, oil resources that were already developed were subject to price controls, but newly developed oil was exempt. In this way he tried to restrain the oil companies from taking advantage of the new scarcity in oil by extracting so-called windfall profits from consumers and also to encourage producers to seek new domestic sources of oil. When price controls on other commodities expired in 1974, Congress allowed the double-tiered oil price control to remain in place.[15]

If anything, this tinkering with the market made the situation worse than it would otherwise have been. By 1973 energy had clearly emerged as one of the nation's major problems. As the demand for oil continued to rise, some oil-refining companies could not get enough oil for their refineries. In the summer of 1973, U.S. oil imports rose to 6.2 million barrels per day, compared to 3.2 million barrels in 1970.

With the United States more dependent on oil, and on foreign oil, than ever before, the situation turned even worse in the fall. In the Arab-Israeli War of October 1973, the United States supported the Israelis. This action alienated the Arab nations in the region, which happened, along with non-Arab Iran, to be the countries with the most conspicuous oil surpluses available for export. In October 1973, delegates from the Gulf states met in Kuwait and decided that the times afforded them the opportunity to raise the price of oil by 70 percent. Then they opted to use oil as a strategic weapon against the United States. In effect, they agreed to supply oil to countries that were friendly to their foreign-policy interests and to cut off other nations. Hence, as American diplomats threaded their way through the Arab-Israeli conflict and tried to get the warring nations to agree to a cease fire, they also had to cope with the fact that Saudi Arabia had decided to cut off oil shipments to the United States. The oil embargo had begun.[16]

It lasted for five months, from October 1973 until March 1974—a time of panic gas buying that sent prices up even further and exacerbated the problems of spot shortages, much as consumers in the Washington area rid the grocery shelves of bread and toilet paper at the first hint of snow. Motorists waited in long gas lines and burned up fuel as they did so. Many bought gasoline more often so as to be sure not to run out. Stations began rationing their product. Even so, many stations ran out of gas faster than the refineries could replenish their supplies.[17]

Richard Nixon, up to his ears in problems related to Watergate, felt the need to calm the nation down in November 1973. He spoke in the language of austerity to a nation unaccustomed to hearing it. He said that the nation was heading toward the "most acute shortages of energy" since the Second World War. As in wartime, the nation would need to conserve, which meant using "less heat, less electricity, less gasoline."

He foresaw changes in school and factory schedules and the cancellation of some airplane flights.

The actions that Nixon recommended struck at the very heart of the postwar American lifestyle. He asked the governors, for example, to reset the speed limits to fifty miles an hour, which would make the traffic that raced across the straight and flat surfaces of interstates in places like Nebraska and Nevada slow to a relative crawl. He urged people to carpool and use mass transit, rather than sitting in stately solitude on the way to work. He sought to put the nation on daylight saving time on a yearly basis, with the result that students would stumble through the dark on the way to school. He announced a 15 percent reduction in the supply of heating oil for homes and businesses, asked everyone to lower their home thermostats by six degrees, and ordered that federal offices be kept at a temperature of between sixty-five and sixty-eight degrees (Nixon himself liked to light a fire and jack up the air-conditioning). He thought that the business hours in what were still called shopping centers, rather than malls, might be cut back.

Nixon also saw the energy crisis as an opportunity to undercut some of the Democrats' regulatory initiatives. He thought that environmental regulations might be relaxed on a case-by-case basis so as to balance shared environmental "interests" with "energy requirements, which, of course, are indispensable." He urged that there be more exploration for oil so as to increase the country's oil reserves and that the Alaskan pipeline be constructed to transport oil from Alaska's north slope to a southern port from which it could be shipped to market. In the face of the energy crisis, Congress put aside its environmental scruples about a pipeline knifing its way through pristine wilderness and approved the project. Nixon wanted the Atomic Energy Commission to speed up the licensing and construction of nuclear power plants and for governments to put an end to regulations that it made it difficult to mine for coal at the surface ("strip-mining"). He also thought that the federal government should support research and development efforts, for example, to extract oil from the oil shale in the western United States.

Nixon reached back to comfortable technological analogies to reinforce his message. He exhorted the United States to achieve energy self-sufficiency by 1980 by engaging in what he called, in words meant to echo the nation's interest in its coming bicentennial, "Project Independence." This project would take the form of a technological challenge, similar to the efforts to develop the atomic bomb, known as the Manhattan Project, and to send a man to the moon, known as Project Apollo.[18]

THE PRODUCTIVITY PROBLEM

The energy crisis provided opportunities for President Nixon to ad-monish the nation and cajole Americans to pull together to overcome their problems. A more subtle economic problem of the seventies that did not lend itself so readily to political speeches was the nation's falling productiv-ity rate. A leading economist in this field noted a relatively constant level of productivity growth from the First World War to the middle of the sixties. Then, starting around 1966, a decline in the level of growth began to occur, so that what began as an annual rate of 2.5 percent in the mid-sixties fell to less than 1 percent in 1979. In that year, the rate of productivity growth was lower than it had been in any year since the depth of the great depression in 1933. The drop in productivity growth meant a slowing down of the previ-ously inevitable process by which each American worker was able to pro-duce more goods per hour and take home more pay each year.[19] One could, of course, produce economic growth by many means, such as a rise in the birth rate, an increase in immigration, or the discovery of new economic resources. But what had catapulted American to the top rank among the world's economies by the end of the nineteenth century was the technical ingenuity of its manufacturing sector.

In the mature economy of the seventies, productivity gains did not come easily to the American economy. One reason was the slowing down of the exodus from the farms to the cities. As farmers became more productive over the course of the nineteenth century, the nation, even with its growing population and foreign markets for its crops, needed fewer farmers. Hence a nation of farmers became a nation of urban and suburban dwellers who did other things. The change, by its very nature, increased the level of na-tional productivity because agricultural productivity, for all of its impres-sive achievements, lagged behind industrial productivity. As people moved from the country to the city, they went, on average, from a less productive to a more productive job and in the process increased the rate of national productivity. The trend continued well into the twentieth century. For ex-ample, as economist Lester Thurow has pointed out, agriculture, consid-ered as a business, reduced its demand for labor by 500 million man-hours per year between 1948 and 1972, with wrenching dislocations but beneficial economic results. The process could not continue indefinitely, however, and by 1972 it had largely reached an end. Although the agricultural sector made many productivity gains, it became too small a sector of the economy to release many workers to the urban economy. [20]

At about the same time, the nature of employment in the urban sector changed from productive factory jobs to less productive service tasks. High rates of mechanization, large machines that produced economies of scale, and teamwork in production all raised productivity levels in factories. In service jobs, people engaged in handicraft pursuits, such as pouring coffee, guarding the parking lot of a shopping mall, or selling things to retail customers. Each of these things could be mechanized—a security guard could, for example, use video equipment to oversee a larger area, and sales clerks benefited from new technology in cash registers and inventory control. Still, on average, the service jobs were less productive than the factory jobs and offered fewer opportunities for productivity gains from year to year. Thurow estimates that 47 percent of all the man-hours that were added to the private economy after 1972 were in services. The service and retail trades accounted for something like 70 percent of all the new private-sector jobs created during the seventies. Since these were less productive jobs than, say, working in the open hearth for U.S. Steel, they were also less remunerative jobs, with shorter hours and lower rates of hourly pay and fewer benefits to enhance that pay.[21]

WOMEN AND DEMOGRAPHIC CHANGE

As U.S. households felt the pinch of declining real wages, they tried to compensate by increasing the number of hours that their members worked. This process led to profound social changes but actually made the nation's productivity rate worse. During much of the postwar economic boom, one sign of affluence was that families consumed more leisure time. Women who had been pressed into employment during the wartime emergency were able to leave the labor force and become full-time homemakers or caretakers. Although a long line of American writers from Sinclair Lewis in *Main Street* (1920) to Sara Davidson in *Loose Change* (1975) questioned the value of enforced domesticity, many husbands considered having a "nonworking" wife to be a symbol of affluence and a sign of progress. In the postwar era, as Americans acquired more confidence in the country's economic future and lost their fears of an impending depression, they began to marry earlier than had the depression-scarred previous generation and to have more children—all of these things were taken as optimistic signs of belief in a better future.

In the seventies, economic stringency altered these trends. Women went to work in record numbers and in so doing transformed the labor force and created a revolution in labor-force expectations. This revolution was not the product of a conscious feminist ideology so much as it was the result of impersonal economic forces. In the words of one writer, it was a subtle revolution, one in which the proportion of prime-aged women at work rose from 43.3 percent in 1970 to 51.2 percent in 1980.[22] In other words, it became the norm for women to work outside of the home during the seventies; workplaces that had the gendered qualities of locker rooms had somehow to be reconfigured to adjust to this reality.

The entrance of women into the labor force, one of the most important overall trends of the era, had a depressing effect on the nation's productivity rate. During the seventies, the size of the work force increased by 28 percent, compared with 19 percent in the sixties. This increase occurred even though the population grew by only 11 percent during the decade, which was the lowest level of population growth for any decade since the 1930s.[23] The section of the adult population working or looking for work outside of the home rose from 59 percent in 1966 to 64 percent in 1979.[24] Most of the people who claimed the new jobs were women or younger workers. They took the jobs that were available, which meant service jobs. Newer workers tended on average to be less productive than older workers because they had less experience and hence less knowledge of the job than their older counterparts. So the economy of the seventies faced a double blow: it had to accommodate new workers with jobs that were less productive than the factory jobs that had been created in earlier decades. The productivity rate suffered accordingly.

The rise in female labor-force participation interacted with the declining state of the economy and influenced other important trends. For one thing, it delayed the baby-boom echo. As defined by demographers, the baby boom "was a 'disturbance' which emanated from a decade and a half long fertility splurge on the part of American couples" that lasted from about 1946 to 1963. The fertility rate, which had averaged roughly 2.1 births per woman in the 1930s, peaked at 3.7 in the late fifties. Then it began to drop, until it fell to 1.8 births per woman in the years between 1975 and 1980.[25]

The factors that accounted for the baby boom help to explain why it took so long for the baby boomers to have children and to produce what demographers called the baby boom echo. The baby boomers were the product of a relatively small cohort of people who had been born or who had come into maturity during the depression. As economist Richard Easterlin has hypothesized, small generations follow large generations in predictable patterns. Small generations create labor shortages, rising wages, more opportunities, more optimism, and more children. Large generations face more competition, falling wages, and more frustration and ultimately decide to have less children. Alternatively, one might argue that the generation that grew up in the thirties developed low expectations that were exceeded by the prosperity of the forties and fifties. Hence, its members elected to have more children. The generation that grew up in the fifties and sixties developed high expectations that were not met in the seventies. Hence, they started their families later and had fewer children.[26] Little Sarah, Emily, or Jennifer who might have been born in, say, 1976 when her parents reached their mid-twenties did not in fact arrive until the mid-eighties, and her parents had neither the time, energy, or desire to replicate the size of the families in which they had grown up.

PLANT CLOSINGS AND ECONOMIC DECLINE: THE DILEMMAS OF THE SEVENTIES

The parents of the baby-bust generation faced a profoundly changed labor market. Industrial jobs were dwindling. With rising international competition, falling rates of productivity growth, and high prices for basic commodities, some industries experienced major dislocations during the decade. In the seventies, plant closings, once thought to be a sign of progress in America's dynamic but destructive economy, became a solemn community ritual that brought only a sense of loss. Elizabeth, New Jersey, for example, a once-elegant town with splendid homes and a strong industrial base, witnessed the slow death of its Singer sewing-machine plant. It was a small part of what some writers have called the deindustrialization of America, a phenomenon that received much attention during the seventies.[27]

Singer sewing machines once stood as an international symbol of America's industrial predominance and superiority. The company, which traced its roots back to before the Civil War, manufactured and sold its products worldwide. Even by 1861 it sold more sewing machines in Europe than in America, and in 1871 it opened what was then the largest factory in Great Britain. In 1891, it had a worldwide market share approaching 80 percent. Women around the world kept sewing machines in their homes to make clothing for their family. The proud company built a landmark skyscraper in New York during the Roaring Twenties to serve as its headquarters. By 1966 the company reached a billion dollars in annual sales.[28]

Increasingly, though, the company began to encounter troubles. In a baby boom household, a sewing machine was something that one's mother had. Modern women were too busy to make their own or their children's clothes or even to repair old clothes or fix a hemline on a dress. If necessary, they asked the dry cleaner to do those jobs as they hastily dropped off the cleaning on their way to work. Most men, outside of those who made their living in the garment trades, never touched a sewing machine even when they were ubiquitous. Sewing became a hobby, not a crucial part of the household economy.

In 1873, the company, which dominated and almost defined the industry, had opened its large factory in Elizabeth. As Katherine Newman writes, Singer tried to react to its postwar troubles by diversifying its product line, but that meant that money was drawn away from the manufacturing plants in places like Elizabeth. What had started as a model of industrial innovation became instead a "dinosaur." First, the company announced a moratorium on new hiring in Elizabeth. Then it started to lay off workers, and finally it closed the factory in the early eighties.[29]

What happened in Elizabeth occurred in, one form or another, in communities across America during the seventies. In this manner the economy joined the Watergate scandal and the end of the Vietnam War as factors in launching the seventies as a distinctive phenomenon. The simultaneous appearance of inflation and unemployment proved perplexing to the nation's economists and to the politicians who relied on their advice. International events created an unfamiliar sense of vulnerability in the United States. The undisputed leader of the free world that had done so much to rehabilitate Europe and Asia's war-torn economies found itself at the mercy of oil-producing countries that did not share the international-policy goals of the United States. Furthermore, economic salvation could not easily come from within, as the declining national productivity rate illustrated. In a weak economy, households needed to increase their working hours just to maintain their previous standards of living. As women entered the labor force in large numbers, they helped to alter the nation's demographic structure not in the optimistic manner of the postwar baby boom but rather in the form of a baby bust. As factories closed, people worried that new ones would not spring up to take their place. The United States was running out of gas.

4

The Frustrations of Gerald Ford

When Richard Nixon resigned in August 1974, he bequeathed the presidency to Gerald Ford, whom he had chosen as vice president after Spiro Agnew's resignation in October 1973. Ford became the only president to serve his entire term during the seventies, and his tenure between 1974 and 1977 reflected the distinctive dilemmas of that era. Ford, rather than Nixon or Agnew, faced the immediate consequences of Watergate, the end of America's involvement in the Vietnam War, the oil shock, and the recession. Although he attempted to deal with each of these problems, he achieved only partial success. The recovery that Ford tried to engineer failed to bring the economy up to the level of its postwar performance. Although the oil crisis eased under Ford's watch, it did not disappear. In the realm of foreign policy, Ford had the singular misfortune of being on hand for the final fall of Vietnam and for the unraveling of the policy of detente designed by President Nixon. Ford, in other words, needed to react to emerging problems without the economic resources to solve them and without many new ideas to confront them. He inherited both the problems of the seventies and the solutions of the sixties.

THE RISE OF GERALD FORD

Gerald Ford, who shared many of the features of the postwar presidents, such as wartime service in the Navy, differed from the more ambitious politicians who had run on the 1960 tickets. Unlike his predecessors, Ford had decided to make his career in the House of Representatives. Where

LBJ, Nixon, and Kennedy were all frustrated by the slow pace of advancement that the House of Representative afforded, Ford settled comfortably into a safe seat from the Grand Rapids area in Michigan and climbed the Republican leadership ladder. Like Kennedy, who also occupied a safe congressional seat, Ford found that his first race was his hardest. Kennedy had run in a crowded field for an open seat. Ford had the more difficult task of unseating a senior member from his own political party. When Ford challenged Bartel Jonkman in 1948 (one election after Nixon and Kennedy were already in Congress and in the same year LBJ ran successfully for the Senate), he faced a four-term congressman and member of the important House Foreign Affairs Committee. Ford won the primary and the seat. After that he coasted through twelve more elections, never receiving less than 60 percent of the vote.

Ford had the sort of congenial personality that made him well liked among those who devoted their lives to congressional service. If he was not a political star in the manner of Kennedy or driven like Nixon, he was not afraid to take risks. In 1963, some of his congressional friends who saw themselves as modern, progressive Republicans, such as Melvin Laird of Wisconsin and Donald Rumsfeld of Illinois, helped him to win the number three spot in the Republican leadership, defeating a more experienced member from Iowa. Two years later, Ford successfully challenged Charles A. Halleck of Indiana and became the House Republican leader. Hence, when Nixon was looking for a new vice president, he was advised that Ford could handle the job and would encounter no obstacles in gaining confirmation. Nixon, who faced considerable difficulties in the Watergate crisis and had no reason to stir up more trouble with Congress, decided to appoint Ford. It was a responsible choice. The new vice president had none of Agnew's criminal taint and had no apparent desire to displace Nixon and become president himself.

The promotion to vice president represented a nice finale to Ford's political career. He had risen about as far as he could in the House leadership. In all of his many terms, the Republicans had run the House of Representatives only once, and the experience did not look as though it would be repeated anytime soon. As matters turned out, Ford never became Speaker of the House, but he did become the president of the United States, one of only nine people who held the job without first being elected to it and the only one of those nine who had never even been elected vice president.

With the cooperation of the media, Ford portrayed himself as an ordinary man who found himself placed in an extraordinary situation. In the 1960s, the nation had wanted its president to be Superman; in the 1970s, the nation appeared willing to settle for Everyman. Gerald Ford tried to oblige, toasting his own English muffins for breakfast, at least for a time, and making every effort not to be an imperial president. Ford optimistically proclaimed that our long national nightmare was over. It was not unlike the succession between Woodrow Wilson and Warren Harding in 1921. One of the first things that Harding did was to order that the curtains and blinds at the White House be opened to let in the light, as if to announce that an invalid no longer lived there. Ford also wanted to let in the light, to show that, unlike Nixon, he was not above the law. Toward that end, Ford testified before a congressional committee, the first sitting president to do so since Abraham Lincoln.[1]

The president liked to say that he was a Ford, not a Lincoln. He might more accurately have said he was a Republican but not a Lincoln. He was not someone who had been called in from the hinterlands to save the republic, in the manner of the Jimmy Stewart character in *Mr. Smith Goes to Washington*. Unlike Stewart, who was awestruck at being in Washington and could not find his way from Union Station to the Capitol, Mr. Ford was an old Washington hand who had been hanging around the corridors of Congress since 1949.

THE PARDON

Gerald Ford made the best of his circumstances. He realized that continuing speculation about whether Richard Nixon would be indicted for criminal activity in the Watergate scandal, followed by a long and dramatic trial, would be a side-show that would swallow up the show. He calculated that Nixon should be pardoned for any crimes he may have committed. That way, Ford, the Republicans, and the nation could all cut their losses and get on with business. Two years of Watergate was enough.

On Sunday, September 8, 1974, Gerald Ford took communion at the St. John's Episcopal Church near the White House. As his staff member Robert T. Hartman describes it, Ford then returned to his office, which he had occupied for only a month. He sat down at his desk and faced a television camera, around which a bunch of reporters had been hastily assembled. He gave a little talk, "earnestly and sometimes eloquently," explaining what he was going to do. Then he signed a "full and absolute pardon" for Richard Nixon.[2]

Ford took a gamble and lost. If he had allowed the prosecution of Richard Nixon to make its way through the courts, he probably would have lost anyway. Whatever the long-term consequences, pardoning

Richard Nixon proved a highly unpopular thing to do in the short run. Ford's honeymoon with Congress and the press, never too passionate to begin with, ended abruptly. His approval ratings fell from 71 percent to 50 percent within a week.[3] The story played itself out very slowly, exposing Ford to the maximum political damage. Three days later, for example, the pardon story still led the *NBC Evening News*; nearly all of the coverage cast Ford in a bad light.

THE CONSEQUENCES OF THE PARDON

Ford's hopes of saving himself and the presidency by posing as an ordinary man faded after the pardon. He had little more than two years before the next election, hardly enough time to reverse the damage that Nixon had done. By election time, he could point to some achievements, such as reducing the inflation rate and keeping the country out of war, but these were largely invisible. They suggested the absence of something negative rather than the accomplishment of something positive.

In the meantime, Ford's image changed from that of an earnest and decent fellow to that of a incompetent bumbler. In college at the University of Michigan, Ford had been a football star, an All-American lineman, and he had coached football while studying law at Yale. If nothing else, then, his athletic competence appeared to be beyond dispute. When the cameras showed him falling down an airplane ramp as he was arriving for a summit in Salzburg, Austria, his reputation also slid. When he went skiing in Vail during the Christmas holiday in 1974, newspapers ran pictures of him falling down.[4] A popular television program featured a performer who began many of the broadcasts by doing an impression of Ford falling over his own feet. Previous presidents had, of course, been satirized. During the Kennedy era, an otherwise obscure comedian named Vaughn Meader made a hit record poking fun at Kennedy and his family, but people could listen to the record, laugh, and still admire the president. In Ford's case, the humor had a nasty element to it, suggesting that he was a joke as president.

Ford, who had come into office with no time for a transition, struggled to put together a staff that was loyal to him rather than to the memory of Richard Nixon, and, at the same time, he tried to regroup for the 1976 election. He also had the difficult task of naming a vice president who would be the second person appointed, rather than elected, to the post. He did not want to pick another Midwestern, country-club Republican, such as Donald Rumsfeld, who had joined the White House staff in September 1974. A few weeks after taking office, Ford settled on Nelson Rockefeller, the former governor of New York, who had been a prominent member of the party's eastern, liberal wing since he was first elected in 1958. On December 18, 1973, he had resigned before the end of his fourth term. As vice president he clashed with Rumsfeld and other members of Ford's staff, as well as with Barry Goldwater and other conservatives in the Senate. Some observers thought that Ford might step aside for Rockefeller in 1976, but even if Ford had been willing, it was clear that the Republican party would choose Ronald Reagan, not Nelson Rockefeller, were he to drop off the ticket. Ford soon disabused people of the notion that he would step down and in the summer of 1975 formally announced his desire to run for a full term in 1976.

FORD AND DETENTE

Much as Ford recognized the necessity of differentiating himself from Nixon, he made no immediate breaks with the Nixon legacy in foreign policy. He did his part to further the process of detente by going to Russia in November of his first year in office to meet with Leonid Brezhnev and the other Soviet leaders. At this summit, he reached the conclusion, as he put it on his return home, that things had gone "very, very well" and laid the basis of a productive personal relationship with Brezhnev. Ford expressed optimism over reaching a new agreement on the limitation of strategic arms that "will constrain our military competition over the next decade." In particular, the two countries signed a joint statement on the limitation of strategic offensive arms that provided a general framework to cover a treaty that would run between 1977 and 1985. The treaty, the two sides hoped, would set a limit on intercontinental ballistic missiles, submarine-launched ballistic missiles, and multiple independently targetable warhead vehicles, known as MIRVs. If such an agreement were reached, it would prove, as the official communiqué put it, "the practical value of the Soviet-American summit meetings and their exceptional importance in the shaping of a new relationship" between the Americans and the Soviets.[5]

The spirit of Vladivostok could not be sustained through the Ford administration. The U.S. bicentennial year appeared to mark a turning point, away from consensus on detente and toward a wary acceptance that the Cold War would continue. By this time, substantial opposition had developed to the very notion of detente. The United States and the Soviet Union clashed over a civil war in Angola, supporting different sides in the conflict. Donald Rumsfeld, named by Ford as secretary of defense in November 1975, and the members of the Joint Chiefs of Staff, who detected a

rising Soviet threat to world peace, expressed their reservations about entering into further SALT agreements. The first SALT treaty had received the
overwhelming support of the Senate in August 1972. A second SALT treaty,
particularly if the military leaders decided to testify against it, faced a much
more uncertain reception. As a consequence of these political factors, Ford,
despite his euphoria over the progress he had made in Vladivostok, decided
to shelve the SALT process until after the election.[6]

SENATOR HENRY JACKSON AND THE
CRITIQUE OF DETENTE

Senator Henry Jackson, a Democrat from Washington, led the opposition to the SALT treaty and detente. In some respects, Jackson's critique
of detente resembled the criticisms that Democrats of the John F. Kennedy school made of Eisenhower's "new look" during the fifties. Just as
Eisenhower hoped to substitute big nuclear weapons for smaller conventional weapons and deliver more bang for the buck, so Nixon and later
Ford hoped to be able, with the aid of the arms agreements, to provide what
Jackson regarded as defense on the cheap. Jackson found a sympathetic
audience among Democrats in the labor unions, such as Lane Kirkland, the
head of the AFL-CIO; some military figures such as Admiral Elmo Zumwalt; and intellectuals who were beginning to discover an identity as neo-
conservatives, such as Jeanne Kirkpatrick, Norman Podhoretz, and Daniel
Patrick Moynihan. In November 1976, Jackson and his followers started a
bipartisan organization (some 40 percent of the members were Republican), known as the Committee on the Present Danger, with the objective of
restoring "the strength and coherence of American foreign policy."[7]

Jackson believed that, just as it was futile to bargain with Hitler, so it
was a mistake to enter into strategic agreements with the Russians. The
Soviet Union, unlike the United States, remained a totalitarian nation,
and this totalitarianism was embedded in the very nature of the society.
Unlike right-wing regimes that used repression as a transitional means of
maintaining order, left-wing regimes systematically repressed dissent as a
normal and desirable function of government. They also sought to export
their model of government abroad, unlike most right-wing dictatorships.
The United States, according to Jackson, would have trouble with any such
regime. Instead of constantly emphasizing common interests, the United
States should not excuse the lack of attention to human rights in Russia,
Cuba, and elsewhere in the communist world. Instead, the country should
be a vigilant defender of human rights around the world and particularly

in communist countries. In other words, this country should not accommodate the domestic politics of the Soviet Union by ignoring human-rights violations and should not hesitate to set itself up as moral exemplar and a countermodel to the Soviets.

Jackson and his intellectual allies thought that Ford and Kissinger surrendered too easily to the spirit of despair that the Vietnam War had engendered. With the proper leadership, such as Jackson himself offered to provide, the American people could be rallied to support increased defense spending. The nation needed the clarion call to duty of a John F. Kennedy, not the dangerous realpolitik of Henry Kissinger. Americans should therefore be strong in their belief that the Cold War was a struggle in which virtue lay on the side of the United States. As Moynihan, an expert on urban affairs and social welfare who morphed into a foreign-policy expert during the seventies and served as ambassador to the United Nations, pointed out, the United States did not have to apologize for being a democratic society and did not need to be lectured on its behavior by autocratic communist or Third World nations. "Democracy has come under increasing attack. I see it every day at the United Nations. Every day, on every side, we are assailed," Moynihan told a sympathetic audience of labor-union members. "We are assailed because of what is right about us," he continued. "We are assailed because we are a democracy."[8]

What separated Jackson from the group of reformed cold warriors that designed detente was a disagreement not over ideology so much as strategy. For example, Jackson criticized Nixon and Ford's idea of entrusting key allies with important roles in containing communism as something expedient but not necessarily wise. America could not rely on surrogate nations to protect its interests but must be prepared to meet threats to its security around the world. As a consequence, there was simply no alternative to a large military force that could be deployed anywhere in the world. The fact that the Soviets had achieved parity with the United States in many areas of defense technology made the need for such a force all the more urgent. To those who looked with despair on a never-ending arms race with the Russians and the endless prosecution of a Cold War that sapped the country's economy and warped its values, Jackson offered the prospect of ultimate victory. The struggle would not be endless. Instead, as his biographer puts it, he "believed that the Cold War was a struggle with a terminal point, which would end with the breakup of the Soviet Union and the collapse of the totalitarian system."[9]

Jackson, then, took a hard-headed but messianic view of the world. Nixon, Kissinger, and Ford, cold warriors and internationalists who perceived themselves as under attack for fighting the Vietnam War and maintaining the nation's military forces, shared Jackson's realism but not his optimistic idealism. Hence, natural allies turned into adversaries. The postwar consensus on foreign policy, strained by the dispute over the Vietnam War, ended. Disengagement prevailed over intervention, much to Jackson's dismay.[10]

THE JACKSON-VANIK AMENDMENT

As a practical means of protesting the process of detente, Jackson decided on the strategy of linking congressional approval of key elements of Soviet-American cooperation with the issue of human rights. If the Soviet Union wanted to gain most-favored-nation status as a trading partner with the United States, it would have to respect the right of its citizens to emigrate and free them of repressive measures such as the exit tax. Although the legislative vehicle embodying this idea, which came to be known as the Jackson-Vanik amendment after its chief sponsors in the Senate and the House, was written in neutral language so as to apply to any ethnic group, it took as its target the emigration of Soviet Jews.

The political potency of the issue lay in the fact that the Soviet Union contained some three million Jews. Furthermore, these Soviet Jews had family connections to American Jewish voters, many of whose parents and grandparents had themselves emigrated from Russia around the turn of the century. These Jewish voters were overwhelmingly Democrats and as likely as any ethnic group to participate in Democratic primaries, a fact that was not lost on Jackson. In Jewish neighborhoods in places like Baltimore and Cleveland, one could find banners in front of temples with the exhortation to free Soviet Jews. Jackson linked himself to this cause. He introduced his amendment to the administration's trade bill in the fall of 1972. Nixon, who hoped to score big among Jews in the 1972 election, made a deal with Jackson in which Jackson agreed not to raise the issue during the campaign and Nixon agreed not to stop Republican senators from supporting the amendment.

In April 1973 the administration renewed its request for Congress to grant most-favored-nation status to the Soviet Union, and Jackson reintroduced his amendment. He managed to interest both liberals who wanted to gain support among Jews and conservatives who opposed trade with communist countries. In Kissinger's words, "conservatives who hated Communists and liberals who hated Nixon came together in a rare convergence."[11] The Soviets, meanwhile, played into Jackson's hands by concluding that international detente needed to be accompanied by internal repression. In the Soviet view, detente was about international relations, not internal affairs. Not surprisingly, then, the House Ways and Means Committee considering the trade bill adopted Jackson's amendment in September, and the full House passed the bill, with the amendment, in December.

By this time, the Nixon-Ford administration realized that it would have to bargain with the Senate on the Jackson-Vanik amendment. In essence, Kissinger negotiated with Jackson and with Soviet ambassador Anatoly F. Dobrynin to reach a compromise. The Soviets agreed to increase Jewish emigration to a level of 45,000 per year, but Jackson, who sensed the potency of the issue, demanded more. Finally, Jackson, Senator Jacob Javits—whose identity as a Republican, a New Yorker, and a Jew gave him standing in the debate—and Representative Charles Vanik met with President Ford and Kissinger in October 1974. The meeting allowed Jackson and Kissinger to engage in an exchange of letters that, it was hoped, would resolve the issue. In these letters, Kissinger reassured Jackson that he had a pledge from the Soviets (who signed nothing and were not directly involved) to permit emigration in the coming year. Jackson replied that this pledge meant that at least 60,000 people would be granted visas, and Kissinger replied that he did not disagree with this assumption. With Jackson thus mollified, the president would be free to grant most-favored-nation status to the Soviets for a period of eighteen months.

Despite Kissinger's efforts, the agreement fell apart. After speaking with Ford, Jackson appeared before the White House press corps and announced that the Soviets had capitulated and he had won a major victory. The Soviets then decided that they did not want to be schooled by Senator Jackson. Although Congress approved the compromise over the trade bill and Ford signed the bill into law at the beginning of January 1975, the Soviets pulled out of the deal. As a consequence, trade between the two nations decreased, and Jewish emigration from Russia fell. The administration suffered a major defeat, having failed to carry through on the commitments it had made to the Soviets and losing the means of influencing Soviet policy through the leverage of foreign trade.[12]

Trade between the United States and the Soviet Union remained a controversial issue during the Ford administration. Conservatives, whose intellectual belief in free trade often conflicted with their desire to use trade policy to reward U.S. industry and punish the nation's adversaries, noted that trade propped up the Soviet regime rather than helping to seal its doom. Furthermore, both liberals and conservatives realized that trade brought Soviet consumers into competition with American consumers. The great "grain robbery" remained fresh in the public's mind. In July and August 1972, the Soviets, plagued by a drought that affected their harvest, played the American commodities market to perfection and purchased over one billion bushels of American agricultural products at favorable prices. At just this time the postwar economic boom weakened, and food prices began to rise in the United States. In effect, the Soviet purchases, along with those made by China and India, contributed to the rising price of food. This domestic feedback of international policy exacerbated U.S. economic problems. That perception, in turn, lent support to Senator Jackson's critique of detente.

At first a rarefied discussion among experts about submarine-launched multiballistic missiles and other lethal but technical arcana, detente became a gut-level political issue that boiled down to the question of whether the Soviets could be trusted to carry out their promises. Detente, which had been a winning issue for President Nixon, looked to be a losing issue for President Ford.

INTERLUDE: THE *MAYAGUEZ*

Gerald Ford made foreign policy during a period of few triumphs in an environment in which Congress challenged the president's power. These conditions increased Ford's assertiveness on the few occasions when he had the freedom to act on his own. The best example concerned the May 1975 *Mayaguez* incident. It occurred at a moment of particularly bad tidings, just when both South Vietnam and Cambodia had fallen into the hands of America's self-professed enemies. The incident began on May 12 when Brent Scowcroft, Kissinger's deputy, told Ford that the *Mayaguez*, an old container ship carrying a nonarms cargo on its way to a military base in Thailand from Hong Kong, had apparently been fired upon and boarded by Cambodian armed forces as it sailed through what the United States regarded as international waters in the Gulf of Siam. The Cambodians took the thirty-nine crew members prisoner. In response to what the president called an act of piracy, he reacted by sending a naval force, including an aircraft carrier, to the site, raising a strong diplomatic protest, ordering photo reconnaissance of the area, and making a public demand for the return of the vessel and the crew.

Before the incident concluded, Ford and his military advisors had the *Mayaguez* seized only to find none of the crew members on board, ordered air strikes on the Cambodian city and seaport of Kampong Som, and sent the marines to invade Koh Tang Island. During the first hour of fighting, the marines met heavy groundfire, sustained fifteen casualties, and lost three helicopters (two others were disabled). The Cambodians tried to signal their willingness to release the crew, but the United States proceeded with the operation. Even after a naval vessel recovered all members of the *Mayaguez* crew unharmed, the bombing of Cambodian targets continued. In the end the *Mayaguez* operation cost some forty-one American lives and fifty Americans were wounded, a dubious price to pay for the rescue of a crew that numbered less than half of that total. These dead Americans became the last names on the Vietnam Memorial Wall, a final testimony to American power in the region, with results that were at best mixed. James Reston, the Washington columnist for the *New York Times*, wrote that the "Administration seems almost grateful for the opportunity to demonstrate that the President can act quickly despite the recent efforts by Congress to limit his authority."[13] Yet what exactly the incident demonstrated remained unclear. For some, though, it provided a moment of old-fashioned exhilaration and an expression of America's military potency. "It was wonderful," said Arizona senator Barry Goldwater. "It shows we've still got balls in this country."[14]

FORD AND THE RECESSION

Economic problems at home compounded Ford's difficulties abroad. Gerald Ford became president at a particularly inauspicious moment for the economy. In July 1974, one month before he took office, consumer prices rose to their highest level since the Korean War and unemployment reached 5.4 percent during his first month in office. By the winter of 1974–75, it had gone much higher, to 7.2 percent, and it would eventually reach 9.2 percent at the height of the recession.[15]

At first, Ford decided to focus on the inflation problem and prescribed the traditional postwar remedies of raising taxes and cutting the federal budget. In December 1974, with the GNP dropping 7.5 percent in constant dollars, he conceded that the economy was in a recession and, as a consequence, he opted to change course. Instead of raising taxes, he now wanted to lower them, but he continued to think in terms of cutting government expenses. Congress reacted more favorably to a tax cut than to a decrease in government expenditures and at the end of the year passed the Revenue Adjustment Act of 1975, which featured a nine-billion-dollar tax cut. At this point, Ford earned a reprieve, in part due to an easing of the oil crisis. The inflation rate as measured by the consumer price index dropped slightly between 1974 and 1975 and significantly between 1975 and 1976.

Then the economy faltered just before the 1976 election, helping to seal Ford's defeat.

FORD AND ENERGY

The energy crisis was one the few things that Nixon passed on to Ford that did not become worse on Ford's watch. Iran and Saudi Arabia moderated their stands toward America, which, although a supporter of Israel, was nonetheless the world's major consumer of oil. The OPEC price hikes in the period between 1974 and 1978 did not match the rises in the general price level, with the result that the real price of oil was actually 10 percent less in 1978 than in 1974.[16]

Gerald Ford tried to give attention to the energy crisis even as he battled other economic ills. He conceded in 1975 that the nation was in a recession and needed to do something about that, yet he added that "we must not lose sight of the very real and deadly dangers of rising prices and declining domestic energy supplies."[17] To bolster those supplies, he thought that the regulatory structure surrounding oil needed to be loosened and automobile pollution standards should be relaxed in the interest of getting more miles to the gallon. Although he hesitated to add new spending programs to the budget, he advocated more money for research into alternative energy sources. He wanted to build more nuclear-power plants, dig more coal mines, generate more power with coal, construct new oil refineries, and create more synthetic fuels. Congress refused to deregulate the price of natural gas, as Ford wished, and kept more of the price controls on oil than he wanted. It did set new fuel efficiency standards and tried to encourage the conversion of utility plants from gas to coal.[18]

Ford, then, attempted to get past the Watergate scandal with the pardon and failed, tried and failed to reinvigorate detente, strove to get the economy on track and failed, and worked to end the nation's dependence on foreign oil and failed. Not surprisingly, he met with repeated political frustration. The 1974 congressional election resulted in a Democratic landslide. In the 1976 battle for the Republican nomination, he faced a stiff challenge from Ronald Reagan, and in the 1976 election, he lost to a neophyte in national politics.

THE ELECTION OF 1976

On November 19, 1975, Ronald Reagan phoned Gerald Ford and told him that he planned to run for the Republican nomination for president.

In the primary campaign that followed, Reagan came as close to capturing his party's nomination from an incumbent as anyone had ever done in the modern political era.[19] Ford took the New Hampshire primary at the end of February, but only barely, winning 51 percent of the vote. Reagan began a concerted attack on Ford's foreign policy, criticizing Ford's efforts to seek detente with the Russians. He hit a particularly hot button with the Panama Canal issue, asserting that the canal belonged to the United States and that he, at least, had every intention of keeping it. Although Ford managed to rally Florida voters to his side by using the powers of his office to put a transit system in Miami, among other things, he stumbled in North Carolina on March 23. Reagan took 52 percent of the vote there. A week later Reagan won all of the delegates from Texas, and a few days later he defeated Ford in Alabama, Georgia, and Indiana. It fast became apparent that the race between Ford and Reagan was real. The two traded states in May and June. Ford won in West Virginia, Michigan, Maryland, New Jersey, and Ohio. Reagan won in Nebraska and his home state of California.

In a close race, Reagan tried one last gambit. He decided to announce his selection of Richard Schweiker, a relatively liberal Pennsylvania senator, as his running mate in advance of the convention. He thought that might shake a few votes from the Pennsylvania delegation or cause Ford to name his vice president and alienate some faction of the party. Pennsylvania and Ford held firm. Eventually Ford won the nomination by the thin margin of 1,187 to 1,070 and tried to placate conservatives by naming Robert Dole of Kansas as his running mate.

For someone who had not been elected to the job, who succeeded a decidedly unpopular, even vilified president, and who ran on the ticket of the less popular party, Gerald Ford did surprisingly well in the 1976 election. He experienced something of a revival during the bicentennial summer, in which the nation's bout of deprecation and cynicism seemed to abate for a moment. Recalling July 4, 1976, Ford remembered, "the sight of Americans hugging each other and shouting for joy. I can still see those seas of smiling faces with thousands of flags waving friendly greetings."[20] Ford had the feeling that evening that he had succeeded in healing America. Harvard would give him an honorary degree for presiding over the nation's birthday party, and Jimmy Carter, who won the general election and later forged a lifelong friendship with Ford, paid tribute to him in his inaugural address "for all he has done to heal our land."[21]

Nonetheless, the immediate legacy of Gerald Ford was that of someone who tried and failed to solve large problems. He became the first incumbent president to lose an election since Herbert Hoover.

5

Congress and Domestic Policy in the Age of Gerald Ford

Gerald Ford had the misfortune to be president in the period right after Watergate when Congress, which was run by the opposition party, sought to control the policy agenda. At the same time, economic stringency made the creation of major new domestic programs difficult. Nineteen seventy-four, as it turned out, became an important dividing line between the expansive domestic policy of Lyndon Johnson's Great Society program and the much more limited domestic policy of the seventies. The congressional elections of that same year, conducted less than three months after Ford took office, resulted not only in a Democratic landslide but also in increased momentum for efforts to reform Congress. Intended as a means of opening up the legislative process so that Congress could more easily act on the people's will, the reforms actually made it more difficult for Congress to pass major legislation.

HEALTH INSURANCE

The battle over national health insurance illustrated how the differences between the Great Society and the seventies affected Gerald Ford. This issue had been a contentious one, almost from the time that it arose during the New Deal. Reformers thought that the government should bring health care within people's financial reach by starting a national program of public health insurance. Members of the medical profession worried that the federal government's entrance into the field would undermine their professional autonomy and lower the quality of care. The results were a stalemate and the expansion of private, rather than public, health insurance. By 1964, however, a consensus had developed that the federal government should finance health care for the nation's elderly.

With the passage of health insurance for the elderly, or Medicare, in 1965, many people assumed that a more comprehensive program would follow. In the optimistic Great Society environment, there was every expectation that Medicare would demonstrate the government's administrative competence. It therefore appeared likely that Congress would expand Medicare to cover other age groups and bring national health insurance to the United States.

Things moved in an incremental manner in the period between 1965 and 1972. In 1968 an idea arose that Medicare should be expanded to cover prenatal and infant care. Such an idea had the virtue of consistency with other Great Society proposals that centered on education and investing in the country's future. Bringing health security to expectant mothers and infants would cut down on infant mortality and developmental disabilities and would pay for itself in the form of reduced illness and increased productivity as the children headed toward adulthood. Philip Lee, a prominent health care official in the Johnson administration (and later the Clinton administration), commented that he and many others believed that kiddy care, as it came to be known, would become the vehicle to move national health insurance forward. "We thought by 1975 there would be national health insurance," he said.[1]

Lee's sentiments reflected a general feeling that national health insurance was inevitable. Even President Nixon, wary of most Great Society programs and no defender of Medicare, felt obligated to offer his own health-insurance proposal. Health, Education, and Welfare secretary Elliot Richardson, the peripatetic member of Nixon's cabinet, appeared before a congressional committee in October 1971 and pronounced himself certain that the hearings would culminate in national health insurance. Richardson presented the Nixon administration's idea of mandating coverage. Each employer would be required to provide a basic health-insurance package to its employees. Provision would be made for the unemployed or others without permanent attachment to the labor force. Liberals, led by Senator Edward Kennedy, countered with a plan that contained more complete health care that was financed through federal funds. The legislative climate was such that even the Health Insurance Association of America, a trade association representing the interests of private health insurers, felt compelled to raise money from its members in order to present its own plan, which it prevailed upon Representative Omar Burleson (D-Texas) to introduce. The industry favored voluntary private health insurance but offered to make special provisions for those who lacked the means to pay for it.[2]

In 1972 the process of expanding the Great Society legislation in health care moved forward. Congress broadened Medicare so that it covered people with disabilities. Veteran social-policy observers recognized this extension of Medicare as a conscious effort on the part of national-health-insurance advocates to have the federal government extend its presence in health insurance beyond the elderly and the poor (who were covered by Medicaid) to reach people of all ages.[3]

The battle for national health insurance continued through the end of the Nixon administration. The effort culminated in 1974 with the appearance of four important health-insurance bills.[4] The first was Senator Edward Kennedy's liberal plan. The second was a catastrophic-healthcare plan that picked up a person's medical expenses once they became burdensome. The third approach came from the Nixon administration, by now tottering in the Watergate scandal but still anxious to leave a social-policy legacy. As before, the administration relied on the strategy of mandating private employers to provide health insurance for their employees. The final bill came from the unlikely pairing of liberal Senator Kennedy and conservative Representative Wilbur Mills. It featured benefits similar to the Nixon plan, including numerous expenses that a patient would have to bear himself, but financed by the federal government through a payroll tax. "I believe this proposal," Senator Kennedy said, "is a major step toward guaranteeing good health care as a right—and can be built upon for future years."

The press reacted as if the passage of national health insurance was only a matter of time. The *Wall Street Journal* reported that "prospects for Congressional action this year" had improved considerably. The *Washington Post* added that "in recent weeks the prospects for national health insurance have brightened suddenly and unexpectedly."[5]

The labor movement, still a force on Capitol Hill, held the key to the success of the Kennedy-Mills bill. If labor retreated from its strong support for the earlier (more liberal and more generous) Kennedy bill and accepted the new bill with the same enthusiasm, it would give the bill a strong liberal base of support. Conservatives might be persuaded to join in on the theory that the bill represented the best deal they could get. The Nixon administration, meanwhile, saw the movement on national health insurance as proof that it was not paralyzed by the Watergate scandal. Some Capitol Hill observers thought that the administration was eager to work something out. Labor, however, had to think in strategic political terms that caused it to speculate in political futures. At a time when the Watergate scandal was a

[handwritten margin note: Ted Kennedy & Healthcare]

strong presence for Americans, maybe the next Congress, which would be elected in 1974, would be more liberal than the sitting Congress and hence more willing to pass national health insurance along the lines that labor preferred. Maybe this next Congress would be strong enough to override vetoes and thus able to render the administration irrelevant. Persuaded by this reasoning, the executive council of the AFL-CIO issued a negative report on the new bill. "While on balance Mills-Kennedy is an improvement over the Nixon bill," the council stated, "it falls short of meeting the needs of America."[6]

The United States never came closer to enacting national health insurance. Soon the political landscape changed beyond recognition, and the economy deteriorated to the point where all ambitious social policy ventures were doubtful undertakings. Here one can see very clearly the end of the expansive social policy of the sixties, with the postscript that Nixon tried to write, and the beginning of the more restrictive and hesitant social policy of the seventies. The year of Nixon's departure, 1974, became the great divide. Gerald Ford's presidency fell on the other side of this break.

THE RISE AND FALL OF WILBUR MILLS

The consequences of Watergate haunted the presidency of Gerald Ford and his successors during the seventies. The most vivid of those consequences concerned institutional changes in Congress that led to the creation of more subcommittees and, in general, to a more fragmented system than had prevailed during Gerald Ford's many years of service in the House of Representatives. When it came to the issue of health insurance, for example, Congress had traditionally ceded a great deal of control to Wilbur Mills, who was invariably described as the "powerful" chairman of the Committee on Ways and Means. Indeed, the battle over Medicare in 1965 and the defeat of national health insurance in 1974 coincided with the rise and fall of Representative Mills. When Medicare was passed, the policymaking system concentrated power in a few hands and permitted Congress to work out the details of the legislation in relative secrecy. As the head of Ways and Means, Mills in effect legislated for the House of Representatives.

Mills was typical of congressional leaders in the period before the seventies. His power stemmed in part from his long tenure in office; he had served in the House since 1939 and on Ways and Means since 1942. He could devote so much attention to the business of Congress in part because he did not have to spend much time worrying about his reelection. He came from Arkansas and from a rural portion of that heavily rural state. He was, of course, a Democrat, since that was the one political party that existed in Arkansas. That did not make him a rube, as some sophisticated Washingtonians assumed, although his slicked-back hair and old-fashioned eyeglass frames made him appear that way at times.

When Mills crafted legislation on such complicated matters as health insurance, he realized he needed considerable staff assistance. For much of the postwar era, this help came from members of the executive branch rather than from Mills' own personal or committee staffs. Mills created Medicare, for example, in close consultation with employees of the Social Security Administration, who drafted committee reports, made actuarial calculations, and did much of the policy planning for the legislation. This close contact between the legislative and executive branches of government, where representatives of executive agencies attended congressional sessions that were closed to the general public, ended in the seventies, after the Watergate scandal increased the level of mistrust between the president and the Congress.[7]

Throughout his tenure, Mills allowed members of the Ways and Means Committee to engage in sensitive political negotiations in private. In considering Medicare and other important legislation, Mills liked to operate in executive sessions that were closed to the public. The executive committee of the Ways and Means Committee was identical to the committee itself—in parliamentary parlance, a committee of the whole. Ways and Means almost never operated through subcommittees and never held open mark-up sessions as it worked its way through the details of tax and social-policy legislation and took votes on important matters. Hence, the actual creation of a bill like Medicare remained hidden from the press and others who wanted to chronicle the legislative process. These features of the policymaking system—the absence of subcommittees and the closed mark-up sessions—would vanish in the seventies, as reformers sought to bring "sunshine" to legislative deliberations.

The downfall of Wilbur Mills played a part in the creation of the new legislative climate. Just as Watergate helped to elevate Ford to the presidency, it also contributed to the scandal surrounding Wilbur Mills and his departure as head of the Ways and Means Committee. What got Mills into trouble was not so much his public performance as his private conduct. Before Watergate, a congressman's private life had, for the most part, remained private. Members of Congress used their colleagues to cover up instances of drunkenness or patches of senility that prevented them from doing their jobs. What one did after hours, particularly in Washington, away from the prying eyes of constituents, remained one's own business. Watergate helped to change that situation. The press now saw uncovering such behavior as an important part of its mission, necessary for getting the story behind the story.

In Mills's case, his problems began with a bad back that led to taking too many painkillers, or maybe they came from a predisposition to alcoholism. By 1973 he was spending an increasing amount of time away from Washington, under a doctor's care. Then his erratic behavior broke out into public view, one of the era's moments that would remain in the public's memory. One night in October 1974, just two months after Ford came into office, Mills rode through Washington in his Lincoln Continental. He was driving too fast and had failed to turn on his headlights. As he passed through the parkland near the Jefferson Memorial at two in the morning, the D.C. Park Police stopped his car. Out ran Annabel Battistella, an exotic dancer who performed under the name of "Fanne Fox, the Argentine Firecracker." Then, with all of her clothes on, she jumped into the Tidal Basin. The police arrested her and an obviously drunk Mills as well. His arrest made national news and, in an election season, he found it necessary to issue a public apology with his wife standing by his side. He won his election, but it would turn out to be his last. At the end of November, he popped back up in the public spotlight. This time he walked on stage while Ms. Battistella was performing in a Boston night club. Once again visibly drunk in public, he proceeded to hold an impromptu news conference. Once again, the media splashed his picture across the nation.

Mills appeared on the stage in Boston only a few weeks after an election in which voters decided to punish the Republicans for Watergate. In such circumstances and in the glare of publicity, Mills's behavior could not be easily overlooked or excused as a manifestation of his illness. Someone who had been outed as a drunk might not be the best person to oversee the nation's income-tax code or its Social Security system. Almost immediately, therefore, the Democrats in Congress took steps to distance themselves from Mills. Just days after the Boston incident, they stripped Mills's committee of its important power to make committee assignments for other Democrats. Ways and Means, in other words, would no longer act as a committee on committees. The next day, Speaker Carl Albert confirmed the stunning news that Wilbur Mills would not seek reelection as chair of the Ways and Means Committee. With that statement, an era in congressional history ended. Mills would finish up his term and then retire, spending much of the rest of his career, before he died in 1992, in a Washington law office. A placard on his desk announcing his position as chairman of

Ways and Means was one of the few reminders of the inordinate power he had once enjoyed.[8]

Gerald Ford dealt with Al Ullman of Oregon as chair of Ways and Means beginning in 1975. In a sense, though, no one replaced Wilbur Mills. He was the last chairman to enjoy the advantages of closed sessions, the absence of subcommittees, and the power to make key assignments on major congressional committees. His downfall underscored the new connections between private and public behavior that the press sought to enforce at a time when the boundaries of public life expanded to include what were previously private activities. A public that could listen in to a president's private conversations did not think it inappropriate to learn the details of a congressman's private life.

CONGRESSIONAL REFORM

Gerald Ford, who became president at the time of the great divide in social policy, became the first of the era's presidents who needed to cope with the consequences of congressional reform. The impulse for congressional reform, like the impulse for the Great Society, came from the insurgent liberalism of the postwar era. In the fifties, many liberals grew frustrated with the apparent inability of Congress to tackle hard social problems, such as civil rights and federal aid to education. In the view of such organizations as Americans for Democratic Action, the will of the majority was being thwarted by a tiny minority in Congress that used the committee system to block social advances. In 1963 political scientist and Kennedy partisan James McGregor Burns wrote that the nation was "mired in governmental deadlock, as Congress blocks or kills not only most of Mr. Kennedy's bold proposals of 1960 but many planks of the Republican platform as well."[9] The solution envisioned by Burns and others was to modify the system to make the committees more responsive to the will of the majority in Congress and to the desires of the people. In this formulation, the country was in fact more liberal than were its laws. One therefore needed to change the process by which the laws got made.

Congressional reorganization was, of course, an ongoing historical concern. What changed from one generation to the next were the perceptions of the problems and the preferred solutions. The Legislative Reorganization Act of 1946, passed at the very beginning of the postwar era, sought efficiency and capability: it sought to streamline congressional operations and expand the size of the staffs available to members of congress. In pursuit of the first objective, the act reduced the number of standing committees and the number of committee assignments for most members to one. These changes strengthened the power of committee chairmen. The number of people who worked for Congress doubled between 1946 and 1956, a sign of success in reaching the second objective.[10]

Opinions on the appropriate level of power for committee chairs changed from one generation to the next. By the seventies, reformers no longer thought it as important to streamline operations and consolidate power. What mattered now was that the system be responsive to the public will. Hence the Legislative Reorganization Act of 1970 looked different from the one passed in 1946. It took up the cause of efficiency, with things like electronic voting, but it also sought to open up the process through such measures as permitting radio and television coverage of House hearings, encouraging committees to hold hearings in public view, and requiring committees to make recorded votes a matter of public record. In addition, the act attempted to protect the rights of junior and minority members, by mandating, for example, that a third of committee funds be used for the minority staff.

THE WATERGATE ELECTION AND DEPOSING COMMITTEE CHAIRS

None of those things got to the problem of committee chairs who used their power to thwart what reformers took to be the popular items on the liberal agenda. In 1971 the Democratic party adopted a significant rule that marked an initial effort to rein in the committee chairs in the House. The rule stipulated that Mills's committee "need not necessarily follow seniority" in nominating the members of committees or, most important, committee chairs. When it came time for the Democratic caucus to vote on the nominations, the members could call for a separate vote on any particular nomination for committee chairman, provided that ten or more members demanded it.[11] It would, of course, take considerable courage for a junior member to stand up in the Democratic caucus and say that he would like to challenge someone like Mills, someone with considerable seniority, lots of chits from other members, and a great deal of power to punish a junior member who dared to oppose him.

Although few members chose to challenge the system in 1971, the cause of congressional reform moved forward. After the 1972 election, the new members of Congress began to grow more assertive. The result was a new series of rules and procedures that further undermined the power of committee chairmen and provided junior members with more rights. If 20 percent of the Democratic caucus requested it, there would be a secret ballot vote on the nomination of a committee chair. All Democratic members of the House would have at least one major committee assignment. If someone served on one of the "big" committees, such as Appropriations or Rules, that person could not be assigned to another standing committee. The caucus also diluted the power of the Committee on Committees by requiring that the party leadership—the Speaker of the House, the majority leader, and the whip—serve on it. Other changes, such as requiring that committee meetings be open to the public unless the hearing was on a sensitive subject such as personal misconduct or national security or a majority of the committee voted to close the hearing, furthered the cause of open government. As a direct result, the public gained the right to attend far more congressional hearings.[12]

Another blow to powerful chairmen such as Mills came in the form of something known as the Subcommittee Bill of Rights. The members of the committee got more say in how vacancies in subcommittees were filled. Each subcommittee gained more budget and staff, which meant that a subcommittee chair need not be totally beholden to the chair of the main committee, and each member of the full committee would get at least one good subcommittee assignment. In 1974 Congress took the even more fateful step of requiring that all committees with more than fifteen members create at least four subcommittees. Ways and Means would therefore be required to establish subcommittees, and it would be enlarged from twenty-five to thirty-seven members. Al Ullman (D-Oregon) would preside over a very different sort of committee than had Wilbur Mills.[13]

What these arcane procedural rules did was to create more points of entry to Congress and less discretionary power for committee chairmen. If a group interested in, say, developmental disabilities received an unsympathetic hearing from a committee chair, that would have ended the matter in the old Congress. In the new Congress, the advocates could take their case to a subcommittee chair, or to the subcommittee staff, and receive, if not an affirmative answer to their request, at least another avenue of appeal. As for the committee chairman, they now needed to appease the heads of the subcommittees if they expected to stay in the good graces of the committee itself. In fact, one way for a committee chairman to make himself popular was to create lots of subcommittees.

The Watergate Election and the Class of 1974

The Watergate election of November 1974 strengthened the pattern of congressional reform that had already been established. The Democrats won a landslide victory over a Republican party that had to defend the record of Richard Nixon and the decision by Gerald Ford to offer him a pardon. Their victory gave them huge margins in the House and Senate. All in all, the Democrats picked up 46 seats in the House, giving them a 290 to 145 edge. The election meant that seventy-five freshmen Democrats entered the House of Representatives in January 1975. The Democrats also gained four seats in the Senate.[14]

The class of 1974 was not united in its outlook, yet it shared a political style. As David Broder noted, nearly half of the class members were political novices who had not served long apprenticeships in their home states. Many had developed a cause during the sixties, such as opposing the Vietnam War or protecting the environment, and, at the time of Watergate, ridden that cause to win elections in districts that were considered safely Republican. According to Majority Leader Tip O'Neill, who had been active first in local and then in statewide Massachusetts politics before taking over John F. Kennedy's old congressional seat in 1953, the new members of Congress were not just people who came in off the street. "We have more Rhodes scholars and more Sorbonnes and more doctorates and more masters of all descriptions," O'Neill said.[15] As he put it, "These youthful able, talented people—they didn't like the Establishment, they didn't like Washington. They didn't like the seniority system. They didn't like the closeness of it, and they came down here with new ideas."[16]

a more educated government [handwritten marginal note]

With the mechanisms put in place during preceding Congresses, the new congressional class proceeded to conduct what amounted to a purge of the old committee leaders. Mills had already bowed out. Early in January, the class of 1974 Democrats in the House, who had formed their own caucus, complete with a staff director, invited every committee chairman to come and address them. The leaders of this class included Norman Mineta, a forty-five-year-old former mayor of the rapidly growing city of San Jose at the base of the San Francisco peninsula and hence politically experienced by the standards of the class, and Tim Wirth, a Colorado politician with a resumé that included two Harvard degrees and a doctorate from Stanford but little practical political experience. Mineta went on to become a cabinet member in two administrations; Wirth graduated to the Senate in 1986. According to Mineta, the committee chairs decided at first that they were too busy preparing for the session to find the time to come and talk with the freshmen. The implicit message was that it was beneath their dignity. It would be more appropriate for a freshman to come, hat in hand, to them in hopes of getting a good committee assignment. When the chairmen heard that the entire class might vote against them if they failed to appear and as it became clearer that such a vote might take place, they reconsidered their positions.[17]

THE GREAT PURGE

The purge began on January 15, 1975. On that day the Steering and Policy Committee met to vote on chairmen for the upcoming session. Tip O'Neill saw the matter as pro forma and asked that all of the chairmen be nominated unanimously. The committee disagreed and took the unusual step of unseating Wright Patman as head of the Banking and Currency Committee, despite his forty-six years of seniority, the longest term in the House, and his fourteen year tenure as head of the committee. The committee replaced Patman of Texas, born in 1893 (he would die in 1976), with Henry Reuss of Wisconsin, born in 1912, a geographical and generational shift. Even if the political views of Patman and Reuss were similar, the change indicated that one could not hold a committee chairmanship for life.[18]

The next day the action shifted to the Democratic Caucus, which met to take up the recommendations of the Steering and Policy Committee. The caucus considered the nominations in alphabetical order, which meant that the Agriculture Committee came up first. The incumbent was W. R. Poage, another Texan born in the nineteenth century who ranked third in seniority in the House and who had chaired the committee for eight years after having served for fourteen years as Harold Cooley's (D-North Carolina) vice chairman. Few people considered Poage to be in jeopardy. To the amazement of many in the crowd, Poage lost his chairmanship by a close vote of 146–141, and a surprised Thomas Foley (D-Washington), the next in seniority but some thirty years his junior, took over for him. Poage accepted the change relatively gracefully and went back to his post of vice chair. When he retired at the end of the seventies, however, he wondered about the efficacy of the new system. "The basic changes in Congress, in my judgment, are very bad," he said. "We have practically destroyed the Committee system in the House. The public doesn't realize it, but committees do not function as they did at one time."[19]

Still on the first letter of the alphabet, the caucus took up the powerful Armed Services Committee, both a sensitive area for national security and an important source of projects that members could win for their districts. Here the incumbent was F. Edward Hebert from New Orleans, who had put in more than thirty-four years in the House. He did not take well to the new arrivals, whom he called "boys and girls." The newer members in turn objected to the way that Hebert protected the interests of the military. He did not see it as his role to investigate such things as Nixon's secret bombings of Cambodia. In sum, he seemed out of step with the interests and desires of the younger members, who organized against him. By a vote of 152 to 133, they succeeded in dismissing Hebert and appointing Melvin Price of Illinois. "We got him. Man, oh, man," said an excited Les Aspin (D-Wisconsin) who had been one of Hebert's critics on the committee.[20]

CONGRESSIONAL BUREAUCRATIC CAPABILITY

Even though the challenges to committee chairmen and the personal scandals grabbed the headlines, more subtle changes occurred in Congress as well. One important development concerned the strengthening of Congress's own bureaucracy. The expansion of subcommittees, the proliferation of subjects that the members were expected to master, the need to show up often in the home district in an age where jet travel meant that distance was no excuse, and the increased demands of media appearances all helped to fuel a rise in the number of people who worked for Congress. In 1972, for example, there were 119 Congressional subcommittees; there were 150 at the end of 1976. Each had a budget and a staff and as congressional authority James Sundquist put it, "the right to proceed independently."[21] As a consequence, committee staffs got larger, since every subcommittee needed at least two professional staff members.

With congressmen expected to know so much more, the increased staff seemed a necessity. In this spirit, junior senators won the right to have a staff member for each of the three committees to which the senator was assigned. In the past, this privilege had extended only to the committee chairs and the ranking members. Between 1972 and 1978, the size of the House committee staffs more than doubled to 2,073 employees, and Senate committee staff members increased by more than a third.[22] As for the personal staffs of the congressmen, they had numbered some 2,000 when Tip O'Neill had entered Congress in 1953. By 1977 this number had more than tripled to 7,000, with many other people assigned to such entities as the Office of the Speaker.[23]

The increased size of the staffs made it possible for Congress to work harder if not more effectively. Veteran Illinois Congressman Dan Rostenkowski used to say that it was Easter before Congress got down to business during the fifties. In those days Congress spent some 230 days in session. In the seventies, Congress could stay in session for nearly the entire year, although with frequent recesses for the members to go on what were usually working sojourns to their districts. The reform of Congress, the extended sessions, and the presence of staff who could offer advice meant that congressmen conducted more formal votes than previously. In the House, the number went from 71 in Tip O'Neill's first year to more than 800 in 1978.[24]

Administrative Capacity and Congress

During the seventies, Congress, having expanded in size and scope, developed the ability to analyze issues independently of the executive branch. Watergate had thrown up a wall between the two branches of government and undermined the confidence that each had in the other. That development put a strain on the sorts of collaborations that were common in the postwar committee era and produced the Great Society legislation. Gerald Ford's job of finding common ground with Congress became harder because Congress was much less dependent on the executive for information and advice.

Congress craved independent sources of information so as to gain a different view on how much a prospective piece of legislation would cost or to gain a sense of how well a particular program was working. To be sure, political bias abounded in all such information. Divided government meant divided policy analysis. The Ford administration might want the cost estimates of a Democratic-sponsored health-insurance plan to be as high as possible to show that it would not be feasible to adopt, and Senator Kennedy might have just the opposite desire. All programs had their defenders that wanted the evaluations to show off that program to best advantage and their detractors who hoped that an independent evaluation might reveal the program to be a failure.

The General Accounting Office fed Congress's need for information from a source removed from the executive branch. Although the General Accounting Office was not a new entity, it experienced a change of mission during the seventies. No longer were its professional staff members primarily accountants. The GAO began to take on sophisticated analytical assignments that went beyond merely counting things. Instead, it evaluated, an action that required the agency to have the capacity to do social-science research of the type being done in the think tanks, such as Brookings, independent contractors such as Abt Associates, or the research arms of major universities.

More congressional staff meant more work for the GAO. So did the increased emphasis that Congress put on oversight. It was no longer enough for the executive agencies to monitor themselves. The expanded post-Watergate Congress wanted to find things out for itself. Often the quest for knowledge meant commissioning the GAO to do a study and then releasing that study as part of an oversight hearing that usually followed some sort of political script and garnered headlines for the head of some subcommittee.[25]

Congress also wanted more control over the budget. In 1974, after the Congress had fought bruising battles with President Nixon over the level of federal spending and over the power of the president to impound appropriated funds, it created a new agency called the Congressional Budget Office. This agency had the delicate task of trying to figure out just how much a particular policy proposal would cost if it were implemented.[26] In the past, large social-policy undertakings, such as Medicare, had been launched with only a vague idea of how much they would cost. Whatever estimates existed came almost exclusively from the executive branch, usually the Bureau of the Budget that worked directly with the president.[27] After the creation of the Congressional Budget Office, future initiatives would be launched with better information, and this information would inhibit the formation of costly social programs.

Congress had still another tool at its disposal in the form of the Congressional Research Service. It originated in the Progressive Era when Senator Robert LaFollette proposed in 1914 that there be a Legislative Reference Division of the Library of Congress. In time the division became the Legislative Reference Service, on call to Congress as it went about its work. In time, also, the LRS became invaluable to a Congress in which professional staff expertise was in very short supply.

The LRS grew steadily in the postwar era. Then, as part of the Legislative Reorganization Act of 1970, the LRS became the Congressional Research Service and grew much larger. Among other things, the CRS issued background reports or issue briefs, as they came to be called, that recapped the legislative action on a particular matter like welfare reform.

This all made for more competence in Congress, a greater ability to deliver complex legislation without relying on the executive branch, and much more capacity to oversee, and hence to criticize, the actions of presidents and executive agencies. The changed nature of Congress could be read as a permanent memorial to the effects of the Watergate scandal. No longer would a Democratic Congress have to depend on manpower and expertise from a Republican president in order to get things done. With the new system in place, Congress would be able to put a check on the power of the no-longer-quite-so-imperial presidency.

The Ironies of Congressional Reform

Whether the new Congress could also produce constructive legislation remained an open question. Its increased capacity should have led somewhere and resulted in more than a flurry of oversight hearings. The Watergate Congressmen wanted to emulate their predecessors who came to Washington during the eras of Wilson, FDR, and Truman and wrote their ideas in the book of law. For the most part, the members of Congress during the seventies failed in that mission, and the failure fit a historical pattern.

Congressional leadership in government was relatively rare in the twentieth century, and the seventies were no exception. Radical Reconstruction, perhaps the best example of congressional government in the post–Civil War era, happened when one party controlled Congress. In this setting, Congress instituted Reconstruction over the active opposition of an unelected president. A somewhat similar situation prevailed in the era of Gerald Ford: another unelected president faced a Congress controlled by the opposite party. Still, there were differences. For one thing, the Republicans of Gerald Ford's era were much stronger than the Democrats of the Reconstruction era. For another thing, Congress in the Ford era simply did not have its own agenda, other than to increase its power and to respond to the requests it received from advocates who favored incremental changes in existing programs. Or maybe it was that Congress had too many agendas that did not cohere into a basis for unified action, which were traditionally the strong suits of presidents. Under the right circumstances, it seemed as if they did not even need the Congress. Wilson and FDR created many of their Progressive Era and New Deal reforms even before the Congress that had been elected with them arrived in Washington. These presidents controlled the action until Congress reasserted itself at the end of the 1910s and 1930s, respectively. Congressional reassertion tended to mean blocking plans, such as the League of Nations and executive reorganization, rather than creating new institutions. The seventies were just such a time of congressional reassertion, and this institutional factor created another problem for President Ford to overcome.

Increased competence, staff, and subcommittees meant that Congress could consider an idea in detail, hear from a wide panoply of people, and work through all the complexities in order to form a bill to be more to its liking. It could absorb more information and assess the measure more thoroughly. But it could not necessarily act more decisively. So much needed to be reconciled across so many subcommittees, interest groups, and experts, and the new congressional system did not offer a ready means for such reconciliation. Nor could Congress make the leaps of faith that were common in earlier reform eras. The fact that Congress did not really know what would happen after it passed Social Security in 1935 and Medicare in 1965 probably made it easier to do so. With the Congressional Budget Office, members of Congress had a much better idea of what a new health-insurance bill would cost. With the improved General Accounting Office and the expanded subcommittee system, congressmen got early bulletins about policy problems in the implementation stage, creating doubts about the efficacy of particular policies. The system developed negative information of the sort that inhibited policy formation much more readily than it produced positive information that created the necessary sense of optimism for reform.

New York and Its Discontents

In this setting of a reformed Congress and a weakened presidency, Gerald Ford dealt as best he could with the domestic problems of the midseventies. One vexing problem concerned the impending bankruptcy of New York, the nation's largest and most important city. During the seventies, New York endured as a financial, entertainment, and retail center, but its municipal services were under severe strain. New York, although a world-class city, emerged as a leading symbol of the urban crisis of the seventies. One sign was that people left New York, just as they left other northeastern and Rust Belt urban centers: during the seventies, the city lost one million residents.[28] People fled in part because jobs were also departing the city; New York lost 10 percent of its private-sector jobs in the first half of the seventies. Another sign of crisis was that the city contained the country's most famous slums. The South Bronx, tantalizingly close to Manhattan's East Side, became the leading symbol of urban blight, in part because it was so accessible to the media outlets.[29] It showcased the fact that, beyond the glamour of Manhattan, the city, which sprawled over five boroughs, contained neighborhoods undergoing rapid deterioration. Such neighborhoods cost the city a great deal in welfare and other social-service costs and, with their diminishing populations and falling property values, returned little to the city in revenues.

By the middle of the decade, the city's government faced a crisis that attracted national attention. In order to pay the city's workers and maintain the pensions of its retirees, New York needed to borrow money. Mayor Abraham Beame, who had been the city's comptroller and had a background in accounting, did what he could to sell bonds and raise money in other ways. Early in 1975 the situation escalated into a crisis as it became apparent that the city had neither the means to continue paying its workers through the year or the ability to borrow enough money to cover its debts.[30] The city sought help in Albany and Washington. The state, which had a Democratic governor with a New York City background, gave the city some funds but not enough to solve the problem. Mayor Beame and Governor Hugh Carey came to Washington in the spring of 1975 asking for more help. In this manner the financial woes of New York City reached the desk of President Ford.

For the president, a financial bailout for New York City marked another call for federal funds from a budget already adversely affected by the recession. Nor was New York a popular political cause among the members of the president's party. Not only did a majority of the residents vote Democratic; they also lived in what many Republicans considered to be a local version of a welfare state. The welfare rolls contained more than a million people; the subways cost a nickel and the city's famed colleges charged no tuition. Hence, President Ford gave New York emissaries Beame and Carey a less than cordial reception.

The New York politicians wanted the president to recommend to Congress that New York City receive a financial bailout. The president suggested that the city do more to improve its finances by raising subway fares or charging tuition at its colleges. The president believed that the city's many social services were simply too costly to maintain in the emerging postindustrial era, particularly when the city and the country more generally faced the worst recession since the Great Depression. Frustrated, the New York politicians fell back on the idea of federal guarantees for municipal bonds, but Ford refused to go even that far. His decision forced the state to adopt a stopgap measure in the form of the Municipal Assistance Corporation, which allowed the city to restructure its debt and obtain temporary financial relief. Ford remained adamant that New York City would have to fend for itself. In a famous appearance at the National Press Club at the end of October 1975, Ford said, "I am prepared to veto any bill that has as its purpose a Federal bailout of New York City to prevent default." His comment elicited the equally famous headline in the *New York Daily News*: "Ford to City: Drop Dead."[31]

In time, Ford reconsidered his position, the newly reformed Congress gave New York City a temporary line of credit, and the city muddled through its crisis.[32] In 1977 Edward Koch became New York's mayor, one of a group of white ethnics who became mayors of northeastern cities in the seventies. Koch, a single man who was married to his city, combined a sensitivity to criticism that often caused him to snap at his detractors, with a contrary desire to please. During his tenure as mayor, his persona shifted from that of an idealistic liberal to that of a fiscal realist and self-proclaimed spokesman for New York's white ethnic communities. He also recognized that New York could no longer maintain its vast panoply of municipal services. Under his leadership, the city pared back its payroll, increased its subway fare, and ended the practice of offering free college tuition. What happened in New York City after Ford left office suggested that his actions in 1975 helped to discipline the city's finances and ease the city through the crisis of the seventies. At the time, however, he received condemnation as a heartless man who did not care about the welfare of the nation's urban residents. And he knew that whatever he did could always be undermined by the highly partisan Congress that was capable of drafting complex legislation, such as a bailout bill for the city of New York, without help from the executive branch of the government.

POSTSCRIPT: WAYNE HAYS

The Wayne Hays scandal showed just how much Congress and Washington itself had changed during the seventies. Those who violated the rules of sexual decorum faced the threat of being outed by an aggressive press corps. Hays was a crusty congressman from Ohio who chaired the Administration Committee, which exercised a great deal of power in Congress since it was responsible for such things as staffing, travel funds, and parking spaces. As head of the Democratic Congressional Campaign Committee in 1974, Hays had handed out some $87,000 to sixty-nine members of the freshman class. Hays was decidedly not a favorite of the good-government types such as public-interest lawyer Ralph Nader, and he frequently earned the disapproval of the *New York Times*. Although Tip O'Neill, the majority leader who aspired to be Speaker of the House, saw him as a rival and an irritant, Hays nonetheless survived the purge of committee chairs that took place in 1975. "Wayne Hays is a son of a bitch—but he is our son of a bitch," said Representative Jim Stanton (D-Ohio).[33]

Wayne Hays got the better of his critics in 1975 but met his match in 1976 at the hands of the *Washington Post*. On April 6, 1976, a woman named Elizabeth Ray dialed the managing editor and tearfully told her that Congressman Wayne Hays was going to marry another of the secretaries in his office. On May 23, 1976, the *Post* ran a devastating story about Hays, full of post-Watergate candor.

The lead of the story confirmed people's worst suspicions about Congress: "For nearly two years, Rep. Wayne L. Hays (D-Ohio), powerful chairman of the House Administration Committee, has kept a woman on his staff who says she is paid $14,000 a year in public money to serve as his mistress." The details made Hays look ridiculous. "I can't type, I can't file, I can't even answer the phone," Ray said. The story described how Ray met Hays twice a week for sex. They would have a quick dinner and then go to her Arlington, Virginia, apartment. "He never stops in the living room," Ray said, "He walks right into the bedroom and he watches the digital clock. He's home by 9:30." Ray also described how Hays told her at one of their dinners that he was marrying someone else but hoped it would not make a difference in their relationship. Hays did say that it would be a good idea if Ray started to show up in the office for two hours a day because he claimed that Bob Woodward of Watergate fame was after him and it would not be good if Woodward found out about Ray. The story, another of the intimate Washington conversations that the public savored during the seventies, also mentioned that Hays had told Ray how, if he had been Wilbur Mills, he would have ended the Fanne Fox affair by putting Fox six feet under the bed of the Potomac River. The story ended with the ironic detail that Hays was scheduled to go to London on a special bicentennial trip to pick up the Magna Carta.[34]

In the atmosphere of the seventies, the personal was the political. Hays abused the public trust by padding his payroll and using federal funds for illegal purposes. He also violated what feminists took to be the norms of appropriate behavior: he used his public position to gain private advantage over a woman. Such behavior might have been routine in previous years, but it was also well hidden from public view. The *Washington Post* now saw such a story as fair game and, even more, as a story of vital news importance that should run on page one. Hays himself mentioned the paper's coverage of Watergate in the story, and the *Post* regarded the Hays story as another instance of the paper taking the lead in exposing capitol corruption. Needless to say, the story ended Hays's career. The members of the freshman class in Congress, now worried about matriculating to the sophomore class, no longer defended him. He was no longer their SOB.

A system capable of exposing Wayne Hays was not necessarily adept at passing legislation or solving social problems. Here, then, was a fine irony of a sort that seemed to define the seventies: a series of reforms designed to make Congress more responsive to the public will also resulted in blocking the passage of many of the liberal measures of which the reformers approved and that they hoped to facilitate through their reforms. In the end, it was the conservative Ronald Reagan and not the liberals of the seventies who ended up using the new Congress to best advantage. Much had changed since the days of Wilbur Mills marking up important legislation without subcommittees in sessions closed to the public and attended by members of the executive branch who worked in tandem with Congress. Neither President Ford nor the members of Congress had easier jobs after Watergate.

6

Jimmy Carter and the Great American Revival

Jimmy Carter, who succeeded Ford after the 1976 election, hoped to lead a great American revival. He wanted to synthesize what was best about postwar America, such as the technological and policy expertise that promoted a form of compassionate efficiency, while also returning America to its bedrock virtues such as the necessity of telling the truth in public life. He hoped that, with the proper moral and political leadership, Americans would be able to face up to their problems, making the necessary sacrifices if necessary, and conquer stagflation, the energy crisis, corruption, and a host of other seventies ills. Although Carter made a difference, he could not overcome a new surge of problems that occurred during his presidency. As a result, the crisis of the seventies, which had begun under Nixon and the Republicans, became associated with Carter and the Democrats.

THE RISE OF JIMMY CARTER

The election of Jimmy Carter marked a pronounced change in the presidency. He was not a member of Congress and, in fact, was the first president without Washington experience since Woodrow Wilson. He also came from a different generation than did his predecessors. Carter, unlike Gerald Ford and the four presidents before him, did not serve in a combat zone during the Second World War. He graduated from high school just before Pearl Harbor and, after further preparation at some Georgia colleges, eventually entered the Naval Academy. By the time he finished at the academy, however, the war had ended, and he did his military service in the peacetime navy. He chose submarines as his area of specialty and helped to train the crew for the USS *Seawolf*, a nuclear-powered submarine. After seven years of service, he left the navy in 1953 with his father ill with cancer and with his chances for long-term advancement in the navy uncertain. After his father died, Carter settled down in his home town of Plains, Georgia, much to the consternation of his wife and brother, and took over the family's farm and warehouse business. Like Harry Truman, who had also been stuck on his family farm, Carter found an outlet in local politics. As a prominent landowner and therefore a leading figure in the county, Carter accepted his duty to serve on county boards that ran local institutions, such as the schools and the library and hospital. In 1962, at the age of thirty-eight, he was elected to the Georgia State Senate and served there through 1966. In that year he made an unsuccessful run for governor; in the next election he ran again and won.[1]

When Carter decided to run for president, therefore, his political experience consisted of a few voluntary offices, two terms in the Georgia State Senate, and a term as governor of Georgia. It was, to say the least, a thin resumé compared to Ford's or Nixon's or any president's in the twentieth century. Even Hoover and Eisenhower, who had never held elective political office before becoming president, were household names in the twenties and forties, respectively.

It did not bode well for a presidential run. Carter could, however, do something that Ford could not, and that was to run as an outsider who was not involved in the political mess that Nixon had created in Washington. This strategy had its obvious limits and could be reduced to absurdity: a complete unknown, whisked off the streets, had no chance of winning. Even Rocky Balboa, the Philadelphia fighter plucked from obscurity to fight the champ, lost his title bout at the climax of a popular movie of the era. For Carter to run and win was beyond fantasy. When Carter first contemplated running in September 1972, the idea struck even his closest staff members as odd. As Carter advisor Hamilton Jordan recalled, "We all knew it looked kind of preposterous. . . . It was hard to really talk about. It was almost embarrassing."[2] Carter's team overcame its embarrassment and flew the candidate all over the country. They studied the mechanics of the Democratic nominating process and decided which primaries were particularly important for Carter to win.

Carter's campaign would later be much studied as a road map for how an outsider should run for the Democratic nomination. If nothing else, Hamilton Jordan and Carter's other advisors understood the importance of keeping the candidate in the media's view, a legacy of Watergate and the new fondness for an open political process. They also understood how important it was for Carter to match the media's expectations. A candidate did not have to win every primary; instead, he had to do as well or better than expected. The trick, then, was to play to expectations. By keeping expectations low but the candidate visible, one could sustain momentum, continue to gather financial contributions, and keep the candidate in the race.

As political analyst Michael Barone has noted, the media operated "as the main transmitter of information about the effectiveness and viability of different candidates and the gauge of their relative success."[3] Instead of simply reporting on the roll-call vote at the convention, the boys on the bus traveled with the candidates and talked with their political advisors. They gained their own feel for who was raising money in New York and who was doing well with voters in Peoria. They sought to foreshadow the results and to explain their significance not in terms of what had happened but in terms of what was about to happen.

The media contributed to the breathtaking process in which Carter came from nowhere to emerge as the leading contender for the Democratic nomination in 1976. Circumstances worked in Carter's favor but guaranteed him nothing. With Ted Kennedy out of the race and having lost the last two presidential elections, the Democrats had no obvious candidate. Many of those who flirted with trying for the nomination, such as Morris Udall of Arizona and Frank Church of Idaho, suffered from the obvious disadvantage of being from small states with few electoral votes. Still, both started with more advantages than did Jimmy Carter, who was out of the national loop, a well-known figure in Atlanta but not in New York City or Los Angeles.

On October 27, 1975, the New York Times ran a front page story about Carter's potentially strong showing in the Iowa caucuses. In the new style of the political prognosticator, R. W. Apple Jr. reported that Carter's campaign had been "considered laughable by many Washington experts" but that he had taken "a surprising but solid lead" in Iowa.[4] When Carter won those caucuses on January 19, he suddenly became a viable candidate in the campaign. On January 20, NBC News devoted six minutes to Carter. Despite the thin number of people involved in the process, John Chancellor, the network anchor, declared that Carter's victory was of great symbolic importance. As reporter Judy Woodruff noted, using themes already developed in the Times story, few had ever heard of Carter when he first came to Iowa a year earlier, but now they praised him for the way he treated them with respect and for the fact that, like many of the Iowa voters, he was a farmer himself. These conclusions came from a sample of about 50,000 Democrats who participated in the Iowa caucuses. Carter won the support of only about 28 percent of those Democrats, or less than 15,000 people, fewer people than listed themselves as uncommitted. But Carter was the story.

It soon became apparent that the Carter phenomenon had legs. In New Hampshire, he received 29.4 percent of the vote in a crowded field and, according to the network analysts, ran well in all voter categories. The Carter campaign stumbled in Massachusetts but righted itself in Florida. There Jimmy Carter defeated George Wallace by a 3 percentage points and bested Henry Jackson by a substantial 10 percent margin. Carter boasted that while George Wallace stood for the interests of a mean-spirited racist old South, Jimmy Carter represented the hope of a tolerant, industrious new South. Carter conveyed to Florida voters that he embodied the anti-Washington sentiment that animated the Wallace campaign but with the significant difference that he, unlike Wallace, had a realistic chance of winning the election.

In all Carter won eighteen of thirty primaries and did not have a primary night on which he did not win somewhere. He withstood late challenges from Frank Church and from California governor Jerry Brown, Reagan's successor and the son of the man who had beaten Nixon for the job, and he captured the Democratic nomination on the first ballot. In November 1974 a Harris poll had not even listed Carter among thirty-five candidates for president. Two years later, he won the presidential election.[5]

THE 1976 CAMPAIGN

In the 1976 presidential campaign, Jimmy Carter did not have the luxury of being the underdog who could surprise people merely with a respectable finish. He now represented the majority party in a year in which the opposition was vulnerable. Television continued to play a large role in the electoral process. Carter believed that a televised debate would help to put him on an equal footing with the incumbent Ford. The president, for his part, knew he was behind and thought that a debate might help him catch up. For the first time since Kennedy faced Nixon, therefore, both candidates gave their approval to televised debates.

The first debate took place on the evening of September 23, 1976, in the Walnut Theater in Philadelphia and did neither candidate much good. Eight minutes before the scheduled end of the debate, a technical glitch occurred, and the sound went out. The incident framed another moment of the seventies in which the presidency lost some of its glamour. For the next twenty-seven minutes, as technicians from the ABC television network scrambled to fix the situation, the two candidates stood frozen in place and did not so much as venture a pleasantry toward one another. Both looked foolish, standing at their podiums and saying nothing in a silent tableau that was broadcast on all three networks before an estimated ninety million people without commercial interruption. The candidates, with their lack of spontaneity, appeared to be two ordinary men caught in an uncomfortable situation.[6] CBS News commentator Eric Severeid, whose job it was to speak the obvious in a serious tone of voice, noted that the format was awkward and the results disappointing.

In the first debate, Carter was on the defensive because of an interview he had given to *Playboy* magazine in which he talked about the lust in his heart and in which he used such racy expressions as "screw" and "shack up." The interview might have been designed to show that Carter was not too sanctimonious to be president, yet it stirred up controversy that detracted from the campaign. During the primary season, Carter had told a North Carolina audience of how a 1967 experience had altered his life: "I recognized for the first time that I lacked something very precious—a complete commitment to Christ, a presence of the Holy Spirit in my life in a more profound and personal way and since then I've had an inner peace and inner conviction and assurance that transformed my life for the better," Carter said. Although postwar presidents invoked God frequently on America's behalf, they seldom dwelled on their personal relationship with Christ. It was expected that presidents would be religious, probably Protestant, and make a show of their faith by attending services on Sunday. Carter spoke in a different religious idiom than these presidents. For those who shared Carter's sense of faith, his strong religious convictions created a bond of trust. But for others who were embarrassed by public piety Carter's religion contributed to what Hamilton Jordan called his "weirdo factor." The *Playboy* interview was Carter's attempt to make himself out to be less of a weirdo. The trouble was that it was hard for a presidential candidate who was being seen nightly on national television to channel his remarks to one set of voters without also attracting the attention of voters with other views. Carter's spokesmen told Walter Cronkite that he was probably not hurt by the interview, but Democrats agreed that it had not helped his campaign. By the end of September, Carter's eighteen-point lead in polling data had slipped to eight.[7]

Ford squandered his momentum by making a mistake in the second debate, which took place on October 6 in San Francisco. Asked a complicated question by Max Frankel of the *New York Times* concerning the country's relationship with the Soviets and its effects on Europe, Ford concluded his answer with the statement that there was "no Soviet domination of Eastern Europe and there never will be under a Ford administration." Before the moderator could move on, Frankel interjected a follow-up question, giving Ford the chance to clarify his answer. Ford then made a longer statement about how the people of Rumania, Yugoslavia, and Poland did not consider themselves under the domination of the Soviets. Each of these countries, he said, was independent and autonomous. Ford seemed to be denying what everyone, including Ford, knew to be true and implying that the people of eastern Europe were communist by choice. Carter had the wit to pick up on Ford's gaffe in his rebuttal. "I would like to see Mr. Ford," he said, "convince the Polish-Americans and the Czech-Americans and the Hungarian-Americans that those countries don't live under the domination and supervision of the Soviet Union behind the Iron Curtain."[8]

Carter made a neat media play by highlighting Ford's mistake and creating doubts about Ford's competence. In the seventies, it was vital that an aspiring president perform well on television, and, under the pressure of the debate, Ford failed the test. The impression mattered more than the substance. A few Polish-Americans in Chicago or Hungarians in Cleveland cared deeply about the issue itself; all Americans worried about the president's ability to project an image of competence in the media.

Ford lost the election by only fifty-seven electoral votes, demonstrating the strength of the Republican party in presidential elections even in an unfavorable year. Carter got about half of the votes from the 54 percent of eligible voters who showed up at the polls. Nearly 80 percent of his votes came from the northeast and the south. Ford carried three more states than did Carter and won every state west of the Mississippi with the exception of Texas and Hawaii. Carter ran well among blacks and union members but still lost the states of Illinois and New Jersey. Although Carter cut into the Republican majority in rural Protestant areas, Ford, despite his gaffe about Eastern Europe, ran well among Catholics who traditionally voted Democrat.[9] Between 1848 and 1960, no candidate of a major political party had come from the South (counting Wilson as from New Jersey, not Virginia). After 1963, no Democrat could be president unless he was from the South.

JIMMY CARTER AS PRESIDENT

In November 1976, Jimmy Carter, the consummate outsider and constant campaigner, had to step inside the circle of power and adapt his anti-Washington rhetoric to the ways of Washington. Hard to place on the political spectrum, he believed that the government had a role in protecting the people's welfare, but he was not a reflexive liberal who thought that big government was the answer to the people's problems. His rhetoric, in which he portrayed himself as an agent of the common good fighting against the "intense concentration of those who have a special interest," had a Progressive Era aura.[10] Like the reformers of the Progressive Era who marshaled their expertise and battled in the name of the people against the interests, he combined a utilitarian sense of efficiency with a Christian sense of ethics. One could say he believed in faith-based efficiency. According to this formulation, government, in a nation that defined itself both in terms of "spirituality and human liberty," should be "competent and compassionate." Carter took a humble view of his own leadership role. He would be a servant of the people and, as he said in his inaugural address, "your strength can compensate for my weakness." He wanted to lead the people on a crusade of "individual sacrifice for the common good."[11]

Defining the common good and creating the conditions for "individual sacrifice" turned out to be hard to do in an era with a weak economy and a constant succession of foreign crises. Carter played the humble servant much better than Ford, and for a time he intrigued the American people enough to maintain favorable ratings. He showed some nice common touches. In a famous symbolic action, he got out of his limousine on inauguration day and walked up Pennsylvania Avenue to his new home in the White House. He proceeded to make a show of getting rid of traces of the imperial presidency. He wore a cardigan when he made a television address about energy. He put his daughter in one of the D.C. public schools, snarling traffic downtown and playing havoc with the routines of the other parents but expressing a sense of solidarity with parents who were forced to send their kids to schools in the inner city. In March 1977, he teamed up with CBS anchor Walter Cronkite to appear on a national radio call-in program aptly named "Ask President Carter." He also stayed in ordinary people's homes during the course of his presidency, just as he had during the campaign when he had carried his own suit bag from town to town. He did not crave luxury, as Richard Nixon did on his frequent trips to Florida and California; nor did he share Nixon's penchant for fine French wines. When Carter made a public appearance, he did not expect the band to strike up "Hail to the Chief." In all these things, he sought to lessen the distance between the president of the United States and the people of the United States.

WELFARE REFORM AND FAMILY VALUES

Carter tried to find themes for his presidency that resonated with common values. He hoped, for example, to make family policy the anchor of his domestic policy and human rights the major motif of his foreign policy. As abstract principles, these themes worked well. As practical guides to everyday presidential problems, the themes left something to be desired. Within weeks of his arrival in Washington, for example, Carter sent his White House staff handwritten notes in which he expressed his concern "for the family lives of all of you." "Rest and a stable home life" would make each staffer more valuable to the president. Staffers should make sure that they were not strangers to their own children and should marry, not just live with, their significant others.[12] In June 1977 Carter extended this homespun advice by telling the Associated Press that "in almost every program that the administration puts forward, the integrity of the family ought to be a factor."[13]

No one opposed the notion of family integrity, yet its application proved tricky. The reporter from the Associated Press wanted to know, for example, what Carter thought of homosexual relationships. Carter gave an equivocal answer, noting that homosexuality did not constitute a "normal relationship" but did not pose a "threat to the family." When the administration proposed to hold a White House conference on the family, it discovered, as Brookings scholar Gilbert Steiner put it, the futility of family policy. When, for example, the administration chose a black, divorced mother of three to head the conference staff, Andrew Greeley, a priest and prominent Catholic intellectual, charged that a divorced woman had no business running a conference on the family. The resulting furor caused the conference to be postponed. Intended as an uplifting, feel-good event, the conference degenerated into arguments over whether one type of family was better than another. Were families headed by women inferior to families headed by men? What about American Indian families and Puerto Rican families? Unable to agree on the definition of a family, conference planners had even more difficulty picking the appropriate tools of family policy. Should such policy include legalized abortion, teenage access to contraception and sex education in the schools, or equal rights for women? In the end, the Carter administration decided not to hold the White House conference on the family, settling instead for a series of regional conferences that took place at the very end of Carter's term.[14]

For Carter the most important application of family policy came in the area of welfare reform, which he made a priority of his administration and in which he took a deep personal interest. The chief welfare program that the federal government financed gave money to single men and, much more often, to single women who were poor and faced the difficult task of raising children by themselves. (Some states, but by no means all, allowed welfare to go to families with two parents present but with the breadwinning parent unemployed.) Such programs appeared to create incentives for mothers and fathers with children to split up in order to get welfare. Carter, in common with all of the presidents of the seventies, sought to correct that problem. His advisors devised an elegant solution, just as President Nixon's advisors had done for him. In Carter's case, the solution involved providing a relatively generous grant for people who were not expected to work and a less generous grant for people expected to work, combined with a guaranteed job that would allow them to pull themselves above poverty. Carter also sought to root out inefficient practices from the welfare system, such as sending a recently widowed mother to four different offices and requiring her to fill out five different forms and answer three hundred different questions if she expected to get welfare. He thought that the savings achieved by being efficient might offset the increased costs that his welfare plan would entail.

He also saw the problem of finding jobs for welfare recipients in highly personal terms, just as FDR had designed the New Deal welfare system with images of the caretaker on his farm at Hyde Park in mind. In Carter's case, the drive to save money often clashed with his advisors' desires to improve the welfare system. When told by his secretary of health, education, and welfare that it would be impossible to have an adequate welfare system without increasing spending, Carter lost his temper: "Are you telling me that there is no way to improve the present welfare system except by spending billions of dollars? In that case, to hell with it."[15] When advised that it might be difficult to find jobs for all of the people who needed them, Carter thought in terms of Plains, Georgia, and reasoned that three jobs could easily be produced in that town. He did not stop to wonder if 150,000 jobs could be found in New York City. In the end, the questions of cost and of finding suitable non-make-work jobs led to conflicts in Congress and the defeat of the measure.[16]

CARTER AND CONGRESS

Even though Carter's administration marked the first combination of a Democratic president and a Democratic Congress since the days of LBJ, Carter could never count on congressional support for his programs.

Part of the problem was personal. Tip O'Neill and Jimmy Carter did not get along very well. O'Neill, the Speaker of the House who expected to make his reputation with the Carter administration, felt slighted from the start. He had little good to say about the staff members from Georgia who accompanied Carter to the White House. "They were all incompetent," O'Neill said. "They came with a chip on their shoulder against the entrenched politicians. Washington to them was evil. They were going to change everything and didn't understand the rudiments of it."[17] O'Neill took to calling Hamilton Jordan, Carter's top aide, "Hamilton Jerkin."[18] Carter, for his part, felt unable to communicate with O'Neill and other Democratic leaders. Still, personal animosity counted for little in a political world founded on marriages of convenience. Whether Tip O'Neill and Jimmy Carter got along with each other meant about as much as whether Franklin Roosevelt enjoyed being in Representative William Bankhead's company or Lyndon Johnson appreciated spending time with John McCormack. FDR and Speaker Bankhead of Alabama worked on the New Deal together because they found it in their mutual interest to do so. LBJ had to do business with Speaker John McCormack of Massachusetts if he expected to pass the measures of the Great Society.

A more important part of the problem was a difference in mission between President Carter and the members of Congress. As the economic situation worsened, Carter's ability to collaborate with Congress on new entitlement programs and other bold domestic programs lessened. Formulating the programs was difficult. Some of Carter's advisors wanted to reign in social spending, and others saw his presidency as a means of advancing social programs that had been thwarted in the Nixon-Ford era. His secretary of health, education, and welfare wanted to cut Social Security, and his White House advisor on aging wanted to expand Social Security. When Carter met with his staff to discuss this issue he said, "social security is not sacrosanct."[19] His domestic-policy advisor sympathized with Carter's position but realized that many in Congress believed Social Security was indeed sacrosanct and a good issue for the Democrats to boot. Hence, getting Carter's programs through Congress proved difficult. Cutting the budget was not something that the post–New Deal Congress was very good at or wanted to do. "You should have seen the stricken expression on the faces of those Democratic leaders when I was talking about balancing the budget," Carter noted in an interview after he left the presidency.[20] As often as not, Carter found himself at loggerheads with congressmen who wanted to start national health insurance but had less interest in hospital cost containment, or who wanted to start a synthetic-fuels program but showed much less interest in energy conservation achieved by raising fuel prices. The congressmen thought that the president was not a good Democrat; the president thought that the congressmen were not good citizens.

Still another part of the problem was the new congressional system itself. The Watergate scandal produced the Democratic landslide in 1974 and the election of Jimmy Carter in 1976. After Watergate, both Congress and the president made a pledge to transact their business in an open and accountable manner. This transparency made it harder for the president to bargain with congressional leaders to produce the necessary compromises on important legislation. A Congress that had difficulties achieving consensus on key matters also had trouble reaching agreement with the president. Watergate helped to revive the power of the Democratic caucus in Congress, as did the departure of many southern segregationists from the Democratic party. But the Democratic caucus was one of many in the new Congress, and each of these groups, whether they represented the interests of women, blacks, or a region of the country, fought to protect their interests. The new system practically guaranteed each member of Congress a good committee or subcommittee assignment that could serve as a venue for generating publicity and raising funds for reelection. That in turn made the junior members, who also saw themselves as an explicit interest group, less in awe of the leadership and more comfortable opposing the leadership on a key vote. Increasingly, these congressmen ran for reelection on the basis of personal recognition achieved by television appearances rather than as candidates whose political appeal came from their party labels. Hence, Tip O'Neill could not deliver for Jimmy Carter in the same way that John McCormack could for Lyndon Johnson.

CARTER AND THE CHANGED IMAGE OF THE PRESIDENT

Carter's lack of success with Congress led to a decline in his popularity by the fall of 1977. In August 1978, 69 percent of those polled by ABC did not approve of Carter's job performance. In the 1978 congressional elections, some of the post-Watergate magic began to wear off, and the Democrats suffered the usual off-year loses of the party in power. Five Democratic senators lost their seats, including such liberals as Dick Clark of Iowa and Wendell Anderson of Minnesota. Neither had been in Congress very long. Clark was a one-termer who could not get a second term, and Anderson, a former governor, was filling the seat vacated by Walter Mondale when he became Carter's vice president. Still, the Democrats ended up with a net loss of three seats in the Senate, and the election heralded the arrival of conservatives such as Roger Jepsen of Iowa and William Armstrong of Colorado. In the House, Republicans picked up fifteen seats.

As Carter's frustration over his lack of success in Congress grew, his image changed. One incident in particular caused the president to be subjected to ridicule and revived the impression people had of him as a weirdo. On April 20, 1979, on a brief vacation in Plains, Carter decided to relax by going fishing. With the level of security that surrounded the president, a fishing trip was not simple to arrange. Carter succeeded, however, in getting a canoe, paddling it out on a pond, and putting his fishing rod into the water. Contemplating the joys of nature, a pleasure that for Carter was genuine, he found himself under assault from a rabbit, described by the Associated Press as "hissing menacingly, its teeth flashing, and nostrils flared." The president lashed out at the rabbit with the paddle of his canoe. An alert White House photographer caught the moment on film. Carter, who was curious about what had happened, ordered that the photo be enlarged so that he could get a better view of the creature that had attacked him. In time, the photo and the story of what Press Secretary Jody Powell called the "swamp rabbit" made its way into the newspapers and on television.[21] At the end of its evening-news program on a slow day in August, ABC News ran a story about what reporter Frank Reynolds called a "killer rabbit," which the Washington Post named "Paws." Ace CBS News reporter Roger Mudd played up the comic aspects of the story, mentioning Harvey, an imaginary six-foot rabbit in a Pulitzer Prize–winning play later made into a movie starring Jimmy Stewart, and the rabbit from the movie "Monty Python and the Holy Grail, " an apparently harmless little bunny that one of the characters describes as a "foul, cruel, and bad-tempered rodent" with a "vicious streak a mile wide." Such stories made Carter look ridiculous.

People started to compare Jimmy Carter and Herbert Hoover. In the comparison, both were engineers who, lacking the heart or the common sense to comprehend people's problems, took the nation to the brink of disaster during a time of economic catastrophe. Both had a naive faith in a self-executing blueprint that excluded political considerations. Arthur Schlesinger Jr., the historian and former Kennedy adviser, made the sophisticated comparison between Carter and Grover Cleveland. Both represented the conservative wing of the party, and neither was a true Democrat. Just as Cleveland vetoed private-pension bills, so Carter resisted programs to implement full employment or create national health insurance. Both had a false sense of rectitude and confused their own priorities with the general welfare.

JIMMY CARTER AND SALT

Foreign policy was a traditional refuge for beleaguered postwar presidents. When Carter entered the White House, however, he faced foreign-policy dilemmas that were every bit as perplexing as those he encountered in domestic policy. As a Democrat, Carter had somehow to reconcile the two foreign-policy wings of his party, which might be described as the Cold War hawks like Henry Jackson and the Cold War doves like Edward Kennedy. His own White House was divided. Carter and Cyrus Vance, his secretary of state, endorsed detente and the SALT process designed to slow the production of nuclear weapons. At the same time, Carter and his national security advisor, Zbigniew Brzezinski, who took a hard line toward the Soviets, wanted to make observance of human rights an important theme of foreign policy. Hence, the United States sought both to cooperate with and criticize the Soviet Union.

Carter ran into problems almost immediately. His selection of Paul Warnke, a strong supporter of arms control, to head the Arms Control and Disarmament Agency and serve as the country's chief negotiator in the SALT process raised the ire of Senator Jackson. Warnke's close confirmation vote cost the president political capital. Human-rights disputes with the Soviets complicated the already strained process of detente. In July of the administration's first year, the U.S. government denied an export license for a computer that was to be used for the 1980 Olympic games scheduled for Moscow. The Soviets, as they had in the past, objected to using trade as a means of conditioning their domestic policy. Within the administration, those sympathetic to business and to the cause of trade pressed for a more liberal policy. Without Carter's knowledge, Secretary of Commerce Juanita Kreps allowed an American company to sell industrial equipment to the Russians. This act, which showed just how hard it was for the administration to maintain consistency on an important element of American foreign policy, angered Jimmy Carter.[22]

Even as Carter tried to send the Russians strong signals on human rights, he continued the SALT process and signed a document that came to be called SALT II in Vienna in June 1979. The Carter-era discussion of SALT occurred at a time of rising tension between the United States and the Soviet Union. The conflicts tended to be centered in remote locations, such as southern Africa and the Horn of Africa on that continent's east coast. The presence of Cuban troops in the horn disturbed many Americans, who felt that, even in the face of detente, the Soviet Union and its clients continued to export socialist revolution around the world. A brief flurry of concern that the Soviets were sending more troops to Cuba added to the fears. Meanwhile, the president faced constant pressure over whether to approve of new weapons or weapon systems, such as the B-1 bomber and the neutron bomb. Confronted, as were his predecessors, with pressure to reduce federal expenditures and contrary pressure to create jobs, Carter, an opponent of nuclear proliferation and something of an expert on nuclear technology, came down against both weapons. Each decision cost him political support. Senator Sam Nunn from Carter's home state of Georgia and an expert on defense policy worried that Carter's 1978 decision to defer production of the neutron bomb would "place in the minds of the Soviets the image of a timid and hesitant America which lacks the courage to confront the difficult decisions ahead."[23]

Nonetheless, Carter persisted in the SALT process. The new treaty he signed in June 1979 extended the previous SALT agreement and put a ceiling on the number of strategic nuclear-delivery vehicles, such as intercontinental and air-to-surface ballistic missiles, that each country was allowed to have. The treaty also banned construction of such weapons as fixed ICBM launchers and placed a ban on increasing the number of warheads on existing ICBMs. As in the previous treaty, the two countries tried to create an effective means for each country to verify the actions of the other and also to institutionalize a process by which the strategic arms limitation talks would continue.

Almost as soon as Carter and Brezhnev signed the agreements, political pundits speculated that Carter, near the absolute nadir of his popularity and more like Nixon in 1974 than in 1972, lacked the votes to get the treaty through the Senate. Even before the treaty was signed, Carter, realizing he would have to create a campaign in favor of the treaty, promoted the establishment of a private group called "Americans for SALT." In the increasingly polarized political environment, this group faced the Committee on the Present Danger and other more focused groups, such as the Coalition for Peace Through Strength, which intervened directly in the political process by making donations to politicians who favored its views.[24]

In the fragmented Congress, there were pockets of support and pockets of opposition to the treaty. Opponents of the treaty, such as Senators Jackson, Jake Garn of Utah, and Jesse Helms of North Carolina, received prominent air play. Still, the Committee on Foreign Relations voted by a three-to-two margin to recommend ratification of the treaty. In the era of Henry Cabot Lodge and the League of Nations that would have been enough to assure Senate passage. In the late seventies, the heads of other Senate committees refused to surrender their sovereignty over foreign-policy issues. The Senate

Intelligence Committee, a creature of Frank Church's investigations into the character and management of the CIA, reviewed the treaty and issued a favorable but tempered report in its favor. The Senate Armed Forces Committee, on which the military had the most influence, took a different tack and advised that the Senate should reject the treaty.[25]

On the SALT issue Carter found himself assailed by Senator Nunn for not exhibiting the bold leadership of John F. Kennedy, even though Edward Kennedy supported the president's position on this issue. It was difficult for Carter to chase dead Kennedys and the living Kennedy at the same time.

THE KENNEDY MYSTIQUE

If Carter was Hoover, then maybe the nation was waiting for Roosevelt. Since Roosevelt was not available, Senator Edward Kennedy represented the next best thing. Despite the impression Carter gave of being above politics, he kept a close eye throughout his presidency on Kennedy's activities, a penchant he shared with every president since 1963. Gerald Rafshoon, a media advisor to the president, warned Carter in the summer of 1979 that people were turning to Kennedy because they perceived that he could solve the economic problems and other crises facing the nation.[26] At that time, speculation was growing that Ted Kennedy would take on Carter for the 1980 Democratic nomination.

The October 1979 dedication of the Kennedy Library became a showdown between Kennedy and Carter. The library, an impressive I. M. Pei–designed structure on Boston Harbor, celebrated the Kennedy legacy in American politics. Although it served the official function of housing the assassinated president's papers, it had the unofficial mission of reminding the public what it had been like to live in Camelot. Most presidential libraries resembled mausoleums—memorials to dead presidents. In the case of the Kennedy Library, there was a living relative who entertained the thought that he might succeed his brother to the presidency. As a result, the library's exhibits described the past with an eye toward the future. The library opening was a gala event, attended by A-list celebrities, including prominent widows Jackie Kennedy, Coretta Scott King, and Lady Bird Johnson. Ted Kennedy served as the host of the occasion, and the featured speaker was President Jimmy Carter.

Carter and his staff treated the Kennedy Library speech as if it were a major event. They prepared a thoughtful text in which Carter paid tribute to JFK but also elaborated on the differences between the postwar era of

JFK and the post-progressive era of the late seventies. Carter argued that America was struggling with a "profound transition" from the days of the New Frontier to a new, still undefined era.[27] High inflation and the need to import oil had changed economic conditions. Inflation meant that "fiscal restraint had become a matter of simple public duty," and hence in the public interest it was necessary to put aside many ambitious social projects. There were, in general, limits to what government could do. "We have a keener appreciation of the limits now—the limits on government, the limits on the use of military power abroad," Carter said. Carter presented the speech forcefully and well. Fidgeting in his seat, Ted Kennedy toyed with replying to Carter and then thought better of it. He was, after all, the host. When his turn came to speak, Kennedy gave a nostalgic tribute to his brother that was more dutiful than poignant. Carter had clearly won the *mano a mano* battle.

AFGHANISTAN

Carter's speech at the Kennedy Library coincided with a growing crisis in Afghanistan that marked a turning point in the relationship between the Soviet Union and the United States. From a partner in detente, Russia once again became a Cold War adversary. The difficulties in Afghanistan began in 1978 when the leader of that country was overthrown and killed in a military coup. In time, this coup came to amount to what one expert calls a "far-reaching national revolution from above" that featured a range of social, political, and economic reforms.[28] Although these reforms were labeled as communist in nature, they could also be regarded as forms of modernization, and as such they ran into opposition from the religious leaders of the country. In March 1979 an uprising occurred in one of the nation's major cities that had a particularly anti-Soviet cast: Soviet military advisors and their dependents were killed and their heads put on spikes for public display. In October, a Soviet-backed Afghan leader was killed, and the Russian ambassador was thrown out of the country. A regime unfriendly to the Soviets consolidated its power, and the Soviet Union, which shared a boundary with Afghanistan and whose population included many people whose ethnic background was the same as those in Afghanistan, decided that its interests were threatened. As a consequence, the Soviets launched an invasion of that country in late 1979.

At first the United States reacted to these developments with relative equanimity. The 1978 coup appeared to be a spontaneous development in Afghanistan and not part of a Soviet conspiracy to take over the country. As the politics within Afghanistan turned against the Soviets, the United States warned that interference in Afghanistan would be regarded as a "serious matter with a potential for heightening tensions and destabilizing the situation in the entire region." The Soviet invasion of Afghanistan decisively changed the emotional tone of the situation and released feelings that had been building up against the Soviet Union since the height of detente in 1972. Crises around the world in places such as Angola, Ethiopia, Yemen, and Cambodia had altered the American attitude toward the Soviet Union. As a consequence, Carter treated the Soviet invasion of Afghanistan as a serious breach of the world peace. He told Brezhnev over the hot line that the invasion "could mark a fundamental and long-lasting turning point in our relations." The president, in the beginning of a difficult campaign year, determined that he would take countermeasures against the Soviet Union. He put ratification of the SALT treaty on hold, as had Ford in the previous election, imposed a grain embargo, played the China card by concluding a grain deal with the Chinese and encouraging tourism with that country, announced that the United States would not compete in the 1980 Olympics in Moscow, and tried to rally other nations to take similar actions.[29]

In the last year of his presidency, Carter moved closer to Jackson's position on the Cold War. Although he strengthened the U.S. relationship with China, he made it clear that the United States, true to its old mission, would seek to contain Soviet communism in places like Southwest Asia and the Persian Gulf. Contrary to the spirit of the SALT process, America would build up its military on land, air, and sea. "An attempt by an outside force to gain control of the Persian Gulf," Carter declared, "would be regarded as an assault on the vital interests of the United States of America, and such an assault will be repelled by any means necessary, including military force."[30]

CARTER AND THE ECONOMY: THE CASE OF STEEL

Managing the economy, like foreign policy, challenged Carter from the very beginning of his administration until the very end. Unlike the presidents of the postwar economic boom, he never enjoyed a period with a robust economy, contending instead with unemployment and inflation. The economy's poor performance put strains on major American industries, such as steel and automobiles, both of which emerged as policy problems for Carter to solve.

At the beginning of the twentieth century, steel represented one of America's great industrial triumphs. When the United States Steel Corporation, which evolved from the holdings of the legendary Andrew Carnegie, was officially founded in 1901, it was the largest corporation in the world. By the time Jimmy Carter got to Washington, however, the steel industry faced precipitous problems. Industry employment reached an all-time peak in the summer of 1974. By the next spring, some 100,000 steel workers had lost their jobs. Despite some recovery, the American steel industry operated at less than 85 percent of capacity in the middle of 1977, with bad prospects ahead.[31]

As the American industry stagnated, the foreign steel industry grew. From 1960 to 1973, for example, global steel production more than doubled, but most of the growth occurred in Europe and Japan. In 1977 imports took up 20 percent of the United States market for steel. The Japanese produced almost as much steel as did the Americans, and they did so in plants that were newer and more efficient. One authority claimed that in 1978 fourteen of the world's largest twenty-two blast furnaces were in Japan and none was in the United States. Hence, with the greater productivity of Japanese steel workers, the Japanese could sell steel at lower prices than could the Americans. U.S. Steel, once the template for the industry, became a marginal firm struggling to compete.[32]

During Carter's first summer and fall in office, the bottom fell out of the U.S. steel industry. In that period more than fourteen major mills ceased operations, and production was suspended in still others. In July 1977 the Bethlehem Steel company laid off 3,500 workers in Lackawanna, New York. Mighty U.S. Steel threatened to close its South Works plant on the south side of Chicago, and Kaiser closed three of its West Coast mills. All in all, 20,000 jobs in the steel industry were lost.[33]

The events of 1977 permanently altered cities that depended on employment from the steel industry. Youngstown, Ohio, a once-prosperous town located on the Mahoning River about halfway between Pittsburgh and Cleveland, suffered a devastating decline. The city, known as Steeltown USA, had a population of 170,000 in 1930. It produced more steel than any place in America other than Pittsburgh. It had its own newspaper and a handsome downtown square that housed attractive department stores. Youngstown also contained more than its share of exotic movie palaces, including one that the Warner brothers, who came from the thriving Jewish community in Youngstown before they triumphed in Hollywood, erected as a regional showplace. Merchants, who sold food and clothing to the families who worked in the mills and more exotic materials to the gentry who ran the mills, prospered. The city contained beautiful residential areas in which prominent families associated with the mills lived and magnificent parks in which everyone played.

The city wobbled during the depression and toppled in the seventies. During the seventies, the city lost more than 25,000 people and by 1980 contained a population of only 115,511. The downtown square withered and died. The Warner Theater could not be sustained as a movie house. Although people moving to the suburbs accounted for some of these changes, the most important factor was the closing of the town's steel mills.[34]

Youngstown Sheet and Tube, the most important of the city's employers, had been taken over by a conglomerate whose out-of-town owners used the company as a source of cash to acquire other companies. The company refused to invest in new equipment because it anticipated no returns on its investment. Management complained that government pollution mandates handicapped Youngstown Sheet and Tube and made it expensive to run the mills. They noted that in Japan the government encouraged the growth of the steel industry and facilitated loans to the industry for expansion and improvement. In the United States, the government appeared to be indifferent to the industry's fate, content to let the production of steel move to Japan and Europe and to gain the benefits of those countries' cheaper and better products. Washington politicians reflexively opposed any price increase in steel, which made it that much harder for the American companies to turn a profit. Hence, the managers of the conglomerate felt they had no choice but to close down the Youngstown steel industry. In September 1977 they announced that the Youngstown Sheet and Tube Company would move out of Youngstown. Some 5,000 Youngstown-area workers would lose their jobs by Christmas. Distressed steelworkers, such as one named Eddie Minor, predicted on the national news that Youngstown would turn into a ghost town. Many workers said they would do almost anything to keep the company in town, even tolerate pollution levels above those officially sanctioned by the government. Another steelworker said that the older workers would get by but younger workers were scared. It looked as though the horrors of the Great Depression were about to be repeated.[35]

After the departure of the steel mills, the city never really recovered. African American families with less cash at their disposal moved to houses that lined once solidly middle-class streets. The town substituted nonprofit service industries, such as Youngstown University and St. Elizabeth's Hospital, for the steel mills and found that these service industries hired far fewer people than had the mills. Youngstown had its share of enterprising entrepreneurs who knew how to operate in the new economy. One of the country's largest developers of shopping centers worked out of the city; the Arbys chain of fast-food restaurants began there. The town had its share of citizens dedicated to its preservation. The newspaper remained in business, and the university took over some of the elegant homes and preserved them. None of these signs of continuity and persistence compensated for the loss of Youngstown Sheet and Tube and the closing of its Campbell works and the subsequent closing of U.S. Steel's Ohio works. Within a few years, all one could see of these plants were slabs of concrete along the Mahoning River Valley. Everything else, including the buildings and the machinery inside, had been cannibalized—sold for scrap or sent to factories in other places.[36]

The abrupt closing of the mills attracted a great deal of notice and became a cause célèbre of the left. Staughton Lynd, a former Yale history professor turned new-left social critic, arrived in town in 1976. He became active in the unsuccessful fight to have the community take over the factories and keep them open. He remained in the area, practicing law and fighting for labor rights. The cause stayed alive, but mostly in people's memories.[37] When popular singer Bruce Springsteen released a 1995 album aptly called "The Ghost of Tom Joad," he featured songs of tribute to America's working past and included a ballad in honor of Youngstown. The song, with its hard, driving rhythm, celebrated Youngstown's history and mentioned "smokestacks reachin' like the arms of god into a beautiful sky of soot and clay."

JIMMY CARTER AND THE DEMOCRATIC RESPONSE TO INFLATION

Carter arrived too late to be able to do much about the steel-mill closings of 1977, yet he knew he had to respond to the lingering recession. Carter's economic advisors, such as former Brookings staffer Charles Schultze, were steeped in the postwar Keynesian dynamic of using the government as a means to induce prosperity. So Carter's advisors brought him what they called a stimulus package. The package contained tax rebates that consumers could take to stores and spend, tax breaks for businesses that they could use, as a later generation would put it, to grow their businesses, and federal funds for state and local governments that would aid communities across the nation. Congress modified but did not derail the president's proposals.[38]

Aware that communities like Youngstown were suffering, the Carter administration expanded the Comprehensive and Employment Training Act, which had been passed in 1973 as a means of consolidating the many manpower programs that had been started during the Kennedy and Johnson administrations. During Ford's term, the Democratic Congress added a new title to CETA that authorized temporary public-service jobs through federal grants to local governments. As part of Carter's stimulus package, he proposed and Congress agreed that more public service jobs be created under CETA. Republicans felt uneasy with this expansion since many believed that Democrats used these jobs as strategic political tools to expand their hold over local governments and to aid Democratic voters down on their luck.[39]

Carter had some luck of his own, before being swamped by the next economic deluge, in his goal of lowering the unmployment rate. Between the time that Carter entered office in 1977 and the second quarter of 1978, the unemployment rate fell from 7.5 percent to 6.0 percent, still quite high by postwar standards but an improvement over the record of the Ford administration.[40]

Just as President Ford eventually had to cope with the problem of unemployment, so President Carter gradually turned his attention to inflation. Early in Carter's administration, Schultze warned him of how inflation could "develop a momentum of its own" but defended the stimulus package as a priority and as something that would not make much of a difference in the inflation rate. As Schultze put it, "We had an anti-inflation program, so-called in April 1977, which had all kinds of bits and pieces in it, none of which meant anything." In 1977 little else seemed to be required, since the inflation rate of 6.5 percent remained about where it was in the Ford administration.[41]

The situation grew worse in 1978 as Carter ran into the same sorts of problems as had affected Nixon and Ford. Early in 1978, for example, the price of food went up because of earlier increases in the price of the feed for cattle and a cold winter. In response to the rise in the price level, the president stepped up his anti-inflation program and in April called for voluntary action to keep price and wage increases below the average increases of the past two years. He proposed to limit pay raises for federal workers to 5.5 percent and called for strenuous efforts to reduce the federal deficit. He gave Robert Strauss, a Democratic party insider and the manager of his 1976 campaign who held the cabinet rank of special trade representative, the task of persuading companies and labor unions to hold the line on inflation, jaw-boning as the economists called it. Not everyone was eager to join in the anti-inflation crusade. Organized labor, led as it had been over the past twenty years by AFL-CIO president George Meany, expressed considerable skepticism about the initiative.[42]

The rate of inflation accelerated, and Carter had to do more about the problem. On October 24, 1978, he spent the day engaged in his usual activities, such as attending a photo opportunity with young Tennessee representative Al Gore and signing into law an important bill deregulating the airline industry. On that same day, Ruhullah Masaui Khomeini spoke in Paris on the theme that the overthrow of the Pahlvai dynasty in Iran was a religious duty. That evening Carter addressed the nation on the subject of inflation.[43] In this speech, he moved inflation to the head of the nation's domestic policy agenda and called it "our most serious domestic problem."

His performance that night was typical of his handling of important moments. He demonstrated his humility by saying that he did not have all the answers to the problem. All he could do was pledge to work hard on it and try to persuade the nation to join him in the effort. He admitted, though, that taming inflation would not be easy because there was no single solution to the problem. All he could offer, he said in his earnest manner, was a "number of partial remedies." These included holding down government spending, slashing federal hiring, eliminating needless regulations, and bringing more competition to the economy. Each of these things, he emphasized, would involve "hard choices" and facing "a time of national austerity." And he wanted more. He asked employees to limit their wage increases to a maximum of 7 percent per year and employers to hold price increases below 5.75 percent. In return, he offered workers that, if they held their wage increases to below 7 percent but inflation rose above that level, they would receive a tax rebate that would provide them with a form of inflation protection.[44]

It was a gloomy message, the sort of belt-tightening once associated with Republicans like Herbert Hoover and Robert Taft. It was also a hard message for many people to grasp. The point that Carter wanted to fight inflation was clear enough, but the mechanics of things like the conditional tax rebate for workers who followed the inflation guidelines should inflation rise above those guidelines were hard to explain and understand.

Another problem with the message was that it was contradictory. On the one hand, Carter wanted to deregulate the economy and encourage competition. On the other hand, he specifically mentioned hospital prices as an important source of inflation and renewed his call that cost controls be put on that sector of the economy. In other words, Carter wanted to deregulate some things and regulate others, with the rationale, perhaps, that he would do whatever worked to make prices go down. That meant in some cases opening up industries to competition and in other industries increasing government oversight.

In trying to rally the American people, Carter invoked neither God nor an American icon like Lincoln. Instead, he quoted Winston Churchill and the way he exhorted the British people to stand up to Hitler. In this case the nature of the sacrifices demanded seemed less clear than they had during the battle of Britain and the consequences of failure less obvious. Even Winston Churchill would have had a hard time charming the inflation out of the late seventies economy, and Carter was no Churchill. As it had earlier in the decade, the inflation rate careened out of control. Food prices and the price of home ownership, an item that was included in the basket of goods and services that formed the consumer price index, continued to rise. In early 1979, just a few months after Carter's inflation speech, the petroleum-exporting countries raised the price of oil. The magnitude of this increase failed to match that of the previous oil shock. This time oil prices merely doubled, but once again the economy suffered terrible consequences. In June 1979, Stuart Eizenstat, the president's chief domestic counselor, caught the mood of near-total despair that gripped the country in a note to Carter. He talked about gas lines that were "growing throughout the Northeast and are spreading to the Midwest." In some of these gas lines, people were getting into fist fights; a recent incident in Pennsylvania had injured forty people. Meanwhile, gasoline prices, which had risen 55 percent since January, affected the entire economy. As Eizenstat put it, "All of this is occurring at a particularly inopportune time. Inflation is higher than ever. A recession is clearly facing us."[45]

Nobody, it seemed, quite knew what to do. Congress, according to Eizenstat, was "growing more nervous by the day over the energy problem." John Updike, describing this same time period in a novel, has his character Rabbit muse about "gas lines at ninety-nine point nine cents a gallon and ninety percent of the stations to be closed for the weekend. The governor of the Commonwealth of Pennsylvania calling for five-dollar minimum sales to stop the panicky topping off."[46]

Carter tried to handle the onslaught of problems he faced at home and abroad. In the end, though, he turned to the tough medicine of monetary policy and agreed to a policy put in place by the Federal Reserve to reduce the money supply. Like Ford he was unable to right the economy in time for the election, and like Ford he lost. As the leading student of Carter's economic policy has observed, interest rates that determined the price of money "went through the ceiling in the first part of 1980, fell in the middle of the year, and rose again during the latter part of the year when the campaign was taking place." By campaign time, all of the economic indicators looked bad: "inflation was in the double-digit range, interest rates were at historic highs, and the employment rate had returned to the level it was at when Carter took office."[47]

As Carter himself put it, in a sort of wistful ode to the days of fine-tuning the economy, there were simply no economic miracles waiting to be performed. When he sought the advice of experts, they told him, in the words of a report from a commission appointed by Carter, that in the future "macroeconomic policy ... should be centered more on the long-term and should de-emphasize attempts at short-run fine-tuning."[48] But as John Maynard Keynes might have reminded Carter, in the long run we are all dead. Certainly Carter's political career was. Although the remedy of high-interest rates worked, the cure came two years too late to save Carter and not before a major and severe recession in 1981 and 1982.

JIMMY CARTER AND THE ENERGY PROBLEM

The energy problem did not sneak up on Carter. On the contrary, it engaged Carter's attention from the very beginning of his administration. His naval work with the nuclear submarine program had made him conscious of the potential of nuclear energy. More important, the energy problem was precisely the sort of issue he thought it proper for the president to address. It was a matter of the president exhorting the people to separate their long-term from their short-term interests and to act in a morally responsible, rather than selfish, manner. As one student of Carter's energy policy has noted, Carter "had an unyielding moral conviction that the nation should act with greater prudence as stewards of the earth's resources."[49]

Early in his administration, Carter delivered the first of his sermons on energy, which he billed as "an unpleasant talk with you about a problem that is unprecedented in our history." Although Nixon and Ford had played on the theme of Americans as wasteful energy consumers, Carter wallowed in it. "Ours is the most wasteful nation on Earth," he said. He elevated energy policy to "the moral equivalent of war" and said that, if the nation failed to act, "we will face an economic, social and political crisis that will threaten our free institutions." He set national energy goals that included reducing the annual growth rate in energy demand to less than 2 percent, establishing a strategic petroleum reserve of one billion barrels, and insulating 90 percent of American homes and all new buildings. It was difficult for some to see the insulation of buildings as the moral equivalent of war, particularly since Carter himself admitted that the gas lines were gone and that spring weather made home heating much less of a priority. Nonetheless, the president chose to spend some of the political goodwill he enjoyed at the beginning of his administration on the creation of a comprehensive energy policy.[50]

Despite the passage of a modified version of Carter's energy plan, the energy problem grew worse in the second half of his term.[51] The first oil shock of the decade had come from the Arab-Israeli war; the second came from the Iranian revolution. As oil exports from Iran came to a halt between December 1978 and the fall of 1979, a shortage of oil developed that led to rapid price increases. For Americans the turn of events was baffling. Although they now understood, after having the point hammered home by three presidents, that the country depended on imported oil, they had difficulty comprehending how a country that supplied the United States with 5 percent of its oil could tie up the entire economy and throw the world oil market out of kilter. At first Carter thought that voluntary conservation might get the United States through the situation. By February 1979, however, James Schlesinger, Carter's secretary of energy, warned that the Iranian crisis might lead to even worse oil shortages than the country had experienced in 1973 and 1974. The oil-exporting countries seized upon the situation to raise their prices, which threatened to throw the economy into turmoil. Carter realized that he would have to return to the theme of energy policy and come up with a new round of proposals. He began to work on a major address on energy.[52]

THREE MILE ISLAND

Then, in a run of bad luck that seemed to plague the Carter administration, an unrelated event made the situation still worse. Implicit in the discussions of energy policy was the promise of a technological salvation, if not immediately then in a few years after government research funds and national willpower combined to produce substitutes for oil. A country with the technical ingenuity and material resources to make fabrics in test tubes could surely cook up a synthetic fuel. Indeed, one promising substitute already existed in the form of nuclear energy. Presidents Nixon and Ford had lauded the nuclear-power industry. President Carter was a little more cautious, noting the industry's potential to ease the energy crisis but worrying about the links between peaceful and military uses of nuclear technology. A few people saw hazards in using nuclear materials to generate electricity, yet the industry's safety was closely monitored by federal authorities.

On the morning of March 28, 1979, the managing editor of a local newspaper gave the Associated Press a story that the state police had been placed on alert in the Harrisburg, Pennsylvania area. Apparently a pump and a valve had failed at a Pennsylvania nuclear power plant near that city. At first the story seemed little more than a sidebar. The problem of leaking radiation appeared to be contained. The next day the situation grew more serious, and the public learned that more radiation had been released into the atmosphere around the plant. The nation faced the possibility of what Walter Cronkite called a "nuclear meltdown." So far as the public could determine, it would be like the slow motion detonation of a nuclear bomb, with horrendous results. Three Mile Island sounded like a remote and bucolic location on the banks of the Susquehanna River. In fact, the plant was located near the state capital, in an area close to some of the country's major population centers. Radiation released into this area could have devastating effects. So the nation watched with trepidation as nuclear-power experts struggled, ultimately successfully, to shut down the plant.[53]

The Three Mile Island incident struck at the heart of the nuclear-power industry and nearly crippled it. Nuclear power from what baby boomers had learned to call "our friend the atom" no longer looked like such a sure bet to replace oil as a means of generating electricity. Even President Carter admitted at the end of 1979 that nuclear power should be the energy source of last resort, not the wave of the future. The bloom was off one of the marvelous technological roses of the postwar era, a prime example of how atomic energy could be put to peaceful purposes. An industry that had been nurtured by a community of government and private-industry experts in atomic energy stood discredited, and people questioned whether it had been wise to put such faith in those experts.

Reinforcing this skeptical mood, a film appeared, nearly simultaneously with the incident, that caught the prevailing tone of cynicism. It was a disaster film about a nuclear power plant, a successor to earlier disaster films like Airport in which technology came through dependably and saved the day. In *The China Syndrome*, hot new Hollywood stars Jane Fonda and Michael Douglas, who were descended from previous Hollywood stars, portrayed a television reporter and camera man, respectively, who, in the post-Watergate manner, use the investigative power of the press to expose corruption in high places and save the world. The nuclear-power industry, the film suggested, was part of the great seventies conspiracy. The experts and the politicians who were in bed with them were not leveling with the people and protecting them from the dangers of nuclear power. As a result of the film and the bad press from Three Mile Island, the industry became discredited. When the creators of *The Simpsons*, putting together a new animated television program at the end of the 1980s, wanted to give their main character a particularly hapless and futile job, they had him work in a nuclear power plant. The once-promising industry had become the punch line of a joke. Bright engineering students at Stanford no longer chose to go into the field of nuclear engineering. As new orders for nuclear power plants fell to zero, future engineers concentrated on other specialities, like computers.

CARTER AND THE MORAL IMPERATIVE

About a week after the start of the Three Mile Island incident and in the middle of a new energy crisis, President Carter once again addressed the nation on the subject of energy policy.[54] He had to reassure his listeners that the energy crisis was real, not some sort of conspiracy, and that the nation needed to do something about it. As usual he did not sugarcoat the medicine or simplify the situation. As with inflation, he asserted that there was no single solution. Instead the nation needed to produce more energy, conserve more energy, and develop new energy sources. The price of domestic oil needed to rise to the price of foreign oil and the nation needed to remain vigilant against the greedy actions of the oil companies who would try to pocket the money as oil prices rose. Congress held hearings to find the "real" causes of the gasoline shortage, but gave Carter little of what he wanted. Perhaps they agreed with one teenager who reacted to the April 5 speech by writing in her diary, "Jimmy Carter is the stinkiest president ever! Gas prices are already out of the world and he says UP they go."[55]

As spring turned toward summer, the energy crisis, which would continue into the autumn, remained a major cause of America's discontents. On June 24, 1979, a Sunday, some 70 percent of the nation's gas stations were closed. When Henry Ford had made the automobile accessible to ordinary Americans, he had a vision of people taking Sunday drives from the city into the country. Such drives, particularly in fine weather, had become a major form of American leisure. On this particular summer Sunday, many Americans wanted to head to the mountains or the beach but worried that they would not be able to find enough gas to get them there and back. "It was a black, dark period," said Carter's domestic advisor Eizenstat.[56]

At this point the energy crisis looked every bit as bad as the one that had occurred in 1973 and 1974. It became the symbol of panic in the economy, just as runs on the bank had symbolized the sense of vulnerability and panic in the 1930s. Then nervous Americans had lined up in banks to withdraw their money before the bank ran out of it. The presence of a line encouraged more people to join the line and withdraw whatever they could. That had the effect of sucking money out of circulation and adding to the deflation. Without money people would not be able to go anywhere or do anything. In the 1970s nervous Americans lined up to buy gas so they could get some before the gas stations ran out of it. Long lines suggested that the gas supply would run out and prompted more people to join the line before that happened. The run on gas added to the shortages and drove up the price, adding to the inflationary pressures on the economy. Without gas people would not be able to leave their homes.

That June OPEC once again raised the price of oil. Jimmy Carter, in Toyko to attend an economic summit conference, skipped a vacation and hurried home with the thought of delivering another message on energy. He requested network time for July 5 but thought better of it. Instead of delivering his speech, he hunkered down at Camp David, met with a wide array of people, and tried to come up with a talk that would, at long last, cut through the nation's mood of despair and rally people to act in the national interest to fight inflation, energy shortages, and the nation's other ills. For the week between July 6 and July 13 he conducted what might be called a domestic summit in which he met daily with between ten and twenty people. The president also made surprise visits to the homes of two or-dinary Americans, as if to symbolize that although he took counsel from the nation's movers and shakers he also wanted to hear from the common man. Lots of people offered the president lots of advice ranging from the spiritual to the practical. His political advisors told him that the matter was relatively simple: people did not like gas lines and wanted them to go away. They thought that waiting in the lines was "pointless" and did not understand the president's energy policy. All they knew was that he had given a lot of speeches on the subject and things had only gotten worse. The president countered with "vague and visionary" words and made al-ternative energy sources "sound as dull as a protracted anti-trust suit." The president, according to these advisors, should stop berating the American people as wasteful and selfish and start finding a way to get them out of the gas lines. Media advisor Gerald Rafshoon told the president that the Ameri-can people wanted to perceive him as "beginning to solve the problems," and that he should "inspire confidence by your actions and lead."[57]

Despite this advice, Carter, resolute in his desire not to talk down to the American people, gave a speech on what he called "a crisis in confidence." "In a nation that was proud of hard work, strong families, close-knit com-munities and our faith in God, too many of us tend to worship indulgence and consumption," he said. But piling up material goods "cannot fill the emptiness of lives that have no confidence or purpose." Having delivered this lament about the loss of the American spirit at a time when many

Americans felt their problems stemmed not from overconsumption but rather from the inability to afford the things they needed, Carter put on his technocratic cap and once again trotted out his solutions for the energy crisis. On his own authority, the president would set import quotas. He asked for a "massive commitment" to develop alternative sources of energy, although he failed to mention nuclear power. In the manner of World War II, he wanted to create an energy mobilization board to lead the conservation effort. Then, in the conclusion of his speech, the president returned to the spiritual theme. He asked Americans to join hands and commit themselves "to a rebirth of the American spirit."[58] He wanted the nation to be born again in a new spirit of selflessness. All in all, the speech featured a remarkable combination of Carter's moralistic themes and his invocation of technocratic expertise, of his search to combine, in the manner of past progressive reformers, morality and efficiency, ethics and economics. It would be his signature moment and for many the summation of the dilemmas the nation faced in the seventies.

In the manner of a summer movie, the hype behind the speech generated some buzz, but not enough to turn it into a blockbuster. Harvard sociologist Daniel Bell, who had met with the president and who would become a member of the President's Commission for a National Agenda for the Eighties that was an offshoot of the speech, put his finger on the problem when he wrote that, "I do not think one can yoke a theme that is primarily moral and cultural to a 'cause' or 'crusade' that is so complex as energy." He thought people were confused about just what was being asked.[59]

In the end, Carter failed to lead the great American revival, and his presidency collapsed amid the economic ruins of the late seventies. He lacked the ability to inspire Americans to overcome their problems. Then again, these problems might have been beyond the reach of any politician or president, the results of structural problems that could not be remedied by moral exhortation or policy expertise. Carter's presidency thus completed a political cycle that Watergate, the energy crisis, Vietnam, and inflation had initiated, and it added to the sense of the seventies as an era of political failure.

7
The Rights Revolution

As presidents tried and failed to cope with the consequences of Watergate, the loss of Vietnam, and the energy crisis, a genuine rights revolution occurred during the seventies. The beneficiaries of this revolution included women, gays, and people with disabilities. Each of these groups profited from the positive example set by the black Civil Rights Movement that culminated in the passage of the civil-rights laws in 1965, 1966, and 1968. These laws of the sixties provided texts for the new civil-rights laws of the seventies. Women and people with disabilities incorporated sections of these laws, such as the requirement that activities receiving federal funds be accessible to blacks, into new laws of direct benefit to them.

An Overview

Even as the events of the sixties served as a preview of and model for the civil-rights-laws movements of the seventies, the two eras differed from each other in their approach to civil rights. The black Civil Rights Movement of the postwar era sought the end of the Jim Crow system of racial segregation in the South. The new civil-rights movements of the seventies involved more fundamental critiques of postwar society. Women sought to reorient gender relations. They toppled an edifice of federal and state laws that distinguished people by sex and as a result barred sexual discrimination in employment, education, job training, and credit. People with disabilities sought nothing less than the physical redesign of America to end the physical barriers that prevented them from full participation in American life. They emphasized that society, rather than the disabled themselves, needed to change. Gays argued that homosexuality not be viewed as a form of deviance that required psychiatric intervention but rather that it be accepted as a legitimate form of sexual orientation.

Each of these new civil-rights movements encountered problems similar to those that beset other domestic-policy initiatives in the seventies. After 1973, civil-rights measures of all types faced a more hostile legislative climate than they had in period from 1963 to 1972. As a consequence, some of the major civil-rights proposals, such as the passage of an equal-rights amendment to the constitution, began with considerable momentum only to be defeated by the end of the era. Ambitious projects, such as making America accessible to people with disabilities, followed a similar trajectory from initial optimism that the goal could be accomplished to a subsequent pessimism that the country simply did not have the economic means to accomplish something so sweeping. Still, the post-Watergate congressional system, with an increased number of subcommittees and a diffusion of power, permitted a wider array of causes to gain a hearing in Washington. Courts and federal agencies, less constrained by economic conditions than the president or Congress, continued to add to the sweep of the rights revolution as the era progressed. Hence, the rights revolution advanced, even though other liberal projects of the era, such as welfare reform and health insurance, foundered.

The civil-rights movements of the seventies, with their pervasive critiques of the status quo, inevitably produced a backlash that also played a prominent role in the politics of the era. As women struggled for equality in the family and the workplace, some questioned the desirability of ending the special accommodations for women that characterized postwar America. They wondered if women would continue to be excused from combat roles in the military or if women would receive preferential treatment in matters regarding child custody. The critics of women's liberation also saw the movement as elitist and undemocratic, the product of federal regulators and judicial appointees who were out of step with mainstream opinion. The movement for gay rights faced even more opposition from people who worried that it would undermine the traditional American family. People ridiculed the disability-rights movement as a costly form of special privilege that would benefit the few at the expense of the many.

These critics tapped into widely held feelings and enjoyed considerable political success. They heightened the conflicts of the era and helped to motivate the turn toward the right that was a feature of America in the seventies and eighties. They failed, however, to derail the movements, and the seventies became an era of profound change in America's attitudes toward women, gays, and people with disabilities.

As evidence of that change, one might take the example of a woman who reported to field-hockey practice at Northwestern University in Evanston, Illinois, in the fall of 1971.[1] Although only a freshman, she entertained hopes of making the starting varsity team and playing intercollegiate field hockey in the widely respected Big Ten Athletic Conference. She had played at a prep school in the east and considered herself a savvy, if not particularly physically gifted, player. During the summers, she had honed her field-hockey skills at special camps in the expectation of playing in college.

The woman waited for the coach to appear on the field and begin the practice. To her surprise, the coach turned out to be a woman who carried a coach's guide to field hockey, a complete novice who knew nothing about the game, who proceeded to read how to hold a hockey stick to the assembled players. Women's field hockey, unlike men's football, basketball, wrestling, or any other male varsity sport, apparently did not merit an experienced coach. As the aspiring athlete discovered, women's field hockey remained a casual activity that was hardly on a par with other intercollegiate sports. Later in her career she went out for Northwestern's women's softball team, which was so underfunded that the players shared their warm-up outfits with the track team.

As the seventies began, women could simply not expect parity with men in intercollegiate sports. From the beginning of their schooling, men and women approached sports differently. Gym classes remained strictly segregated by gender, with different standards of participation for girls and boys. Girls who claimed cramps or other female maladies could be excused from gym, and few bothered to work up a sweat. In one suburban high school, girls received extra credit if they took showers after class, but no one was required to do so.[2] Boys had to take showers, just as they were required to wear jockstraps. Gym teachers, invariably men who had served in the military and carried a military-drill style into their classes, conducted regular jockstrap inspections. The boys often engaged in games with names like Hungarian mayhem that showcased their strength and encouraged their sense of aggression. A typical exercise involved throwing a rubber ball at an opponent from a short distance away. Girls pursued gentler activities.

Indeed, the high-school experience of girls and boys differed considerably, as befit a world in which women and men would go to different colleges and enter different job markets. In New Jersey, for example, Rutgers, the state university, limited its undergraduate admissions to men and provided a separate college, located at the other end of town, for women. The big Midwestern universities were, as the expression had it, coed, but many of the exclusive eastern schools were segregated by sex. Yale, Princeton, and Columbia admitted only men; Vassar accepted only women. Newspapers featured separate job advertisements for men and women.

In 1970 a new high school opened in Randallstown, Maryland, to accommodate the growing population of the suburban area around Baltimore.[3] A perusal of the school's yearbook showed that although boys and girls attended many of the same classes, they participated in different activities when school ended. The Pep Club, a traditional institution designed to bolster the spirit of the new school, had three male and thirty-four female members. The members of the Pep Club whipped up enthusiasm for the school's sports teams. The elite players on those teams joined the Varsity Club, which had no female members. Neither the Radio Club nor the Chess Club, standard hangouts for the technically inclined sort who would later be called geeks or nerds, contained a female member. All of the cheerleaders were women, as were all of the members of Nurses Aides.

Girls and boys took standard academic subjects together, but the vocational courses contained a heavy dose of sexual segregation. In 1971 boys started what was called the Boys' Gourmet Cooking Class. They were the only male enrollees in home-economics courses that included Clothing I and Clothing II and a course called Living in the Home. Boys who wanted to emerge from high school with a practical skill took courses from the Industrial Arts Department which "engenders respect for the instruments of a trade ... and prepares individuals for future jobs after graduation." In other words, the girls learned how to cook and sew, and boys learned some of the skills that would lead to a blue-collar job. Girls who sought similar jobs thought in terms of barber and beauty school, known as cosmetology, or took business-education courses where they trained for secretarial and clerical work.

In 1971, as the woman went out for the field-hockey team at Northwestern and the Boys Gourmet Cooking Class started in Randallstown, a student born with no arms or legs entered college at Princeton. To reach the main lecture hall of that school, students climbed a steep set of steps. It was nearly impossible to study at Princeton without taking a course that met in this lecture hall. When this student with physical disabilities wanted to go to a class in this hall, he had to prevail upon a group of his fellow students to carry him up the steps. Such was the nature of physical accommodation as the seventies began.

At the time, many people understood homosexuality as a disease. *Time* magazine described it in 1966 as "a pathetic little second-rate substitute for reality, a pitiable flight from life. . . . But it deserves no encouragement, no glamorization, no rationalization, no fake status as minority martyrdom, no sophistry about simple differences in taste—and, above all, no pretense that it is anything but a pernicious sickness."[4] John Macy, the civil service commissioner who served in the Kennedy-Johnson era of major black civil-rights initiatives, believed that "homosexuals are not suitable for appointment or retention" in federal employment.[5]

During the 1970s many of these overt aspects of discrimination ended. Women began to gain parity with men in all aspects of education, and this led to Northwestern and other institutions needing to take women's sports seriously. One scholar estimates that in 1971 women accounted for about 7 percent of high-school athletes. By 1978, however, nearly one-third of these were female.[6] Separate physical-education and vocational-educational programs for boys and girls were modified. In Randallstown, Maryland, over the course of the decade, the local high school started softball, track, badminton, and lacrosse teams for girls and added girls to the school's cross-country and indoor track teams. By 1978 the Varsity Club contained boys and girls, as did the Randallstown Athletic Association. At the same time, universities and many other American institutions inventoried their buildings in an effort to see if they could be made handicapped accessible. The medical community changed its understanding of homosexuality so that it no longer was regarded simply as a disease amenable to treatment. Gays gained status as members of a minority group.

WOMEN'S RIGHTS AND TITLE IX

The rights revolution of the seventies started with the women's liberation movement. As part of the epochal Civil Rights Act of 1964, Congress made it unlawful to discriminate against women in employment. In other words, an employer did not have the right not to hire someone for a job merely because she was a woman. This provision came as an afterthought in a legislative process that focused nearly exclusively on racial, rather than sexual, discrimination. As civil-rights historian Hugh Graham has detailed, the Equal Employment Opportunity Commission, in charge of enforcing the employment provisions of the Civil Rights Act, regarded ending racial discrimination as its primary mission and did little on behalf of women. Women were not completely neglected in the civil-rights movements of the sixties, however. In December 1961, President Kennedy created the President's Commission on the Status of Women and charged it with making recommendations on a wide array of matters affecting women.

When the commission completed its work in 1963, its activities were continued through such venues as the Citizen's Advisory Council on the Status of Women. In these and other forums, women tried to get the EEOC to focus on employment discrimination against women. In June 1966, women attending the National Conference of Commissions on the Status of Women urged the EEOC "to take sex discrimination as seriously as race discrimination." The resolution failed, leading some in attendance to believe that a new organization needed to be formed "to take the actions needed to bring women into the mainstream of American society." As a direct result, the National Organization for Women started in October 1966 and became a focal point for what came to be called the movement for women's liberation.[7]

During the late sixties and early seventies, the women's liberation movement made a major impression on America. In the aftermath of the 1968 Democratic convention in Chicago, with its confrontations between young Vietnam war protesters and police, the women's movement staged its own protest. It took place at the Miss America Pageant, a beauty contest traditionally held in Atlantic City, New Jersey, after Labor Day. As part of the pageant, women donned bathing suits and paraded before judges who graded their relative beauty. The protesters, in the spirit of the Yippies who had nominated a pig for president in Chicago, crowned a sheep as Miss America. They also threw objects that they regarded as emblematic of their oppression, such as dishcloths, confining underwear, cosmetics, and high-heeled shoes, into what they called a Freedom Trash Can. It all made for good television and helped to bring the movement to the attention of mainstream America.[8]

Women had always been the object of advertising in the mass media. In 1970 the tone of this advertising changed to reflect a new image of women. That year a cigarette company launched a new product, known as Virginia Slims, with the slogan, "You've come a long way, baby." Apparently women had come so far that their nicotine consumption could now match that of men. The campaign was traditional in its emphasis on women as a separate class of consumers from men yet modern in its celebration of women's achievements outside the home.

Another product that was traditionally aimed at women was the woman's book or magazine, such as *Lady's Home Journal*. These magazines contained beauty tips, recipes, advice on dating and marriage, and other features designed to appeal to housewives. At the end of 1971, a new woman's magazine appeared with a different emphasis. *Ms.* aspired to be the periodical for the newly liberated woman who did not care to be immediately identified as married or single but preferred the more ambiguous title of "Ms." Indeed, by the middle of the seventies, this new identifier for women became a standard form of address in journalism and in private correspondence. The magazine itself featured the usual assortment of features about the public and private lives of women, although with a modern twist. In 1975, for example, the magazine ran a piece on how the experience of being raped had changed a woman living in Philadelphia. Instead of acting "like a good girl," she began to respond to the insults she heard on the streets by initiating comments of her own and making rude gestures with her hands. One day a businessman approached her on her way to work and asked, crudely, if she wanted to "fuck." She took her heavy copy of *The Gulag Archipelago*, itself a symbol of oppression and redemption, and smacked the man with it. She described the look on his face as "delicious" and her own feelings as "wonderful." A man had been put in his place by a woman's hard-won self assertion; a book could be both a source of ideas and a weapon.[9]

This article in *Ms.* dealt, in part, with the physical differences between the sexes at a time when subjects such as rape in marriage, battered wives, and sexual harassment were gaining media attention. The interplay of women's liberation and this interest in how physical characteristics shaped the limitations of men and women produced one of the era's signature events. The "battle of the sexes" took place in the Houston Astrodome in the fall of 1973. It featured a tennis match between Billie Jean King, the best female tennis player in the world, and Bobby Riggs, a middle-aged tennis player whose triumphs had come on the courts at Wimbledon and Forest Hills at the beginning of the Second World War. King, a role model for many women and young girls who proudly put up her poster on their bedroom walls, hoped to upgrade the status of women's professional tennis and bring the earnings of female professionals to parity with those of men. As for Bobby Riggs, it was never entirely clear how serious he was about his contention that the best women tennis players were not the equals of the best men tennis players and that he would prove it by volunteering as a middle-aged man to take on and defeat the champion King.

At first Billie Jean King refused to take the bait. Riggs played leading professional Margaret Court instead and beat her in straight sets in June. Court's defeat prompted King to agree to Riggs's challenge in an atmosphere in which the public's imagination had been piqued. The September event attracted a large television audience. Riggs treated the match, in the words of ABC correspondent Ann Medina, as a circus, something like the stunts of the 1920s, such as sitting on a flag pole. King, by way of contrast, practiced quietly but intensely. For her the game was a solemn mission and a challenge, something like Lindbergh's flight over the Atlantic in 1927. The country, in the process of settling into its fall routines and confronting considerable political turmoil in the scandals involving Richard Nixon and Spiro Agnew, treated the event as a noteworthy diversion.

If the country needed a reminder of how its postwar sense of innocence and triumph was coming to an end, it received it on the day of the match. Willie Mays, arguably the greatest baseball player of the postwar era and a good example of how the entrance of blacks into Major League Baseball had raised its caliber, announced his retirement. That evening Billie Jean King, a new kind of hero, defeated Bobbie Riggs by out-hitting him and running him ragged across the court. She won in three straight sets and took home the $100,000 prize. She refused a rematch on the theory that the point had been made: a woman could beat a man.[10]

At the same time that Bobbie Riggs challenged the best female tennis players in the world and attracted the insatiable interest of the media, Congress and the executive branch dealt with issues related to women and education in more substantive terms. The origin of Title IX of the Education Amendments of 1972 lay in the relatively arcane field of civil-rights law. In 1964, as part of the Civil Rights Act, Congress created a provision that made it illegal for recipients of federal funds to discriminate on the basis of race, color, or national origin.[11] The part of the same law that prohibited discrimination in employment on the basis of gender, race, color, or national origin, exempted colleges and universities from its reach. After 1964, therefore, advocates for women's rights probed ways of extending the law so that, for example, the ban on discrimination for recipients of federal funds covered discrimination against women or the scope of the employment provisions was broadened to colleges.

In 1970, Congressman Edith Green (D-Oregon), who had already served eight terms, used her seniority on the House Education Committee to investigate sexual discrimination in education. She had in mind amending the employment title of the Civil Rights Act to cover colleges and collected more than a thousand pages of information on the subject.[12] These hearings helped to create a favorable climate of opinion for changing another key law of the 1960s, the Elementary and Secondary Education Act of 1965 (over which Green and her committee had direct control), in order to end discrimination in education on the basis of sex. The resulting Title IX of the Education Amendments of 1972 stated that "no person shall, on the basis of sex, be excluded from participation in, denied the benefits of, or be subjected to discrimination under any education program or activity receiving Federal finance assistance."[13]

Without much discussion or debate, Congress included this sweeping statement in a law that contained a grab bag of other provisions. At the time, the busing of students to achieve racial balance in local school districts generated considerable controversy; Title IX slipped by unnoticed. Depending on how the federal government chose to implement the new title, however, it had the potential to be the source of sweeping changes in education. Nearly every school district in the country received federal funds; hence the law could be applied to the entire country and end such things as separate high schools for boys and girls. Therefore, what mattered about this title was not only its congressional passage but also the way that the executive branch, in this case the Department of Health, Education, and Welfare, implemented the law and the ways in which the courts interpreted it.

Not surprisingly, then, the process of writing the regulations to implement the title took a considerable amount of time as the executive branch pondered its implications. Passed in the summer of 1972, the title's regulations did not appear in their final form until the winter of 1975, and the president did not sign them until the spring. Unlike the simple and boldly stated law, the regulations went into considerable detail. They exempted fraternities and sororities from the reach of the law and preserved the single-sex status of colleges such as Smith and quasi-educational institutions such as the YMCA and the Girl Scouts. Within the realm of athletics, the regulations exempted sports that featured bodily contact, such as wrestling and football, from their reach.[14] Nonetheless, the title supplied an important part of the impetus for changes in the ways that male and female students related to one another in elementary schools, high schools, and colleges. By the end of the millennium, women wrestled on high-school teams and people watched women's college and professional basketball games on television. A considerable change had occurred in a quiet way.

THE EQUAL RIGHTS AMENDMENT

A far more visible battle for women's rights during the seventies concerned the effort to add an Equal Rights Amendment to the Constitution. The ERA, as nearly everyone called it, represented a long-standing goal of feminist groups. First proposed in 1923 and introduced in every session of Congress from then until 1972, when Congress approved it, the amendment stated that "equality of rights under the law shall not be denied or abridged by the United States or any state on account of sex." The amendment initially appeared after the success of women's groups in persuading the states to ratify women's right to vote in 1920. That amendment had corrected what these women viewed to be a defect in the fifteenth amendment, passed in the era of Reconstruction, that provided black *men* with the right to vote (if not the reality of voting). The proposed ERA would assure that the fourteenth amendment's provision guaranteeing equal protection under the law applied to women.

Americans, as it turned out, were ambivalent toward matters related to the rights of women. Some conservative men supported the ERA, which was introduced in 1923 by two Republicans. Some liberal women were concerned that the law would eradicate the protective labor laws passed in the Progressive Era that provided minimum wages, maximum hours, and such things as rest periods and rest-room facilities to women but not to men. Although the measure came to a vote in the Senate on two occasions, Congress never sent it to the states for ratification until 1972. The successful campaign that culminated in that year resulted from the resolution of the questions related to sex-specific labor laws. The Equal Employment Opportunity Commission ruled that the employment title of the Civil Rights Act barred state protective labor laws and the federal courts agreed. With the issue of protecting labor legislation removed, everyone, it seemed, rallied around the ERA. It supporters included liberal Edward Kennedy, moderate Richard Nixon, and conservatives Strom Thurmond and Barry Goldwater. Despite this broad base of support, Emanuel Celler, the Brooklyn congressman with considerable seniority and substantial clout as head of the House Judiciary Committee, stubbornly resisted the measure. Martha Griffiths, the same Michigan congresswoman who played a key role in the passage of Title IX, filed a successful discharge petition.[15]

For the next ten years the states debated the Equal Rights Amendment, which became the most visible of all issues associated with feminism and women's rights. At first the measure enjoyed bipartisan support and seemed like a logical affirmation of women's newfound status in the labor force and the country's new consciousness of civil rights. In 1972, twenty-two states ratified the measure. The media ran stories that anticipated the ERA's passage, such as a CBS news story about how the Navy planned to gear up for the amendment by assigning women to positions on ships. By late 1973, however, as the crises of the seventies came into clearer view, the drive toward ratification stalled. Three states ratified the measure in 1974, then only one in 1975, and one in 1977.[16]

The states failed to ratify the ERA for at least four reasons. The first was that the movement for the ERA became entangled with the drive to legalize abortion. People who worried about the ethical implications of abortion grew concerned that the ERA would somehow further the cause of abortions on demand, and that feeling gave them a reason to oppose the ERA. The second reason had to do with the simple passage of time. The process of state ratification took place over a long period of time, and as a consequence the ratification drive launched in optimistic times and under good economic conditions extended into the adverse economic conditions of the seventies. As time passed, opponents of the ERA worried more about its potential costs, such as taking jobs away from men and giving them to women. The third reason for the failure of the ERA had to do with the loss of consensus as the issue encountered opposition from antiabortion and other conservative advocates. What had begun as a bipartisan issue acquired an ideological edge. The fourth and final reason was that the opponents of the ERA demonstrated considerable political skill in communicating their message.

The ERA, then, started as an issue that enjoyed widespread support and ended as a highly partisan issue. On one side stood liberals such as Bella Abzug; Betty Friedan, the head of NOW; and Coretta King, the widow of the assassinated civil-rights leader. Abzug, who served in Congress from 1971 to 1976, was a particularly polarizing figure, an outspoken New York Jew with experience in the antiwar movement and links to many liberal causes. On the other side stood conservatives such as Phyllis Schlafly, a Catholic from St. Louis with a gift for political organization and rhetoric. Born in 1934, she had received a Catholic education, finishing up her undergraduate education at Washington University and supporting herself since her father had lost his job. She did graduate work at Radcliffe, as the women's division of Harvard was known, before coming home to marry a wealthy lawyer from an Illinois community across the river from St. Louis. Even as the mother of a growing family, Schlafly remained active in politics, twice serving as president of the Illinois Federation of Republican Women. She ran for Congress on two separate occasions, losing both times, and then became a crusader for conservative causes.[17]

The ERA had once gained conservative support because it promised to end the special treatment of women in the labor market and thus seemed to further such causes as freedom of contract and free-market economics. Schlafly, described by one feminist writer as "intelligent, attractive, self-confident, and the mother of six children," read the measure differently. Beginning in 1972, she argued, in effect, that the ERA would disrupt the family, disturb gender relations, and in general deteriorate the quality of American life. Passage of the ERA, according to Schlafly, could mean such things as unisex toilets, abortion on demand, rights for homosexuals—whom she called "perverts"—the end of the exemption of women from military service, the ordination of women as Catholic priests, and the elimination of a legal system that protected the rights of mothers and housewives. In support of her convictions, she mobilized groups of women, such as the National Committee to Stop ERA, and lobbied at the grassroots level to defeat the measure in the states—a sort of modern day version of the crusading Dorothea Dix petitioning the nineteenth-century state legislatures on behalf of the mentally ill.[18] After Schlafly testified in Georgia, Virginia, Missouri, and Arkansas, those states rejected the ERA. In 1979 the period that had been allotted for ratification of the measure ended. Supporters managed to gain a three-year extension, but by then it was clear that the drive to pass the ERA had run out of momentum. The measure died in 1982.[19]

Although Schlafly and her supporters managed to defeat the ERA, the spirit of the measure survived in many of the laws and court decisions of the seventies. Federal programs that had once made overt distinctions by gender became gender neutral during the seventies and early eighties. Social Security, the most important domestic benefit program, had once made explicit references to widows, who required financial assistance after the death of their husbands. These provisions implied that women were dependent on men for support and made no similar provisions for men who were dependent on women for support. After a series of court decisions in the seventies, Congress changed the language of the law and eliminated references to widows in 1983.[20] Other laws of the period marked explicit attempts to provide women with equal rights in seeking loans from banks and to bar discrimination in the housing market on the basis of sex. Despite the defeat of the ERA, women gained the right to be admitted to military academies. Hence the defeat of the ERA failed to stop the process of accommodating women in the labor force and in other spheres in which their previous participation had often been as the dependents of men. Both Congress and the courts made it clear that the protections of the fourteenth amendment applied to women, with or without the ratification of the ERA.

This hidden consensus did not diminish the visible conflict between supporters of women's liberation and proponents of a more traditional view of women. At key moments in the late seventies, the two sides directly confronted one another. One such moment occurred at the First National Women's Conference, held in Houston in 1977. The United Nations had declared 1975 International Women's Year. In response, Congress allotted money for the women's conference in Houston. Supporters of the ERA controlled the conference apparatus and did all they could to publicize the conference as a vehicle for women's liberation. To mark the beginning of the conference, women carried a torch from Seneca Falls (site of the 1848 convention at which Elizabeth Cady Stanton recomposed the Declaration of Independence to affirm that all men *and women* were created equal) to Houston (the site of Billy Jean King's triumph over Bobby Riggs). Abzug, Friedan, and King all attended the convention. Across town a rival gathering of some 15,000 women, including Schlafly, held their own convention. When, predictably, the conference endorsed the ERA, Schlafly charged that its composition was slanted in favor of the measure and failed to reflect the sentiments of most women.[21]

ABORTION

The fight over abortion became even more emotional than the battle to ratify the ERA. During the seventies, as before and after, many people held strong convictions on this matter, which emerged as a key issue in women's rights. Some, in the manner of nineteenth-century abolitionists who were convinced of the moral sanctity of their cause, were prepared to die for these convictions. From the beginning of the century until 1970, all states made performing an abortion a crime, although not all states enforced their laws with vigor. Some, for example, unofficially recognized extenuating circumstances, and some tacitly approved of abortion if it was performed by someone deemed to be a competent practitioner. By the end of the sixties, furthermore, fourteen states had passed laws to permit what were called "therapeutic" abortions in circumstances involving rape, the deformity of the fetus, or situations in which a pregnancy would threaten the health of the mother.

The presence of these laws indicated that by the 1960s abortion, linked to modern medical practice, had become a public health issue every bit as much as it was a moral issue. Many of the states that permitted abortion in special circumstances, for example, followed a recommendation of the American Law Institute that two doctors be required to certify that bringing a pregnancy to term would harm the mother's health. Advocates of abortion rights argued that, whether or not abortion was made legal, women faced with an unwanted pregnancy would take steps to abort that pregnancy. The state had a choice between keeping abortion a hazardous procedure, performed as one observer put it "by unskilled and untrained personnel working under dangerous septic conditions," and making abortion safe by requiring that its practice be limited to licensed professionals.[22] In the seventies, these arguments, which fed on the postwar perception of the efficacy of medicine and other forms of professional expertise, were tied to other arguments concerning women's rights. The Boston Women's Health Book Collective wrote in 1971 that "Abortion is our right—our right as women to control our bodies." Referring to the public health rationale for legalizing abortion, the group also noted that illegal abortions were "one of the most common causes of maternal death in this country."[23]

Equity considerations also played a part in the movement to make abortion legal. Simply stated, rich people had better access to abortions than did poor people, which also meant that whites could more readily obtain abortions than blacks. People of means could, for example, travel abroad to places like Mexico, England, Sweden, and Japan and receive safe abortions there. For those whose personal circumstances did not permit them a trip abroad, one could also find an abortion practitioner with a reputation for competence closer to home, provided one was able to pay the premium that that practitioner received for the risks he or she took.

Abortion advocates enjoyed considerable success in the states and in the courts at the beginning of the seventies. By 1971, four states, including New York and Washington, had passed laws that allowed women to receive abortions on demand.[24] Essentially, those laws legalized abortion in the United States, since New York was a cosmopolitan center to which people from across the country, at least those with the price of a ticket, could travel. Those on the west coast could go to Seattle and receive an abortion there. In New York, in particular, the law did not pass without controversy, yet once it was enacted many women took advantage of its provisions. Within nine months of its passage, more than 100,000 legal abortions were performed in the state.[25] At the same time, the courts began to declare that restrictions on a woman's reproductive choice were unconstitutional.

Then came the Supreme Court's decision on January 22, 1973, in the case of *Roe v. Wade*. Neatly combining the discourse of rights and the prevailing belief in the efficacy of medicine, the court ruled seven to two that, during the first three months of a pregnancy, abortion was a matter between a woman and her doctor. Justice Harry Blackmun's opinion relied on a constitutional "right to privacy," "broad enough to encompass a woman's decision whether or not to terminate her pregnancy." The court permitted states to pass laws that outlawed abortion in the last trimester, except in cases where an abortion was necessary to preserve a woman's health or save the woman's life. Blanket prohibitions against abortion, such as existed in Texas and Georgia, were unconstitutional.[26]

The decision brought people's feelings about abortion out into the open. Some applauded it enthusiastically, and others were appalled by it. Dr. Alan Guttmacher, a physician and a spokesman for Planned Parenthood who became a strong advocate of abortion rights, cited the decision with approval, calling it extraordinary. Cardinal Terence Cooke, the archbishop of New York, described the decision as shocking, and Cardinal John Krol, the archbishop of Philadelphia, said it was tragic. For Catholic leaders and many others, the decision, with its talk of trimesters and its discovery of a right to privacy, put a scientific and legalistic gloss on a moral problem. As law professor Robert Burns expressed the idea, a fetus is alive, and that makes abortion murder.[27] The fact that the Supreme Court, the ultimate arbiter of American law whose members served for life, condoned this form of murder was reason for particular concern.

The Catholic Church hierarchy had been closely monitoring the events of the late sixties that led to the *Roe* decision. In 1970, for example, the archdiocese of Washington had ordered its parishes in Maryland to back the congressional campaign of Lawrence Hogan, who opposed abortion. After the decision, the church increased its level of participation and its visibility in the antiabortion campaign, creating a blueprint in 1975 that it called the "Pastoral Plan for Pro-Life Activities" and forming organizations such as the National Commission for the Human Life Amendment. This commission and a host of other groups sought constitutional relief from the decision in the form of a constitutional amendment that would ban abortions. Other proposed legal remedies included extending the reach of the fourteenth amendment, with its promise of equal protection under the law, to the fetus. If the fetus were endowed with rights, those might supersede the rights of the mother, particularly if the case in point involved the extinction or, as some would have it, the murder of that fetus. The same policy tool in the feminists' kit that produced the Equal Rights Amendment would now be used for conservative purposes. Antiabortion forces also lobbied on the state level to pass laws that would restrict abortion to the maximum degree that the Supreme Court permitted.[28]

Congress hesitated to touch such a sensitive subject, on which people's feelings ran so high that compromise was nearly impossible. Still, just as a feminist network used the nooks and crannies of the legislative process to advance such causes as Title IX, so a conservative and Christian network attempted to put that process in the service of the antiabortion cause. Mimicking a strategy that civil-rights advocates had once used, Henry Hyde, a respected Republican congressman from Illinois, placed what lawmakers called a "rider" on an appropriations bill. The Hyde Amendment, as it came to be known, banned federal funding for abortions, just as Representative Adam Clayton Powell had once used a similar device to ban federal funding for segregated schools. As a practical matter, Hyde's rider meant people who received federally funded health care, such as people on welfare, could not receive abortions. For abortion-rights proponents, such a practice harked back to the worst days of the world before *Roe*. As a reminder, these advocates sent coat hangers, a symbol of the crude and dangerous tools people used to perform abortions before they were made legal, to representatives who supported the Hyde Amendment.

The Hyde Amendment became one of the capitol's featured annual battles, which moved in synch with each year's budget process. In 1977, for example, the House passed the amendment in June. The Supreme Court soon bolstered the House's position by ruling that the Hyde Amendment was constitutional. The Senate adopted a similar but less sweeping amendment, allowing federal funds for abortions in extreme circumstances, such as pregnancies that resulted from incest or rape or pregnancies that endangered the life of the mother. A five-month standoff ensued over which version of the law to accept. The National Conference of Catholic Bishops sided with Hyde, and both Joseph Califano, President Carter's secretary of health, education, and welfare, and President Carter himself were on record as "personally" opposed to abortion. Abortion-rights advocates, associated with organizations such as Planned Parenthood, argued that the heavy involvement of the Catholic Church in the debate violated the American conception of the separation of church and state. After a protracted fight that lasted until December, President Carter signed a measure that banned federally funded abortions but accepted the Senate's limitations on the ban.[29] But just as soon as the controversy ended for 1977, it arose again in 1978. Ironically, the same appropriations bill that elicited the abortion controversy contained unnoticed items secured by feminists to advance their causes.

The pattern of shifting attitudes in the abortion-rights debate was similar to that confronted by advocates of the Equal Rights Amendment. In both cases, influential policymakers' favorable attitudes toward an item on the women's rights agenda became much more qualified and conflicted over time. In both of these cases, the clout of the liberal factions waned and the influence of the conservative factions strengthened as the decade progressed, with the economic recession years of 1973 and 1974 as something of a dividing point. The right-to-life movement drew on a wide and growing pool of potential supporters who lost their faith in the conventional postwar reliance on secular experts, versed in science and technology, to act as stewards for the rest of society. The issue resonated not just with Catholics but with evangelical Protestants as well, people with a distrust of governmental and professional authority who saw in the so-called rights revolution a willful disregard of the majority. An unborn child could not defend itself against the tyranny of Supreme Court justices or federal bureaucrats. Hence, many conservatives believed that abortion needed to be banned.

GAY RIGHTS

The emergence of the women's liberation movement during the seventies raised the delicate question of discrimination based on one's sexual orientation. Betty Friedan, whose 1963 book *The Feminine Mystique* helped to launch the women's movement and who herself played a key role in the 1966 creation of the National Organization for Women, regarded lesbianism as a side issue that would derail the cause of women's liberation. Friedan saw the movement as engaging the causes and concerns of mainstream America and did not want its detractors "to dismiss the women's movement as a bunch of man-hating dykes." Others within the women's movement disagreed. They argued that at the root of women's problems was oppression by men. If women could free themselves of their dependence on men, not just as a source of economic support but as a source of love and sexual satisfaction, they could achieve true freedom. Between 1970 and 1975, according to Ruth Rosen, "countless women's liberationists made the 'political choice' to live life as lesbians." Popular author Erica Jong whose books took women's sexual liberation as one of their major themes, complained that "you got the feeling that unless you had the trappings of radical lesbianism about you, you would be shunned."[30]

These feelings undoubtedly reflected a view of life from the relatively rarified vantage point of Manhattan's Upper West Side. They nonetheless responded to a growing awareness during the seventies of a gay-rights movement. Like other minorities, gay and transgendered people insisted that they should not endure discrimination because of their differences from other people. Just as African Americans should not be stigmatized for having black skins, so gays should not suffer because of their sexual orientation. Yet many of the same people who found the treatment of African Americans in the postwar era shameful and who viewed it as a failure to live up to American ideals and as something that detracted from the nation's performance in the Cold War freely indulged in prejudice against gays. The official views of organizations such as the New York Academy of Medicine, which regarded homosexuality as a disease that endangered the welfare of society, bolstered these feelings. "The exclusive homosexual is a psychopath," declared respected psychiatrist Albert Ellis in 1963. He and many others believed that homosexuality was something to be cured—in the optimistic manner of other postwar assaults on physical diseases and mental disorders—not an identity to be celebrated. Gay rights faced potential opposition from the Right and the Left. The Catholic Church condemned homosexuality because it "excludes all possibility of transmission of life"; conservatives such as Phyllis Schlafly did not want "perverts" to be given "the same legal rights as husbands and wives." It was no wonder that gays enjoyed fewer rights than other Americans. Two gay people who sought to marry were not allowed to do so. Homosexuals also faced discrimination when they went to buy a house or apply for a job.[31]

Since homosexuals were being deprived of the civil rights that had been defined by statute and judicial opinion in the sixties, it made sense for members of this group to seek the same sorts of remedies that other minority groups received. In terms of economics, if not attitudes, the matter seemed simple enough. Unlike blacks who demanded the dismantling of Jim Crow public facilities or people with disabilities who called for expensive changes like curb cuts to make the physical environment accessible, gays wanted only an end to legal discrimination. They did not see themselves as a class of economically deprived individuals, as did many blacks and Hispanics, who would require federal financial assistance in addition to the relief provided by civil-rights statutes.

To launch a civi-rights movement, however, gays needed to gain a sense of their own identity and feeling of group solidarity. In June 1969 an event occurred that brought new attention to the gay community and its grievances. The incident took place in Greenwich Village on the evening of June 28. That night the New York City police received orders to raid the Stonewall Inn just off Sheridan Square. Such raids were hardly unusual because bars like Stonewall brought together a volatile mixture of public displays of affection and dancing by same-sex couples, the patronage of men who dressed as women, the sale of alcohol without the proper liquor license, and the presence of members of the "mob" who owned the bar and bribed the police to overlook the laws being violated. In the previous fortnight, two similar bars had been visited by the police. At the Stonewall, there was even a warning system that allowed gay couples who had been dancing to leave the dance floor before the police arrived. The usual drill was for the patrons of the bar to exit and for some of the employees to be arrested. But things did not go as usual that night. Instead, as the New York Times reported, "hundreds of young people went on a rampage"; thirteen people were arrested, four policemen were injured.[32] The next evening police remained in the area until four in the morning, dealing with "a crowd of 400 youths, some of whom were throwing bottles and lighting small fires." The crowd taunted the police and chanted slogans such as "support gay power" and "legalize gay bars."[33] Incidents continued throughout the next week.[34] The event marked the emergence of gay pride as an important new theme of the rights revolution.

To be sure, the gay-rights movement had a long history that preceded Stonewall. Still, the Stonewall riots served as a catalyst for the movement in the seventies, just as the Rosa Parks incident in Montgomery helped to rekindle interest in the black Civil Rights Movement during the fifties. The two "founding" incidents revealed both similarities and differences between the two movements. Both were acts of self-assertion in the face of official harassment of groups previously considered passive. Rosa Parks sat down on a bus, a symbol of mobility. The Stonewall riots took place outside a bar, a symbol of leisure time and social solidarity. Blacks fought for upward mobility, the right to share in America's abundance. Gays strived for the right to enjoy a social life with others who shared their sexual orientation and, in a sense, to act differently from the prevailing "straight" community. Blacks sought their rights in the name of Christian morality. Gays appealed to a new sensibility that held that sexual orientation was key to one's identity. Blacks were oppressed by the town authorities. Gays faced persecution from the police but also economic extortion from the mafia. Montgomery was a small Southern town. Greenwich Village was part of America's most cosmopolitan city.

Leaders of groups like the Gay Liberation Front built upon the Stonewall riots. One year after the event, the gay community staged a commemoration. The organizers urged gay people to join in the activities and, in the words of Michael Brown, founder the Gay Liberation Front, "stop hiding in closets and in the shelter of anonymity." He entreated such people to "come out" and claim the civil rights that they deserved "as human beings."[35] As the mainstream New York Times reported, the appeal succeeded. Thousands of gay men and women marched from the Village to Central Park. The march indicated that an increasing number of people identified themselves as homosexuals and took pride in their homosexual identity, embracing such slogans as "out of the closets and into the streets" and "gay is good." Still, not everyone approved of this newfound pride. "Homosexuality is a psychiatric or emotional illness," insisted Dr. Lionel Oversey, a professor of clinical psychiatry at Columbia. According to the Harris Poll, more than 65 percent of the population regarded homosexuals as "harmful to society."

Oversey believed it was "part of the American culture that anything non-manly is looked upon with disgust." Such views, countered the leaders of the gay community, were out of step with the times. If homosexuality was an illness, then it was an illness shared by some 10 percent of the population. The women's movement gave "nonmanly" activities, whatever that term was supposed to mean, a new legitimacy.[36]

As the gay-rights movement gained momentum in the seventies, its members lobbied to end such practices as prohibiting homosexuals from working in public schools. Gay-pride marches became municipal staples. In response, cities passed ordinances that granted equal protection to homosexuals, and, between 1969 and 1973, six states removed laws that banned sex between two members of the same sex from their books.[37]

As with the women's rights movement, however, opposition to these manifestations of gay rights mounted in the period after 1973 as the economic problems of the era became more evident. The issue came to a head in Miami, a city that represented many of the contrary trends of the seventies. It was a southern city but with the demographic characteristics of a northern one; a city that had been racially segregated until the civil-rights revolution but one that contained the largest concentration of Jews outside of New York City; a city that was losing white population but rapidly gaining Latino population. Neighboring Miami Beach, described as a "gay paradise in the fifties," had long welcomed gays who coexisted with Jews on vacation from New York and Canadians thawing in the warm sun. A resort with a permissive life style, Miami Beach was also influenced in the seventies by Latin ideals of masculinity.[38] In 1976 gay activists won an impressive political victory in which they helped elect a majority of the members of the Metro-Dade (county, including Miami and Miami Beach) Commission. This commission followed the lead of other communities and passed a gay-rights ordinance in January 1977.

This action prompted Anita Bryant, a thirty-six year old Miami resident, to take action. Bryant was a celebrity, a beauty queen—a former Miss Oklahoma—and a professional singer and commercial spokesman for the Florida orange juice industry. She was also a practicing Southern Baptist, who at the age of eight accepted Jesus Christ as her savior, and a patriot who had supported the Vietnam War, entertained the troops with Bob Hope, and been invited to the White House by Lyndon Johnson.[39] Bryant instinctively understood what advocates for other moralistic crusades such as prohibition had come to learn. In gaining public support, it helped if a cause was linked with the welfare of the community's children. In that spirit, Bryant charged that the gay-rights advocates really wanted "to propose to our children that there's an acceptable alternate way of life." "Before I yield to this insidious attack on God and his laws, I will lead such a crusade to stop it as this country has not seen before," she said. Bryant won the battle of Miami, whose voters decided to overturn the gay-rights ordinance that June (1977).[40]

The Supreme Court refused to take up the cause, deciding not to review a Washington state law that allowed a teacher to be fired for being a homosexual. By the end of the seventies, other cities, such as St. Paul, Minnesota, and Eugene, Oregon, had decided, in a manner reminiscent of the sagging support for the ERA, to follow Miami's example and repeal their local antidiscrimination laws that protected gays. Even in this chilly climate, however, pockets of warm support for gay rights remained. Seattle passed a gay-rights ordinance in 1978. That same year, George Moscone, the mayor of San Francisco, signed a gay-rights ordinance. It proved to be his death warrant. Later in the year, he was assassinated, along with an openly gay city supervisor named Harvey Milk, by a politician who had voted against the ordinance. In this way the gay-rights movement acquired its martyrs.[41]

To be sure, San Francisco and New York remained the vanguard of the gay-rights movement. Still, this movement established a national presence during the seventies, one that could be felt in smaller, more typical communities such as Atlanta and Cleveland. Being gay became something like being Jewish or Italian. People recognized the category as describing a distinctive ethnic group, one that, like the other groups, had left its mark on the American culture. Gay rights lingered into the eighties as a controversial issue with the potential to drive a wedge between liberals and conservatives, culturally permissive and cultural proscriptive people. Nonetheless, it gained a permanent place on the American political agenda during the seventies that it never lost.

DISABILITY RIGHTS

One might have thought that controversies over the Equal Rights Amendment, abortion, and gay rights would have stopped the rights revolution dead in its tracks, yet that was not the case. On the contrary, at just the moment that women and gays were encountering staunch opposition from Phyllis Schlafly and Anita Bryant, new minority groups arose to claim their civil rights. The disability-rights movement serves as a case in point.

In the postwar era, disability fell into a realm of public policy devoted to medicine, vocational guidance, and income maintenance. These strategies had the common characteristic of putting people with disabilities in the hands of professional caretakers or consigning them to a life of inactivity.[42] In the seventies, a feeling began to grow, first among the parents of children with disabilities, then among people who had once had polio, and finally among those with other disabilities, that a different response was required. These members of the disability community sought education, jobs, and other tangible benefits not as discretionary privileges to be granted by doctors, rehabilitation counselors, school administrators, or other gatekeepers but as fundamental rights. The rights strategy shifted the burden of adjustment from people with disabilities to society itself. In this distinctively seventies view, the deficits of people with disabilities mattered less than did the defects in the environment. Contrary to the postwar wisdom, people with disabilities did not need to be changed or simply maintained. Instead, the environment that surrounded them needed to be altered in order to accommodate them. Physical barriers, such as high curbs and steep steps, had to be removed; attitudinal barriers, such as prejudices on the part of employers who interpreted difference as inability, needed to be broken down.[43]

The disability-rights revolution first took hold in the courts. In the late sixties and early seventies, lawyers who worked in such settings as the Mental Health Law Project advocated legal protections for people who lived in insane asylums or facilities for the mentally retarded. The crusading lawyers won favorable judicial rulings on such subjects as "minimum constitutional standards for adequate treatment." In 1972, public-interest lawyers and the parents of children with disabilities gained significant victories in the field of education for the handicapped. In the cases of *Mills v. Board of Education* and *PARC v. Pennsylvania*, the federal district courts held that disabled children had a right to a "free and appropriate public education." With these rulings in hand, the advocates went to Congress and asked the legislators to put the wording of these decisions into statute law. In response, Congress passed the Education for all Handicapped Children Act of 1975, which ignored the fiscal stringencies of the era and President Ford's desire not to create new entitlement programs and ordered school districts across the nation to provide a free appropriate education for all handicapped children.[44]

This law never commanded the attention of the general public. Instead, it was created and implemented by a small circle of advocates and policymakers who followed disability policy. Hence, few people made the argument that the difficulties that public school systems were having in implementing earlier civil-rights law portended trouble for the new laws and argued against their passage. Instead, the civil-rights revolution quietly entered a new area of endeavor, just as it had in 1972 with the creation of Title IX of the Education Amendment.

The most important of the disability-rights laws followed the strategy of Title IX in extending Title VI of the Civil Rights Act into new areas. In 1972 the reauthorization of an established disability program known as vocational rehabilitation became enmeshed in a political controversy between Richard Nixon and the Democratic Congress. Nixon vetoed two different versions of the law before Congress came up with an acceptable alternative. Somewhere in the middle of this protracted battle, someone got the idea of using the legislation to extend the provisions of Title VI to people with disabilities. That suggestion sent an aide to Senator Jacob Javits scurrying out of the room to look for the wording to Title VI. In this manner, what became Section 504 of the Rehabilitation Act of 1973 was inserted into the bill. Unlike the later 1975 laws, no group of legal advocates or anyone else pushed to include this provision. Section 504 elicited almost no attention in congressional hearings and congressional committee reports. It was an afterthought, one that seemed in keeping with the still liberal spirit of the times.

After passage of the law and with the onslaught of the economic and political troubles that ushered in the seventies, the Republicans in the executive branch began to view Section 504 with alarm. They realized that its innocuous language—"No otherwise qualified handicapped individual in the United States shall, solely by reason of his handicap, be excluded from participation in, be denied the benefits, or be subjected to discrimination under any program or activity conducted by an Executive agency"—masked its long reach. The new law meant that all hospitals, schools, colleges, urban transportation systems, and a host of other institutions would have to be accessible to people with disabilities. As a consequence, officials in the Department of Health, Education, and Welfare hesitated to put the law into operation. They stalled for the rest of the Ford administration, worried that it might cost as much as $26 billion to make facilities that received federal funds accessible to the handicapped. During the life of the Ford administration, disability-rights groups such as the American Coalition of Citizens with Disabilities, which had been created in 1975, education groups such as the American Council of Education, and groups representing particular interests of local governments such as the American Public Transit Association all became aware of the law and tried to influence the regulations. In the end, Secretary Joseph Califano of the Carter administration signed the regulations but only after protestors from the

ACCD picketed in front of his house and in front of the San Francisco headquarters of his department.[45]

These demonstrations, like the Stonewall riots, were important to the creation of a disability-rights movement. They helped to establish group solidarity and conveyed the message to the public that people with disabilities were acting without the aid of rehabilitation doctors or vocational rehabilitation counselors and taking control of their lives. Unlike the leaders of the gay-rights movement, people with disabilities were affirming a law that had, in effect, been created for them rather than protesting against and eliminating a law that had been used to oppress them. In the case of the women's movement, the inclusion of women in the employment title of the Civil Rights Act of 1964 served as a catalyst for the creation of the National Organization for Women, but feminists soon expanded on the narrow enforcement of this title and established their own distinctive policy agenda. The disability-rights movement was unique. The federal government created the modern disability-rights movement without having any intention of doing so. The process demonstrated how the courts, Congress, and people at the grassroots all added momentum to the rights revolution, even after the shift toward bad economic conditions in the seventies and the presence of active opposition to the liberal initiatives of the Great Society and its immediate aftermath.

In the case of disability rights, this opposition centered not so much on the legitimacy of the group itself, as it had with gay rights, but rather on the prohibitive costs associated with accommodating people with disabilities. One publicized case concerned the small rural town of Rudd, Iowa. Even a town of some 500 hundred people could not escape the reach of the federal government's grant-in-aid programs. Its public library, for example, received federal funds. As a consequence, officials from the regional office of HEW's Office of Civil Rights informed town officials that the Rudd public library had to be made accessible. These officials objected and wondered why they should install a ramp at a cost of $6,500 when there was no obvious need—another example of what cynical journalists called costly and pointless dicta from Washington.

One might dismiss the disability-rights movement as far less important than the causes of women's rights or gay rights. Women, who made up more than half of the population, constituted a larger group, but the number of people with disabilities, depending on how one defined the concept, was, according to a 1978 estimate, on the order of 36 million people, or one person out of every six.[46] If that were true, then people with disabilities were a larger minority group than either blacks or Hispanics, and their political independence made them a political prize worth courting. Although not everyone with a functional limitation identified himself or herself as disabled, the group also benefited from an image of being worthy of state and charitable aid, in sharp contrast to members of other groups who were sometimes perceived as malingerers. Each of these factors aided the cause of disability rights.

As a direct consequence, the physical design of America changed in the seventies. Curb cuts began to appear on the corners of city streets. Rest rooms acquired wider toilet stalls, urinals mounted lower on the walls, and faucet handles that could be pushed or pulled. Ramps appeared in public buildings. Subway systems no longer depended solely on stairs and escalators to move people in and out of stations. Elevators and public buses had audio devices that called out the stops to facilitate the use of public facilities by people with visual impairments. Automatic teller machines, which were just beginning to appear during the seventies, acquired instructions written in Braille. Theaters and ball parks contained sections with no seats for the convenience of patrons in wheel chairs. The relatively unheralded disability-rights movement, therefore, succeeded in making major changes in the built American environment.

CONCLUSION

An account of the seventies, then, must take into account not only the problems created by Watergate, economic recession, and the loss of American prestige abroad but also the opportunities that the rights revolution made possible. The women's movement helped to bring about lasting changes in education and in the workplace that opened up a new range of professional and vocational possibilities and went far toward ending gender discrimination in hiring and promotion. The gay-rights movement helped to ease the stigma associated with homosexuality and to make Americans more accepting of differences in sexual orientation and less willing to exclude gays from jobs and other forms of public life. If the black Civil Rights Movement of the sixties produced, with great fanfare, the country's most important civil-rights legislation, a more broad-based rights revolution occurred in the seventies. It started with little public notice, encountered heated clashes as the seventies progressed, and still left its imprint on the era.

8

The Me Decade and the Turn to the Right

Respected commentators Tom Wolfe, Christopher Lasch, and Lester Thurow, who wrote about the seventies as they were happening, believed that the rights revolution demonstrated what was wrong with the era. People clamoring for their rights were acting in a self-absorbed, hedonistic, narcissistic, selfish, and uncompromising manner. The rights revolution represented a retreat away from the social purpose that marked the liberal postwar era. It was less about improving the whole society and more about one part of America gaining an advantage over another in a slow-growth economy in which one person's victory meant another person's loss. The rights revolution meshed at the personal level with the rush to join self-help and human-potential movements, such things as psychotherapy, existential philosophy, Scientology, and EST, which asked people to expend energy on themselves rather than on one another.[1]

These respected critics, who proclaimed the seventies "the Me Decade," a culture of narcissism, and the zero-sum society, were on to something. They correctly picked up on the bleak economic prospects of the seventies and on the fact that baby boomers in their twenties, concerned about finding their way in a difficult job market and beginning their families, turned inward. The result was self-absorption, which implied a lack of social purpose and a disengagement from public affairs.

At the same time, the critics also missed a great deal. What some saw as selfish acts of self-protection were to others altruistic gestures to make a better future for their children. Group conflict, by its very nature, also produced group solidarity and led to an engagement with civic affairs.[2]

The trouble was that the commentators accorded far more respect to the liberal aspirations of the Great Society than they did to the efforts of white ethnics and urban Catholics who protested against the Great Society's legacies. Civil rights, if not the rights revolution to which it gave rise, was a noble cause. The fights against busing, bilingual education, and affirmative action were manifestations of a defensive selfishness that harked back to the inherently paranoid style of American conservatism. Women's rights helped to open up American society in ways that improved the quality of American life. Other minority groups that tried to assert their rights fared less well at the hands of the social critics. If gays, women, and people with disabilities created a rights revolution in the seventies, the era also featured the emergence of other groups, such as evangelical Protestants, who vocally asserted their rights and who began to see themselves as an embattled minority. The evangelicals, once thought to be relatively docile in terms of political participation, became mobilized to protest such causes as abortion and the Equal Rights Amendment. In general, the liberal critics gave conservative ideas short shrift, as if they were something alien, the products of self-interested businessmen and socially irresponsible Sun Belt entrepreneurs, who had no interest in acting as stewards for the rest of society. Yet conservative ideas, such as government deregulation and supply-side economics, were espoused by people every bit as earnest and sincere as Thurow and the other advocates of government planning. In short, Wolfe, Lasch, and Thurow, blinded by an overwhelming sense of despair about America's inevitable decline that afflicted many intellectuals in the seventies, misunderstood America's turn toward the right and overreacted to it.

Tom Wolfe and the Third Great Awakening

Of these three social commentators, Tom Wolfe, a perceptive journalist and pop historian with a particularly sensitive eye for uncovering social trends, attracted the most attention with an essay on "The Me Decade and the Third Great Awakening" that he included in a book of his collected journalistic pieces. It appeared during the nation's bicentennial year, when Americans made concerted attempts to reflect on their accomplishments and shortcomings. Wolfe pointed to two important changes between the seventies and the postwar era. The first concerned alterations in family structure. In the postwar era, only the very privileged got to "shuck overripe wives and take on fresh ones." Divorce, as Wolfe pointed out, had damaged the careers of politicians Adlai Stevenson and Nelson Rockefeller, and divorce disqualified people for important postwar missions, such as becoming an astronaut. During the "Me Decade," it became normal for people of all social classes to divorce, and the divorce rate soared. Indeed, the percentage of married Americans in their forties fell from 84 percent in 1972 to 67 percent in 1982.[3] Wolfe noted that when Eugene McCarthy, a Catholic politician with wide public visibility, obtained a divorce, few people bothered to take notice.[4] Had he written a few years later, he might have commented on the fact that Ronald Reagan became the nation's first divorced president in 1981 while simultaneously proclaiming the virtues of family values. Wolfe's description of divorce as "wife shucking" also failed to pick up on the related pattern of "husband shucking," a more positive attribute of the rights revolution. A society in which women were gaining equal rights was also one in which women, as well as men, might wish to terminate a marriage. What some might reflexively condemn as a sign of moral decline was for others an example of liberation.

The second change Wolfe described concerned religion and what he called the "third great awakening." During the seventies, people were finding God in record numbers and in odd places. In the postwar era, according to Wolfe, if a serious person had "'announced for Christ' people would have looked at him as if his nose had been eaten away by weevils." Religious conviction, in America's politely tolerant postwar society, was something always present but seldom mentioned except in the ritual endings to political speeches and in the invocations of religious leaders for religious tolerance. It was certainly not something much discussed outside of church, and few people who aspired to any sort of sophistication dared to call God by his Christian name in mixed company. In the seventies, those sorts of inhibitions ended, and all sorts of famous people in mainstream rather than religious careers announced for Christ, including politicians like Jimmy Carter, astronauts, and popular entertainers like Anita Bryant. The locus of this activity was not the fancy Episcopal church in a tony section of New York or Philadelphia or the simple, yet socially upscale Quaker meeting house in northwest Washington. Instead, Wolfe noticed that in the midst of all of this religiosity, the organized Protestant sects that had predominated after the Second World War were "finished, gasping, breathing their last," and new evangelical congregations were on the rise.[5]

More dispassionate observers noticed similar trends. In the age of the great postwar crusade against godless communism, Americans joined churches and synagogues in record numbers. Nearly all Protestant denominations, for example, grew between 1955 and 1965, with Methodists, Southern Baptists, Presbyterians, and Lutherans being the largest. Then in the sixties, for the first time in 150 years, church membership as a percentage of the total population began a gentle decline. But religion, as historian Leo Ribuffo has noted, remained as important as ever: "The number of Americans who told pollsters that religion was increasingly important in their lives rose from 14 percent in 1970 to 44 percent in 1978."[6] What was happening could best be observed among Protestants. After 1965 the evangelical denominations of Protestantism increased in membership, and "liberal" denominations declined. Many of these evangelicals worshiped in small, intimate, unaffiliated congregations of the sort one associated with back-roads America, but others drove on the interstates to large suburban churches that were sophisticated business enterprises. Catering to the suburban crowd, such churches allowed people to dress casually and made sure they were surrounded by plenty of parking spaces. The Melodyland Christian Center in Anaheim, California, boasted 8,000 members.[7] Other Protestants showed their interest in religion by watching preachers such as Billy Graham, Oral Roberts, Rex Humbard, Jimmy Swaggart, Pat Robertson, Jim Bakker, Jerry Falwell, and Robert Schuller on television. In 1972 Rex Humbard could be seen on 300 stations. He and his colleagues offered viewers the chance for eternal salvation if they gave themselves over to Christ.[8]

Many, such as Wolfe, found the emphasis on being born again as further evidence of the era's self-absorption, yet paradoxically they also worried about the increased involvement of what came to be called the new Christian right in politics. The traditional view of theologically conservative Protestants who believed in the Bible as the inerrant word of God, in the divinity of Christ, and in the hope that Christ offered for the salvation of the human soul was that they were disengaged from politics. In the Cliff Notes version of American history, they had tried and failed to make America a Christian nation and had retreated to their own congregations in the twenties. As one social scientist expressed this notion, these conservative Protestants were "almost uniformly politically quietistic" in the 1950s and 1960s. Then, in the seventies, evangelical Protestants became "the most likely group to be politically motivated."[9]

By the seventies people who had been born again were just as likely to vote as other churchgoers. As these evangelicals became better educated, they felt more of a sense of political entitlement. Questions of morality, rather than abstract considerations of social justice, engaged them in particular. When they perceived the government condoning abortion, according rights to homosexuals, protecting pornography, and banning prayer and Bible readings in schools, they felt the need to join in the public debate and oppose such initiatives.[10] Thus the American culture wars, a recurring feature of American history, were renewed in the seventies. In the postwar era, liberal Protestant churches attached themselves to the widely acclaimed liberal causes of the era, such as civil rights for African Americans and an end to the nuclear arms race. In the seventies, members of the evangelical sects, joined by Catholics concerned about abortion and even religiously orthodox Jews, nudged Protestants to take on the visible manifestations of the rights revolution.

For left-leaning intellectuals and the liberal leaders of the rights revolution, the rise of the new Christian right came as more bad news in an era of bad tidings. It signaled the rebirth of the cardinal sins of the postwar era: intolerance and anti-intellectualism. For many despairing intellectuals, it marked a throwback to the age of William Jennings Bryan and the Scopes Trial. In this view, America was a religious society that had risen above religion and now seemed posed to sink back into it. Postwar America self-consciously rejected the notion of an official religion. One could be a Protestant, Catholic, or Jew and still meet the unofficial requirement for religious participation. The leaders of the new Christian right, by way of contrast, wanted to make America a Christian nation, a vague notion but one that put the groups in direct opposition to the manifestations of the rights revolution.

Whether or not a monolithic new Christian right existed was, as one authority noted, irrelevant. The mere fact that groups such as the Moral Majority (founded in 1979) attracted members stimulated dissent from liberal groups such as the National Organization for Women and other groups that sought to raise money to combat "the new political menace."[11]

CHRISTOPHER LASCH AND NARCISSISM

Christopher Lasch, another of the era's influential critics and a brilliant historian who could not easily be pigeonholed as leaning toward the left or right, worried that the uncivil behavior unleashed by the culture wars reflected a deterioration in the quality of life. The wars provided another reason for people to sink within themselves and focus on self-preservation, the characteristic mode of the seventies, rather than self-improvement, the characteristic attitude of the postwar era. Lasch saw the seventies as an age of diminishing expectations, in which inflation eroded the value of investments and advertising legitimized indebtedness. The future had become menacing and uncertain. Some sought refuge in God and the promise of eternal salvation, which caused them to disengage from efforts to improve the future. Others lived by their wits and took refuge in the pleasures of the moment.[12] Neither contributed much to the improvement of society.

Lasch believed that "narcissism emerges as the typical form of character structure in a society that has lost interest in the future." Parents no longer lived through their children. People experienced a "pervasive uneasiness about reproduction—to widespread doubts, indeed, about whether our society should reproduce itself at all."[13] Such a society, Lasch implied, was one with profound misgivings about the efficacy of its "public institutions and welfare agencies."[14]

LESTER THUROW AND THE ZERO-SUM SOCIETY

Tom Wolfe was a journalist who observed the passing scene but did not much interact with it. For him the descriptive epithet mattered more than prescriptive action. Christopher Lasch was an intellectual and a social critic who tried to make sense of disparate trends through the use of historical analysis and other intellectual tools. He called attention to the malaise of the era, worried about it, yet despaired of his or anyone's ability to counteract deep historical forces. The science of studying society required that the investigator not influence the experiment. Lester Thurow, a third influential commentator, was, like Wolfe, deeply interested in finding an arresting image that would put the era into perspective. Like Lasch, he was an intellectual and a member of the professoriate with a prestigious post in the economics department of the Massachusetts Institute of Technology, yet he came from a much more activist tradition. Economists, unlike historians, were expected to cure the ills they diagnosed. So, although Thurow wanted to write for a popular audience, like Wolfe, and uncover the era's master trends, like Lasch, he also was expected to enter the realm of policy and make practical suggestions to put America back on track.

He began, as did Lasch, with the diminishing expectations that contributed to the sense of decline that was pervasive in the seventies. These diminishing expectations reflected pessimism about the prospects for economic growth and a renewed emphasis on scarcity as a factor in the global economy. Searching for the master metaphor, Thurow hit upon an image from game theory that, despite its arcane origins, also appealed to people's common sense. In a 1979 book, Thurow called attention to America as a zero-sum society. A growth society eased conflict by increasing the size of its economy. In a zero-sum economy, one person's gain was another person's loss. America, Thurow warned, needed to find a way of coping with this condition. The solution required not clashes in popular forums but rather a means of establishing a "modicum of speedy, disinterested decision-making capacity in a political process where everyone has a direct self-interest." In particular, a democratic government needed to find a way "To have the labor and capital to move into new areas" and withdraw from "old, low-productivity areas." Hence Thurow, turning from social prophet to policy wonk, thought to cure the country's economic maladies by creating a self-conscious industrial policy that would transfer capital from sunset to sunrise industries.[15]

THE MARKET FOR ECONOMIC IDEAS: INDUSTRIAL POLICY AND JAPAN

Industrial policy was not something that Thurow invented. Instead, he hitched himself to a popular bandwagon among liberals of the era. The idea followed from a well-worn liberal mantra: the proper response to chaos was coherence; the best way to counter disorganization was planning. The trouble was that the trendy idea of industrial policy had no single sponsor and it could mean almost anything—from government investment in declining Rust Belt steel plants to deregulating the airline industry. Lots of people hoped that industrial policy would benefit them. Residents of Youngstown, Ohio, wanted federal money to keep the steel mills operating in that town. The Chrysler Corporation, which had lost close to a billion dollars in 1978 and 1979, understood industrial policy to be a $1.5 billion loan guarantee.

As it turned out, Chrysler received its loan guarantee and survived into the next century, although as part of a multinational conglomerate. Youngstown, in contrast, lost its steel industry and much of its self-esteem. To Thurow such actions proved that America already practiced industrial policy, but badly. The concept, although a good one, needed to be implemented in a thoughtful and consistent way. Liberals, less likely than conservatives to privilege America in their thinking, cast around for a good model to follow. In one of the era's significant developments, they discovered the wonders of Japan. Once a country stereotyped as making cheap knockoffs of watches and other goods, Japan emerged in the seventies as the newfound envy of American intellectuals. Once Americans had given the Japanese advice on things like democracy and industrial management with a clear conscience. Americans had helped to reconstruct the Japanese economy after the Second World War. Now, it seemed, the Americans needed to study what the Japanese were doing and apply Japanese wisdom to the restructuring of the American economy.

In another of the era's widely read books, Ezra Vogel, a Harvard social scientist, encouraged Americans to think of Japan as the leading country in the world and to ponder what lessons Japan held for America. Japan led the world in its standard of living, political power, and cultural influence. The Japanese were the healthiest people in the world, with a life expectancy that surpassed America's or Sweden's. According to Vogel, the Japanese were also politically savvy. They would never have elected the hapless Jimmy Carter as their leader because he had no experience in the bureaucracy or in the national capitol. Japanese bureaucrats were experts in consultation and, as a consequence, they cut through the interest group conflicts that so hampered the United States.[16] The Japanese disparaged the American way of government, in which "individual contributors pressure individual politicians to their own ends and some groups are better organized than others," as leading to "haphazard results that do not necessarily reflect the major interests of the largest number." America should, therefore, be more like Japan, a place where workers still worked hard, where long-term economic growth was not sacrificed for short-term profits, where minority groups had to live up to the standards of the majority, where drug offenders were pursued with vigor, and where the crime rate was low. In short, Japan did not suffer from the hedonism, narcissism, and lack of social purpose that intellectuals insisted hindered the United States.[17]

A key instrument that the Japanese had and the Americans lacked was an industrial policy, similar to the one advocated by Thurow. An organization known as MITI kept pushing the Japanese economy in the right direction. Officials in this government agency took as their mission to help declining companies merge with more successful companies or go out of business. At the same time, MITI encouraged new companies to move into the areas that the unsuccessful companies had vacated and to employ the workers who had been laid off. The experts of MITI identified losers and winners in the national economy and through prudent planning and consultation gave the country a winning economic record. America, some believed, needed something similar if it ever expected to have a steel industry that could compete successfully with foreign operations and if it ever expected to put its economy back into shape.[18] The idea held particular appeal to those people who fancied themselves the sort of person who might work at a place like MITI. It harkened back to the progressive ideal of removing important decisions from the rough and tumble of popular politics and leaving things to disinterested experts, while somehow simultaneously preserving the benefits of democracy and the marketplace.

CONSERVATIVES AND DEREGULATION

In a disagreement that stretched back at least as far as the 1912 election between Teddy Roosevelt and Woodrow Wilson, liberal economists like Thurow wanted to combine the benefits of state planning and private enterprise. Conservative thinkers believed that this conjunction of opposites was impossible. They saw the problem of economic malaise in much different terms. In their view, the American economy suffered not from too little central direction but from too much. The model of Japan to the contrary, conservatives insisted that no one could predict economic winners or losers in advance. The best thing to do was to take the government out of the picture and unshackle the power of the free market. The deflationary 1930s had seen the start of many federal regulatory programs that, responding to the problems of the times, sought to prop up industries by maintaining the prices of products. Over time the regulations led to inefficiencies, such as prices that were higher and supplies that were lower than the market would otherwise yield. In an era of stagflation, with the twin problems of high prices and underutilized capacity, the situation might be improved by deregulating American industry.

Deregulation represented one of the era's few successful liberal-conservative collaborations. Conservatives believed that deregulation was inherently a good idea; liberals thought that deregulation in some industries might benefit consumers and become part of a larger, more comprehensive industrial-policy effort. The discussion tended to focus on a few heavily regulated industries rather than on American industry more generally. The best example of a successful collaboration came in the airline industry.

By the seventies, travel by air no longer had the hazardous connotation of previous decades; nor was air travel the exclusive province of the rich. The regulatory structure in the industry reflected the earlier struggle to get air travel established in the face of competition from trains and trucks and the need to protect the public's safety. In 1938 Congress created an agency to control which companies ran particular routes and to regulate air fares.

Federal regulation applied to interstate travel but not to travel within states, such as between San Francisco and Los Angeles. Hence, states began to experiment with deregulating these intrastate markets. These experiments attracted the interest of federal policymakers, who realized that it might be possible to lower air fares and improve service if interstate routes were also deregulated. The price of interstate flights tended to be higher than flights that covered the same number of miles within a single state.

In the mid-seventies, Senator Edward Kennedy used a subcommittee of the Judiciary Committee as a platform from which to publicize the achievements of the states in lowering air fares. Rising prices for airfare and nearly every other consumer good in the seventies made people receptive to policies that might lower fares. Jimmy Carter, who fancied himself a new-style Democrat not stuck in the New Deal mode, announced that he was in favor of airline deregulation during the 1976 campaign. He followed up his victory by appointing a Cornell economist known to favor deregulation to head the Civil Aeronautics Board. Alfred Kahn realized that the industry had remained frozen in place since 1938, with no major carriers having been added since then. The airlines, like other industries in the seventies' economy, faced troubles brought on by the recession and by the rising cost of jet fuel. Kahn understood that airlines needed to increase the number of people who flew on each flight. The cost of serving one passenger was quite high, but the extra, or, as Kahn, who thought of airplanes as marginal costs with wings, would have put it, the marginal cost of serving the thirty-fifth passenger was much lower. If the airlines were freed of cumbersome regulations, they could adjust their fares so as to increase their passenger loads and in the process raise their total revenues. In addition, they could take advantage of the fact that different people had different preferences with regard to air travel. Some needed to be in a particular place, no matter what: they might be willing to pay more for a ticket than the casual traveler who just wanted to see the sights. In a looser regulatory structure, one could more effectively discriminate between these two passengers and gain the maximum revenues from a flight.

Airlines worried about the potential of price competition to drive them all out of business but in the end could not overcome the bipartisan coalition in favor of deregulation in a time of inflation. Congress passed the Airline Deregulation Act in 1978, which opened up fares and routes to competition and allowed new companies to enter the air-transportation industry.[19]

Supply-Side Economics and Tax Revolts

Agreement came far more readily in microeconomics than in macroeconomics. Conservatives opposed an industrial policy that involved self-conscious government planning. Their favored remedy for the malaise and self-indulgent behavior that so worried the intellectuals involved lowering taxes as a means of spurring people's productive energies and invigorating the economy. This general idea became known as supply-side economics.

According to historian Robert Collins, "Supply siders believed that the non-inflationary way to achieve prosperity was to expand supply by increasing the incentives for individuals to work and invest—and that could be done by cutting tax rates."[20]

The supply-siders, who lacked the access to the liberal press enjoyed by Wolfe, Lasch, and Thurow (each of whom, ironically, had many ties to conservative intellectual traditions), publicized their ideas through the conservative press, the editorial pages of *The Wall Street Journal* in particular. They also published popular books such as *The Way the World Works* by Jude Waniski (which it was popular to own and discuss, if not actually to read). In time they gave their support to a legislative vehicle that Congressman Jack Kemp of New York and Senator William Roth of Delaware introduced in the summer of 1977. The legislators proposed a 30 percent reduction in personal income taxes to be phased in over a period of three years.

With the Democrats still dominating Congress, the Kemp-Roth bill gained little traction during the seventies. At the local level, however, the drive for tax reduction became one of the most popular causes of the era. The vigor of this movement belied Lasch's and Wolfe's notion that narcissism bred indifference to public affairs. To be sure, campaigning on behalf of lower taxes was in some sense a pleasure-seeking activity that was compatible with selfishness. At the same time, it required that people band together in a great crusade.

Many people, other than those with a very direct interest, neither understood nor cared much about the intricacies of the tax code. They grasped the implications of rising property taxes much more readily. A key component of inflation during the seventies involved housing. If one were lucky enough to own a home, it had a good chance of appreciating, as the baby boomers tried to enter the housing market and as people perceived owning a home as a good hedge against inflation. The trouble was that local tax assessors tracked the sales and as property values went up, so did property taxes. For someone who owned a home but who was faced with declining real wages, the rising property taxes took another big bite out of the household income. Even if a house's value appreciated, that increase was not money that someone could put in his or her pocket. Property taxes, by way of contrast, were a tangible means by which the government took money away from people. In states where real estate appreciated the most, such as California and Massachusetts, the conditions were ripe for a taxpayer revolt, one that mirrored on a local level the supply-side revolution at the federal level.

In California, a state that had given the nation all sorts of crazy tax schemes, such as the Depression-era Townsend Plan that promised to take money from the young and give it to the old, a conservative activist named Howard Jarvis worked to put Proposition 13 on the California ballot. His proposal would put a cap on property taxes and prohibit the state or local government from raising tax rates without the consent of two-thirds of the people affected. When Jarvis succeeded in getting his proposal on the ballot, few thought it would pass. They failed to appreciate the popular appeal of property tax cuts. On June 6, 1978, Californians approved Proposition 13 by a margin of two to one.[21]

BILINGUAL EDUCATION

The turn to the right, a mid- to late-seventies phenomenon, extended well beyond tax revolts to touch on the key social questions of the era, such as bilingual education, affirmative action, and busing to achieve racial integration. The people who participated in these grassroots protests were hardly the affluent but purposeless young members of the "me" generation described by Tom Wolfe, nor were many of them likely to have heard of Wolfe, Lasch, or Thurow. They saw themselves as hard-working people devoted to their families, not as celebrants in a culture of narcissism. If America suffered from a lack of purpose and drive, these people tended to locate the cause in the various forms of social engineering, which had never received popular ratification, that made things too easy for minority groups. Things like bilingual education, affirmative action, and busing sapped the initiative of the groups they were supposed to help and lowered the welfare of all. Far from improving social conditions, the measures lowered the quality of education in cities and undermined productivity in the workplace. Members of what Richard Nixon had called the silent majority and what commentators would soon describe as the Reagan Democrats made vocal protests in the face of compensatory measures designed to level the playing field between whites and nonwhites.

One might consider bilingual education in this regard. In 1968, at the tail end of the Great Society and without much enthusiasm from a tired Lyndon Johnson, Congress passed the Bilingual Education Act. It was a political gesture on behalf of Hispanic constituents who were important swing voters in places like Texas where a two-party system was becoming a new reality. Under the terms of this act, school districts could receive federal money for projects aimed at helping students with limited English proficiency. Congress never funded it lavishly, and neither Johnson nor Nixon paid much attention to it. Hence, the passage of this act assured individual school districts or particular Hispanic students of nothing.

Then, on its own motion, the Department of Health, Education, and Welfare's Office of Civil Rights announced the discovery of a new civil right for limited English proficiency children in 1970. It targeted districts in which 5 percent of the student body belonged to what the Office of Civil Rights defined as a national-origin minority group. It ordered such school districts to take "affirmative steps to rectify the language deficiency to allow 'effective participation' in district educational programs for students who could not speak or understand English."[22] The courts affirmed this notion and put students with limited English proficiency on the civil-rights map. Then, in 1974, the Supreme Court reaffirmed that national-origin minorities did indeed have rights that related to language in education. That decision, in turn, led the bureaucracy to issue what were called, after the Supreme Court case, Lau remedies, the chief of which involved bilingual education.[23]

Somehow implementation of the widely acclaimed Civil Rights Act of 1964 intended to end the Jim Crow racial arrangement in the South had come to mean bilingual education for some 1.1 million students. In the zero-sum society during the sensitive seventies, urban residents feared that the new mandate for bilingual education would mean transferring money from English-speaking students to non-English-speaking students. For the parents of these English-speaking students, many of whom were the children of immigrants who came to the country in the late nineteenth and early twentieth centuries, it appeared that federal bureaucrats were changing the rules of the game in an unfair manner. When the great mass of Italian, Jewish, and Eastern Europeans arrived in the United States, few dared to suggest that the New York public schools offer instruction in Italian, Yiddish, and Greek so as not to disadvantage their children. Instead, these children learned by total immersion at school. Despite the hardships that such a policy imposed, it became a point of pride among the members of these groups that they had learned English and taken their place in American culture.

Bilingual education offended the white ethnics. It struck them as self-indulgent. "Today it's all your rights, your rights, everything is your rights. You've got a right to this, and you got a right to that. In other words, you do as damned well please," said a cab driver in Brooklyn. Others saw bilingual education as impinging on their rights. "I believe in black pride but don't step on my white Italian pride. We've all been discriminated against," said a resident of the Canarsie section of Brooklyn.[24]

Affirmative Action

The fight over bilingual education paled beside the debate over affirmative action. Affirmative action was also the product of the courts and officials in the executive branch of the government, not the Congress.[25] The Department of Labor had the responsibility of assuring that federal government contractors obeyed laws that governed the wage levels on federal projects and followed hiring practices that did not violate the civil-rights laws. That assignment led, at the beginning of 1970, to a requirement, based on a plan that had been worked out in Philadelphia for the construction trades, that for projects that cost more $50,000 contractors supply hiring goals and timetables to achieve those goals based on the percentage of minorities in the local workforce. In other words, the contractor should take affirmative steps to increase the number of its minority and female employees up to an agreed limit. Failure to make a good-faith effort would mean the contractor could lose the contract.

Defined in this manner, affirmative action placed a considerable strain on hiring practices among the many federal contractors in communities across the nation. It was no longer enough for these companies not to discriminate against a given individual; they now had to achieve positive results in the racial composition of their workforce in order to satisfy officials in the Office of Federal Contract Compliance in the Department of Labor. During the seventies, with opportunities constricting for all workers, affirmative action, like bilingual education, thus had the potential to be a very divisive policy. Increasingly, it became perceived as a special benefit for African Americans (even though it applied to all racial minorities and to women as well), just as bilingual education was perceived as a special benefit for Hispanics (even though it applied to all students with limited English proficiency).[26]

Affirmative action received some sanction from the judiciary but never in the clarion manner of the court's support for integrated schools. The case that came to symbolize the problem involved a medical school—one of the many that opened up with public encouragement at a time when people believed that the country did not have enough doctors—started by the University of California on its Davis campus in 1968. By 1971 the school had one hundred students, the overwhelming majority of whom were white. This racial homogeneity concerned the faculty, which sought to diversify the student body by establishing a special program to attract and retain minority applicants. Under the terms of this program, the school reserved sixteen places for minorities in each entering class of one hundred. At the time, no better ticket to a secure and prosperous life existed than admission to medical school, a fact that did not go unnoticed among those with a bent toward science and a desire to live a comfortable life. One aspiring doctor was a man named Alan Bakke who applied for admission to Davis in 1973. Although his grades and test scores were higher than the averages obtained by people admitted under the special program for minorities, he was rejected. He tried again the next year and was rejected again. He sued, claiming he had been denied admission because he was white. He argued that he had not received equal protection under the law and that the university had violated the terms of the 1964 Civil Rights Act by discriminating against him on the basis of race. In the parlance of the day, Bakke claimed to be a victim of reverse discrimination.

The Bakke case attracted a great deal of attention as it made its way through the California courts to the U.S. Supreme Court. The Court heard the case at the beginning of its 1977 term and issued its opinion at the end of June in 1978. The decision sent a much less clear message than had the 1954 *Brown* case, which had been decided by a vote of nine to zero. The Court provided no single majority opinion. Instead, four justices held that the University of California maintained a racial quota system that violated the Civil Rights Act. In a separate opinion, Justice Lewis Powell agreed, although on different grounds, thus creating a majority in favor of admitting Bakke. The other four justices each wrote dissenting opinions in which they stated that race could be used as a criterion for admissions decisions. Powell, whose opinion turned out to be the judgment of the court, joined those opinions as well. In other words, the court found that there were constitutional and unconstitutional ways to use race as a factor in admissions decisions. Hence, the court found for Bakke because what the University of California had done was unconstitutional but did not invalidate the concept of affirmative action because there were permissible ways of doing it—a decidedly mixed message that illustrated that even the Supreme Court, the bastion of civil-rights protection in the postwar era, was conflicted over the issue.[27]

Another leading case, decided around the same time, contained a stronger defense of affirmative action in employment. The case arose at a Kaiser aluminum plant in Gramercy, Louisiana. Kaiser required that the craftsmen it hired from the local workforce have five years of experience. In part because of restrictive practices that prevented blacks from entering skilled trades in Louisiana, only 5 of the 273 craftsmen at the Kaiser plant were black, and the OFCC found these numbers inadequate. Working with the union, the company agreed to a plan to remedy the situation that allowed unskilled workers in the plant to train for the craft jobs. The idea was to select an equal number of whites and minorities, including blacks and women, for this training until the workforce measured up to the federal standards. The company followed seniority in picking people for the training but maintained a separate list for blacks and whites. In 1974 the company selected seven whites and six blacks. One of the white people who had been rejected, despite having more seniority than most of the blacks who were selected, sued the company and won his case in both the district and appeals court.[28] He argued that he had been discriminated against because he was white, a violation of Title VII of the Civil Rights Act. By a vote of five to two the Supreme Court held in June 1979 that the program did not violate the law because the 1964 Act "did not intend to prohibit the private sector from taking effective steps" to reach the goals defined by Title VII.[29]

URBAN CONFLICT AND GRASSROOTS RESPONSE

Many blue-collar white workers saw affirmative action as a direct threat to their jobs at a time when jobs were not plentiful. But the threat that affirmative action posed to their welfare was selective and often remote. A white worker was not likely to be fired for being white. A much more tangible threat to his welfare came in the form of busing and other remedies to achieve racial integration in urban school systems. Such measures, these workers believed, would lower the quality of their children's education and make it that much harder for their kids to get good jobs in a job market where affirmative action put whites at a disadvantage. If many grumbled about bilingual education and some took legal action against affirmative action, busing brought people out into the streets in vocal and often violent protest. Here again was evidence of vigorous, if not exactly civil, involvement in public life, not a sense of apathy or malaise. Contrary to the feelings of Christoper Lasch, the residents of Boston and their urban counterparts in other places cared deeply about their children's future.

By the seventies it had become apparent that cities and urban school districts were changing rapidly in ways that heightened policy conflicts. Thurow's zero-sum society seemed to be taking hold. Black migration from the rural South to the urban North continued in force, even as the industrial base of many cities weakened. Blacks came and whites left. Although many cities, particularly those in so-called Rust Belt areas of the east and Midwest, experienced declining populations, the percentage of black residents in those cities increased. To cite just one example among many, the black population in Boston more than doubled between 1960 and 1980.[30]

Because black families tended to be relatively young and the white families that persisted in the city relatively old, because of differences in family size, and because of unequal access to private schools, the proportion of black students in urban school districts increased even more rapidly than did their numbers in the populations of major urban centers. By the end of the decade, even cities with a majority of white residents had school systems in which a majority of the students were people of color. In Los Angeles, for example, less than a third of the enrolled students were white by 1980, and in Chicago fewer than one in five were white. In cities with black majorities, such as Detroit, the imbalances were even greater.[31]

Hard-pressed cities experienced significant political changes that helped pave the way for busing. Blacks began to gain more political power in cities, which had traditionally contested elections along ethnic lines. In some cities, typically those with black majorities, a black became mayor. In 1973, for example, the city of Atlanta elected Maynard Jackson, the son of a minister with connections to the Civil Rights Movement, as mayor. In other cities, even those with white majorities or in which white politicians held on to the mayor's office, blacks achieved a greater amount of influence over the administration of the city's schools. In cities in which patronage often took ethnic forms, the schools became areas ceded to blacks. Hence, even before there were black mayors in cities such as Baltimore, there were black school superintendents, and white politicians increasingly saw schools as an area of patronage for blacks.

THE BATTLE OF BOSTON

In Boston, opponents of busing carried their protests to the point of violence in a series of ugly confrontations that attracted the nation's attention and became another of the enduring moments of the seventies. It was difficult to reconcile the events of Boston and the picture of an apathetic decade painted by the social commentators.

The city of Boston, like so many others, consisted of a series of small but well-defined neighborhoods, each of which had its own ethnic character. The city contained a large Italian population that lived in places like East Boston, across the bay from the city center, and large Irish enclaves such as South Boston to the south and east of the downtown. As the seventies began, some of the neighborhoods were undergoing substantial changes. Jewish neighborhoods in Dorchester and Roxbury were rapidly becoming black neighborhoods. Boston contained the usual urban mixture of great wealth, such as the stately mansions of Beacon Hill, and relative poverty in such locations as Roxbury. The fact that these neighborhoods were so close together added to the sense of tension.

Segregated neighborhoods meant segregated schools in cities large enough to have neighborhood schools. In a series of rulings, the Supreme Court ordered that northern cities needed to take immediate steps to end this form of de facto segregation. In the 1971 *Swann v. Charlotte-Mecklenberg* decision, for example, the Court ruled that the preservation of neighborhood schools could no longer be used as a rationale to justify racial imbalance. It noted that the remedy of busing students from one neighborhood to another was legal.[32]

These rulings created a hospitable climate for groups who sought to use legal action to bring about the desegregation of northern urban schools. Early in 1972, a group of black parents, with the active participation of the NAACP, filed a class action suit in Boston that demanded that their children attend suitable (and hence integrated) public schools. In June 1974, U.S. District Court Judge Arthur Garrity found the Boston School Board, the independent but highly political body that administered the schools, guilty of segregation. He ordered the board to come up with a desegregation plan. The board refused to comply, which led Garrity to work with the state Board of Education on his own plan. His plan paired white South Boston and black Roxbury, which were close together on a map but far apart in their attitudes toward the question of school desegregation. As the city waited with apprehension for the start of the school year, proponents and opponents of busing organized in order to influence public opinion.[33]

Giving the rhetoric of the rights revolution an ironic spin, Louise Day Hicks helped start Restore Our Alienated Rights, known by its assertive acronym, ROAR. A native of South Boston, Hicks was both well educated and an experienced politician. She had a degree from a local teacher's college as well as two degrees from Boston University, including a law degree. During the sixties, she had served on the Boston School Committee as its treasurer and chairman. In 1967 she ran for mayor and placed second. Three years later, after having served on the Boston City Council, she won election to Congress against a formidable array of opposing candidates in the primary. For all of her sophistication, Hicks knew how to speak the local language. "It is against our children's best interest to send them to school in crime-infested Roxbury," she said. "There are at least one hundred black people walking around the black community who have killed white people during the past two years . . . any well informed white suburban woman does not pass through that community alone, not even by automobile."[34]

School opened on September 12, 1974. Many South Boston parents held their students out of class. As black students arrived in South Boston on buses from Roxbury, some of the local residents hurled rocks and bottles at the buses and taunted the black students as they disembarked and entered the school. As the students reboarded the buses at the end of the day, demonstrators again threw stones. Police made four arrests that day, and two policemen were injured. Throughout the fall, skirmishes between white and black students at South Boston High School were common. On December 11, 1974, a black student stabbed Michael Faith, a seventeen-year-old white student, at South Boston High School. As word spread of the stabbing, mobs gathered outside, preventing blacks from leaving the school. Fights broke out, and eleven people were injured. An ugly situation turned uglier. A black student told of getting hit in the head with a brick. "Why should niggers come over here and wreck the city?" asked one South Boston resident. "Why should I go to Roxbury when there's a school right up the street? Why should I go unprotected?" a high school student from South Boston wanted to know.[35]

On December 27, Judge Garrity held three members of the Boston School Committee in contempt for failing to comply with his desegregation order. Finally, the School Committee submitted a desegregation plan to Garrity in January, and the tension began to subside. Eventually, after further riots, Boston achieved a measure of peace.[36] The permanent result of the battle of Boston was that the white population in Boston's public schools dropped precipitously as parents put nearly half of the white students in private, parochial, or suburban schools. Those actions made achieving racial integration that much harder, and indeed it was never achieved. Critics pointed out that the local politicians—such as Edward Kennedy—editorial writers at the Boston Globe, and judges who urged people to act responsibly and accommodate the civil-rights revolution sent their own children to private or suburban schools. In a shrinking economy, issues such as busing, which involved the next generation's future, held the potential to divide people in dangerous ways. Socially engineered solutions to society's problems met greater opposition than they had in the flush postwar era.

CONCLUSION

It was difficult to reconcile the image of the residents of South Boston, battling to preserve their community from outside assault, with the

images of the seventies as the "Me Decade" or a decade of mindless narcissism. In this era, as in any other, people cared about the well-being of
their children and the stability of their communities. What had happened
was that the remedies for avoiding conflict of the postwar era, such as the
extension of civil-rights protections and Keynesian economics, no longer
seemed to work. That failure did not prevent people of all types—from
black residents of Roxbury, to gay citizens of Greenwich village, to suburban housewives—from asserting their rights. The result was both a rights
revolution *and* a resurgence of conservative values that was itself a means
by which evangelicals, Irish Catholics in South Boston, and Eastern European ethnics in Baltimore could assert *their* rights. In the past the growth
of the economy and groups' ability to avoid one another had helped to
avert ethnic conflict. In the seventies, neither remedy was available. A fal-
tering economy limited economic growth and inhibited people's ability to
move from the troubled cities to the more promising suburbs. The result
was a series of conflicts in which engaged citizens confronted one another.
Far from the impression left by the commentaries of Wolfe, Lasch, and
Thurow, it was an era not of narcissism but of activism, as much the "We
Decade" as the "Me Decade."

9

The Movies as Cultural Mirror

As intellectuals tried and failed to see the seventies as a whole and people of all sorts fought for their rights, movies offered tantalizing vignettes of the era. Watergate, the oil crisis, economic stagnation, urban conflict, and ethnic solidarity and pride all received perceptive movie treatments. The best films of the seventies used the form of established genres such as the detective movie or the gangster movie to comment on the state of American life.

In the seventies, going to the movies was not the universal experience that it was in the twenties, thirties, or forties. Television had replaced the movies as the most ubiquitous form of common culture. No longer turned out on a mass-production basis by studios that controlled all aspects of production and distribution, the movies of the seventies reflected the creativity of a new generation of directors who enjoyed unprecedented freedom to realize their artistic ambitions. The results were some of the best American films ever made, such as *Chinatown* and *The Godfather*.

For Americans the seventies marked the last time that one needed to go to a theater to see a movie. Soon after the seventies, video tapes would make watching movies on demand possible in one's living room and change the nature of the moviegoing experience forever. By then, too, the industry would be in thrall to the summer blockbuster that would crowd out the market for the smaller and more experimental products of the seventies. Hence, the seventies represented a unique era in the history of the movies; even critics who pointed to the dreary aspects of the period recognized the seventies as a time of great cinema.

Movies as Selective Experience

By the seventies, television had long since overtaken the movies in popularity. Between 1946 and 1962, the years in which America embraced television, the amount of money that the movies took in at the box office fell by half.[1] Americans, it seemed, had lost the moviegoing habit. Previously, the studios had kept the theaters supplied with enough pictures to satisfy this regular habit. It helped that some of the major studios also owned a block of theaters in which they could show their movies. At the end of the forties, not only did television enter the picture, but the studios lost the right to own movie theaters. The courts broke up this arrangement. In the face of these changes, the studios began to flounder. They tried gimmicks, such as enhanced color processes, improved sound, and larger screens that made the pictures seem three dimensional, all in an effort to create an experience that television could not duplicate. None of that reduced television's appeal. Studios had no choice but to enter into an uneasy relationship with television, using their lots to film television programs, selling some of their backlist of movies for television viewing, and using television to promote movies.

The advent of television and the changes it brought meant that Americans became much more selective about the pictures they went to see. Movies still held an important place in American culture: Teenagers still liked to make out in the dark, something that was easier to do in a movie theater than at home. Teen idols like James Dean, Elvis Presley, and later the Beatles made movies that teenagers on dates were practically obligated to see. Younger children still watched Disney cartoons through the 1950s and 1960s. Their parents were, however, much more diffident about which movies they went to see, relying on word of mouth to interest them in a particular film. Studios making fewer pictures took fewer chances and, even more than before, imitated one another. When *Mary Poppins* and *The Sound of Music* became a runaway hits in 1964 and 1965 for Disney and Fox, respectively, other studios hastened to sign up Julie Andrews, who had starred in both of these movies, in order to make their own lavish musicals. They discovered that the success of these films could not easily be transferred to other movies, gambling on large productions and often losing.[2]

The Rise of the New Hollywood

In 1967 two movies appeared that did well at the box office, helped to establish a new generation of stars, and spotlighted the talents of new directors. *Bonnie and Clyde*, a movie about the notorious bank robbers from the 1930s, starred Warren Beatty and Faye Dunaway and created a national mania of thirties nostalgia, showing how good economic times could blot out bad economic memories. The picture took full advantage of relaxed censorship standards to feature Bonnie without too many clothes and to portray Clyde's battles with sexual impotence. It ended with a much-copied slow-motion shower of bullets riddling the bodies of Bonnie and Clyde. Director Arthur Penn, it seemed, had come up with something that was visually arresting and not easily duplicated on television. That same year Mike Nichols, who had previously gained fame as part of an improvisational comedy team and as a director on Broadway, released *The Graduate.* The picture took America by storm. It featured Dustin Hoffman in the role that made him a star as young Benjamin Braddock, a privileged kid from Los Angeles who had graduated from college and faced an uncertain future—not because there were no jobs, as had been the case for the depression generation, but because there were no meaningful jobs.[3]

Instead of looking for a job, Benjamin spends his summer having an affair with his neighbor, the wife of his father's business partner. He discovers true love in the form of a chaste relationship with the neighbor's daughter and proceeds to follow her from Los Angeles to Berkeley and to save her from the clutches of her mother and the prospect of an empty marriage. In addition to Hoffman's wonderfully understated performance, the film features a stunning turn from Ann Bancroft, a talented actress whose beauty on the screen waxes and wanes in synch with Benjamin's rising and falling attraction to her, and a soundtrack by Simon and Garfunkel that showcases their harmonic, folk-influenced form of rock and roll. Mike Nichols gives the film highly stylized direction, with many special effects and shots that call attention to the film's meaning.[4]

The arrival of these films appeared to usher in a new golden age of American cinema that lasted through the seventies.[5] With the studios in disarray, the executives lost some of their power to shape the movies. They no longer had a stable of stars, directors, writers, and production assistants whose services were available to them on demand. Instead, each movie became a complex package whose financing and production had to be assembled piece by piece. The process put a premium on the contribution of directors to the creative process. Unlike a previous generation of honored Hollywood directors who earned their kudos for putting their distinctive stamps on the mass-produced studio product, the new directors became stars in their own right, important figures in what some called "the new Hollywood," with a great deal of personal discretion to influence the look, design, and even the marketing of a film. These directors created a series of profitable films that reversed the declining financial fortunes of the industry and that demonstrated that movies could coexist profitably with television.

For television, the seventies was the era before cable fragmented the audience into hundreds of pieces. In the movies, something similar happened with the advent of videotapes. By the middle of the eighties, America had more stores that rented videotapes than it had movie theaters.[6] At first, the videotape industry consisted of mom-and-pop operations that depended on a piece of software to keep track of the inventory. As such stores proliferated, movie theaters consolidated. Neighborhood movie houses turned into stages for religious revivals or retail stores, if they were not torn down altogether. The new movie theaters, built in shopping centers and malls, invariably boasted more than one screen. At the multiplex a person could choose from nearly all the current offerings. By the eighties, though, renting a tape and selecting from a representative selection of all the movies ever made became an alternative to going to the movies. As film scholar Peter Lev has noted, "the 1970s might have been the last time people were together in a movie house to see significant movies."[7] Catching a masterpiece like *Citizen Kane* meant watching it in a revival house or risking seeing it on television, cut with commercials.

MOVIES AT WAR

Movies at the beginning and again at the end of the seventies offered insights about the nation's experience in Vietnam. The earlier pictures, filmed and released when the war was still being fought, made an implicit contrast between Vietnam and previous wars. *M*A*S*H*, a commercial success that received five Oscar nominations, portrayed the comic adventures of doctors in an army hospital close to the front lines of the Korean War. Pauline Kael, an influential critic whose pieces in the *New Yorker* were widely read in the seventies, wrote an ecstatic review of the film, which she thought "the best American comedy since sound came in."[8] She also praised Robert Altman, its director, a forty-five-year-old man who had kicked around for a considerable period of time directing industrial films and making television shows before scoring his first big success with *M*A*S*H*. Altman, a key figure of the seventies who created the masterpiece *Nashville* in 1975, gained fame as a director who was adept at working with large ensemble casts and letting the actors have a hand in the creation of the film. He specialized in creating sound tracks that allowed the audience to hear layers of sound and overlapping dialogue. *M*A*S*H* was a comedy that portrayed the military bureaucracy with contempt and did not cover up the gore that was a daily product of war. It was a far stretch from such movies as John Wayne's *Ballad of the Green Berets* (1969) that celebrated the American cause in Vietnam.

M*A*S*H took second place to another war movie at the 1971 Academy Awards. *Patton*, a biopic about the famous Second World War general, won the Oscar for best picture of the year. It did not have the free-flowing, experimental quality of Altman's film and looked like a picture out of the 1950s with its epic length of nearly three hours, its vivid use of color and the large screen, and its exotic battlefield scenes shot on location. *Patton* relied on George C. Scott's acting talents to keep the viewer's attention as it traced the general's exploits from North Africa, up the boot of Italy, to the Battle of the Bulge, and the end of the war. The movie made the point that Patton, who believed in reincarnation, was a warrior in the classic tradition, who thought he was engaged in a noble profession. His views differed from those of his colleague Omar Bradley, who told Patton that he did his job because he had been trained to do it. Patton, by way of contrast, fought because he loved war, a view that was out of place well before the Second World War.[9] *Patton* glorified war and dramatized the loneliness of command. President Nixon, who saw himself shouldering the unpopular burdens of a necessary war in the manner of Abraham Lincoln, watched the movie repeatedly and supposedly took inspiration from it. Others saw it as an anti–Vietnam War film because it contrasted a good war with a bad one, a war fought with all of America's talent and might compared to one that was conducted in a halting and limited manner.

The appearance of these two pictures at the beginning of the decade showed how the movies offered independent commentary on current events in a way that was far removed from America's experience in earlier wars. The comparison between the 1940s and the 1970s was particularly stark. During the Second World War, the studios enlisted in the war effort and made movies, such as the 1943 Howard Hawks film *Air Force*, that rallied the American spirit. Unlike *Patton*, *Air Force* focused on the fighting men, not the generals.[10] It followed the adventures of the crew of a B-17 bomber that had the misfortune of landing in Pearl Harbor on the morning of the attack and getting swept up into the action of the war. The movie had an explicit propaganda purpose, which was to show how the war forged a mix of ethnic characters into a collective fighting unit and to raise American morale at a time when victory seemed less than certain.[11]

M*A*S*H did none of that. It made war out to be the horrible institution that it was and featured a crew of distinctive individuals who never meshed into a group or took the American cause too seriously. The seventies, in this regard, had the feel of the thirties, in which writers and movie directors reconsidered the First World War and questioned whether the results were worth the sacrifice.

The Movies and Conspiracy

As the seventies progressed, the movies began to focus on Watergate, the next big story. At first they commented on the scandal in a metaphorical way in such masterpieces as *Chinatown*, which appeared in 1974, the year of Nixon's resignation, and then they addressed the scandal in a literal way, as in the 1976 dramatization of the Woodward and Bernstein account. *Chinatown* went into production in the fall of 1973 as the revelations about Watergate were coming into public view. One of the era's conspiracy films, similar to *The China Syndrome* in that respect, it suggested that an unspeakable evil lay at the core of American life.[12] *Chinatown* used the idiom of movies, in particular the genre known as "film noir," to portray this evil. It took the form of a classic private-investigator film that automatically suggested a time, the 1930s, and a place, Los Angeles.

Jack Nicholson, in a role that would make him a superstar, plays a private detective named Jake Gittes who makes it his business to stick his nose into other people's business. In a famous scene with director Roman Polanski, Gittes nearly has his nose cut off by one of the film's unsavory characters but not even that can throw him off the scent of the bad guys. Instead, Gittes tangles with Noah Cross, whose first name suggests a survivor of the Flood—the picture is about water and floods—and whose last name alludes both to his tough temperament—one would not want to cross him—and to his symbolic role in the movie as a cross that the female lead, played by Faye Dunaway, has to bear. In the end Gittes discovers the corrupt way in which businessmen like Cross, in league with the city's politicians, have manipulated the water supply so as to make a fortune and influence the city's future. He also comes upon the horrible secret that unites Dunaway and Cross, played by John Huston who had, appropriately enough, directed *The Maltese Falcon*, the first great film noir. The discovery of this secret leads, in ways that Gittes can neither fully understand nor control, to Dunaway's death in the mysterious setting of Los Angeles's Chinatown. The movie nicely captures the sense of corruption that appeared to pervade American life.

JAWS AND STEVEN SPIELBERG

After Watergate came the oil shortages, which some people interpreted as another of the decade's conspiracies, and the downward spiral of the economy. Once again, the movies responded, both with escapist fare, such as fanciful science fiction that transported the viewer into another world and nostalgic tributes to the fifties, and with films that tried to capture the sense of fear caused by the breakdown of the economy. Steven Spielberg, the most successful of the decade's directors, found a cinematic representation of this fear in his movie based on a best-selling novel by Peter Benchley, *Jaws*. The film played upon an old cultural theme: the idea of alien forces traveling across the ocean to invade America and ruin it. Permeating American history, the idea went back to the days of the American Revolution, continued through the tidal wave of immigration from Europe, and persisted to the era of oil shortages induced by the country's dependence on Arabian oil. In Spielberg's movie, it was a shark that upset the balance of things by swimming close to the shore and gnawing at the vacationers idling in the surf.

Like Jack Nicholson in *Chinatown*, Roy Scheider in *Jaws* plays a former city cop who has decided to get into an easier line of work. He takes over as the police chief of a rural beach community with the inviting name of Amity. After the shark attacks the citizens and the tourists of Amity, Scheider has no choice but to hunt it down. The authorities of the town, in the manner of the Nixon White House, want to cover up the danger and pretend that nothing has happened, but Scheider, a man of principle, cannot knowingly put people in harm's way. Like Jake Gittes, he has to track down the source of evil. Although he is not a natural sailor, he boards a boat, captained by the macho Robert Shaw, and sails out with the technologically adept young scientist, played by boyish Richard Dreyfuss, to seek out the shark. In the end, it is this simple man of the people, a hero in the cinematic tradition of Frank Capra, who destroys the shark and restores tranquility to Amity. The picture suggests that there is a reserve of morale character and good common sense in the American people that, properly motivated, will enable the nation to overcome its troubles. Neither macho military might, as personified by the boat captain, nor scientific knowledge alone, as represented by the Dreyfuss character, is as powerful a force as patriotic Americans going about their business in a quiet and determined manner.

Jaws made a huge impression on America and brought considerable fame to Steven Spielberg, who ascended to the very top ranks of American directors. On August 7, 1975, CBS ran a story about how the movie had created a real-life scare that made people on beaches along the Atlantic Coast reluctant to go in the water. Tourism, according to CBS reporter Bernard Goldberg, was down because of *Jaws*, not sharks.[13] The movie, it seemed, exercised a powerful hold on the imaginations of Americans in middecade.

Steven Spielberg, the man who put the fear of the surf in Americans, was a baby boomer who was born in the city and moved to the suburbs. When his family relocated from Cincinnati to an area near Phoenix in the middle of the 1950s, he was a self-described loner who said he wanted nothing more than to make it through the school year without getting his face pushed into the water fountain.[14] He did not do particularly well in school, refusing to participate in the academic competitions that were traditional for Jewish families of Spielberg's sort. In the manner of the outsider with time on his hands and a father who was an engineer, Spielberg began to fiddle around with gadgets, in his case a movie camera.

In the style of an earlier generation of Jewish movie moguls, Spielberg became so successful that a legend about him developed. The story went that while staying with an uncle who lived near Los Angeles he visited the Universal Studios, a common tourist experience. Instead of tagging along with the group, he ventured off to the sound stages by himself and happened upon a Universal executive to whom he talked for an hour. Two days later Spielberg came back, dressed in a suit, set himself up in a vacant office, and became a squatter on the lot.[15] Whether or not the story is true, Spielberg did eventually get a contract from Universal on the strength of a feature he made as a student at Cal State, Long Beach. In the late sixties, at the tender age of twenty-one, he started directing for television. He worked on *Marcus Welby, MD*, a top-rated program starring veteran actor Robert Young, and on *Columbo*, a detective series that allowed Peter Falk to rummage around in the pockets of his ill-fitting raincoat and shamble his way through a case. Then Spielberg made *Duel*, a 1971 television movie that attracted favorable critical attention. His first theatrical feature appeared in 1974.[16]

Spielberg saw himself as the representative of a new generation of Hollywood directors who constituted a creative community that made Hollywood over in its own image. He told a journalist who wrote about the phenomenon of the new Hollywood that, "the 70s was the first time that a kind of age restriction was lifted and young people were allowed to come rushing in with all their naiveté and their wisdom and all the privileges of youth. It was just an avalanche of new ideas, which is why the 70's was such a watershed."[17]

THE CIRCLE OF DIRECTORS

When the directors of the new Hollywood met one another at the University of Southern California and other gathering places, they experienced a shock of recognition at finding there were others passionately devoted to making movies. Spielberg fell in with George Lucas and Francis Ford Coppola, who helped produce Lucas's *American Graffiti* and became renowned for his direction of the *Godfather* films. Lucas, in turn, knew Brian De Palma, who would cast his breakthrough movie *Carrie* side by side with Lucas as the latter was beginning work on *Star Wars*.

Carrie (1976), although less well known than the other movies, showed how the new directors were close students of the products of the old Hollywood. Where such pioneering directors as Howard Hawks and John Ford had invented new cinematic techniques on the spot, as it were, the new directors could study the old masters in film school and profit from their example. Some, like De Palma, made a conscious effort to pay tribute to the old masters in their movies. *Carrie*, for example, owed much to Hitchcock's *Psycho*. Both movies contained a shower scene that ended with blood going down the drain. In Hitchcock's case, a woman is stabbed with a knife; in De Palma's case a woman is stabbed by the onset of puberty. Carrie, the girl with telekinetic powers, attends Bates High School, which also happens to be the name of the hotel that Anthony Perkins runs in *Psycho*. In common with the other new directors, De Palma did not invent a new cinematic form in *Carrie* but rather brought new touches to an old one. His movie, based on a book by popular novelist Stephen King, might be described as a high-school horror film, a dark version of a Mickey Rooney–Andy Hardy picture.

Just as the novelists of Norman Mailer's generation after the second world war eagerly anticipated the appearance of the next important novel from Hemingway, Faulkner and their successors, so the film makers of Steven Spielberg's generation followed the work of their colleagues with a sense of excitement. Spielberg later called the years between 1971 and 1976 the best because he and the others were just starting out. "We couldn't wait for our friends' next pictures, Brian's next picture, Francis's next picture to see what they were doing," he said.[18]

THE GODFATHER AND THE ETHNIC REVIVAL

Francis Ford Coppola produced the first conspicuous success of this group of young directors with his film adaptation of Mario Puzo's 1969 novel *The Godfather*. It appeared in 1972, while Spielberg was still working in relative obscurity at Universal. Like the best of the seventies movies, *The Godfather* allowed the director to engage in an extended dialogue with the history of the movies, with the work of his fellow directors, and with the events of the time.

Puzo's novel was itself a cultural landmark. Mario Puzo was a man of John F. Kennedy's generation who was born poor in the Hell's Kitchen section of New York, the son of Italian immigrants who could barely read and write. When he came of age, the Second World War began and he joined the Army Air Forces. He took advantage of the GI Bill to get an education at the New School for Social Research and Columbia. He struggled to survive as a writer. He had enough perseverance and talent to publish two well-received novels, neither of which sold well. Determined to write a best-seller, Puzo pitched the idea of a book about the mafia to a New York publisher who expressed mild interest in the idea and gave him a $5,000 advance. By the time he had finished his book, Puzo was already forty-nine, well past the usual age of success in America. The book became the best-selling novel of the seventies, with more than twelve million copies in circulation by 1975. Puzo was finally in the money.

The book's appeal lay in the inherent fascination of the subject matter, combined with an agreeable sentimentality that caught the mood of the rising interest in ethnicity. At the time of the civil-rights revolution, minority groups that were seemingly left behind, such as the Italians, welcomed treatments of their history that showed how aspects of their past that they had once shunned and tried to put aside were in fact affirmations of what was best about their culture. Italians felt they no longer needed to apologize for their immigrant past but could look back upon it with a nostalgic pride. In this spirit, Don Vito Corleone, the godfather in the book, emphasizes the values of ethnic solidarity, family, and friendship. It is he who is warm hearted, not his critics, who preach the cold-hearted values of American individualism and capitalism. "Friendship is everything. Friendship is more than talent. It is more than government. It is almost the equal of family. Never forget that," the don tells the character modeled after Frank Sinatra who has come to him for advice.[19] *The Godfather*, then, fed into the rise of a new ethnic consciousness based upon what Michael Novak would soon describe as "disillusionment with the universalist, too thinly rational culture of professional elites."[20]

Coppola used his own childhood in an Italian family as an inspiration for the movie. His personal vision often clashed with that of the Paramount studio executives who were nervous about putting a relative unknown, whose only solid credit was as a script writer for *Patton*, in charge of such an important production. The executives entertained the idea of replacing him before and even during filming. Coppola filmed one scene, in which Connie Corleone, played by Coppola's sister Talia Shire, fought with her husband, while another director with more experience with action sequences stood by on the set ready to take over the production. The studio also considered changing the story so that it took place in modern times and did not like Coppola's choice of the then-unknown actor Al Pacino to play the lead character, Michael Corleone. The studio worried that Marlon Brando, considered washed up after his great triumphs in the fifties, was too much of a liability to play the aging don. In the best tradition of the artist struggling to defend the integrity of his creation, Coppola persevered and produced what was universally recognized as a masterpiece. His movie was a sentimental gangster film in which the audience sympathized with the Corleone family as it battled other crime families and did business with the corrupt police and judicial systems of New York. In the end, Michael Corleone, who is Ivy League–educated, who had enlisted in the U.S. military, and who has a fiancée whose last name does not end in a vowel, turns his back on the American mainstream and takes his place as the head of the Corleone family.

The *Godfather* became one of the most celebrated successes in the history of the American cinema. Paramount proved particularly astute in booking the long movie in several theaters in the same city, with the start times for the picture staggered throughout the day. No less a personage than Secretary of State Henry Kissinger, then at the very peak of his popularity, attended the March 1972 premiere. The picture opened in 5 different theaters in New York alone and in 316 nationally. The picture helped revive Paramount and, as Peter Biskind notes, it was "like a jolt of electricity for the industry, which was still awakening from the half-decade-long coma that began after *The Sound of Music*."[21] Coppola took his revenge on the studio executives by stipulating that he would have complete control over the sequel, which filled in more of the story about the godfather's rise to power and showed what happened as Michael moved the family's interests to Las Vegas. Both films won the Academy Award for best picture in their respective years. In the mid-seventies, with three films nominated for Academy Awards, Coppola was the biggest thing in Hollywood.

THE BLOCKBUSTER

The *Godfather*, with its wide release, and *Jaws*, with its television-advertising campaign, helped create the phenomenon of the blockbuster, which would dominate the distribution of movies after the seventies. Universal promoted *Jaws* not only through the traditional print ads but also through $700,000 worth of thirty-second spots on prime-time network television, something done only very rarely before June 1975. As Paramount did with *The Godfather*, Universal gave *Jaws* what the industry called a "wide break," opening it in 409 theaters across the nation. Before the seventies, most studios restricted movies that were in their first runs to a small number of theaters. If people wanted to see an important picture when it opened, they often had to travel to a downtown movie house that would have exclusive access to the picture for a fifty-mile-radius surrounding area. The idea was that the picture would build up a reputation in its first run, when it was shown in plush movie palaces that could display the movie to best advantage—the sorts of theaters, like the Fox Theater in downtown Atlanta or the Chinese Theater in Hollywood, that had large lobbies, spacious balconies, ushers in uniform, and ornate decorations. Then the picture would go into its second and third runs, branching out from downtown to the neighborhoods. *Jaws*, which became the first movie in American history to take in $100 million at the box office, marked the beginning of the summer blockbuster in America and changed all these strategies.[22]

After *Jaws*, television advertisements that announced that a particular movie was opening "everywhere" heralded the arrival of a potential blockbuster. Summer held the best chance for a blockbuster to develop because that was the season in which television offered the least competition. Without exception, the networks aired reruns during the hot summer months. During the summertime, a movie could also benefit from the repeat business of schoolchildren on summer vacation, and repeat business was essential for a box-office smash. Some people never went to see even the most popular of movies. Others went repeatedly, and they tended to be people with time on their hands, like schoolchildren on holiday, who during the school year had to do their homework, go to the dance, or root for their high-school team on Friday nights. Perhaps most important of all, a blockbuster had to be even more escapist in nature than most movies, something that appealed to the mass audience.

ROCKY'S REDEMPTION AS AMERICAN CELEBRATION

After *Godfather*, stories about Italians who lived in declining Northeastern communities became hot commodities in the motion-picture business. An actor and writer named Sylvester Stallone, who was relatively unknown, convinced United Artists to produce his script about a boxer. During the celebration of America's bicentennial, *Rocky* became the feel-good movie of the year. It portrayed a fighter named Rocky Balboa who proved his worth by rising from the streets of Philadelphia and going the distance with the heavyweight champion of the world.

As with the other films of the seventies, *Rocky* plays upon the history of the movies and contemporary history. As a fighter in a port city who asserts and redeems himself, the character of Rocky is a direct descendent of Marlon Brando's character Terry Malloy from *On the Waterfront* (1954). Both Rocky and Terry work for the mob in jobs that lower their feelings of self-worth and keep them from realizing their true potential. Both gain confidence and inspiration from their girlfriends who are virtuous creatures and somehow out of place in their brutal environments. Adrienne, Rocky's girlfriend, receives constant abuse from her brother, a butcher who works in a freezing meat locker and relies on snorts from a bottle of whiskey to get him through the day. Rocky himself gets no respect from the tough Irish trainer at the local gym, who derides him for spending time collecting money for the mob. The Irish trainer says that if Rocky had applied himself, he could have been a contender.

Then, in an act of fate, Rocky gets his chance to fight Apollo Creed, the well-heeled and business-savvy heavyweight champion of the world. Creed resembles Mohammed Ali, and his gesture of letting an unknown fight him is a reverse form of affirmative action. Rocky takes advantage of the opportunity that has been offered to him. As the camera pans through shots of Philadelphia, he trains hard, triumphantly running to the top of the steps at the Philadelphia Museum of Art, jogging past the Italian market. The old and tired city begins to look beautiful just as Rocky himself is revitalized. In the final scenes, Rocky acquits himself honorably in the ring and shows that he is indeed a contender. Like his fellow Italian residents of Philadelphia, Rocky has nothing to apologize for, just as a beleaguered America could be proud of itself in its bicentennial year.

One interesting aspect of *Rocky* is that both the Italian character and the black character manage to maintain their dignity. The picture suggests that there is room for both the black champion and the Italian challenger in the world of boxing. In this manner, *Rocky* builds on a series of seventies pictures with black heroes who are the antithesis of the old Stepin Fetchit movie stereotypes. The best example of these reversals in cinema is the 1971 movie *Shaft*, which stars Richard Roundtree as a black private eye hired to find the kidnapped daughter of a Harlem gang lord. Shaft, who personifies the notion of cool, stands out as a powerful, intelligent figure on the urban scene who receives the respect of the good guys and the bad guys. He has an uncanny ability to maneuver between the white world of the cops and the black world of the gangs. He never loses his identity as a back man who knows that the world is stacked against him yet who asserts his own form of control over that world. In the end, Shaft and a New York City police lieutenant cooperate to foil the mafia, return the gang lord's daughter to him, and keep the peace in Harlem.

SATURDAY NIGHT FEVER

For the most part, however, Italians played better than African Americans at the box office in the seventies. In 1977 John Travolta joined Al Pacino and Sylvester Stallone in the circle of new Italian heroes. The source for the movie *Saturday Night Fever* was a 1975 *New York Magazine* article on the disco phenomenon. It referred to a revival of interest among young people in going out to clubs and dancing to recorded music in places that in the sixties were known as discotheques. The places, first associated with gay culture and only then assimilated into the American mainstream, featured strobe lights and other visual effects that were intended to transform an often quite ordinary place into a glamorous setting. The music played in these warehouses and other mundane settings had a driving, insistent beat that dancers could follow. Just as Benny Goodman turned jazz into swing in the 1930s and reignited an interest in dancing among the young, so disco brought young people onto the dance floor as a form of recreation, social ritual, and cheap entertainment that allowed people to escape from dreary economic conditions.

Saturday Night Fever had much more depth than previous rock-and-roll films such as Elvis Presley's *Blue Hawaii* (1961) or Frankie Avalon's *Beach Blanket Bingo* (1965). Like Rocky, the characters in *Saturday Night Fever*, who lived in the Brooklyn white-ethnic neighborhood of Bay Ridge, owed something to those in *On the Waterfront* in terms of their working-class lifestyles and ethnic identities. But *Fever* was also a dance movie, cinematic territory that had been explored in *West Side Story* (1961) and in the Fred Astaire–Ginger Rogers movies of the thirties. Like those movies, it emphasized bright songs and exquisite partnership on the dance floor.

A group known as the Brothers Gibb, or Bee Gees, supplied the songs for the Travolta movie. In the past this group had featured close harmonies that resembled rock arrangements of folk songs. In the music for the new movie, the group reinvented itself as a disco group, with a high-pitched falsetto lead voice and louder and more rhythmic orchestral backgrounds. As it turned out, the album of the movie's music became a smash hit and

helped to give legs to the disco craze that would later become as emblematic of the seventies as the Charleston was of the twenties. "Stayin' Alive," a
song used in *Saturday Night Fever*, became part of an album that eventually
sold thirty million copies.

In *Saturday Night Fever*, John Travolta plays Tony (shades of *West Side
Story*) who works in a hardware store in Bay Ridge in the shadow of the
Verrazano-Narrows Bridge. Like the others in the community, he seems
isolated, unable to take the big bridge over to Staten Island and from there
to the American mainland and also unable to cross over from provincial
Brooklyn into cosmopolitan Manhattan. Both he and his friends often drive
halfway over the bridge and then turn around. Tony and his friends lead
lives riddled with prejudice and a brutal form of sexuality that limits their
outlook and keeps them from realizing their true potential. Everyone in the
picture appears to be at a dead end. Tony's dad is an unemployed construction worker, his masculinity compromised by his inability to work. Tony
also lives with his sister, his mother, and his very Italian grandmother who
speaks little or no English. These women exist to serve the men, who sit
around the table and talk after dinner, as the women, who have cooked
the meal, clear the dishes from the table. The father forbids the mother
from working outside of the house. The family thinks of Tony's brother, a
priest, as a hero, but during the movie he returns home to announce that
he is quitting the priesthood. He, too, is out of faith and out of work. In
one scene, Tony puts on his brother's collar and pretends it is a noose.
Tony's fellow workers at the hardware store also appear to be at the end of
their ropes. One has a bad back, and all look as if they are injured in some
way. No member of the older generation offers much in the way of hope
for the future to Tony and his friends, who lead squalid lives and face tragic
dilemmas. One of Tony's pals gets his girlfriend pregnant. He cannot bring
himself to marry her and knows that getting an abortion is wrong. He ends
up throwing himself off the bridge, symbolizing his inability, and that of his
friends, to reach a safe destination in life.

Tony's hope for salvation lies in his talent. Every Saturday night he
dresses up and becomes the king of disco. His love interest and dance partner, played by Karen Gorney, has a job in Manhattan and, although she
has no polish, she has aspirations to leave Bay Ridge. In the movie, she gets
an apartment in Manhattan, and Tony finally crosses the river and joins
her. His ability to move on with his life stems from his realization that, like
Rocky and Terry Malloy, he must transcend his immediate environment,
where people have sex in cars and indulge in gang bangs and where racial

prejudice blinds people to the truth. In the movie's climactic dance-contest scene, Tony and his partner win the prize, but Tony realizes that the black and Puerto Rican contestants are actually better dancers. The judges have rigged the contest in his favor but done him no real favor. Just as taking a dive in a fight turns Terry Malloy from a contender to a bum, so throwing the contest robs Tony of his dignity. He gets away in the nick of time to make his own way in Manhattan.

The movie, shot on location in Bay Ridge in March 1977, contains nice glimpses of a declining neighborhood on the fringes of the urban action. The neighborhood owes its identity to its segregation from the black and Puerto Rican communities that were filling up Brooklyn. The people in the neighborhood lead out-dated lives, eating chop suey in Chinese restaurants and wearing clothes that the audience recognizes as cheap and loud. All dressed up to go out dancing, Travolta wears a three-piece white suit and a dark shirt with an open collar that exposes the hair on his chest, a mannered pose of casual elegance that has become the single most famous image from the seventies.

Director John Badham, put in charge of the project because John Avildsen, who had just finished *Rocky*, was otherwise occupied, proved himself adept at capturing the dance sequences. When the film opened on December 1, 1977, at Mann's Chinese Theater, it became a smash, staying at the top of the box office for weeks and ultimately grossing $285 million in revenues.

WOODY ALLEN AND THE ROMANCE OF *MANHATTAN*

Saturday Night Fever celebrated Manhattan as the pot of gold at the end of the rainbow without centering the action on Manhattan itself. It was part of a late-decade revival of New York City's image. Plays and movies about New York traced a change in the city's reputation from romantic in the 1940s and 1950s to menacing in the 1970s, as the differences between the Broadway musical *Guys and Dolls* (1950) and Martin Scorsese's 1973 movie *Mean Streets* indicated. Based on Damon Runyon's picaresque short stories, *Guys and Dolls* has a sweet tone and a benign view of New York street life. During the second act, one of the lead characters stands in the middle of Times Square at four in the morning and sings of its romantic virtues. Although Scorsese's movie also deals with the lives of gamblers in New York City, it has a much darker tone and presents a much less upbeat portrait of New York life. His New York is a place where the locals take advantage of the suburban kids who come cruising into town looking for drugs and where people have vendettas against one another that lead to violent murders.

It fell to Woody Allen to complete the project of restoring the city's romantic image. At a time when the city was experiencing severe fiscal troubles, he made a valentine called *Manhattan*, a movie that critic Andrew Sarris described as "the only truly great film of the seventies." Allen himself was a product of many of the city's outdated traditions. Born in 1935, with the name Allan Stewart Konigsberg, he grew up in Brooklyn. Like Steven Spielberg, he showed little interest in school and made it a point of pride not to do his homework. Instead his interests centered on sports, playing the clarinet in a traditional New Orleans jazz manner, doing magic tricks, and going to the movies. Movies, which he began to see in the early forties, offered him a means of escape from a childhood that he otherwise found oppressive. As he got older, Manhattan became the place at the other end of the subway line, a wide world of amusements and sophistication. Allen developed a gift for writing jokes, and in his early career he was a gag writer. Earl Wilson, the Broadway columnist, printed some of the jokes that Allen, still in high school, sent to him at the *New York Post*, beginning in November 1952. Allen then started to write gags for David Alber, who was a personal publicist who tried to get his clients mentioned in the Broadway columns. In 1953, at the insistence of his parents who were determined that he put his obvious talents to some practical use, he entered New York University and, after failing there, City College. College, the postwar generation's ticket to prosperity, never took with Allen.

The Broadway culture, already well past its prime, fascinated Allen. He thought of someone like George Kaufman, the famous playwright, drama critic, director, and wit who personified the sophistication and glamour of the New York show-business scene, as someone worth emulating. Woody Allen came to maturity long after the era of Kaufman's greatest triumphs, one of the last of which was directing the Broadway smash *Guys and Dolls*. He had to put his talents to work not in theater but in television. In late 1955 he secured a position in NBC's writer-development program and worked on the *NBC Comedy Hour*, a show that featured comic Jonathan Winters, among others, and allowed Allen to interact with Danny Simon, mentor to other television writers and brother of Neil Simon, who was soon to graduate from television writing to Broadway and become a theatrical legend. Danny Simon helped Allen get a position at Tamiment, a summer resort in the Pocono Mountains that featured live shows for which Simon and others wrote. The Jewish summer resort was another institution that was waning in popularity; many Jewish families could afford more upscale vacations and no longer felt the need to surround themselves with other Jews. In the course of a career as a television writer, Allen also wrote for Buddy Hackett and Carol Burnett in a short-lived situation comedy; for Sid Caesar. who by 1958 was nearing the end of his television run but still maintained a large stable of some of the best writers in television; for Pat Boone; and for Garry Moore. Always, it seemed, Woody Allen was a bit behind the cultural curve.

By the end of the decade, he began to tire of the highly collaborative world of television writing and thought of performing some of his own material as a stand-up comic. He joined a new wave of performers that included Mike Nichols and Elaine May, Mort Sahl, and Lenny Bruce. They appeared in bars and coffee houses in the Bohemian sections of New York, such as Greenwich Village, and in the areas of cities that were being retrofitted from places of production to places of consumption with a nostalgic feel, such as Old Town in Chicago and Gaslight Square in St. Louis. Allen dreaded live performance but persevered. Soon he was good enough to play the *Ed Sullivan Show* in 1962 and to host the *Tonight Show* in 1964. He had a highly personal style: he did not tell jokes in the rapid-fire way of Bob Hope; instead, he spoke in a halting and stuttering manner, his voice high pitched and infused with a Brooklyn accent, and told stories that were fanciful accounts of his own life or parodies of literary situations. His humor had a postwar sensibility, with references to psychoanalysis, divorce, and existential philosophy as in his mention of taking "Death 101" in college but cheating on the exam by looking into the soul of the boy seated next to him.[23]

In the sixties, Allen made the leap into movies and by the end of the decade was writing, directing, and starring in his own films. In the seventies, he created a series of classic comedies that included *Bananas* (1971); *Sleeper* (1973), a hilarious comedy about a bleak future where everything is advanced and people have orgasms by fondling machines yet nothing really works; *Love and Death* (1975), an elaborate parody of nineteenth-century Russian literature in which Allen tosses off references to the novels of Tolstoy and Dostoevski; and *Annie Hall* (1977), a bittersweet romantic comedy that won the Academy Award for best picture. Despite the trendy subjects, such as revolution in Latin America and the nature of modern relationships, Allen's work showed an appreciation for the comedy of Bob Hope and the Marx brothers. In the climax of *Sleeper*, for example, Woody Allen and his sidekick Diane Keaton, despite having no medical experience whatsoever, find themselves forced to clone the body of the repressive dictator, known as the Fearless Leader, working only with his nose. Allen approaches the operating room with Bob Hope's self-deluded bravado. "We're doctors, not imposters," he says. He and Keaton then blunder their way through the operation in a comic manner, just as Groucho and his brothers blunder their way through the medical examination of Margaret Dumont in *Day at the Races* (1937).

After *Love and Death*, Woody Allen tried his hand at more serious drama in the manner of Ingmar Bergman, and the result was a somber and self-indulgent piece called *Interiors* (1978). Promising to return to comedy, he then made *Manhattan*, in which he juxtaposed the romance and allure of the city with the messy and incomplete nature of the lives of the people living there. Allen's Manhattan is far removed from John Travolta's Brooklyn. Instead, he transports the audience into the smart and sophisticated world that he had imagined Manhattan to be when he was a kid in Brooklyn. To underscore that association, Allen uses the music of George Gershwin from the twenties and thirties for the soundtrack of the movie (something once thought to be more worthy of Paris than New York as the Academy Award–winning *An American in Paris* [1951] demonstrated). At the beginning of the movie, Ike Davis, the movie's hero and narrator, played by Allen, concedes that New York may be "a metaphor for the decay of contemporary culture" but that he adores New York and idolizes "it out of all proportion." And New York is quite beautiful in this handsomely shot black-and-white movie about people whose names—Ike, Yale, Mary, and Tracy—link them to previous eras.

Allen's movie takes place far away from New York City's fiscal crisis. The problems of Ike and his friends are more existential than economic. They have the usual problems with love and relationships. Tracy is in love with Ike who is in love with Mary who is in love with Yale. Ike's former wife has entered a lesbian relationship and written a book that Ike worries will expose all of his sexual foibles. She assures him that being raised by two mothers will not harm their son, to which he replies that he thought few people survive having one mother. For solace, Ike has turned to Tracy (played by Mariel Hemingway, the granddaughter of the famous author), a suitable mate who shares many of his interests and enthusiasms but who is nonetheless still in high school. "I'm dating someone who does homework," he laments. She goes to a fashionable private school and lives in a fancy apartment with a doorman, but her mother and father never seem to be around. Pygmalion-like, Ike mentors Tracy, yet in the end she is the one who gives him good advice, telling him he needs to show a little more faith in people. Yale, as the name suggests, is an academic who cannot commit to having a child with his wife but can make a decision to buy a sports car. Mary Wilke, Diane Keaton's character, with whom both Yale and Ike have an affair, knows she is quite talented and that she could sleep with the entire MIT faculty but finds herself writing cheap novelizations of film scripts. As she puts it, "I have everything going for me, except I'm all fucked up." She and Yale have a game in which they nominate artists for something they call the "academy of the overrated" that includes, among others, F. Scott Fitzgerald and Gustav Mahler. Although they can disparage the work of others, they cannot seem to create their own. No one in the book produces anything but words. Everyone, it seems, is writing but not necessarily finishing a book.

CONCLUSION

The remarkable thing about *Manhattan* was that it got made at all. An intensely personal film that reflected many of Woody Allen's own artistic preoccupations and personal idiosyncrasies, *Manhattan* indicated the vitality of the movie scene in the seventies and demonstrated how a creative director could address the problem of the era in his own terms. Like *Chinatown*, *The Godfather*, and *Jaws*, Allen's film was backward looking in its use of elements from cinema's past but present minded in its subject matter. The possibility for creating such movies peaked in the seventies because those who financed the pictures were willing to take a chance on talented directors. In the future, Hollywood would go off in search of blockbusters, hoping for more hits like *The Godfather*, *Jaws*, or *Star Wars* and willing to open them in theaters across the country with a blitz of television advertisements. In the future, people who wanted to see the new Woody Allen or Robert Altman or Martin Scorsese film would have to rush to the theater where it would play for only a short time or catch it on videotape or in Europe. The seventies was indeed the last era in which people sat together in the dark and watched some of the best movies ever made.

10
Television and the Reassurance of the Familiar

During the seventies, since not everyone went to the movies, a selective audience created a niche for quality pictures offering incisive vignettes of the era. Television, by way of contrast, was unavoidable: 97.1 percent of American households contained a TV set in 1975. Because television was ubiquitous, it served as America's principal medium for the dispersal of both entertainment and news. It therefore contributed to the ways in which Americans experienced the seventies. They learned about Watergate, the energy crisis, and the end of the Vietnam War and escaped from the sobering legacies of those events primarily through television. TV images of gays, people with disabilities, women in the work place, and African Americans reinforced their impressions of the rights revolution.

The fact that so many people watched the same shows heightened television's role as a source of common images and sounds. The three television networks, enjoying the largest audience they would ever have, dominated the airwaves. As commercial entities that needed to satisfy a large audience, the networks sought to offer popular and inoffensive programs to the public. ABC, CBS, and NBC, according to the industry credo of the postwar era, aimed for the least objectionable programming to fill the prime-time hours.[1] Between 1948 and 1970, they saturated the airwaves with variety shows, westerns, and situation comedies that featured suburban households confronting the problems of a prosperous society. By the end of the sixties, however, the networks realized that they could make even more money in prosperous postwar America by catering to the younger members of the household. The variety shows, with their emphasis on reaching a consensus on entertainment values within a household, disappeared, and in their place came a new generation of situation comedies and detective and police shows. In response to this demographic imperative, many television performers of long standing, such as the comedian Red Skelton and the variety impresario Ed Sullivan, left the air, and new shows that more accurately reflected generational change and conflict, such as *All in the Family* and *Mary Tyler Moore* took their place. The status quo no longer ruled on television.

As the social and economic upheavals of the seventies proceeded, however, the networks retreated from or modified these new shows and began to put overtly escapist programs, such as *Charlie's Angels* and *Happy Days*, on the air. These new shows resembled the older postwar programs, minus the emphasis on variety and with relaxed standards for language and sexual content that reflected the influence of the sixties. Hence *Three's Company*, a situation comedy in which one of the characters claimed to be gay and therefore a suitable roommate for single girls Suzanne Somers and Joyce DeWitt, made it to air in 1977 and became a major hit. Media critic Josh Ozersky has noted that a broad retreat from "controversy and 'relevant' programming occurred in 1974" and that the "Ford years enveloped television like cascading billows of cotton."[2] In this way, television maintained its mass character yet still embodied the spirit of the high sixties between 1970 and 1973 and reflected the chastened seventies beginning in 1974.

For all of television's light and fluffy character in the seventies, it continued to be America's most important source of news, information, and sports throughout the era. As a consequence, it replaced the mass-circulation magazines and evening newspapers that had once been the principal means by which America learned of national and world events. It also influenced the look and feel of spectator sports and altered America's leisure habits. Monday night, for example, was no longer just a time to recover from the beginning of a long work week. In 1970 it became a night to party and watch professional football on TV.

TRADITIONAL TELEVISION IN 1970

In 1970, Americans watched the same television shows because their choices were limited by the number of available channels. Furthermore, the programs they saw differed little from the ones they had watched ever since television first came into their homes in the late forties and early fifties. Even in New York, the nation's largest television market, most viewers had only seven channels from which to choose. The three networks owned and operated stations in New York. The other four independent stations filled up their air time with sports, cartoons, movies, and reruns of network television programs. The Mets games appeared on channel 9, and the Yankees played on channel 11.

Most people in New York and elsewhere chose to watch the first-run offerings on the three major television networks, which nationally attracted some 90 percent of the evening audience by the late seventies.[3] Since these networks broadcast programs for such a wide-ranging audience, they served as important forces of national integration, arraying their programs throughout the day somewhat like a great department store displayed all of its merchandise under one roof. Just as different floors and sections in the department store served different clienteles, according to age, gender, and ability to pay, so networks designed their schedules according to the characteristics of the audience that watched at any particular time. In the morning the stations aired news and information programs that prepared people for the day. Later in the morning, a station might run programs aimed at kids who were not old enough to go to school, such as a cartoon program, and follow that with soap operas intended for housewives who remained at home. There followed more cartoons and juvenile programming for kids returning from school at the end of the day, a block of news programs in the early evening, and prime-time entertainment programs, designed to appeal to a wide range of tastes, later in the evening.

Prime time, which lasted from seven-thirty until eleven in the evenings on the east and west coasts and from seven until eleven on Sundays, constituted the most important segment of the broadcasting day because the audiences were largest during those hours. Consequently, the networks reserved those hours for themselves, rather than letting their local affiliates control them and keep all of the advertising revenues. Beginning in 1971, however, local stations did manage to regain the half hour from seven-thirty until eight on weekdays.

The prime-time shows that aired in September 1970 did not contain much to surprise or alarm the audience.[4] On Sunday night, for example, a family could begin its evening viewing at seven with *Lassie*, a series about a collie that had a talent for rescuing humans from the direst situations. Like its canine star, the program had an impressive entertainment pedigree. It had begun as a novel in 1940, served as the basis for a popular 1943 movie with Elizabeth Taylor, and been a radio series in the late 1940s and a television series since 1954. It was, therefore, thoroughly familiar to the postwar audience and a good example of the continuity in programming from television's very beginnings through the 1960s.

Other Sunday programs reflected the persistence of old shows in a new decade. NBC proudly featured the *Wonderful World of Disney*, a variety series containing cartoons, true-life adventures, and other products of the Walt Disney studios and theme parks that had been on television as long as *Lassie*. Ed Sullivan's variety program aired at eight on CBS. Broadcast from New York's theater district, it allowed viewers from around the country to see the nation's top performers, selections from Broadway shows, and cultural attractions such as the Bolshoi Ballet. Launched in 1948, the program provided a window on the New York cultural scene and harked back to the days when the talk of Broadway captured the nation's attention. Each week Sullivan, a gossip columnist for a New York paper—with no discernible performing talent—who moved stiffly and spoke in an odd cadence that impressionists loved to imitate, put together a variety package for the nation's viewers, hoping that a rock-and-roll act would satisfy the teenagers in the house and someone like singer Lena Horne might appeal to older viewers.

The *Ed Sullivan Show* was a cultural landmark of the postwar era but not of the seventies. It had trouble surviving into the seventies and would end its long run in 1971 because it attracted an audience that in advertising parlance skewed old and was less valued than a younger audience. In the late sixties and into the seventies, reconciling the cultural styles of the young and the old became harder than it had been in the fifties. The younger segment of the audience did not want to sit through the Yale Marching Band or a routine from borsht-belt comedian Henny Youngman just to get to a four-minute song by the Rolling Stones.

Sullivan's show, viewed today on old films and video tapes, has a sort of East Coast formality that was a distinctive feature of the times. The members of the audience, throughout the run of the show, dressed up for the occasion, as if they were going to the theater and were aware that their images might be broadcast across the nation. Some twenty years later, CBS used the same theater for David Letterman's late-night show. Despite the New York location, the audiences in Letterman's time almost never dressed up; other than Dave himself, a snazzy dresser, the male guests seldom wore ties and jackets. Between the era of Ed Sullivan and David Letterman, between the nineteen seventies and today, a new informality had entered the national scene. This informality extended to the material on the shows. Sullivan's show used Broadway shows, nightclub acts, operas, ballets, and movies as reference points. The material on Letterman's show referred most often to other television shows, and many of the guests were television performers.

If the Sunday night prime-time schedule had a well-worn feel, the rest of the broadcast week in 1970 also featured stars and programs with long historical roots in television. Monday's CBS programs included not only *Gunsmoke*, the venerable western that had been on television since 1955 and had premiered on radio in 1952, but also programs starring such enduring television and movie performers as Lucille Ball, Andy Griffith, and Doris Day. *Here's Lucy* showcased the comic antics of Lucille Ball, a fixture on television since *I Love Lucy* went on the air in 1951. What was remarkable was that Ball, entering her sixties and without the support of her former partner Desi Arnaz, continued to hold such a large audience week after week. In the 1970–1971 season, her show was the third most popular on the air. The *Doris Day Show* provided the former movie star, who was well-known to the audience, with a television vehicle. Whether or not the television series, which had a situation-comedy format, represented her best work, the audience took to it and gave it a five-year run from 1968 to 1973.

The Tuesday-night schedule in 1970 featured new comedies that reflected old situations. *The Beverly Hillbillies*, one of television's most popular programs during the sixties and still popular in 1970, spotlighted the members of the Clampett family who had moved from the rural Ozarks to sophisticated Beverly Hills—from the world of the *Grapes of Wrath* to the home of the Hollywood stars—when oil was discovered on its Ozark property. The humor of this program depended on the ability of the rural folks, dressed up in a wardrobe that Ma and Pa Kettle might have worn in 1947, to show up the urban folks with their common sense and their ability to see through pretense. *Green Acres* reversed the premise to allow urbanites Eva Gabor and Eddie Albert, she of the exotic Hungarian accent and voluptuous body and he a long-time featured player in movies, to move to the country and cope with the problems of adjustment in humorous ways. The program followed in the tradition of movies such as *George Washington Slept Here* (1942, adopted from an earlier play) and *Mr. Blandings Builds His Dream House* (1948). As such, the audience recognized the form instantly.

Initial Changes in the Seventies

If television emphasized a sense of continuity with the past, it was not a static medium. Changes were already evident in 1970. Detective shows remained a staple, but beginning in 1967 one of the detectives was a paraplegic who worked from his wheelchair. Variety shows continued to be popular, but some offered new twists on the format by featuring African American stars or taking advantage of technological advances in broadcasting. The variety show hosted by comedian Flip Wilson that lasted from 1970 to 1974 was the most popular one on the air in 1970. Wilson, the first African American to have a successful variety television program, exaggerated the characteristics of stock figures from the black ghetto, such as Reverend LeRoy of the Church of What's Happening Now, for comic effect. He worked in the tradition of comics who appeared on the black entertainment circuit in venues like the Apollo Theater in New York and the Royal Theater in Baltimore. He let white audiences in on the black jokes in a way that was new for the mass media.

Rowan and Martin's Laugh-In, another innovative variety show that ran from 1968 to 1973, played against *Gunsmoke* and *Lucy* on Monday nights in 1970. Displaying the medium's ability to differentiate itself from live performances of the Ed Sullivan variety, it depended on fast-paced editing of video tape to produce a stream of jokes. Many of these jokes had a modern look and sensibility, such as gags written on the body of a girl in a bikini or the repeated use of apparently hip expressions such as "sock it to me," followed by a vaudeville-style punch. Among the many performers who appeared regularly on the show during its five year run were Goldie Hawn and Lily Tomlin, who were to emerge as major stars during the seventies.

MONDAY NIGHT FOOTBALL AND THE WORLD OF SPORTS

Another television innovation that survived the decade and became one of television's longest-running programs involved football, a television staple since 1950 that received a new twist in 1970. Every Monday night in the fall and early winter, ABC, which remained mired in third place in the ratings and could afford to depart from the conventional formats in an effort to induce change, broadcast a prime-time professional football game that attracted a large, primarily male audience. The men preferred to watch football rather than Doris Day on CBS or the movie on NBC. As a prime-time broadcast, *Monday Night Football* incorporated entertainment values not associated with other sports broadcasts, such an extra commentator in the booth to provide comic relief and an elaborately produced sports newsreel designed to hold the audience during halftime, narrated by Howard Cosell, who became one of the era's major stars. The program illustrated how television altered both the format and the entertainment value of sports in the seventies.

Cosell, with his bombastic style, turned the Monday-night games into major events—ways for the male audience to shake off its Monday lethargy at the local bar or at home in front of the television set. Cosell, who had a thick New York accent and looks that could charitably be described as ordinary, contrasted nicely with his fellow commentator Don Meredith, twenty years his junior and a former Dallas Cowboy quarterback, who played the role of the laid-back Texas good ole boy to perfection. It was the same dynamic of city meets country that worked so well on the *Beverly Hillbillies* and *Green Acres* and that had always been an important part of sports in which country boys played before city crowds.

It was significant that ABC's *Monday Night Football* broadcasts did much better than its Monday-night baseball broadcasts, which began in 1976 and lasted through 1988. Baseball, once the nation's most popular game, commanded the entire nation's attention only during the period of postseason play in October. For the rest of the year, it served either as form of local programming, with an emphasis on the hometown team, or as marginal summer programming that could not be relied on to garner high ratings. It was symbolic of football's dominance over baseball during the 1970s that such proud baseball franchises as the Pittsburgh Pirates, St. Louis Cardinals and Cincinnati Reds were forced to play their games in stadiums designed primarily for football and affording many poor views of the baseball action.

Although television tended to frame the nation's interest in sports and boosted the level of interest in nearly all sports, it benefited football more than baseball. Football is a slow-paced game with short bursts of furious action. Its frequent breaks permit television producers to show replays that allow the analysts like Meredith and Cosell a chance to comment on the action. Baseball, as broadcast on the radio, features constant, low-key patter from an announcer who functions as a fan filling other fans in on the action. Football is a game in which the analysts, who surpassed the play-by-play announcers in fame and who carried the broadcast, get to give fans the inside story on what really happened. The physical design of football, with most of the action taking place near the line of scrimmage, also allows plays to be framed by television in ways that baseball does not permit, with its players spread out over the field and the ball traveling at great speeds from pitcher to catcher across a significant distance.

For viewers of *Monday Night Football*, the game was more of a special event and treat than baseball. Hardcore fans listened to baseball games on the radio nearly every evening for half of the year, "six months out of every year," as the neglected baseball wife in the Broadway musical *Damn Yankees* laments. Professional football teams played less than twenty games a year, nearly all of them on Sunday, a day that remained one of leisure and on which most of the stores were closed. Each game therefore became an event eagerly anticipated over the course of the work week. In places like Washington, which failed to support two different professional baseball teams, tickets to the Washington Redskins were a status item. Football was a network sport that made it into prime time during the seventies. Baseball was much more often broadcast on regional chains of stations composed of local affiliates.

ALL IN THE FAMILY

Networks, which dominated the television scene during the seventies, proved to be lucrative enterprises. During the decade the revenues of the three networks tripled to reach $3 billion dollars. To buy a minute of commercial time on a hit program cost $60,000 at the beginning of the decade and $200,000 by its end.[5]

The vast amounts of money coming into the three networks did not encourage experimentation or risk taking. As the 1970 schedule demonstrated, the network executives stayed with what worked. At the same time, the networks recognized that they could always make more money by raising their ratings and gaining a greater share of the audience. In the sixties and seventies, they also acquired better tools to measure the spending habits of the public. Those tools allowed them to sell shows to advertisers based not just on the number of people who would watch but also on the type of people who would watch. This type of demographic information accounted for the presence of such sports as tennis and golf on network television. Not everyone played or even understood the scoring system for those games, but those who did tended to have a lot of disposable income and made good targets for advertisers interested in selling luxury cars or stocks and bonds.

In a change of considerable importance to the cultural history of the seventies, Robert Wood, the president of ratings-leading CBS, believed that his network could do better if it increased its appeal to younger viewers, who were prime consumers. He sought to change the schedule so that it retained its popularity but contained more programs with "better" demographics. Hence Wood announced in 1970 that the schedule would be revamped, and he proceeded over the next few years to drop such shows as the *Beverly Hillbillies* and *Ed Sullivan* and replace them with new situation comedies that featured more contemporary settings, such as *The Mary Tyler Moore Show* and *All in the Family*. By 1974 CBS had made the changeover and still had nine of the top ten shows.[6]

Between 1971 and 1976, *All in the Family* won the annual ratings race five times in a row, something that no other show has duplicated. Introduced at the beginning of 1971, it attracted a great deal of critical attention and found an audience that summer. In the fall of 1971, the show started the season at number twelve in the ratings and took the top spot the next week. It went on to become the most popular television show of its era.

All in the Family, filmed before a live studio audience using one basic set, takes place in the Corona section of Queens. Archie Bunker, the central character, is the dock foreman for the Prendergast (a nod toward the days of the big city political machine) Tool and Die Company.[7] The program's topical humor utilizes ethnic stereotypes and plays upon the conflict be-tween the generations.[8] In a sense, Archie Bunker, like Jed Clampett on the *Beverly Hillbillies*, is a man displaced in time. The difference is that both Jed and his wealthy Beverly Hills neighbors come out of the world portrayed in the movies of the 1930s, with its comic hillbillies and society matrons, whereas Archie Bunker seems a much more real presence whose dilem-mas spring from exaggerated versions of the problems that Americans in big cities were facing. As a member of what would later be proclaimed the "greatest generation," Archie, unlike Jed Clampett, cannot accept the reali-ties of modern life with genial good humor. He is out of step with his times, railing, for example, about the fact that a black family has moved in down the block and circulating a petition meant to stop blacks from further "in-filterating," as the malapropism-tending Archie puts it, the neighborhood. His son and daughter, who live with him and his wife Edith, accept the fact that the neighborhood is changing and welcome the diversity that the new family, named the Jeffersons, brings. Archie, however, simply cannot be reconciled to change.

In a typical episode from the program's early run, Edith accepts an in-vitation from Mrs. Jefferson for dinner. Archie panics and invents excuses not to go. In the characteristically blunt language of the program, he refuses to break bread with a "jungle bunny." Through a series of situation-com-edy misunderstandings, the Jeffersons end up bringing the dinner over to Archie's house, just at the moment when Archie's comrade in the fight to keep blacks out of the neighborhood is in the living room. When Edith sets the table, Archie frets that "that ain't gonna be enough light" and says that they will only be able to see their guests when they smile. It later comes out that Mr. Jefferson is also a bigot and, like Archie, he refuses to eat with his nemesis, whom he calls "whitey." Instead of going to the Bunkers' for dinner, Mr. Jefferson goes to the ball game, which, as it turns out, is where Archie also wants to be. Later, Archie's enlightened son-in-law and daughter ask him and Edith about the evening. They want to know if Mrs. Jefferson prepared soul food for them to eat. "No, it wasn't fish," replies Mrs. Bunker. In another episode, Archie seeks a lawyer and makes sure that the lawyer he hires is from a Jewish firm. To his disappointment, however, the lawyer sent to his house is a Wasp. Archie prefers a Jew because he is convinced that only a very wily, aggressive lawyer will be able to win the case.

Such material put a modern gloss on the traditional situation comedy. Archie's ethnic jokes and racial epithets carried much more sting than did Jed Clampett's references to his swimming pool as the "see-ment" pond. At the same time, Archie was not a simple bigot but, in the style of a medium that sought wide acceptance for its programs, a loveable bigot. Some people could relate to Archie as a source of ironic wisdom, a wise fool in the tradition of Shakespeare's Polonius or, to use a more down-home example, a plain-spoken ethnic character in the tradition of Mark Twain or the Chicago journalist Peter Finley Dunne. Others thought him a fool but a humorous one and delighted in the program because they were in on the joke. The program also aged well. It began with a decidedly sixties flavor, including references to the Vietnam War, such as in the joke that Archie lied so well that he should work for the Defense Department, and the generation gap, as in Archie's horror that his daughter would appear in public wearing hot pants. As the economy turned sour and these concerns faded, Archie's situation as an aging white male who had missed the sexual revolution and who had few real skills acquired a certain poignancy to which audiences responded. Indeed, by 1974 the program had lost much of its topical edge. Instead it evolved into a "highly affectionate family sitcom, a sort of 'Father Knows Least.' "[9]

As a sign of television's influence in the seventies, the very name "Archie Bunker" entered the English language. An Archie Bunker was a white ethnic bigot, a close relative of Joe Six-Pack, but more likely to live in the city than the suburbs. Archie was a lower-class version of Sinclair Lewis's Babbitt, another character who lent his name to the language. It was perhaps significant that Babbitt came from a novel of the 1920s and Archie Bunker from a television show of the seventies. Despite the fifty years that separated the two characters, both had trouble understanding their children, and both were capable of making the same sort of ethnic references. For Archie, Michelangelo is "that dago artist." Babbitt, in his more literary rather than visual medium, learns that Dante is the "wop poet" who conducts "the Cook's Tour of hell."[10] Just as Babbitt lives in a fictional world that the author embellished in subsequent novels dealing with the inhabitants of Babbitt's hometown, so the characters in Archie

Bunker's world became the subjects of new television shows spun off from the original. These included *Maude* (1972–1978), concerning Edith's cousin, who was her exact opposite—liberal and upper middle class, suburban rather than urban—played by the brassy Beatrice Arthur, as well as *The Jeffersons* (1975–1985) who moved from Queens to Manhattan's East Side for their series.[11]

MARY TYLER MOORE

Another CBS situation comedy created in the period when the network tried to improve its demographic starred an attractive young actress whom the audience knew as Dick Van Dyke's wife from an earlier show. Although *The Mary Tyler Moore Show* followed the rules of the genre, with the usual coincidences and sources of embarrassment, it depicted the novel situation, at least for television, of a young woman living on her own in a big city. Following what became an established convention of the seventies sitcom, it took place in Minneapolis, a Rust Belt city featured in the opening credits. The series itself, like most television series, was shot in Los Angeles, although the producers were careful to show snow falling outside the window of Mary's apartment at the appropriate times of year.

Mary, contrary to the chill of the climate, had a warm and sunny disposition. Unlike other female characters left to fend for themselves in the big city, like Lily Bart in Edith Wharton's *House of Mirth* or Carrie Meeber in Theodore Dreiser's *Sister Carrie*, Mary Richards, as the theme song reminded viewers, just might "make it, after all." The show conveyed a hopeful message to the many female baby boomers who were setting out on their own in the early seventies and, in the cautious manner of television, played to their nascent feminist leanings.

In the pilot episode, Mary Richards is thirty years old and on her way to Minneapolis, after a failed affair with a medical student whom she has helped support.[12] When he comes to Minneapolis, she takes things into her own hands and breaks up with him, establishing her strength of character and independence of mind. She seeks work in Minneapolis and finds it as an associate producer in a local TV newsroom, run by the paternalistic and overbearing Lou Grant, who drinks and is brusque in manner but also, in that oxymoronic television way, endearing. Mary, in common with other single women, wants to be married and much of the show centers on her social life.

The show takes place on two primary sets. One is the newsroom where Mary works, an environment dominated by men such as Ted Baxter, the handsome but empty-headed anchorman who depends on others to put the right words in his mouth. Mary, along with many other working women in the 1970s, frequently must decide whether to ignore or protest the reflexive sexism of her boss and coworkers. To modern eyes, the newsroom is not only sexist but surprisingly low tech. Lou Grant watches the news not from some slick monitor in the control room but from a television set perched on a desk. The work space also holds two manual typewriters at which Mary and her sidekick Murray Slaughter write copy for Ted. The other set is Mary's apartment, which is populated almost exclusively by women who worry about their social lives. Rhoda Morgenstern is a Jewish woman of Mary's age who comes from New York and seems a little out of place in the Midwest. Forced in one of the episodes to go on a camping trip, Rhoda comes away tired and disgruntled. Mary, always cheerful, reminds Rhoda that at least she learned something about survival on the trip. "I learned about survival on the New York subways," Rhoda replies. Another person who shows up at the apartment is Phyllis Lindstrom, played by accomplished actress Cloris Leachman. Phyllis is raising her child according to the latest psychological wisdom, which the show ridicules.

In a typical adventure, Mary and Rhoda, who are smart, savvy updates of Lucy and her sidekick Viv, go to a meeting of a group of divorced people, on the theory that it is easier to catch a man if you are divorced than if you have never been married. Through the usual comic misadventures, Mary ends up as the vice president of the club. But it is apparent that the people in the club are self-seeking losers, like the dentist who is obsessed with people's teeth, and the show makes it clear that Mary is better off single than married to one of these men. With the exception of Murray, none of the married people on the show has a particularly good marriage, and the series' memorable finale episode, broadcast in the late spring of President Carter's first year in office, emphasized the joys of friendship, rather than marriage.

Retro Comedies and Jiggle

By the time *The Mary Tyler Moore Show* left the air in 1977, the topical situation comedies from CBS no longer dominated the television scene. The audience, no doubt beleaguered by the new economic realities of the seventies, no longer had the same taste for programs that confronted contemporary problems, even the situation-comedy versions of those problems. The full-blown arrival of the seventies in the period after Nixon's resignation, the end of the Vietnam War, and the first oil shock permitted last-place ABC to make its ratings move. Between January 1974 and January 1976, the network unleashed a string of hits that included *Laverne and Shirley, Happy Days, Charlie's Angels* and *Welcome Back Kotter*. ABC benefited from a new agreement by which the networks set aside the hour from eight to nine as a time for family viewing. The rule meant that CBS had to reschedule some of its established shows, such as the police drama *Kojak*, an hour later and aided ABC's strategy of starting the evening with situation comedies that appealed to younger viewers. By the spring of 1977, CBS managed to place just two of its shows in the top ten, and ABC held its lead during the 1977–1978 season.[13]

The ABC shows played upon a middecade fascination with the 1950s. In times of rampant inflation and high unemployment, perhaps, audiences liked to be reminded of an era when the economy seemed to function better and life seemed more innocent. People who were alive in the fifties and watching television in the seventies were looking back on a time when they were much younger and in retrospect happier. Their personal dilemmas of the fifties were conveniently forgotten. Younger viewers had even more license to construct their own images of the fifties based on what they saw on television.

Retro comedies demanded retro settings. As a consequence, both *Laverne and Shirley* and *Happy Days* took place in Milwaukee—a textbook Rust Belt city that was experiencing the usual urban problems of the decade. Laverne and Shirley worked in a Milwaukee brewery. The gang on *Happy Days*, which reconstructed the fifties conflicts between the straight arrows (as personified by Ron Howard, whose television pedigree included a turn as the cute young boy on the *Andy Griffith Show*) and the greasers (as represented by the character known as the Fonz, played by Henry Winkler, who took America by storm), went first to high school and then to college in Milwaukee. *Welcome Back Kotter* took place in present time but was set in an inner city Brooklyn High School, just the sort of place that people were making every effort to leave in the seventies.

Another aspect of ABC's success depended on selling sex. Programmers called it "jiggle" or "t and a." Shows with this formula substituted exotic locations and pretty girls for the gritty look of the urban-based shows. *Charlie's Angels*, which featured the exploits of three women who undertook dangerous missions and solved puzzling cases, found lots of situations to put its female leads in bathing suits or other revealing clothing. Critics called it "schlock" and "stupid"; a prominent journalist described the show as a "massage parlor in the living room." Audiences loved it, and Farrah Fawcett-Majors became a breakout star. Men worshipped her as a sex symbol and bought her poster; women found her adorable and imitated her hair style.[14] Soon after the program premiered in 1976 it became a major hit, ranking fourth in the 1976–1977 ratings; *Laverne and Shirley* and *Happy Days* held down the first two positions. *Charlie's Angels* appealed to men, who liked the sexy features of the program, and to women, who appreciated the notion of seeing women in action. It spiced up an otherwise dull Wednesday night.

Critic Robert Sklar summed up the changes that had taken place over the course of the seventies. He argued that *All in the Family* and similar productions were "responses to contemporary realities." *Happy Days* and the associated ABC programs were "in another way responses to the fatigue and retreat from years of turmoil—but with the critical proviso that they did not reject the changes those turbulent years wrought, [and] they were able to incorporate at least some of them into genre forms."[15]

ROOTS

One almost inadvertent ABC success helped to insure the success of the miniseries as a new television form. On January 23, 1977, the miniseries *Roots* appeared on television. The date was significant. ABC executives, riding the crest of considerable success, decided that *Roots* would not draw large enough ratings to risk putting it on during the February sweeps period (which helped establish advertising rates for the year). The subject matter made the executives nervous, and they tried to hedge their bets by casting Alex Haley's story about his African ancestors, their coming to America, and their struggles to maintain their dignity in the face of slavery with white stars who were familiar to the audience, such as Ed Asner of *The Mary Tyler Moore Show*.

As it happened, the program, which ran for eight consecutive nights and a total of twelve hours, caught America's attention and became the most popular television program ever. One reason was that cold weather kept people at home. Another reason was that the program ran during the same week that Jimmy Carter was inaugurated, which perhaps got people to thinking about the place of the South in American culture and about changes in American politics. Whatever the reason, *Roots* became an important cultural phenomenon in its own right, establishing the new television form of the miniseries. Such series ran over successive nights, rather than once every week as did most television programs, in a manner similar to the baseball World Series, which attracted large audiences every October. *Roots* gave blacks an immigration story to match that of other ethnic groups, and its phenomenal ratings success reinforced the commercial viability of African Americans as lead players on television.[16]

SATURDAY NIGHT LIVE

When producer Garry Marshall created *Happy Days*, he said he wanted to be the "Norman Rockwell of television" and come up with "warm, humorous entertainment" for the whole family.[17] His success did not spell the end of programs aimed primarily at the baby-boom generation, as the phenomenon known as *Saturday Night Live* illustrated.[18] Late-night programming on Saturday night was a wasteland, with reruns and anything else that stations could find to fill in the time. In 1974, Johnny Carson, the late-night host whose *Tonight Show* was extremely important to struggling NBC, told the network that he wanted to pull the reruns that were showing on Saturday nights and use them during the week, allowing him to do fewer programs. That decision prompted NBC to develop a program for Saturday night into Sunday morning. The network chose Lorne Michaels, born in Canada as Lorne Lipowitz, to be the executive producer for the project. He had worked on *Laugh In* and a number of Lily Tomlin specials.

Michaels came up with a program that seemed very old-fashioned, something like a reprise of the *Ed Sullivan Show*, and yet it was also groundbreaking. Each week a prominent guest would host a variety show, with musical groups and comedy sketches, to be broadcast live from New York. Doing live television from the large NBC Studio at 30 Rockefeller Center that had once housed Arturo Toscanini and his orchestra was such an old concept that, in the age of video tape and filmed situation comedies, it appeared new. It would give the New York production facility a place on the schedule that it had long since lost to Los Angeles, at a time when New York was at the very nadir of its financial fortunes, and might also boost the fortunes of NBC.

Saturday Night Live premiered in the fall of 1975. Despite the presence of a famous guest host and a cutting-edge rock-and-roll group on the program each week, the program came to be dominated by its resident troupe of young comedians, known as the Not Ready for Prime Time Players. They were recruited from improvisational companies in Chicago and Toronto and were adept at sketch comedy. Like the performers on the legendary *Sid Caesar Show* of the fifties, such as Carl Reiner, they could both write and perform. Chevy Chase often opened the show with a bit that made fun of President Ford as a bumbling, ineffective leader and ended with a pratfall. Later in the program he appeared as the anchor of the show's mock news broadcast that consisted of a series of topical jokes combined with a parody of television news broadcasts. Other sketches might feature John Belushi, a talented comic presence, as a Greek lunch counter worker in Chicago or Dan Ackroyd and Lorraine Newman as the Coneheads, aliens from outer space who claimed to be from France. The sketches often had a surreal, drug-induced feel to them, but many took the form of television parodies, whether of commercials or of the programs, such as *I Love Lucy*, that baby boomers had watched as kids. If Sid Caesar made fun of the movies of the thirties and forties in the early fifties, the cast of *Saturday Night Live* satirized the television of the fifties and sixties in the seventies. Both programs reached viewers live from New York.

The hip sensibility of the cast and the lateness of the hour proclaimed the program as a haven for teenagers and young adults. *SNL* launched the careers of important performers. Chase, Belushi, Ackroyd, Gilda Radner, Newman, Jane Curtin, Garrett Morris, Bill Murray, Albert Brooks, Jim Henson, and Paul Shaffer all appeared on the program during the seventies, and other stars, such as Julia-Louis Dreyfuss, Eddie Murphy, Billy Crystal, Chris Rock, Mike Myers, and Adam Sandler were to follow. The show helped reinstate New York as the place to begin a career in show business and added a sense of glamour to a city thought to be in trouble.

As a long-term survivor, *Saturday Night Live*, with its changing casts, illustrated what happened to the television audience after the seventies. The show enjoyed its biggest audiences in the seventies, just as network television itself did. The show reached a peak in 1978 with an average rating of 12.6, which meant that more than one set out of ten was tuned to the program, and a huge audience share of 39, which meant of all the sets on at the time, more than one of every three was tuned to the program. In the 2000–1 season, these numbers had slipped to a rating of 5.4 and a 15 share.[19] In part, the program was no longer the cutting-edge phenomenon of the mid-seventies. In part, also, the nature of television had changed. In the year 2000 *SNL* faced direct competition from *Mad TV* on the Fox Network and from hundreds of cable stations that presented viewers with a plethora of choices. Neither Fox nor the many cable channels existed in the seventies.[20]

Broadcast News

Like the evening paper in one era and radio in another, television served not only as a source of entertainment but also as the nation's most important source of news. In Chicago, for example, some 1.1 million people tuned to Channel 7 during the seventies for the local news each evening, making that station the most important news source for the city. The *Chicago Tribune*, the leading morning newspaper, only reached about three quarters of a million people each day.[21] Channel 7 used a format known as Happy Talk that emphasized the entertainment aspects of television news. Joel Daly and Fahey Flynn did not try to pretend they were anywhere else than in a television studio. They were entertainers, not the descendants of the hard-bitten Chicago newspaper men portrayed in the classic play *The Front Page*. They bantered with each other and with John Coleman, the weatherman who delivered his reports in front of a gigantic map and other eye-popping graphics.

The Happy Talk format proved so successful that other stations owned by ABC began to copy it for their local news shows. Consultants who worked in the local news business sold other stations distinctive formats such as Action News and Eyewitness News. The result was that local news became a homogeneous product that looked pretty much the same everywhere.

Local news became a much more important part of the broadcast day during the seventies than it had been before, and it provided the most lucrative source of revenues for the local stations. In some cities, one could watch two full hours of local news followed by a half-hour of national news. Technological improvements made it possible for a local station to switch via satellite for a report from its Washington bureau that allowed local politicians to speak live to their constituents at home. During the seventies, cameras became lighter in weight and required less light to operate, making television news a far more mobile operation. Stations featured remote live broadcasts so that the viewer could be on the scene of a major accident or crime, and they made much more use of video tape, which could be processed more quickly than film. No longer was the weatherman dependent on a series of charts that he often had to draw himself. Now his segment of the program featured a slide show of current weather information. Sports coverage was up to the minute and often accompanied by video highlights. These things made the coverage and features of the evening papers seem stale and unnecessary.

Of all the aspects of television, local news was one of the most heavily criticized. Media critic Edwin Diamond complained of "disco news" in which "what is said—the reporting and narration, the content—becomes less and less important: what counts is how people look when they are saying it."[22] Much of this criticism came from cultural conservatives who regretted that newspapers and other printed materials had lost their influence as a source of news. Local news broadcasts took advantage of the particular nature of the medium and its technological capabilities to differentiate themselves from newspapers. Unlike the newspapers, television could broadcast the news live, and it made constant reference to that fact. It was a much more dynamic medium. Once the columns of the newspaper were set and the headlines written, they stayed that way forever. Television could be much more spontaneous and adjust to the feeling of the minute. The way that the anchors talked to one another and to the reporters in the field emphasized that fact. Happy Talk, then, was a way of bringing a sense of immediacy to the viewers. At the same time, television took away some of the freedom that newspaper readers enjoyed and made the viewer experience the news at the pace and in the order that the producer intended. It was, in the end, a different medium but one that people preferred as their source for news.

NETWORK NEWS

The nightly network news broadcasts took a more serious approach to their subject than did their local counterparts. The network news anchors occupied an important place in American life during the seventies. They were the people who narrated the public events of the era, both on their regular news broadcasts and during special events such as elections or extraordinary moments such as the arrival of President Nixon in China or his departure from office. During previous eras, radio reporters or newsreel announcers served these purposes. The nation bonded even more closely with the network anchors because they could see them, see them often, and see them as the events were taking place. The 1970s, before the advent of cable and the development of cable news stations, represented the apex of the anchors' influence over American life.

NBC News anchor John Chancellor and CBS anchor Walter Cronkite brought the events of the seventies to the American people. Walter Cronkite, who took over the CBS anchor chair in 1962, was the industry leader. Like his counterparts, he was a middle-aged white man from middle America. He spoke without any appreciable regional accent. He came from a comfortable background. Born in St. Joseph, Missouri, he moved with his family to Texas where he attended the University of Texas. Not as brilliant as the academically accomplished journalists around CBS radio reporter Edward R. Murrow, Cronkite did not stay in Austin to graduate. Instead, he began a career as a reporter for the *Houston Post* and the *Kansas City Star* that led to an assignment as a wartime correspondent for the United Press International. In 1950 he joined CBS News and only two years later became the network anchor for the 1952 political conventions. Cronkite took to the job with a natural ease. He had the ability to ad-lib and to fill in the ample spaces that the convention, which the networks covered, as the expression went, from gavel to gavel, provided. Although not handsome in a movie-star sense and with a mustache that seemed to mark him as a member of the older generation, in contrast to the clean-shaven Murrow, Cronkite radiated a sense of authority in front of the camera. He spoke in a deep, broadcast-quality voice and managed to combine, as one writer put it, "the sense of your favorite uncle with a world statesman."[23] He became the person whom Americans trusted to take them through the many ups and downs of the seventies, the decade in which he became the "undisputed king of TV news."[24]

SIXTY MINUTES

Television news helped to end the life of the evening newspaper and the general-interest mass-circulation magazine as well. Just as the seventies saw many evening newspapers go out of business, so the era also witnessed the demise of magazines that had once enjoyed an immense popularity. Well into the fifties, middle-class Americans read a group of mass-circulation magazines that were delivered to their doors. Colliers and the Saturday Evening Post attempted to offer a little something for everyone, much the way the television networks later did.[25] In the sixties, a showdown occurred in which the television networks and the mass circulation magazines competed for advertisers. The networks, able to deliver far more viewers than the magazines could readers, won the battle, and despite the large circulations that the magazines enjoyed, they began to experience financial difficulties. Look, Life, and the Saturday Evening Post all struggled during the sixties and eventually went out of business.[26] Sports Illustrated, People, and Playboy enjoyed large audiences in the seventies, but the rest of the surviving magazines fit narrow niches, such as advice for brides or tips on bodybuilding or news for hot-rod enthusiasts.[27]

The demise of the mass-circulation magazines left a void that television filled. The most conspicuous example was Sixty Minutes, which was first broadcast in 1968. The brainchild of Don Hewitt, a producer who had worked in television news since 1948, the show attempted to blend news and entertainment in a manner similar to Life or the Saturday Evening Post. The idea was to have a few longish feature stories each week that were different from the news stories on the evening news or the hour-long documentaries that CBS broadcast on a sporadic basis. The show would also have the equivalent of back-of-the-book pieces in magazines, such as short opinion pieces or debates on current issues. The broadcast would begin with a ticking stop watch, emphasizing the ability of television to compress the news into a short period of time and perhaps playing up the similarity to *Time* magazine.[28]

Nothing much happened at first. Although the show had the advantage of being cheap to produce compared with a situation comedy or variety show, few people bothered to watch it on Tuesday evenings at ten. It came in last in the ratings. Then, as the show changed time slots, first to six on Sunday evenings and then to the seven o'clock Sunday time slot once held by *Lassie*, it slowly began to gain an audience. By the end of the 1975–76 season it had risen halfway up the rankings to reach number 52. Then in the spring of 1977, the show cracked the top twenty, and in another year it was in the top ten. It remained one of America's most popular television shows, a remarkable accomplishment for a program produced by a news division.

Sixty Minutes became a national habit that people talked about on Monday morning. Here one got the story behind the story and experienced a feeling of intimacy with America's most famous people. In 1975, for example, First Lady Betty Ford revealed that she would not be surprised if her unmarried daughter had an affair or smoked marijuana. The show also became famous for its exposés, such as the story of a California doctor accused of swindling his patients or the piece on an enterprise that sent people diplomas in the mail in exchange for money. These stories and others like them resulted in people going to jail. The show delighted in profiling con men and in ambushing unsuspecting people with evidence of their wrongdoing on television.[29]

Always the program offered an entertaining mix of stories. On January 22, 1978, for example, viewers saw a piece on how oil companies made money from the Arab oil embargo, a report on apartment complexes that did not take kids, and a profile of film director Robert Altman. In 1978 Andy Rooney, an experienced reporter and writer, started to offer humorous essays that showed his befuddlement with modern life. These soon became a regular feature at the end of the show.

The public got to know the correspondents and their various styles. The whimsical Morley Safer, confrontational Mike Wallace, the intense Dan Rather, and the wry Harry Reasoner became the television heirs to investigative reporters Carl Bernstein and Bob Woodward of the *Washington Post*.[30] The producers, who were the people who did much of the leg work and actual reporting, remained off camera. Television, unlike the print medium, demanded that a face go with the story. The reporters on *Sixty Minutes* became familiar faces who joined Mary Richards, Archie Bunker and a host of other characters in the nation's living rooms each week.

CONCLUSION

During the seventies television offered a reassuring form of cultural continuity to a nation that sorely needed it. The three networks, for the last time in the nation's history, monopolized the viewer's attention. Although the networks strived hard to be inoffensive and to gain the largest possible audiences, they nonetheless offered programs that reflected the characteristics of the era in which they were broadcast. In the early seventies, programs with topical humor appeared, playing off the situations of single women in the labor force or older married men in declining urban neighborhoods. As the crises of the seventies deepened, the programs took on a more escapist air yet still featured the beneficiaries of the seventies rights revolutions in what for television were new settings. Television itself was the means by which people viewed the political and cultural events of the era. Programs like the local news and *Sixty Minutes* offered entertaining and often compelling coverage of the era's events, creating points of common interest in a nation battered by a bad economy and fragmented among different groups and cultural concerns. Although television never achieved the artistic level of movies in the seventies, it nonetheless served a more important cultural function.

11

The End of the Seventies

The seventies came crashing down on Jimmy Carter's head in 1979. One catalyst was a foreign-policy crisis in Iran that reflected the changed nature of American foreign policy in the seventies. During the Second World War, the United States defended Europe against the Nazis and Asia against the Japanese. In the postwar era, the major causes of confrontation between the United States and the Soviet Union were disputes over the disposition of the countries that had been reclaimed from German and Japanese influence during the war. The United States and the Soviet Union had a long and tense standoff over the fate of Berlin and used proxy nations to wage war in the former Japanese empire. In the seventies, as oil from the Middle East became a more important commodity in the American economy, the locus of the disputes between the United States and Russia shifted to that region.

As in Asia, the Middle Eastern disputes had internal causes, rather than simply being reflections of world geopolitics and political economy. The civil wars in the Middle East concerned battles between modernizers who looked to the west to develop the economies of their nations and traditionalists who wished to preserve Muslim values in those nations. Because of oil, Cold War politics, and the particular concern of the United States for the survival of Israel, these civil wars became matters of international concern. If in the postwar era the United States fought wars in Korea and Vietnam; in the new era that began in the seventies the United States would stage wars in places like Iraq and Kuwait.

TROUBLE IN IRAN

The United States had made the shah of Iran one of its principal regional allies. During Nixon's triumphant trip to Moscow in 1972, he had returned home by means of Iran, so that he could toast the shah and reassure him of his country's continuing support for his regime. Jimmy Carter also went out of his way to visit with the shah and pledge his friendship. Visitors to Iran in the postwar era frequently remarked on its modern, by which they meant western, character. Here was a country of handsome hotels and an educated populace with strong ties to America. Upper-class Iranians flocked to American universities to study subjects such as economics, and Iranians, even Iranian women, wore what westerners perceived as modern dress. The character of Iran appeared to be more like that of Turkey, with its assimilated Muslim population and lax pattern of religious observance, than Saudi Arabia's, whose leaders looked to Americans as though they had just stepped off the set of *Lawrence of Arabia*.

Still, American students and others who went to Iran in the late seventies began to notice a spirit of unrest in that country. Official reporting from such agencies as the CIA, which maintained strong ties to the shah and tended to reflect his point of view, failed to pick up on this trend, but some events were unmistakable. In August 1978, for example, a fire in a movie theater in Abadan left more than 350 people dead and lead to riots and demonstrations across the country. The shah cracked down on dissent and forced violent showdowns with the protestors, one of which resulted in the deaths of as many as 700 people in the heavily westernized capital city of Tehran. At the beginning of 1979 the shah fled to Egypt, and Ruhullah Masaui Khomeini arrived from foreign exile to proclaim an Islamic revolution.

The United States found itself in a position similar to that of the Russians in Afghanistan. A government sympathetic to its interests, one that had received direct support and military aid, served as a buffer against the Soviet Union, and supplied the United States with oil, stood repudiated. The association between the United States and the shah, once a prized asset, became a distinct liability. The United States exacerbated the situation by maintaining its allegiance to the shah until the last minute, making the U.S. a convenient target for the antiwestern, but not procommunist, sentiment that motivated the revolution. Demonstrations against the shah in the old regime became demonstrations against the United States in the new regime. On February 14, 1979, for example, Iranians marched on the American embassy in Tehran and detained the American ambassador. Khomeini repudiated the incident and apologized. On that same day, rebels in Afghanistan seized and ultimately killed the American ambassador, demonstrating how events in Iran were intertwined with events in Afghanistan.

In this unstable atmosphere, Carter made a decision to admit the peripatetic shah into the United States so that he could be treated for cancer. He did so at the urging of many sturdy internationalists with appropriate Cold War credentials such as David Rockefeller, Nelson's brother and the head of the Chase Manhattan Bank, and Henry Kissinger who told him told that, if he refused to do so, the shah would die. Carter believed he had a deal with the Iranians that there would be no retaliatory action if the shah came to the United States only for medical treatment. That understanding paved the way for the shah to enter the country on October 22, 1979. Only a few weeks later, on November 4, Iranian militants again stormed the American embassy, and this time they took what ultimately became sixty-six American hostages. The Iranian prime minister ordered the militants to withdraw from the embassy, but unlike in the previous incident Khomeini refused to back him up. Instead, the prime minister resigned. The hostage crisis, which became a daily story in America until the very end of the Carter administration, had begun.[1]

Carter, faced with a widely publicized incident at the beginning of an election year, had to decide whether the hostage crisis was a matter for diplomacy and international cooperation in the manner of detente or a matter for military action in the manner of the *Mayaguez* incident. It was the quintessential hard choice. Carter knew he did not have much diplomatic leverage against the Iranians; nor did he have easy military options. If he invaded Iran, then the Iranians could simply kill the hostages. At the same time, negotiations with the Iranian militants were perceived as signs of weakness; it was well known, for example, that the Israelis did not negotiate with terrorists and instead sought revenge elsewhere. The situation was further complicated by the fact that it was not clear to the Americans who, if anyone, was in charge of the situation in Iran and just where in Iran the hostages were being held. Nor would the matter simply disappear and be buried by other stories in an election year. Walter Cronkite signed off on his popular nightly news broadcast by reminding Americans how many days had passed since the beginning of the hostage crisis, and ABC began a late night news program that provided a daily recap of events in Iran.

THE KENNEDY MISTAKE

At just that moment, Senator Edward Kennedy decided he would challenge Carter for the Democratic nomination in 1980. In an interview with

Roger Mudd of CBS that aired on Sunday evening, November 4, Kennedy tried to explain why he was running. In the interview, Kennedy spoke in a halting, inarticulate manner, as if he did not quite know why he was in the race. Even worse, the Iranian events overshadowed the Kennedy challenge and allowed Carter to act presidential as he coped with a major foreign-policy crisis.

Carter, confronted by economic and foreign-policy crises and a political challenge from a popular figure within his party, tried to act both responsibly and decisively. In April 1980, he signaled a new willingness to get tough with the Iranians and announced that he was breaking off diplomatic relations with Iran. He also approved a military raid on Iran in order to rescue the hostages. Rather than a full-scale invasion, the raid resembled Ford's popular rescue of the *Mayaguez* crew or, in Cold War parlance, a surgical strike to remove the hostages. The rescue attempt took place on April 25. Since it was earlier in Iran than in the United States, Americans awoke to the news that the rescue attempt had failed. The helicopters involved in the mission had gotten bogged down in the sands of the Iranian desert, and Carter had to call off the mission. It was his version of the Bay of Pigs, and no redemptive Cuban missile crisis was to follow. It was the *Mayaguez* with all of the confusion but without the ultimate prize of the crew.[2] The foreign policy of the United States, already hobbled by the loss of the Vietnam War, appeared to be in total disarray.

It came as a small consolation to Carter that he prevailed in the contest with Kennedy and won the Democratic nomination. Despite his decisive victory, voters signaled their unhappiness with Carter by voting for Kennedy in the primaries once it became clear that Kennedy had no chance of getting the nomination. After a stumbling start, Kennedy won primaries in New York, Connecticut, California, and New Jersey. As the primary season ended in June, Carter gave a joyless speech to his followers at a public square across from the White House. The president seemed tense and withdrawn. When a representative of a labor union that had endorsed the president came up to him and shook his hand, Carter took a step back, as if he were embarrassed by the attention.

At the Democratic convention in New York, Carter did not equal the fine performance he had given at the Kennedy Library in the late fall of 1979. At one point in his acceptance speech, he stopped as an aide whispered something in his ear. At another point, he fumbled over a tribute to Senator Hubert Humphrey, calling him Hubert Horatio Hornblower in an unconscious reference to the novels of C. S. Forester. Adding to Carter's problems, Kennedy never really reconciled with Carter. His speech to the convention roused the delegates far more than Carter's. At the end of the convention, he appeared to be running away from Carter as the president sought to pose with him for a unity photograph on the podium.

THE 1980 ELECTION

Watching on television, Ronald Reagan, claiming his place on the Republican ticket that he had been denied in 1976, realized that the Democrats were a divided party. He pressed his advantage by bringing voters a message of joy, rather than Carter's doom. Jack Kemp, a New York congressman and conservative colleague of Reagan's, captured the spirit of the effort when he said that in the past the Republicans had been "the ones who said to the people, 'Don't come to our table for dinner. All we're going to do is tighten your belt.'"[3] Under the tutelage of Kemp and other post-Goldwater conservatives, the Republicans laid claim to being the growth party and came closer than did Carter to capturing the style and substance of the New Frontier. They were the ones who believed unambiguously in the pursuit of the Cold War and in stimulating the economy through tax cuts. At a debate during the last week of the campaign that clinched his victory, Reagan, an eloquent and composed speaker, looked voters in the eye and asked them if they were better off under Carter than they had been before his presidency. The line resonated with the viewers and gave them hope that things might be better under Reagan.

The election of 1980 closed the era's circle of presidential politics. None of the presidents fared well, and Carter fared worst of all. He had the unwanted honor of being the first president elected to office to lose a bid for reelection since Herbert Hoover and the election of 1932. In the end, Reagan got 51 percent of the popular vote and won every state except for the very short list of Rhode Island, West Virginia, Georgia, Minnesota, and Maryland. Reagan piled up electoral votes from all regions and took back the South and much of the Northeast from Carter.

The Watergate interruption appeared to be over, and the emerging Republican majority, which Nixon had so coveted, became the dominant political force in America. In 1972 Richard Nixon, in gathering a larger percentage of the vote than Reagan, won in a personal but narrow landslide. Reagan took other Republicans with him. The party won as many seats in the House as it did in Nixon's landslide and gained thirteen seats in the Senate, enough to take control of that body for the first time since the election of 1952. Liberals with substantial seniority and national visibility, such as George McGovern and Frank Church, lost their races. Church had been the boy wonder of American politics, first winning his seat in 1956 at the age of thirty-two and getting reelected three consecutive times after that. The election of 1980, unlike the other elections of the 1970s, was, as Barone puts it, "a solid defeat for the Democrats."[4]

THE CONVENTIONAL WISDOM AT THE END OF THE ERA

Before the humiliation of this solid defeat, Jimmy Carter made repeated attempts to try to comprehend what was happening and to take steps to inspire people to work together toward common goals. One of his efforts in this direction consisted of a presidential commission whose task it was to come up with a coherent agenda for the decade ahead. The genesis of this commission was the president's domestic summit in the summer of 1979 that led to his famous address to the American people, which journalist George Will described as President Carter's "lamenting and lamentable 'malaise speech.'"[5] The president invited a group of about fifty distinguished people to join the President's Commission for a National Agenda for the Eighties and asked William McGill, the president of Columbia University, to chair.

In December 1980, after the president had already lost the election to Ronald Reagan, the commission issued its report. Coming as it did at the end of the decade from a group of people who were influential in their respective fields, it neatly embraced the conventional wisdom of the time. It provided a valuable snapshot of how the events of the 1970s had altered the truths of the postwar era. As a central motif, the report emphasized tradeoffs. "We no longer have the luxury of recommending more of the same in a variety of areas," the commissioners wrote. The nation faced instead an era of discontinuity and hard choices in public policy.

The commission also denigrated the ineffective way in which Congress operated. Too many subcommittees considered too many things for too long, inhibiting the passage of needed legislation. The commission noted, for example, that 119 congressional committees and subcommittees and 17 executive departments and agencies had some sort of jurisdiction over the nation's welfare system. It was no wonder that welfare reform was so difficult to achieve, particularly when "the committee structures have helped to lock legislators into a program-by-program view of social policy."[6] No one wanted to part with his pet program.

Having so many committees and subcommittees in Congress increased people's disaffection with government, according to the Carter commission. Its report cited data that showed that the percentage of people who expressed dissatisfaction about the government doubled between the mid-1960s and the late 1970s.[7] The commission wanted to reverse that trend by undoing many of the congressional reforms instituted during the decade. Hence, there should be fewer subcommittees and committees, and there should be more ways for the leadership to get bills through Congress.

The commission also tackled the troubled area of economic policy. The commission noted that during the seventies total output had expanded not because of productivity gains, as in years past, but because of a rapid growth of the labor force. The commission lamented the slowdown in productivity growth and hoped to restore the pattern of postwar economic growth in the decade ahead. At the same time, the commission did not share the confidence in economists as policy advisors that had prevailed for much of the postwar era. It noted that macroeconomic policy should look toward the long term and "should de-emphasize attempts at short-run fine-tuning."[8] Economists, like so many of the experts of the postwar era, had lost much of their allure. The economic misfortunes of the seventies indicated that some new form of wisdom was required.

One notion that the commission endorsed was leaving more economic policy to the natural forces of the market. This view marked another clear challenge to the wisdom of the postwar era. Classic accounts of economic policy from the Populist Era at the end of the nineteenth century to the New Deal and beyond described it as a revolt against laissez-faire. In the post-postwar era, the leaders of American society seemed to be saying that a little laissez-faire might not be a bad thing or, alternatively, that there needed to be a revolt against the revolt against laissez-faire. The regulation of economic activity by means of an expert commission had not produced such salutary results. As the commission's report stated, "economic regulation often retards innovation, productivity, and competition that would normally lead to better service at lower prices." The commission pointed to successful efforts to deregulate the airlines and the brokerage industries.[9]

One area that might benefit from deregulation would be the nation's energy policy. The commission regarded the energy crisis as one of the most important developments of the seventies. It stated flatly that an era had come to an end and the age "of cheap and plentiful oil" was over. The nation somehow needed to find new energy sources or, put another way, go back to older energy sources such as coal. This view implied that the nation could not depend on technology alone to rescue it from its energy dilemma. Whether synthetic fuels could be developed remained an open question. As for nuclear power, the clear favorite of many experts in the postwar era, the commission wrote that "the nuclear option cannot be counted upon to contribute extra power … beyond what is already available and coming on line."[10] There was no technological quick fix to the energy problem. Instead, old-fashioned conservation held the key.

Although the commission embraced many themes that Ronald Reagan would have found congenial, no one paid much attention to its report, coming as it did at the end of an administration that had been soundly defeated in the November elections. People wanted to know what Ronald Reagan would do, not what Carter would have done. Nonetheless, the report did manage to spark some controversy with its recommendations in urban policy. The usual thing for groups associated with the Democratic party to say was that programs needed to be put in place that would help to rebuild the nation's great cities, such as New York, Philadelphia, and Chicago. The commission came up with a different slant and argued that the government should not spend money trying to preserve cities like objects under glass. Cities changed, and the government could make things worse by interfering. Using Darwinian language, the commission noted that "growth and decline are integral parts of the same dynamic process in urban life. When the federal government steps in to alter these dynamics, it generates a flood of demands that may sap the initiatives of urban governments via the expectation of continuing support." So the commission wanted the nation to recognize that New York and Cleveland and their counterparts would never again be thriving nineteenth-century cities and urged that the government help people rather than places. It was better to give a New Yorker money to relocate to the Sun Belt than to throw money at New York in a futile effort to prop up a nonexistent industrial base.

Even after the great urban travails of the seventies, such recommendations still had the power to shock. As the *Washington Post* reported in a page-one story on Christmas Eve, 1980, "the United States must accept the inevitable decline of cities in the Northeast and Midwest and adopt a radically new urban policy that encourages people to move to the expanding sunbelt." The reaction from the nation's mayors was immediate. "Sheer nonsense," said Mayor Richard Hatcher of Gary, one of the decade's new African American urban politicians who did not like the idea of the federal government pulling the plug on the cities just when he and his ethnic group had come to a position of power. The city manager of Cincinnati agreed that the commission's report was "horrible" and deputy commerce director of Philadelphia described it as "intellectual claptrap."

The reaction to the report showed that the seventies had been a painful decade of transition. The previously accepted dogma of urban renewal no longer enjoyed universal acceptance and would undergo a major change in the eighties. In general, the nation no longer possessed the postwar sense of confidence that economic growth and a steady national purpose would set things right in the cities, the suburbs, or elsewhere.

WAITING FOR BILL GATES

Thus the seventies ended on a note of despair and even panic among the sophisticates on the president's commission and among the more common folks who gave up on Jimmy Carter and voted for Ronald Reagan. In time the sense of crisis would lift, but the United States never did return to the conventional wisdom of the postwar era. Ronald Reagan ushered in a long period of Republican ascendancy in which tax cuts to stimulate economic activity and the vigorous prosecution of the Cold War became the order of the day. Although on the surface that development looked like a return to the status quo of the postwar era, with the Republicans taking the place of the Democrats, it was nonetheless different in tone and content. Reagan wanted tax cuts to stimulate the economy, as did President Kennedy, but he did not join the tax cuts to a campaign to have the federal government invest money in the nation's education and healthcare systems. Instead, he pursued a course of deregulation and of enthusiasm for the private market as the best engine of economic growth and the achievement of social goals. To be sure, like Presidents Roosevelt, Truman, Eisenhower, Kennedy, Johnson, Nixon, and Carter, he presided over a measure that strengthened the Social Security system, but he also took steps to arrest the growth of spending for Medicare and made a concerted effort to restrict welfare to the deserving poor. Even when the economy recovered in the period after 1982, there would be no reprise of the New Deal or Great Society. That process stopped in 1973 and never returned in the same form. Reagan was president after the great divide in social policy that occurred in 1974 and separated postwar and modern America.

Reagan also wanted to end what observers called the Vietnam syndrome—the feeling that American intervention in the affairs of other countries was always counterproductive. He was less conflicted than President Carter over the need to confront the Russians in the Third World and elsewhere. At the same time, the Reagan years, despite the military buildup of the times, did not mark a full-scale return to the heyday of the Cold War and American military might. The effects of Vietnam lingered in the preference of politicians for short-term, relatively bloodless military engagements rather than the extended commitments of the Korean and Vietnam Wars. The departure from Vietnam in 1973, another of the era's great divides, ended that style of military combat and, although a later president would involve the United States in what looked to be a long and bloody occupation of Iraq, the United States went out of its way to avoid a Vietnam-style quagmire after the seventies.

Ronald Reagan also presided over what many hailed as the rebirth of the American economy in the 1980s, thus eliminating what had been the major reason for despair during the seventies. Key to this process was the easing of the demographic dilemmas posed by the entrance of the baby boom into the labor force, a momentary freedom from oil shocks, and the clamping down on inflation by the Federal Reserve Board. As it happened, the next great wave of American billionaires was already on the scene in the 1970s, although few people recognized that fact at the time.

The man who would later be identified as the symbol of American wealth made significant gains in the seventies, yet he labored in relative obscurity. Bill Gates was a member of the baby boom, born in 1955 into an upper-middle-class family near Seattle.[11] He attended the Congregational Church, participated in the Boy Scouts, and went to a fancy private school. Despite this background of privilege, he had many of the self-taught characteristics of the other great businessmen-thinkers in American history, such as Henry Ford and Thomas Edison. As with those two Americans, who had helped and admired each other, the life of Bill Gates would become the stuff of admiring biographies that held him up as an example to awe and inspire others. Young Bill Gates and his friend Paul Allen acquired a passion for computers. Because no one at their posh high school knew much about them, they taught themselves how to program. Before graduating from high school, Gates, a mathematical wunderkind who got a perfect score on the math section of the SAT, learned how to put the computer to use in creating the schedule of classes. A project analyzing the flow of Seattle traffic followed, and even before he graduated from high school Gates was earning more than most people made in a year through his computer expertise.

Gates went off to Harvard. His friend Paul Allen took a job with Honeywell and asked to be transferred to Boston to be near Gates. The two became involved in the process of designing software for what would become known as the personal computer. In July 1975, while Gates was still a Harvard student, he and Allen started a company they called Microsoft that would develop computer languages for the microcomputer, as it was then known. Significantly, they began the company not in Boston but in Albuquerque, which was closer to the action in microcomputers. Across the nation, but particularly around Menlo Park, California, the smart kids in math who once carried around slide rules and fooled around with ham radios began to get interested in computers. They formed clubs in which they shared their enthusiasm and exchanged ideas. It was not a visible phenomenon that an industrial-policy enthusiast like Lester Thurow would have noticed, but more of a hobby among people who were far from the social mainstream and did not look to be the advanced cohort for the next stage of capitalism.

In December 1976 Gates dropped out of Harvard to enter this subculture full-time. He moved to Albuquerque to work at Microsoft. The scene resembled a high-tech version of the garage in which Henry Ford and an assistant fiddled around with automobiles in the 1890s. At Microsoft a studied informality infused the atmosphere, and the notion of hierarchy was downplayed. People wandered from one office to another, kept an edge by drinking coffee or Coca-Cola freely provided from a communal refrigerator, and observed no formal hours or many rules. Meanwhile, the environment for the software on which they were working improved with the introduction of more reliable machines such as the Apple II, which appeared in 1977. Late in 1979 the first killer application, as the computer geeks called it, arrived in the form of VisiCalc, a spread sheet that could be used to manage a business.

By that time, Microsoft was already a player in the young industry. In 1977 Microsoft made a half a million dollars in sales. By the middle of 1978, Gates's company had pocketed its first million and had a workforce of thirteen. That year Gates and Allen decided to move the company from Albuquerque to Seattle. By the next year Microsoft sales reached $2.5 million, and Gates and Allen decided to try their hand at what was called application software. On November 6, 1980, Microsoft signed a contract with IBM in which it agreed to supply software for the company's new personal computer. In February 1981, Microsoft ran what it called MS-DOS, a disk operating program, that was used in the IBM PC introduced to the world in the summer of 1981. Everyone who purchased an IBM PC, a product that became wildly popular, or a similar machine, that came to be known as an IBM clone, also purchased a copy of MS-DOS. The software program, available on a floppy disk, became a key structural part of the industry and the avenue to unimagined fame and fortune for Gates.

Bill Gates became the late-twentieth-century version of Henry Ford. Like Ford, he created a company that emerged from the chaos of a crowded market and became a dominant player in a field that did not even exist twenty years before. Nor did the parallels stop there. Gates, like Ford, became known as a progressive employer who rewarded innovative ideas and got the most from his workers by paying them well and giving them good working conditions, although in time he was perceived, as was Ford, as something of a bully who used his competitive advantages unfairly. Just as Ford led the early-twentieth-century economic resurgence from the depression of the 1890s with products such as the Model T, so Gates and his industry helped to pull the nation out of the economic doldrums of the seventies. Just as people grew rich by investing their money in Ford's company—its stock was not publicly traded for many years—so could one have grown rich by buying a piece of Microsoft in the seventies.

Summing Up

So the seventies were the era of economic hardship that also allowed Bill Gates to flourish. They differed from both the self-confident sixties and the swaggering eighties. In the sixties, the children of the baby boom rebelled against the authority of their elders. In an emblematic moment, Benjamin Braddock, in the 1967 movie *The Graduate,* refused to accept an unfulfilled life making money from plastic. For all of his disaffection, though, he was a polite kid who ran on the track team, wore his hair short, had a penchant for sports cars, and dressed neatly. In a pinch he could pass for a kid from the fifties. His successors in the seventies would have longer, less kempt hair, wear far more informal clothes, and be much less polite to their elders.

During the sixties, as Benjamin Braddock graduated from college, the most exclusive colleges remained all-male bastions, as they had since the colonial era.[12] Such male enclaves disappeared forever in the seventies. Gone forever were scenes such as regularly occurred at Princeton University in 1968. A student would bring his date to dinner at the university commons, and as she walked past the rows of tables to take her seat in the high-ceilinged, faux-Gothic room, someone in attendance would call attention to her presence by banging on his glass with his spoon, a custom known as "spooning." Soon everyone would join in, creating a din in the room that rose above the chatter. If a student brought a girl into the dining hall merely to be ostentatious or if the crowd judged a woman to be homely, students sometimes commented on that fact by refraining from spooning. In an all-male environment, women were almost inevitably sex objects.

The seventies, not the sixties, changed that pattern of behavior. Women gained entrance to Princeton, Yale, and many other selective colleges. The very presence of women tended to diminish, if not eliminate, the juvenile high jinks—food and water-balloon fights—that had been so prevalent only a few years before. Perhaps more importantly, the curriculum changed as well. Such fields as women's studies entered the college scene and the notion of gender began to figure seriously in the work of historians and many other academics and intellectuals.

The concern with gender as a category of analysis was an enduring legacy of the seventies. Other artifacts of the era, such as long sideburns and disco dancing, were more ephemeral. The key triggers of the seventies, Watergate, the fall of Vietnam, and the oil shock and economic crises left permanent marks on America, although not quite in the ways perceived by the members of the President's Commission for a National Agenda and other prominent Americans at the time. By 1980, after Watergate, the office of the presidency no longer enjoyed the same level of prestige as it had in the postwar era. That phenomenon turned out to be temporary. Ronald Reagan and Bill Clinton served two full terms, unlike the presidents of the seventies, and, despite Reagan's apparent inattention to details and Clinton's predilection for bimbos, restored the image of the president as a capable leader of America. Yet the seventies nonetheless affected the long-term development of the presidency. Those who held the office were no longer recruited from the ranks of the U.S. Senate. Instead they tended to come from the ranks of the nation's governors.

Vietnam, as already noted, had a long-term effect on U.S. foreign policy. Presidents elected after the seventies repeatedly trumpeted the end of the Vietnam syndrome while all the time worrying that their foreign-policy initiatives would be compared with America's involvement in Vietnam. China, although very much a subject of concern to the architects of the Cold War, reemerged as a central consideration in foreign policy. Once lost, China was again found in the seventies. The Cold War, which lingered, even became reinvigorated, toward the late seventies, ended in the eighties. At the same time, the seeds of future conflicts in the Middle East were clearly visible in Israel, Iran, Afghanistan, and Iraq during the seventies.

As for the oil crises and the notorious problems of stagflation, they, too, turned out be relatively temporary problems, although the oil crisis reasserted itself in the twenty-first century as oil prices once again soared. At the same time, the seventies had a permanent effect on the conventional economic wisdom. Where policymakers once concentrated on the risks of unemployment and deflation, they now turned a watchful eye toward the problem of inflation. Inflation shock motivated many of the economic policies of the eighties and nineties. Such an outlook had a profound effect on how people viewed the efficacy of government spending. What was once regarded as a mainstay of the economy and a source of investment in America's future became in the eighties and nineties the source of now-dreaded government deficits. The seventies, in this regard, reoriented economic thought and increased the acceptability of such things as industrial deregulation, tax cuts at all levels of government, and policies such as managed care in health and personal savings accounts in retirement. After the great divide in social policy of 1974, ambitious federal social programs were off the table, as Jimmy Carter learned when he pushed welfare reform in 1977 and Clinton discovered when he advocated national health insurance in 1993.

The seventies turned out differently than many people expected. As time passed, the era lost its dreary and depressing aura. If the seventies looked dated in a quaint way to new generations of Americans who watched situation comedies about the era on television, they were nonetheless the source of enduring changes. Wide ties went out of fashion, but what Tom Wolfe called "wife shucking" became a permanent part of American life. That development reflected a new and long-lasting informality that remained long after leisure suits became curiosity pieces. Formal institutions, such as marriage, lost some of their sway. Instead, marriages were considered voluntary commitments that, like less-formal living arrangements, could be altered as circumstances changed. That development also reflected the rights revolution that played such an important part of the seventies. As women entered the labor force in record numbers and began to approach parity with men in the workplace, they acquired more say over their living arrangements. Some chose to live alone. Others chose to end their marriages.

Some women decided to form households with other women, not just in the age-old manner of the Boston marriage in which two working women shared a house but as life partners who shared a sexual intimacy. Although homosexuality was not universally accepted in modern America, it nonetheless gained much of its legitimacy during the seventies. In a major paradigm shift, homosexuality went from a malady requiring treatment in the postwar era to a recognized and condoned form of sexual orientation in the seventies. Similarly, people with disabilities hardly existed as a visible group in American life for much of the postwar era. They were cripples or patients or sick people in need of a cure. The rights revolution of the seventies brought a new recognition to people with disabilities as a member of a minority group. No subsequent controversy over special privileges or the costs of the welfare state succeeded in dislodging this impression.

Culturally, the seventies were distinct, as one might expect. Movies enjoyed a renaissance in a momentary lull that allowed directors to gain artistic control over the motion pictures they made. Soon, an all-consuming search for the summer blockbuster would reorient the industry and once again limit the range of creativity. After the seventies, also, people started to watch movies at home, on their television sets. In the seventies, people sat in the dark and watched films that reflected the artistic style of the day but also offered commentaries on contemporary events. One could observe the changing fortunes of white ethnics in America through movies such as *The Godfather*, *Rocky*, and *Saturday Night Fever*. Meanwhile, television, which reached more people, offered a more homogeneous product than the movies. The three networks controlled the airwaves in the era just before the emergence of cable television on a grand scale. They put on the traditional situation comedies, yet even television changed to reflect the new realities of American life, with the result that Americans got to see Mary Tyler Moore as she made her own way in the workforce and Flip Wilson as he brought a black idiom to the venerable variety show.

Patterns of continuity and discontinuity shaped the seventies as they did any era. The unique thing about the seventies was that it marked the end of the conventional postwar wisdom, which was never put together in quite the same way again.

Notes

A Note on the Notes

I have tried in the notes that accompany this book to keep the references to a bare minimum. That practice has meant that the notes are not bibliographic essays on the topics covered by the book, fragments of material cut from the main body of the text, or indications to potential reviewers that I have read their books. They simply list my direct debts to other works.

Readers who want to learn more may want to consult the books in the bibliography, chosen because they were helpful to me and accessible to a general audience. As the bibliography makes clear, there is an abundance of books about various aspects of the seventies.

Two other types of sources should be mentioned. The first is the Internet, which is teeming with information about the seventies. One can find convenient summaries of network-news programs; the biographies of people who have served in Congress; the text of Supreme Court decisions; the texts of Nixon's, Ford's, and Carter's presidential speeches; and much else besides on the Web. It seems to me that historians can no longer afford to ignore this valuable resource, and I have tried to include links to at least some of the major Web sites in the notes.

The second type of source that has proved valuable to me are the many movies and television programs that are on DVD. I have found the commentary on these DVDs to be particularly helpful.

Although the great bulk of the information used in this book comes from secondary sources, such as the ones listed in the notes and bibliography, I have inevitably fallen back on the knowledge I have gained from previous projects and on material from the National Archives, the presidential libraries of Ford and Carter and the presidential materials of Richard Nixon, and the Wisconsin State Historical Society.

INTRODUCTION

1. See *Statistical Abstract of the United States*, annual editions, 1970–1981 (Washington, D.C.: U.S. Bureau of the Census). For a secondary source that collects this data in a convenient table, see Sheryl R. Tynes, *Turning Points in Social Security: From "Cruel Hoax" to "Sacred Entitlement"* (Stanford, Calif.: Stanford University Press, 1996).

2. See Daniel Yergin, *The Prize: The Epic Quest for Oil, Money, and Power* (New York: Simon and Schuster, 1991).

3. See, for example, Becky M. Nicolaides, *My Blue Heaven: Life and Politics in the Working-Class Suburbs of Los Angeles, 1920–1965* (Chicago: University of Chicago Press, 2002); Thomas J. Sugrue, *The Origins of the Urban Crisis: Race and Inequality in Postwar Detroit*, pbk. ed. (Princeton, N.J.: Princeton University Press, 1998).

4. David Farber, *The Age of Great Dreams: America in the 1960s* (New York: Hill and Wang, 1994).

5. Peter N. Carroll, *It Seemed Like Nothing Happened* (New York: Holt, Rinehart, and Winston, 1982; reprint, New Brunswick, N.J.: Rutgers University Press, 1990).

6. Tom Wolfe, *Mauve Gloves and Madmen, Clutter and Vine* (New York: Farrar, Straus and Giroux, 1976).

7. Arthur M. Schlesinger Jr., *The Crisis of the Old Order, 1919–1933* (Boston: Houghton Mifflin Company, 1957).

8. Steven F. Hayward, *The Fall of the Old Liberal Order, 1964–1980* (Roseville, Calif.: Prima Publishing, 2001).

9. On the persistence of conservatism and comments on Trilling and Hofstadter, see the work of Leo P. Ribuffo, including "Conservatism and American Politics," *The Journal of the Historical Society* 3 (Spring 2003): 438–49; "Why Is There So Much Conservatism and Why Do So Few Historians Know Anything About It?" *American Historical Review* 99 (April 1994): 438–49; "The Discovery and Rediscovery of American Conservatism," *OAH Magazine of History* 17 (January 2003): 3–10.

10. David Frum, *How We Got Here: The 70's: The Decade That Brought You Modern Life (For Better Or Worse)* (New York: Basic Books, 2000).

11. Ruth Rosen, *The World Split Open: How the Modern Women's Movement Changed America* (New York: Penguin Books, 2000), 195.

12. Bruce J. Schulman, *The Seventies: The Great Shift in American Culture, Society, and Politics* (New York: Free Press, 2001), xvi–xvii.

13. Carroll, *It Seemed Like Nothing Happened*, 235.

14. Boston Women's Health Book Collective, *Our Bodies, Ourselves: A Book by and for Women* (New York: Simon Schuster, 1971; reprint, 1973), 1.

15. Winifred D. Wandersee, *On the Move: American Women in the 1970s* (Boston: Twayne, 1988), 85, 89.

16. Carroll, *It Seemed Like Nothing Happened*, 240.

17. Roger Bulger to Robert Glaser, October 10, 1975, Institute of Medicine Records, National Academy of Sciences Archives, Washington, D.C.

18. Dr. Lewis Thomas, quoted in Edward D. Berkowitz, *To Improve Human Health: A History of the Institute of Medicine* (Washington, D.C.: National Academy Press, 1998), 61.

19. James T. Patterson, *The Dread Disease: Cancer and Modern American Culture* (Cambridge, Mass.: Harvard University Press, 1987), 256, 279, 263.

20. For an account of this dispute and for all of the quotations see Berkowitz, *To Improve Human Health*, 122–23.

1. Nixon, Watergate, and Presidential Scandal

1. Max Lerner, *Philadelphia Bulletin*, July 13, 1979, quoted in "The White House News Summary," July 17, 1979, Jimmy Carter Library, Atlanta, Georgia.

2. Roger Morris, *Richard Milhous Nixon: The Rise of an American Politician* (New York: Henry Holt, 1990).

3. Richard Nixon, *The Memoirs of Richard Nixon* (New York: Warner Books, 1978), 63–87.

4. Irwin F. Gellman, *The Contender: Richard Nixon: The Congress Years, 1946–1952* (New York: Free Press, 1999).

5. Richard Nixon, *Six Crises* (New York: Doubleday, 1962), 105.

6. For a good, accessible source of information on the 1968 elections and on other presidential elections, see http://www.presidency.ucsb.edu/showelection.php?year=1968.

7. Garry Wills, *Nixon Agonistes: The Crisis of the Self-Made Man* (Boston: Houghton Mifflin, 1970), 267.

8. Bruce J. Schulman, *The Seventies: The Great Shift in American Culture, Society, and Politics* (New York: Free Press, 2001), 35–37.

9. Dan T. Carter, *The Politics of Rage: George Wallace, The Origins of the New Conservatism, and the Transformation of American Politics* (New York: Simon and Schuster, 1995), 424.

10. For more on Muskie, go to http://bioguide.congress.gov/scripts/biodisplay.pl?index=M001121. In general, the website, http://bioguide.congress.gov/biosearch/biosearch.asp, provides an excellent means of finding basic biographical information for anyone who has ever served in Congress. I have used this resource extensively in this book.

11. Winifred D. Wandersee, *On the Move: American Women in the 1970s* (Boston: Twayne, 1988), 22.

12. Carter, *Politics of Rage*, 427.

13. Michael Barone, *Our Country: The Shaping of America from Roosevelt to Reagan* (New York: Free Press, 1990), 507.

14. Barone, *Our Country*, 508.

15. Stanley I. Kutler, *The Wars of Watergate: The Last Crisis of Richard Nixon* (New York: Knopf, 1990), 103.

16. Kim McQuaid, *The Anxious Years: America in the Vietnam and Watergate Era* (New York: Basic Books, 1992).

17. Alfred E. Lewis, "Five Held in Plot to Bug Democrats' Office Here," *Washington Post*, June 18, 1971.

18. Ron Power, *The Newscasters* (New York: St. Martin's Press, 1977), 66.

19. Alicia C. Sheppard, "Off the Record: Glimpses Into the Lives of Woodward and Bernstein from the People Who Know Them Well," *Washingtonian*, September 2003, available online at http://www.washingtonian.com/people/woodward_bernstein.html; "Woodward and Bernstein's Watergate Archive Acquired by the University of Texas at Austin," University of Texas Press Release, April 7, 2003.

20. Bob Woodward and Carl Bernstein, "GOP Security Aide Among Five Arrested in Bugging Affair," *Washington Post*, June 19, 1972.

21. Carl Bernstein and Bob Woodward, "Bug Suspect Got Campaign Funds," *Washington Post*, August 1, 1972.

22. Carl Bernstein and Bob Woodward, "FBI Finds Nixon Aides Sabotaged Democrats," *Washington Post*, October 10, 1972.

23. For a concise overview of Agnew's career, see http://www.angelfire.com/zine2/baltimorehistory/spiroagnew.html. For his resignation, see Richard M. Cohen, *A Heartbeat Away: The Investigation and Resignation of Vice President Spiro T. Agnew* (New York: Viking Press, 1974).

24. Fred Emery, *Watergate: The Corruption and Fall of Richard Nixon* (London: Jonathan Cape, 1994), 225, 241.

25. "Judge John Sirica: Man of the Year," *Time*, January 7, 1974.

26. For the text of this speech, see http://www.watergate.info/nixon/73-04-30watergate-speech.shtml.

27. Laurence Stern and Haynes Johnson, "Three Top Nixon Aides, Kleindienst Out; President Accepts Full Responsibility; Richardson Will Conduct New Probe," *Washington Post*, May 1, 1973.

28. Emery, *Watergate*, 359.

29. Carl Bernstein and Bob Woodward, "Dean Alleges Nixon Knew of Cover-Up Plans," *Washington Post*, June 3, 1973; Bob Woodward and Carl Bernstein, "Break-In Memo Sent to Ehrlichman," *Washington Post*, June 13, 1973.

30. To hear Dean say this, go to http://www.watergate.info/sounds/dean-cancer-on-the-presidency.ram.

31. Peter N. Carroll, *It Seemed Like Nothing Happened* (New York: Holt, Rinehart, and Winston, 1982; reprint, New Brunswick, N.J.: Rutgers University Press, 1990), 145.

32. Richard Nixon, "Address to the Nation," August 15, 1973, available at http://www.watergate.info/nixon/73-08-15watergate-speech.shtml.

33. Carroll Kirkpatrick, "Nixon Forces Firing of Cox; Richardson, Ruckelhaus Quit," *Washington Post*, October 21, 1973; Jules Witcover, "Pressure for Impeachment Mounting," *Washington Post*, October 21, 1973; McQuaid, *The Anxious Years.*

34. For transcripts of the network-news broadcasts here and throughout I have relied on the materials in the Television News Archives, Vanderbilt University, Nashville, Tennessee. The archives also maintains an excellent Web site that allows the researcher to look at a summary of each evening's broadcast on each of the major networks.

35. Carroll Kirkpatrick, "Nixon Tells Editors, 'I'm Not a Crook,'" *Washington Post*, November 18, 1973.

36. George Lardner Jr., "Haig Tells of Theories of Erasure," *Washington Post*, December 7, 1973.

37. Richard Nixon, "Address on the State of the Union Delivered before a Joint Session of the Congress," January 30, 1974, in *Public Papers of President Richard Nixon, 1974* (Washington, D.C.: Government Printing Office, 1975), available through the Richard Nixon Library online at http://www.nixonlibrary.org/Research_Center/PublicPapers.cfm?BookSelected=1974#P6_76.

38. Richard Nixon, "Address to the Nation Announcing Answer to the House Judiciary Committee Subpoena for Additional Presidential Tape Recordings," April 29, 1974, *Public Papers of President Richard Nixon, 1974.*

39. Haynes Johnson, "President Hands Over Transcripts; Initial Reaction on Hill Divided Along Party Lines," *Washington Post*, May 1, 1974.

40. Harold Rosenberg, "Up Against the News," *New York Review of Books*, October 31, 1974.

41. Quoted in John A. Farrell, *Tip O'Neill and the Democratic Century* (Boston: Little Brown, 2001), 369.

42. Richard Nixon, "Remarks on Departure from the White House," August 9, 1974, *Public Papers of President Richard Nixon, 1974.*

2. VIETNAM AND ITS CONSEQUENCES

1. Walter Isaacson, *Kissinger: A Biography* (New York: Simon and Schuster, 1992), 239.

2. Peter N. Carroll, *It Seemed Like Nothing Happened* (New York: Holt, Rinehart, and Winston, 1982; reprint, New Brunswick, N.J.: Rutgers University Press, 1990), 4.

3. Robert Dallek, *Flawed Giant: Lyndon Johnson and His Times, 1961–1973* (New York: Oxford University Press, 1998), 459.

4. Martin Luther King, "Beyond Vietnam: A Time to Break the Silence," April 4, 1967, Riverside Chapel, New York, text available at http://www.hartford-hwp.com/archives/45a/058.html.

5. Seymour Hersh, *My Lai 4: A Report on the Massacre and Its Aftermath* (New York: Random House, 1970), 48–75.

6. Tom Johnson, "Notes of Meeting," March 26, 1968, Lyndon Johnson Presidential Library, Austin, Texas; available online at http://www.state.gov/r/pa/ho/frus/johnsonlb/vi/13703.htm.

7. Isaacson, *Kissinger*, 160.

8. Isaacson, *Kissinger*, 176.

9. Richard Nixon, "Address to the Nation on the Situation in Southeast Asia," April 30, 1970, item 139, *Public Papers of President Richard Nixon, 1970* (Washington, D.C.: Government Printing Office, 1971).

10. See, for example, the transcript of the NBC News broadcast for April 1, 1970, with Chet Huntley reporting on international reaction and Paul Duke reporting on the congressional reaction (transcript available from Television News Archives, Vanderbilt University).

11. See, for example, David Brinkley's report on the NBC Nightly News broadcast for May 4, 1970.

12. Vincent J. Cannato, *The Ungovernable City: John Lindsay and His Struggle to Save New York* (New York: Basic Books, 2001), 448.

13. "The President's News Conference of May 8, 1970," item 144, *Public Papers of President Richard Nixon, 1970* (Washington, D.C.: Government Printing Office, 1971).

14. Ronald L. Ziegler, "News Conference," 9:04 am, Saturday, May 9, 1970, addendum to May 8, 1970, press conference, in *Public Papers of President Richard Nixon, 1970* (Washington, D.C.: Government Printing Office, 1971). Bob Schieffer report on CBS Evening News, Sunday, May 10, 1970, Television News Archives, Vanderbilt University.

15. H. R. Haldeman, *The Haldeman Diaries: Inside the Nixon White House* (New York: Putnam, 1994), 163.

16. Richard Nixon, "Address to the Nation on the Situation in Southeast Asia," May 8, 1972, item 147, *Public Papers of President Richard Nixon, 1972* (Washington, D.C.: Government Printing Office, 1973); Dale Andrade, *America's Last Vietnam Battle: Halting Hanoi's Easter 1972 Offensive* (Lawrence: University Press of Kansas, 1995).

17. Isaacson, *Kissinger*, 439–40.

18. Raymond L. Garthoff, *Detente and Confrontation: American-Soviet Relations from Nixon to Reagan* (Washington, D.C.: Brookings Institution, 1985) 260; Richard Nixon, "Address to the Nation Announcing Conclusion of an Agreement on

Ending the War and Restoring Peace in Vietnam," January 23, 1973, item 12, *Public Papers of President Richard Nixon, 1973* (Washington, D.C.: Government Printing Office, 1974).

19. Richard Nixon and Henry Kissinger, quoted in Robert M. Collins, *More: The Politics of Economic Growth in Postwar America* (New York: Oxford University Press, 2000), 108, 105.

20. Garthoff, *Detente and Confrontation*, 229.

21. Garthoff, *Detente and Confrontation*, 200, 214.

22. Garthoff, *Detente and Confrontation*, 231.

23. Richard Nixon, "Remarks to the Nation Announcing Acceptance of an Invitation to Visit the People's Republic of China," July 15, 1971, item 231, *Public Papers of President Richard Nixon, 1971* (Washington: Government Printing Office, 1972).

24. "Memorandum of Conversation, [Nixon-Mao Meeting] Chairman Mao's Residence, Peking," February 21, 1972, TOP SECRET, National Security Archives, Washington, D.C.

25. "Joint Statement Following Discussion with Leader of the People's Republic of China," February 27, 1972, item 71, *Public Papers of President Richard Nixon, 1972* (Washington, D.C.: Government Printing Office, 1973); Stephen Ambrose, *Nixon: The Education of a Politician, 1913–1962* (New York: Simon and Schuster, 1987), 513.

26. Henry Kissinger, *White House Years* (New York: Little Brown, 1979), 1092.

27. Garthoff, *Detente and Confrontation*, 255.

28. Message, White House to U.S. Liaison Office, Peking, August 9, 1974, National Security Archives, Washington, D.C.

29. Burton I. Kaufman, *The Presidency of James Earl Carter* (Lawrence: University of Kansas Press, 1993), 129.

30. Isaacson, *Kissinger*, 500.

31. Stanley Karnow, "Changing (Mis)Conceptions of China," in *The American Image of China*, ed. Benson Lee Grayson (New York: Frederick Ungar, 1979), 286; originally published as "China Through Rose-Tinted Glasses," *Atlantic Monthly* (October 1973): 73–76,

32. Garthoff, *Detente and Confrontation*, 24.

33. Garthoff, *Detente and Confrontation*, 71–73.

34. "Chronology of Visit to Austria, the Soviet Union, Iran, and Poland," May 20–June 1, 1972, item 162A, *Public Papers of President Richard Nixon, 1972* (Washington, D.C.: Government Printing Office, 1973).

35. Isaacson, *Kissinger*, 425.

36. Richard Nixon, "Radio and Television Address to the People of the Soviet Union," May 28, 1972, item 176, *Public Papers of President Richard Nixon, 1972* (Washington, D.C.: Government Printing Office, 1973).

37. Reports by John Chancellor and Rebecca Bell, NBC Nightly News, May 28, 1972, Vanderbilt Television News Archives.

38. "Text of the 'Basic Principles of Relations Between the United States of America and the Union of Soviet Socialist Republics,'' May 29, 1972, item 177, *Public Papers of President Richard Nixon, 1972* (Washington, D.C.: Government Printing Office, 1973).

39. Reports from Walter Cronkite and Roger Mudd, CBS Evening News, May 29, 1972, Vanderbilt Television News Archives; Garthoff, *Detente and Confrontation*, 289.

40. Report by Roger Mudd on CBS Evening News, June 19, 1973, Vanderbilt Television News Archives; report by John Chancellor on NBC Nightly News, June 19, 1973, Vanderbilt Television News Archives.

41. Report from Ron Nessen, NBC Nightly News, June 24, 1973, Vanderbilt News Archives.

42. Report from Alvin Rosenfeld, NBC Nightly News, June 25, 1973, Vanderbilt News Archive.

43. Report from Marvin Kalb, CBS Evening News, June 25, 1973, Vanderbilt News Archives.

44. Garthoff, *Detente and Confrontation*, 377.

45. Isaacson, *Kissinger*, 516.

46. Richard Nixon, "Address to the Nation on Returning from the Soviet Union," July 3, 1974, item 211, *Public Papers of President Richard Nixon, 1974* (Washington, D.C.: Government Printing Office, 1975).

47. John Robert Greene, *The Presidency of Gerald R. Ford* (Lawrence: University Press of Kansas, 1995) p. 140.

48. Isaacson, *Kissinger*, 488.

49. Greene, *The Presidency of Gerald R. Ford*, 104.

50. Isaacson, *Kissinger*, 488.

3. Running Out of Gas

1. I am grateful to Betsy Blackmar of Columbia University for pointing these things out to me and to my colleague William H. Becker, on whose paper "Lean and Mean," delivered to the faculty of Singapore University, I have relied heavily.

2. Michael A. Bernstein, "Understanding American Economic Decline: The Contours of the Late Twentieth-Century Experience," in *Understanding American Economic Decline*, ed. Michael A. Bernstein and David E. Adler (New York: Cambridge University Press, 1994), 17.

3. David M. Gordon, "Chickens Home to Roost: From Prosperity to Stagnation in the Postwar U.S. Economy," in *Understanding American Economic Decline*, ed. Michael A. Bernstein and David E. Adler (New York: Cambridge University Press, 1994), 44.

4. Gordon, "Chickens Home to Roost," 42; W. Carl Biven, *Jimmy Carter's Economy: Policy in an Age of Limits* (Chapel Hill: University of North Carolina Press, 2002), 113–14.

5. Gordon, "Chickens Home to Roost," 42.

6. Ezra F. Vogel, *Japan as Number One: Lessons for America* (Cambridge, Mass.: Harvard University Press, 1979), 9.

7. John Updike, *Rabbit Is Rich* (New York: Knopf, 1981), 3–4.

8. Group Interview of the Council of Economic Advisors, Oral History Collection, John F. Kennedy Library, Boston, Massachusetts; Herbert Stein, *The Fiscal Revolution in America* (Chicago: University of Chicago Press, 1969).

9. Aaron Wildavsky and Naomi Caider, *The New Politics of the Budgetary Process*, 4th ed. (Boston: Addison Wesley, 2000).

10. Quoted by Paul Light in "The Politics of Assumptions," unpublished paper. See also Paul Light, *Artful Work: The Politics of Social Security Reform* (New York: Random House, 1985), 50.

11. Herbert Stein, *Presidential Economics* (Washington, D.C.: AEI Press, 1994).

12. Robert M. Collins, *More: The Politics of Economic Growth in Postwar America* (New York: Oxford University Press, 2000). 118; Allen J. Matusow, *Nixon's Economy: Booms, Busts, Dollars, and Values* (Lawrence: University Press of Kansas, 1998).

13. Collins, *More*, 127; Matusow, *Nixon's Economy*, 214–75.

14. Daniel Yergin, *The Prize: The Epic Quest for Oil, Money, and Power* (New York: Simon and Schuster, 1991), 567.

15. Matusow, *Nixon's Economy*, 241–75.

16. Yergin, *The Prize*, 591, 605.

17. Peter N. Carroll, *It Seemed Like Nothing Happened* (New York: Holt, Rinehart, and Winston, 1982; reprint, New Brunswick, N.J.: Rutgers University Press, 1990), 117–18.

18. Richard M. Nixon, "Address to the Nation About Policies to Deal with the Energy Shortages," November 7, 1973, reprinted in Senate Committee on Energy and Natural Resources, *Executive Summary Documents* (Washington, D.C.: Government Printing Office, 1978), 81–93.

19. Biven, *Jimmy Carter's Economy*, 256–57.

20. Lester C. Thurow, *The Zero-Sum Society: Distribution and the Possibilities for Economic Change* (New York: Basic Books, 1980), 87.

21. Thurow, *Zero-Sum Society*, 87; Bernstein, "Understanding American Economic Decline," 20.

22. Winifred D. Wandersee, *On the Move: American Women in the 1970s* (Boston: Twayne, 1988), 127; Ralph E. Smith, "The Movement of Women into the Labor Force," in *The Subtle Revolution*, ed. Smith (Washington, D.C.: Urban Institute, 1979), 1–30.

23. Michael Barone, *Our Country: The Shaping of America from Roosevelt to Reagan* (New York: Free Press, 1990), 564.

24. Gordon, "Chickens Home to Roost," 45.

25. Paul Light, *Baby Boomers* (New York: W. W. Norton, 1988).

26. Richard A. Easterlin, *Birth and Fortune: The Impact of Numbers on Personal Welfare* (Chicago: University of Chicago Press, 1987).

27. Jefferson Cowie et al., eds., *Beyond the Ruins: The Meanings of Deindustrialization* (Ithaca, N.Y.: Cornell University Press, 2003).

28. D. C. Bissell, *The First Conglomerate: 145 Years of the Singer Sewing Company* (New York: Biddle, 1999).

29. Katherine S. Newman, "Troubled Times: The Cultural Dimension of Economic Decline," in *Understanding American Economic Decline*, ed. Michael A. Bernstein and David E. Adler (New York: Cambridge University Press, 1994), 336.

4. THE FRUSTRATIONS OF GERALD FORD

1. John Robert Greene, *The Presidency of Gerald R. Ford* (Lawrence: University Press of Kansas, 1995), 57.

2. Robert T. Hartman, *Palace Politics: An Inside Account of the Ford Years* (New York: McGraw-Hill, 1980), 240.

3. Greene, *Presidency of Gerald Ford*, 53.

4. Greene, *Presidency of Gerald Ford*, 62.

5. Gerald R. Ford, "Remarks Upon Returning from Japan, the Republic of Korea, and the Soviet Union," November 24, 1974, item 259, *The Public Papers of President Gerald Ford, 1974* (Washington, D.C.: Government Printing Office, 1975); Ford, "Joint United States–Soviet Statement on the Limitation of Strategic Offensive Arms," November 24, 1974, item 257, *The Public Papers of President Gerald Ford, 1974* (Washington, D.C.: Government Printing Office, 1975).

6. Raymond L. Garthoff, *Detente and Confrontation: American-Soviet Relations from Nixon to Reagan* (Washington, D.C.: Brookings Institution, 1985), 544.

7. Robert G. Kaufman, *Henry M. Jackson: A Life in Politics* (Seattle: University of Washington Press, 2000), 296.

8. Godfrey Hodgson, *The Gentleman from New York: Daniel Patrick Moynihan* (Boston: Houghton Mifflin Company, 2000), 240.

9. Kaufman, *Jackson*, 248.

10. Walter Isaacson, *Kissinger: A Biography* (New York: Simon and Schuster, 1992), 239.

11. Garthoff, *Detente and Confrontation*, 327.

12. Garthoff, *Detente and Confrontation*, 356, 357, 402, 455, 461.

13. James Reston, " 'Twas a Famous Victory' " *New York Times*, May 16, 1975.

14. Peter N. Carroll, *It Seemed Like Nothing Happened* (New York: Holt, Rinehart, and Winston, 1982; reprint, New Brunswick, N.J.: Rutgers University Press,

1990), 167; Greene, *Presidency of Gerald Ford*, 143–48; Richard Neustadt and Ernest May, *Thinking in Time* (New York: Free Press, 1988), 63.

15. Robert M. Collins, *More: The Politics of Economic Growth in Postwar America* (New York: Oxford University Press, 2000), 155.

16. Daniel Yergin, *The Prize: The Epic Quest for Oil, Money, and Power* (New York: Simon and Schuster, 1991), 646, 657.

17. Gerald Ford, "Speech to the Nation on Domestic Policy," January 13, 1975, *Public Papers of President Gerald Ford, 1975* (Washington, D.C.: Government Printing Office, 1976), available online at http://www.presidency.ucsb.edu/ws/index.php?pid=4916&st=&st1=.

18. Gerald Ford, "Statement on the Energy Policy and Conservation Act," December 22, 1975; Ford, "Remarks Upon Signing the Energy Policy and Conservation Act," December 22, 1975, *Public Papers of President Gerald Ford, 1975*, available online at http://www.presidency.ucsb.edu/ws/index.php?pid=5451&st=&st1=; Yergin, *The Prize*, 660; W. Carl Biven, *Jimmy Carter's Economy: Policy in an Age of Limits* (Chapel Hill: University of North Carolina Press, 2002), 155–56.

19. Greene, *Presidency of Gerald Ford*, 161–170.

20. Greene, *Presidency of Gerald Ford*, 190.

21. Jimmy Carter, "Inaugural Address of President Jimmy Carter Following His Swearing in as the 39th President of the United States," January 20, 1977, in *Public Papers of the Presidents, 1977* (Washington, D.C.: Government Printing Office, 1978), available online at http://www.presidency.ucsb.edu/ws/index.php?pid=6575.

5. CONGRESS AND DOMESTIC POLICY IN THE AGE OF GERALD FORD

1. Philip Lee, interview by author, November 27, 1995, Washington, D.C., Health Care Financing Administration Oral History Collection.

2. Quoted in Edward Berkowitz, "The Burleson-McIntyre Bill," report prepared for the Health Insurance Association of America, May 1992. For more on the health insurance politics of this period, see Paul Starr, *The Social Transformation of American Medicine* (New York: Basic Books, 1982).

3. Edward D. Berkowitz, "History and Social Security Reform," in *Social Security and Medicare: Individual Versus Collective Risk and Responsibility*, ed. Sheila Burke, Eric Kingson, and Uwe Reinhardt (Washington, D.C.: National Academy of Social Insurance, 2000), 42–47.

4. I base this account of the Kennedy-Mills bill on Edward D. Berkowitz, *Robert Ball and the Politics of Social Security* (Madison: University of Wisconsin Press, 2003), chapter 6.

5. "New Health Bill Aids Prospect for '74 Passage," *Wall Street Journal*, April 3, 1974; "Health Plan Progress," *New York Times*, April 7, 1974; "National Health Insurance," *Washington Post*, April 8, 1974, Robert Ball Papers, Wisconsin State His-

torical Society, Madison, Wisconsin; Richard D. Lyons, "What Can Be Expected from Health Insurance," *New York Times*, April 7, 1974, Ball Papers.

6. "Statement by the AFL-CIO Executive Council on The Mills-Kennedy Bill," May 9, 1974, attached to Larry Smedley to Bob Ball, May 30, 1974, Ball Papers.

7. Berkowitz, *Robert Ball.*

8. John A. Farrell, *Tip O'Neill and the Democratic Century* (Boston: Little Brown, 2001) 406–7; Report from Roger Mudd, CBS Evening News, December 2, 1974, Television News Archives, Vanderbilt University.

9. James McGregor Burns, *The Deadlock of Democracy*, quoted in Edward Berkowitz, "The Great Society," in *The Reader's Companion to the American Congress*, ed. Julian Zelizer (New York: Scribners, 2004).

10. Julian E. Zelizer, *Taxing America: Wilbur D. Mills, Congress, and the State, 1945–1975* (New York: Cambridge University Press, 1998), 40.

11. James L. Sundquist, *The Decline and Resurgence of Congress* (Washington, D.C.: The Brookings Institution, 1981), 378.

12. John Jacobs, *A Rage for Justice: The Passion and Politics of Phillip Burton* (Berkeley: University of California Press, 1995), 242.

13. Sundquist, *Decline and Resurgence*, 382.

14. Michael Barone, *Our Country: The Shaping of America from Roosevelt to Reagan* (New York: Free Press, 1990), 533.

15. David S. Broder, *Changing of the Guard: Power and Leadership in America* (New York: Simon and Schuster, 1980), 34–36.

16. Farrell, *Tip O'Neill and the Democratic Century*, 385.

17. Farrell, *Tip O'Neill and the Democratic Century*, 399–400; Broder, *Changing of the Guard*, 54; Jacobs, *A Rage for Justice*, 267.

18. Jacobs, *A Rage for Justice*, 268.

19. Sundquist, *Decline and Resurgence of Congress*, 380; Farrell, *Tip O'Neill and the Democratic Century*, 401; for the quotation see the material that accompanies Poage's collection of papers at Baylor University, available on the Web at http://www3.baylor.edu/Library/BCPM/Poage/poage_retire.htm.

20. Farrell, *Tip O'Neill and the Democratic Century*, 401.

21. Sundquist, *Decline and Resurgence of Congress*, 403.

22. Sundquist, *Decline and Resurgence of Congress*, 408.

23. Farrell, *Tip O'Neill and the Democratic Century*, 420.

24. Dan Rostenkowski, interview by author, Chicago, Illinois, November 22, 2003, Centers for Medicare and Medicaid Services Web site, http://www.cms.hhs.gov/about/history/Rostenkowski.asp; Farrell, *Tip O'Neill and the Democratic Century*, 420.

25. Sundquist, *Decline and Resurgence of Congress*, 324.

26. Sundquist, *Decline and Resurgence of Congress*, 334.

27. Wilbur Cohen, "Reflections on the Enactment of Medicare and Medicaid," *Health Care Financing Review* 1983 Annual Supplement, 3.

28. Barone, *Our Country*, 566.

29. Thomas J. Sugrue, "Carter's Urban Policy Crisis," in *The Carter Presidency Policy Choices in the Post–New Deal Era*, ed. Gary M. Fink and Hugh Davis Graham (Lawrence: University Press of Kansas, 1998), 145.

30. Barone, *Our Country*, 566.

31. Robert T. Hartman, *Palace Politics: An Inside Account of the Ford Years* (New York: McGraw-Hill, 1980), 354–55.

32. John Robert Greene, *The Presidency of Gerald R. Ford* (Lawrence: University Press of Kansas, 1995), 90–93.

33. Farrell, *Tip O'Neill and the Democratic Century*, 401.

34. Marion Clark and Rudy Maxa, "Closed Session Romance on the Hill: Rep. Wayne Hays' $14,000-a-Year Clerk Says She's His Mistress," *Washington Post*, May 23, 1976.

6. JIMMY CARTER AND THE GREAT AMERICAN REVIVAL

1. Burton I. Kaufman, *The Presidency of James Earl Carter* (Lawrence: University of Kansas Press, 1993). I am also grateful to Leo Ribuffo for sharing his thoughts on Carter's prepresidential life with me.

2. Jules Witcover, *Marathon: The Pursuit of the Presidency, 1972–1976* (New York: Viking Press, 1977), 109.

3. Michael Barone, *Our Country: The Shaping of America from Roosevelt to Reagan* (New York: Free Press, 1990), 546–47.

4. R. W. Apple Jr., "Carter Appears to Hold a Solid Lead in Iowa as the Campaign's First Test Approaches," *New York Times*, October 27, 1975.

5. For a succinct analysis of the 1976 campaign, see Charles O. Jones, *The Trustee Presidency: Jimmy Carter and the United States Congress* (Baton Rouge: Louisiana State University Press, 1988), 20, 31.

6. John Robert Greene, *The Presidency of Gerald R. Ford* (Lawrence: University Press of Kansas, 1995), 181; Barone, *Our Country*, 555.

7. Witcover, *Marathon*, 271–72.

8. The transcript of the Carter-Ford debate is available on the Web at http://www.pbs.org/newshour/debatingourdestiny/76debates/2_b.html.

9. Greene, *The Presidency of Gerald R. Ford*, 187; Barone, *Our Country*, 556–57.

10. Jimmy Carter, *Why Not the Best?* (Fayetville: University of Arkansas Press, 1996), 89–90.

11. Jimmy Carter, "Inaugural Address," quoted in Jones, *The Trustee Presidency*, 125.

12. See the coverage in the *Washington Post*, February 4, 1977.

13. Quoted in the *New York Times*, September 12, 1977.

14. Gilbert Steiner, *The Futility of Family Policy* (Washington, D.C.: Brookings Institution, 1981).

15. Quoted in James T. Patterson, "Jimmy Carter and Welfare Reform," in *The Carter Presidency: Policy Choices in the Post–New Deal Era*, ed. Gary M. Fink and Hugh Davis Graham (Lawrence: University Press of Kansas, 1998), 125.

16. Laurence Lynn Jr. and David Whitman, *The President as Policymaker: Jimmy Carter and Welfare Reform* (Philadelphia: Temple University Press, 1981).

17. John A. Farrell, *Tip O'Neill and the Democratic Century* (Boston: Little Brown, 2001), 446.

18. Patterson, "Jimmy Carter and Welfare Reform," 123.

19. Wilbur Cohen, quoted in Edward D. Berkowitz, *Mr. Social Security: The Life of Wilbur J. Cohen* (Lawrence: University Press of Kansas, 1995), 301.

20. Melvyn Dubosky, "Jimmy Carter and the End of the Politics of Productivity," in *The Carter Presidency: Policy Choices in the Post–New Deal Era*, ed. Gary M. Fink and Hugh Davis Graham (Lawrence: University Press of Kansas, 1998), 97.

21. Cecil Adams, "What Was the Deal with Jimmy Carter and the Killer Rabbit?" in *The Straight Dope*, syndicated column, November 10, 1995, available on the Web at http://www.straightdope.com/classics/a4_019.html.

22. Raymond L. Garthoff, *Detente and Confrontation: American-Soviet Relations from Nixon to Reagan* (Washington, D.C.: Brookings Institution, 1985), 608, 611.

23. Kaufman, *The Presidency of James Earl Carter*, 95.

24. Garthoff, *Detente and Confrontation*, 730, 732.

25. Garthoff, *Detente and Confrontation*, 742.

26. Jerry Rafshoon, "Memorandum to the President," July 10, 1979, Speechwriters, Chronological, box 50, Jimmy Carter Presidential Library.

27. Robert M. Collins, *More: The Politics of Economic Growth in Postwar America* (New York: Oxford University Press, 2000), 159.

28. Garthoff, *Detente and Confrontation*, 898.

29. Garthoff, *Detente and Confrontation*, 942–48.

30. Garthoff, *Detente and Confrontation*, 976.

31. W. Carl Biven, *Jimmy Carter's Economy: Policy in an Age of Limits* (Chapel Hill: University of North Carolina Press, 2002), 232.

32. Ezra F. Vogel, *Japan as Number One: Lessons for America* (Cambridge, Mass.: Harvard University Press, 1979), 9.

33. Judith Stein, *Running Steel, Running America: Race, Economic Policy, and the Decline of Liberalism* (Chapel Hill: University of North Carolina Press, 1998), 235.

34. Office of Strategic Research, Ohio Department of Development, "Population of Ohio and Ohio's Top Ten Cities, 1800 to 1990" (Columbus, 1995).

35. Stein, *Running Steel, Running America*, 241; report from Bob Kur, NBC News, September 20, 1977; Report from Jerry Bowen, CBS News, September 20, 1977, Television News Archives, Vanderbilt University.

36. Sherry Lee Linkon and John Russo, *Steeltown USA: Work and Memory in Youngstown* (Lawrence: University Press of Kansas, 2003).

37. Staughton Lynd, *Fight Against Shutdown: Youngstown's Steel Mill Closings* (New York: Singlejack Books, 1982).

38. Biven, *Jimmy Carter's Economy*, 61, 72, 82.

39. Margaret Weir, *Politics and Jobs: The Boundaries of Employment Policy in the United States* (Princeton, N.J.: Princeton University Press, 1992).

40. Biven, *Jimmy Carter's Economy*, 200.

41. Biven, *Jimmy Carter's Economy*, 134.

42. Biven, *Jimmy Carter's Economy*, 138.

43. "The Daily Diary of President Jimmy Carter," October 24, 1978, Jimmy Carter Library, Atlanta, Georgia.

44. Jimmy Carter, "Anti-Inflation Program," October 24, 1978, *Vital Speeches of the Day* 45, no. 3 (November 15, 1978): 66–69.

45. Stu Eizenstat to the president, June 28, 1979, Handwriting Files, Box 137, Jimmy Carter Library.

46. John Updike, *Rabbit Is Rich* (New York: Knopf, 1981), 3.

47. Biven, *Jimmy Carter's Economy*, 244.

48. President's Commission for a National Agenda for the Eighties, *A National Agenda for the Eighties* (New York: New American Library, 1981).

49. John C. Barrow, "An Age of Limits: Jimmy Carter and the Quest for a National Energy Policy" in *The Carter Presidency: Policy Choices in the Post–New Deal Era*, ed. Gary M. Fink and Hugh Davis Graham (Lawrence: University Press of Kansas, 1998), 161.

50. Jimmy Carter, "The Energy Problem," April 18, 1977, *Public Papers of the President, 1977* (Washington, D.C.: Government Printing Office, 1978), available from http://www.presidency.ucsb.edu/ws/index.php?pid=7369&st=&st1=.

51. Biven, *Jimmy Carter's Economy*, 163.

52. Kaufman, *Presidency of James Earl Carter*, 135–38; Daniel Yergin, *The Prize: The Epic Quest for Oil, Money, and Power* (New York: Simon and Schuster, 1991), 639.

53. Biven, *Jimmy Carter's Economy*, 83, 85; Peter N. Carroll, *It Seemed Like Nothing Happened* (New York: Holt, Rinehart, and Winston, 1982; reprint, New Brunswick, N.J.: Rutgers University Press, 1990), 218.

54. "The Daily Diary of President Jimmy Carter," April 5, 1979, Jimmy Carter Library, Atlanta, Georgia.

55. Biven, *Jimmy Carter's Economy*, 76; for the diary item, see http://www.geocities.com/stuckinthe70s/april79.htm.

56. Yergin, *The Prize*, 694.

57. Kaufman, *Presidency of James Earl Carter*, 143; Achsah Nesmith, Walter Shapiro, Gordon Steward to Jerry Rafshoon and Rick Hertzberg, "Energy Speech," June 29, 1979, Speechwriters Chronological Files, box 50, Jimmy Carter Presidential Library, Atlanta, Georgia; Jerry Rafshoon, "Memorandum to the President," July

10, 1979, Speechwriters Chronological Files, box 50, Jimmy Carter Presidential Library, Atlanta, Georgia.

58. Jimmy Carter, "Energy and National Goals," July 15, 1979, *Public Papers of the Presidents of the United States, Jimmy Carter, 1979*, book 2 (Washington, D.C.: Government Printing Office, 1979), 1235–41.

59. Daniel Bell to Patrick Caddell, August 28, 1979, Daniel Bell Papers, cited in Daniel Horowitz, *Jimmy Carter and the Energy Crisis of the 1970s* (New York: Bedford/St. Martin's, 2005), 152.

7. THE RIGHTS REVOLUTION

1. I am grateful to Emily Frank, associate dean of students at the Peabody Institute of Johns Hopkins University, for bringing this story to my attention.

2. I am grateful to Kathy Fella for providing me with this information.

3. I am grateful to Ms. Frances Kleeman, a teacher in this school, who provided me with copies of the yearbooks, known as the *Horizon* after 1972, for Randallstown High School, from which I have developed the following section.

4. *Time*, January 21, 1966, 21, quoted in John D'Emilio, *Sexual Politics, Sexual Communities: The Making of a Homosexual Minority in the United States, 1940–1970* (Chicago: University of Chicago Press, 1983), 138.

5. Quoted in D'Emilio, *Sexual Politics*, 155.

6. Bruce J. Schulman, *The Seventies: The Great Shift in American Culture, Society, and Politics* (New York: Free Press, 1971), 159.

7. Rosalind Rosenberg, *Divided Lives: American Women in the Twentieth Century* (New York: Hill and Wang, 1992), 168.

8. Rosenberg, *Divided Lives*, 192–93; Ruth Rosen, *The World Split Open: How the Modern Women's Movement Changed America* (New York: Penguin Books, 2000), 160.

9. Rosen, *The World Split Open*, 213.

10. Schulman, *The Seventies*, 159; Winifred D. Wandersee, *On the Move: American Women in the 1970s* (Boston: Twayne, 1988), 150–52; Report by Ann Medina, ABC News, September 20, 1973; report from George Lewis, NBC News, September 20, 1973, Television News Archives, Vanderbilt University.

11. Wandersee, *On the Move*, 104.

12. Wandersee, *On the Move*, 105–6.

13. John D. Skrentny, *The Minority Rights Revolution* (Cambridge, Mass.: Harvard University Press, 2002), 255.

14. Wandersee, *On the Move*, 106, 118, 119; Skrentny, *Minority Rights Revolution*, 255.

15. The National Organization for Women, one of the principal advocates for the ERA, provides good information on the background of the measure at http://www.now.org/issues/economic/cea/history.html.

16. David S. Broder, *Changing of the Guard: Power and Leadership in America* (New York: Simon and Schuster, 1980), 272–73; Schulman, *The Seventies*, 168; Donald T. Critchlow, "Mobilizing Women: The 'Social' Issues," in *The Reagan Presidency: Pragmatic Conservatism and Its Legacies*, ed. W. Elliot Brownlee and Hugh Davis Graham (Lawrence, University Press of Kansas, 2003), 299.

17. Lawrence Lader, *Politics, Power, and the Church: The Catholic Crisis and Its Challenge to American Pluralism* (New York: Macmillan, 1987), 127–28.

18. Rosenberg, *Divided Lives*, 224; Lader, *Politics, Power, and the Church*, 130.

19. Rosenberg, *Divided Lives*, 227.

20. See Edward Berkowitz, "Family Benefits: A Historical Commentary," in *Social Security and the Family: Addressing Unmet Needs in an Underfunded System*, ed. Eugene Steurele and Melissa Favreault (Washington: Urban Institute, 2002), 19–46.

21. Wandersee, *On the Move*, 175, 177–78; Report from Eric Engberg, CBS News, November 21, 1977; Report from George Lewis, NBC News, November 20, 1977, Television News Archives, Vanderbilt University; Rosen, *Divided Lives*, 291–93.

22. Mark A. Graber, *Rethinking Abortion: Equal Choice, The Constitution, and Reproductive Politics* (Princeton, N.J.: Princeton University Press, 1996), 56, 61.

23. The Boston Women's Health Book Collective, *Our Bodies, Ourselves: A Book by and for Women* (New York: Simon and Schuster, 1973), 138.

24. Graber, *Rethinking Abortion*, 65.

25. Donald T. Critchlow, *Intended Consequences: Birth Control, Abortion, and the Federal Government in Modern America* (New York: Oxford University Press, 1996), 136.

26. *Roe v Wade*, 410 U.S. 113 (1973); Graber, *Rethinking Abortion*, 65; Critchlow, *Intended Consequences*, 148.

27. Report from Lem Tucker, ABC News, January 22, 1973; Report from George Herman, CBS News, January 22, 1973, Television News Archives, Vanderbilt University.

28. Critchlow, *Intended Consequences*, 202; Lader, *Politics, Power, and the Church*, 57–58.

29. Critchlow, *Intended Consequences*, 205; Wandersee, *On the Move*, 183.

30. Rosen, *The World Split Open*, 166–69, 234.

31. D'Emilio, *Sexual Politics*, 144, 155, 163; Lader, *Politics, Power, and the Church*, 61, 122.

32. "Four Policemen Hurt in 'Village' Raid," *New York Times*, June 29, 1969; Martin Duberman, *Stonewall* (New York: Plume Books, 1994).

33. "Police Again Rout 'Village' Youths," *New York Times*, June 30, 1969.

34. "Hostile Crowd Dispersed Near Sheridan Square," *New York Times*, July 3, 1969.

35. Lacey Fosburgh, "Thousands of Homosexuals Hold a Protest Rally in Central Park," *New York Times*, June 29, 1970.

36. Steven V. Roberts, "Homosexuals in Revolt," *New York Times,* August 24, 1970.

37. Skrentny, *Minority Rights Revolution,* 316; Peter N. Carroll, *It Seemed Like Nothing Happened* (New York: Holt, Rinehart, and Winston, 1982; reprint, New Brunswick, N.J.: Rutgers University Press, 1990), 290.

38. Alex Stepnick, Guillermo Grenier, Max Castro, and Marvin Dunn, *This Land Is Our Land: Immigrants and Power in Miami* (Berkeley: University of California Press, 2003); Rosen, *The World Split Open,* 165.

39. Dudley Clendinen, "Anita Bryant, b. 1940, Singer and Crusader," *St. Petersburg Times,* November 28, 1999.

40. Carroll, *It Seemed Like Nothing Happened,* 290.

41. Carroll, *It Seemed Like Nothing Happened,* 292, Skrentny, *Minority Rights Revolution,* 316; Broder, *Changing of the Guard,* 146.

42. Edward D. Berkowitz, *Disabled Policy: America's Programs for the Handicapped* (New York: Cambridge University Press, 1987).

43. Jacqueline Vaughn Switzer, *Disabled Rights: American Disability Policy and the Fight for Equality* (Washington, D.C.: Georgetown University Press, 2003).

44. Doris Fleischer and Frieda James, *The Disability Rights Movement: From Charity to Confrontation* (Philadelphia: Temple University Press, 2001); *Pennsylvania Association for Retarded Children (PARC) v Pennsylvania,* 334 F. Supp. 1257 (E.D. Pa. 1971); *Mills v Board of Education of Washington, D.C.,* 348 F. Supp. 866 (1972); *Wyatt v Stickney*344 F. Supp. 387 (M.D. Ala. 1972). I am grateful to Jennifer Erkulwater for sharing some of her research on this subject with me.

45. Richard Scotch, *From Goodwill to Civil Rights* (Philadelphia: Temple University Press, 2001); Berkowitz, *Disabled Policy.*

46. See Frank Bowe, *Handicapping America: Barriers to Disabled People* (New York: Harper and Row, 1978), 16–18.

8. THE ME DECADE AND THE TURN TO THE RIGHT

1. Leo P. Ribuffo, "1974–1988," in Stephen J. Whitfield ed., *A Companion to Twentieth-Century America* (New York: Blackwell, 2004), 108.

2. Donald T. Critchlow, "Mobilizing Women: The Social Issues," in *The Reagan Presidency: Pragmatic Conservativism and Its Legacies,* ed. W. Elliot Brownlee and Hugh Davis Graham (Lawrence, University Press of Kansas, 2003), 293.

3. Ribuffo, "1974–1988," 109.

4. Tom Wolfe, *Mauve Gloves and Madmen, Clutter and Vine* (New York: Farrar, Straus and Giroux, 1976), 142.

5. Wolfe, *Mauve Gloves,* 140.

6. Ribuffo, "1974–1988," 104.

7. James Davison Hunter, *Evangelicalism: The Coming Generation* (Chicago: University of Chicago Press, 1987), 6; Robert Wuthnow, *The Restructuring of Ameri-*

can Religion: Society and Faith Since World War II (Princeton, N.J.: Princeton University Press, 1988), 159.

8. Wuthnow, *The Restructuring of American Religion*, 176, 194–95.

9. James Davison Hunter, *American Evangelicalism: Conservative Religion and the Quandary of Modernity* (New Brunswick, N.J. Rutgers University Press, 1983), 7; Hunter, *Evangelicism*, 124, 126.

10. Wuthnow, *The Restructuring of American Religion*, 198–200.

11. Hunter, *Evangelicals*, 127.

12. Christopher Lasch, *The Culture of Narcissism: American Life in an Age of Diminishing Expectations* (New York: Norton, 1979), 53.

13. Lasch, *Culture of Narcissism*, 211.

14. Lasch, *Culture of Narcissism*, 225.

15. Lester C. Thurow, *The Zero-Sum Society: Distribution and the Possibilities for Economic Change* (New York: Basic Books, 1980), 16, 77, 95.

16. Ezra F. Vogel, *Japan as Number One: Lessons for America* (Cambridge, Mass.: Harvard University Press, 1979), 64, 95.

17. Vogel, *Japan as Number One*, 116–17.

18. Vogel, *Japan as Number One*, 70.

19. W. Carl Biven, *Jimmy Carter's Economy: Policy in an Age of Limits* (Chapel Hill: University of North Carolina Press, 2002), 218, 220, 224; Thomas McCraw, *Prophets of Regulation* (Cambridge, Mass.: Harvard University Press, 1987).

20. Robert M. Collins, *More: The Politics of Economic Growth in Postwar America* (New York: Oxford University Press, 2000), 183.

21. Burton I. Kaufman, *The Presidency of James Earl Carter* (Lawrence: University of Kansas Press, 1993), 106; Peter N. Carroll, *It Seemed Like Nothing Happened* (New York: Holt, Rinehart, and Winston, 1982; reprint, New Brunswick, N.J.: Rutgers University Press, 1990), 324.

22. Quoted in John D. Skrentny, *The Minority Rights Revolution* (Cambridge, Mass.: Harvard University Press, 2002), 216.

23. Bruce J. Schulman, *The Seventies: The Great Shift in American Culture, Society, and Politics* (New York: Free Press, 2001), 70; Skrentny, *Minority Rights Revolution*, 211–26; *Lau v Nichols*, 414 U.S. 563, 94 S.Ct. 786 (1974).

24. Jonathan Rieder, *Canarsie: The Jews and Italians of Brooklyn Against Liberalism* (Cambridge, Mass.: Harvard University Press, 1985), 138, 121.

25. Skrentny, *Minority Rights Revolution*, 126.

26. Skrentny, *Minority Rights Revolution*, 89; Schulman, *The Seventies*, 69.

27. *Regents of the University of California v Bakke*, 438 U.S. 265 (1978); Skrentny, *Minority Rights Revolution*, 173.

28. Judith Stein, *Running Steel, Running America: Race, Economic Policy, and the Decline of Liberalism* (Chapel Hill: University of North Carolina Press, 1998), 186.

29. *United Steel Workers of America v Weber* 443 U.S. 193 (1979).

30. Schulman, *The Seventies*, 56.

31. Carroll, *It Seemed Like Nothing Happened*, 261.

32. Schulman, *The Seventies*, 57; *Swann v Charlotte-Mecklenberg Bd. of Ed.*, 402 U.S.1 (1971); *Keyes v School District No. 1*, 413 U.S. 189 (1973).

33. John Robert Greene, *The Presidency of Gerald R. Ford* (Lawrence: University Press of Kansas, 1995), 85–86.

34. Quoted in Steven J. L. Taylor, *Desegregation in Boston and Buffalo: The Influence of Local Leaders* (Albany: SUNY Press, 1998), 73; John A. Farrell, *Tip O'Neill and the Democratic Century* (Boston: Little Brown, 2001), 520–21

35. Report from Chris Kelley, CBS Evening News, December 11, 1974, Television News Archives, Vanderbilt University.

36. Farrell, *Tip O'Neill and the Democratic Century*, 525.

9. THE MOVIES AS CULTURAL MIRROR

1. Michael Schumacher, *Francis Ford Coppola: A Filmmaker's Life* (New York: Three Rivers Press, 1999), 234.

2. James L. Baughman, *The Republic of Mass Culture: Journalism, Filmmaking, and Broadcasting in America Since 1941* (Baltimore, Md.: Johns Hopkins University Press, 1992), 241.

3. Peter Biskind, *Easy Riders, Raging Bulls: How the Sex-Drugs-and Rock'n'Roll Generation Saved Hollywood* (New York: Simon and Schuster, 1998), 15.

4. Unless otherwise noted, my comments on the movies discussed in this chapter come from my own viewing of the movie on videotape or DVD. When I have watched a movie on DVD, I have also taken advantage of the available commentary by the movie's director.

5. Peter Lev, *American Films of the '70s: Conflicting Visions* (Austin: University of Texas Press, 2000), 185.

6. Baughman, *Republic of Mass Culture*, 208.

7. Lev, *American Films of the '70s*, 184.

8. Biskind, *Easy Riders, Raging Bulls*, 97.

9. Roger Ebert, "Patton," March 17, 2002, available from RogerEbert.com, http://rogerebert.suntimes.com/apps/pbcs.dll/article?AID=/20020317/REVIEWS 08/203170301/1023.

10. I am grateful to Greg Doherty of Brandeis University for pointing this out to me.

11. *Air Force* had a script written by William Faulkner among others, and it was directed by Howard Hawks. For commentary on the Web, which contains a great deal of information about this and other American movies, see David Perry, Cinema-Scene.com 5, no. 8, 21 February 2003, http://www.cinema-scene.com/archive/05/08.html#Air.

12. Biskind, *Easy Riders, Raging Bulls*, 188–89.

13. Reports from Roger Mudd and Bernard Goldberg, CBS Evening News,

August 7, 1975. On December 8, 1975, Howard K. Smith reported on ABC News that *Jaws* had grossed $40 million in the United States and was poised to do monster business in Japan. Both reports are housed in the Television News Archives, Vanderbilt University.

14. Biskind, *Easy Riders, Raging Bulls*, 256.

15. Philip M. Taylor, *Steven Spielberg: The Man, His Movies, and Their Meaning* (London: Batsford, 1999), 256.

16. Taylor, *Steven Spielberg*.

17. Quoted in Biskind, *Easy Riders, Raging Bulls*, 14–15.

18. Biskind, *Easy Riders, Raging Bulls*, 273.

19. Mario Puzo, *The Godfather* (New York: Putnam, 1969), 36.

20. Quoted in Peter N. Carroll, *It Seemed Like Nothing Happened* (New York: Holt, Rinehart, and Winston, 1982; reprint, New Brunswick, N.J.: Rutgers University Press, 1990), 68.

21. Biskind, *Easy Riders, Raging Bulls*, 162.

22. Biskind, *Easy Riders, Raging Bulls*, 277.

23. John Baxter, *Woody Allen: A Biography* (New York: Carroll and Graf, 1998).

10. Television and the Reassurance of the Familiar

1. Josh Ozersky, *Archie Bunker's America: TV in an Era of Change, 1968–1978* (Carbondale: Southern Illinois University Press, 2003), 6.

2. Ozersky, *Archie Bunker's America*, 107.

3. Sally Bedell Smith, *In All His Glory: The Life of William S. Paley* (New York: Simon and Schuster, 1990), 494.

4. For information on individual shows, I depend here and throughout on Tim Brooks and Earle Marsh, *The Complete Directory to Prime Time Network and Cable TV Shows, 1946–Present*, 6th ed. (New York: Ballantine Books, 1995).

5. James L. Baughman, *The Republic of Mass Culture: Journalism, Filmmaking, and Broadcasting in America Since 1941* (Baltimore, Md.: Johns Hopkins University Press, 1992), 144.

6. Smith, *In All His Glory*, 494; Baughman, *Republic of Mass Culture*, 144; Steven D. Stark, *Glued to the Set: The Sixty Television Shows and Events That Made Us Who We Are Today* (New York: Free Press, 1997), 162.

7. Stark, *Glued to the Set*, 164–67.

8. I base my analysis of *All in the Family* on my direct observation of the programs from its first season, which I saw on a DVD, *All in the Family: The Complete First Season*, Columbia Tristar Home Entertainment.

9. Ozersky, *Archie Bunker's America*, 79.

10. Actually, it was one of Babbit's friends who makes this observation at a dinner party at Babbit's house.

11. Stark, *Glued to the Set*, 167.

12. I base my observations of *The Mary Tyler Moore Show* on Stark, *Glued to the Set*, 169, and of my direct observation of the show on DVD, including *The Mary Tyler Moore Show: The Complete First Season*, Twentieth Century Fox, 2000. The DVD includes commentary from the creators of the series.

13. Smith, *In All His Glory*, 516, 536; Baughman, *The Republic of Mass Culture*, 154.

14. Mary Ann Watson, *Defining Visions: Television and the American Experience Since 1945* (Belmont, Calif.: Thompson Wadsworth, 1998), 113, 192.

15. Quoted in Ozersky, *Archie Bunker's America*, p. 110.

16. "Why *Roots* Hit Home," *Time*, 14 February 1977. For more information on the Roots phenomenon and for background information about the show see http://www.museum.tv/archives/etv/R/htmlR/roots/roots.htm.

17. Ozersky, *Archie Bunker's America*, 111.

18. I base this account of *Saturday Night Live* largely on Tom Shales and James Andrew Miller, *Live from New York: An Uncensored History of* Saturday Night Live (Boston: Little Brown, 2002), which provides an oral history of the show.

19. Shales and Miller, *Live from New York*, 511.

20. Baughman, *Republic of Mass Culture*, 62.

21. Ron Powers, *The Newscasters* (New York: St. Martin's Press, 1977), 33.

22. Edwin Diamond, *Sign Off: The Last Days of Television* (Cambridge, Mass.: MIT Press, 1982), 4.

23. Diamond, *Sign Off*, 71.

24. Stark, *Glued to the Set*, 129.

25. Diamond, *Sign Off*, 224.

26. Baughman, *Republic of Mass Culture*, 128, 190.

27. Diamond, *Sign Off*, 224, 229.

28. Frank Coffey, *Sixty Minutes: Twenty-five Years of Television's Finest Hour* (Los Angeles: General Publishing Company, 1993). This book contains a complete log of all of the *Sixty Minutes* shows up to the point of publication.

29. Stark, *Glued to the Set*, 189–91; Baughman, *Republic of Mass Culture*, 159.

30. Stark, *Glued to the Set*, 192–93; Smith, *In All His Glory*, 545.

11. THE END OF THE SEVENTIES

1. Burton I. Kaufman, *The Presidency of James Earl Carter* (Lawrence: University of KansasPress, 1993), 124–28, 160–61.

2. Kaufman, *Presidency of James Earl Carter*, 173.

3. David S. Broder, *Changing of the Guard: Power and Leadership in America* (New York: Simon and Schuster, 1980), 171

4. Michael Barone, *Our Country: The Shaping of America from Roosevelt to Reagan* (New York: Free Press, 1990), 596.

5. This quotation and much of the material on the President's Commission for National Agenda for the Eighties comes from Edward D. Berkowitz, "Commissing the Future," in *History and Public Policy*, ed. David Mock (Malabar, Fla.: Krieger, 1991), 7–22.

6. Report of the President's Commission for a National Agenda for the Eighties, *A National Agenda for the Eighties* (New York: New American Library, 1981), 102–3.

7. President's Commission, *A National Agenda for the Eighties*, 105.

8. President's Commission, *A National Agenda for the Eighties*, 30.

9. President's Commission, *A National Agenda for the Eighties*, 38.

10. President's Commission, *A National Agenda for the Eighties*, 44

11. I base this account of the life of Bill Gates on Daniel Ichbiah and Susan L. Knepper, *The Making of Microsoft: How Bill Gates and His Team Created the World's Most Successful Software Company* (Rockin, Calif.: Prima, 1991), and on views about more traditional American entrepreneurs, such as Edison and Ford, expressed in Jonathan R. T. Hughes, *The Vital Few: The Entrepreneur and American Economic Progress* (New York: Oxford University Press, 1986).

12. I base this account of Princeton on *The 1972 Nassau Herald: A Record of the Class of Nineteen Hundred and Seventy-Two, Princeton University*. This is a privately printed book that was prepared by Princeton University and given to members of the class when they graduated. It consists of a narrative of the class's history and photographs and brief biographies of each graduating senior.

Selected Bibliography

Andrade, Dale. *America's Last Vietnam Battle: Halting Hanoi's Easter 1972 Offensive.* Lawrence: University Press of Kansas, 1995.

Barone, Michael. *Our Country: The Shaping of America from Roosevelt to Reagan.* New York: Free Press, 1990.

Barnouw, Eric. *Tube of Plenty: The Evolution of American Television.* New York: Oxford University Press, 1975.

Baughman, James L. *The Republic of Mass Culture: Journalism, Filmmaking, and Broadcasting in America Since 1941.* Baltimore, Md.: Johns Hopkins University Press, 1992.

Baxter, John. *Woody Allen: A Biography.* New York: Carroll and Graf, 1998.

Berkowitz, Edward D. *Robert Ball and the Politics of Social Security.* Madison: University of Wisconsin Press, 2003.

——. *America's Welfare State: From Roosevelt to Reagan.* Baltimore, Md.: Johns Hopkins University Press, 1991.

——. *Disabled Policy: America's Programs for the Handicapped.* New York: Cambridge University Press, 1987.

——. "Family Benefits: A Historical Commentary." In *Social Security and the Family: Addressing Unmet Needs in an Underfunded System,* ed. Eugene Steurele and Melissa Favreault, 19–46. Washington: Urban Institute, 2002.

——. "History and Social Security Reform." In *Social Security and Medicare: Individual Versus Collective Risk and Responsibility,* ed. Sheila Burke, Eric Kingson, and Uwe Reinhardt, 42–47. Washington, D.C.: National Academy of Social Insurance, 2000.

——. *Mr. Social Security: The Life of Wilbur J. Cohen.* Lawrence: University Press of Kansas, 1995.

Bernstein, Michael A., and David E. Adler, eds. *Understanding American Economic Decline*. New York: Cambridge University Press, 1994.

Berman, William C. *America's Right Turn: From Nixon to Bush*. Baltimore, Md.: Johns Hopkins University Press, 1994.

Biskind, Peter. *Easy Riders, Raging Bulls: How the Sex-Drugs-and-Rock'n'Roll Generation Saved Hollywood*. New York: Simon and Schuster, 1998.

Bissell, D. C. *The First Conglomerate: 145 Years of the Singer Sewing Company*. New York: Biddle, 1999.

Biven, W. Carl. *Jimmy Carter's Economy: Policy in an Age of Limits*. Chapel Hill: University of North Carolina Press, 2002.

Boston Women's Health Book Collective, The. *Our Bodies, Ourselves: A Book by and for Women*. New York: Simon and Schuster, 1973.

Bowe, Frank. *Handicapping America: Barriers to Disabled People*. New York: Harper and Row, 1978.

Broder, David S. *Changing of the Guard: Power and Leadership in America*. New York: Simon and Schuster, 1980.

Brownlee, W. Elliot, and Hugh Davis Graham, eds. *The Reagan Presidency: Pragmatic Conservatism and Its Legacies*. Lawrence: University Press of Kansas, 2003.

Califano, Joseph M. *Governing America: An Insider's Report from the White House and the Cabinet*. New York: Simon and Schuster, 1981.

Cannato, Vincent J. *The Ungovernable City: John Lindsay and His Struggle to Save New York*. New York: Basic Books, 2001.

Carter, Dan T. *The Politics of Rage: George Wallace, The Origins of the New Conservatism, and the Transformation of American Politics*. New York: Simon and Schuster, 1995.

Carter, Jimmy. *Why Not the Best?* Fayetville: University of Arkansas Press, 1996.

Carroll, Peter N. *It Seemed Like Nothing Happened*. New York: Holt, Rinehart, and Winston, 1982. Reprint, New Brunswick, N.J.: Rutgers University Press, 1990.

Coffey, Frank. *Sixty Minutes: Twenty-five Years of Television's Finest Hour*. Los Angeles: General Publishing Company, 1993.

Collins, Robert M. *More: The Politics of Economic Growth in Postwar America*. New York: Oxford University Press, 2000.

Cowie, Jefferson, et al., eds., *Beyond the Ruins: The Meanings of Deindustrialization*. Ithaca, N.Y.: Cornell University Press, 2003.

Critchlow, Donald T. *Intended Consequences: Birth Control, Abortion, and the Federal Government in Modern America*. New York: Oxford University Press, 1996.

Dallek, Robert. *Flawed Giant: Lyndon Johnson and His Times, 1961–1973*. New York: Oxford University Press, 1998.

D'Emilio, John. *Sexual Politics, Sexual Communities: The Making of a Homosexual Minority in the United States, 1940–1970*. Chicago: University of Chicago Press, 1983.

Diamond, Edwin. *Sign Off: The Last Days of Television*. Cambridge, Mass.: MIT Press, 1982.

Easterlin, Richard A. *Birth and Fortune: The Impact of Numbers on Personal Welfare*. Chicago: University of Chicago Press, 1987.

Emery, Fred. *Watergate: The Corruption and Fall of Richard Nixon*. London: Jonathan Cape, 1994.

Farrell, John A. *Tip O'Neill and the Democratic Century*. Boston: Little Brown, 2001.

Fink, Gary M., and Hugh Davis Graham, eds. *The Carter Presidency Policy Choices in the Post–New Deal Era*. Lawrence: University Press of Kansas, 1998.

Fleischer, Doris, and Frieda James. *The Disability Rights Movement: From Charity to Confrontation*. Philadelphia: Temple University Press, 2001.

Frum, David. *How We Got Here: The 70's: The Decade that Brought You Modern Life (For Better or Worse)*. New York: Basic Books, 2000.

Garthoff, Raymond L. *Detente and Confrontation: American-Soviet Relations from Nixon to Reagan*. Washington, D.C.: Brookings Institution, 1985.

Gellman, Irwin F. *The Contender: Richard Nixon: The Congress Years, 1946–1952* (New York: Free Press, 1999.

Graber, Mark A. *Rethinking Abortion: Equal Choice, The Constitution, and Reproductive Politics*. Princeton, N.J.: Princeton University Press, 1996.

Greene, John Robert. *The Presidency of Gerald R. Ford*. Lawrence: University Press of Kansas, 1995.

Haldeman, H. R. *The Haldeman Diaries: Inside the Nixon White House*. New York: Putnam, 1994.

Hartman, Robert T. *Palace Politics: An Inside Account of the Ford Years*. New York: McGraw- Hill, 1980.

Hersh, Seymour. *My Lai 4: A Report on the Massacre and Its Aftermath*. New York: Random House, 1970.

Hodgson, Godfrey. *The Gentleman from New York: Daniel Patrick Moynihan*. Boston: Houghton Mifflin Company, 2000.

Hunter, James Davison. *American Evangelicalism: Conservative Religion and the Quandary of Modernity*. New Brunswick, N.J.: Rutgers University Press, 1983.

——. *Evangelicalism: The Coming Generation*. Chicago: University of Chicago Press, 1987.

Isaacson, Walter, *Kissinger: A Biography*. New York: Simon and Schuster, 1992.

Jacobs, John. *A Rage for Justice: The Passion and Politics of Phillip Burton*. Berkeley: University of California Press, 1995.

Jones, Charles O. *The Trusteeship Presidency: Jimmy Carter and the United States Congress*. Baton Rouge: Louisiana State University Press, 1988.

Karnow, Stanley. "Changing (Mis)Conceptions of China." In *The American Image of China*, ed. Benson Lee Grayson. New York: Frederick Ungar, 1979. Originally published as "China Through Rose-Tinted Glasses,." *Atlantic Monthly* (October 1973): 73–76.

Kaufman, Burton I. *The Presidency of James Earl Carter*. Lawrence: University of Kansas Press, 1993.

Kaufman, Robert G. *Henry M. Jackson: A Life in Politics*. Seattle: University of Washington Press, 2000.

Kissinger, Henry. *White House Years*. New York: Little Brown, 1979.

Kutler, Stanley I. *The Wars of Watergate: The Last Crisis of Richard Nixon*. New York: Knopf, 1990.

Lader, Lawrence. *Politics, Power, and the Church: The Catholic Crisis and Its Challenge to American Pluralism*. New York: Macmillan, 1987.

Lasch, Christopher, *The Culture of Narcissism: American Life in an Age of Diminishing Expectations*. New York: Norton, 1979.

Lev, Peter. *American Films of the '70s: Conflicting Visions*. Austin: University of Texas Press, 2000.

Light, Paul. *Artful Work: The Politics of Social Security Reform*. New York: Random House, 1985.

——. *Baby Boomers* . New York: W. W. Norton, 1988.

Linkon, Sherry Lee, and John Russo. *Steeltown USA: Work and Memory in Youngstown*. Lawrence: University Press of Kansas, 2003.

Lynd, Staughton. *Fight Against Shutdown: Youngstown's Steel Mill Closings* . New York: Singlejack Books, 1982.

Lynn, Laurence, Jr., and David Whitman. *The President as Policymaker: Jimmy Carter and Welfare Reform*. Philadelphia: Temple University Press, 1981.

Marsh, Earle. *The Complete Directory to Prime Time Network and Cable TV Shows, 1946–Present*. 6th ed. New York: Ballantine Books, 1995.

Matusow, Allen J. *Nixon's Economy: Booms, Busts, Dollars, and Votes*. Lawrence: University Press of Kansas, 1998.

McCraw, Thomas. *Prophets of Regulation*. Cambridge, Mass.: Harvard University Press, 1987.

McQuaid, Kim., *The Anxious Years: America in the Vietnam and Watergate Era*. New York: Basic Books, 1992.

Morris, Roger. *Richard Milhous Nixon: The Rise of an American Politician*. New York: Henry Holt, 1990.

Neustadt, Richard, and Ernest May. *Thinking in Time*. New York: Free Press, 1988.

Nixon, Richard. *The Memoirs of Richard Nixon*. New York: Warner Books, 1978.

——. *Six Crises*. New York: Doubleday, 1962.

Ozersky, Josh. *Archie Bunker's America: TV in an Era of Change, 1968–1978*. Carbondale: Southern Illinois University Press, 2003.

Parmet, Herbert S. *Richard Nixon and His America*. Boston: Little Brown and Company, 1990.

Power, Ron. *The Newscasters*. New York: St. Martin's Press, 1977.

President's Commission for a National Agenda for the Eighties. *A National Agenda for the Eighties*. New York: New American Library, 1981.

Puzo, Mario. *The Godfather*. New York: Putnam, 1969.

Rieder, Jonathan. *Canarsie: The Jews and Italians of Brooklyn Against Liberalism*. Cambridge, Mass.: Harvard University Press, 1985.

Rosen, Ruth. *The World Split Open: How the Modern Women's Movement Changed America*. New York: Penguin Books, 2000.

Rosenberg, Rosalind. *Divided Lives: American Women in the Twentieth Century*. New York: Hill and Wang, 1992.

Schulman, Bruce J. *The Seventies: The Great Shift in American Culture, Society, and Politics*. New York: Free Press, 2001.

Schumacher, Michael. *Francis Ford Coppola: A Filmmaker's Life*. New York: Three Rivers Press, 1999.

Scotch, Richard. *From Goodwill to Civil Rights*. Philadelphia: Temple University Press, 2001.

Shales, Tom, and James Andrew Miller. *Live from New York: An Uncensored History of* Saturday Night Live. Boston: Little Brown, 2002.

Skrentny, John D. *The Minority Rights Revolution*. Cambridge, Mass.: Harvard University Press, 2002.

Smith, C. Fraser Smith. *William Donald Schaefer: A Political Biography*. Baltimore, Md.: Johns Hopkins University Press, 1999.

Smith, Ralph E. "The Movement of Women into the Labor Force." In *The Subtle Revolution*, ed. Smith, 1–30. Washington, D.C.: Urban Institute, 1979.

Smith, Sally Bedell. *In All His Glory: The Life of William S. Paley*. New York: Simon and Schuster, 1990.

Spector, Ronald H. *After Tet: The Bloodiest Year in Vietnam*. New York: Free Press, 1993.

Stark, Steven D. *Glued to the Set: The 60 Television Shows and Events That Made Us Who We Are Today*. New York: Free Press, 1997.

Starr, Paul. *The Social Transformation of American Medicine*. New York: Basic Books, 1982.

Stein, Herbert. *The Fiscal Revolution in America*. Chicago: University of Chicago Press, 1969.

——. *Presidential Economics*. Washington, D.C.: AEI Press, 1994.

Stein, Judith. *Running Steel, Running America: Race, Economic Policy, and the Decline of Liberalism*. Chapel Hill: University of North Carolina Press, 1998.

Steiner, Gilbert. *The Futility of Family Policy*. Washington, D.C.: Brookings Institution, 1981.

Stepnick, Alex, Guillermo Grenier, Max Castro, and Marvin Dunn. *This Land Is Our Land: Immigrants and Power in Miami*. Berkeley: University of California Press, 2003.

Sundquist, James L. *The Decline and Resurgence of Congress*. Washington, D.C.: Brookings Institution, 1981.

Switzer, Jacqueline Vaughn. *Disabled Rights: American Disability Policy and the Fight for Equality*. Washington, D.C.: Georgetown University Press, 2003.

Taylor, Philip M. *Steven Spielberg: The Man, His Movies, and Their Meaning.* London: Batsford, 1999.

Taylor, Steven J. L. *Desegregation in Boston and Buffalo: The Influence of Local Leaders.* Albany: SUNY Press, 1998.

Thurow, Lester C. *The Zero-Sum Society: Distribution and the Possibilities for Economic Change.* New York: Basic Books, 1980.

Updike, John. *Rabbit Is Rich.* New York: Knopf, 1981

Vogel, Ezra F. *Japan as Number One: Lessons for America.* Cambridge, Mass.: Harvard University Press, 1979.

Wandersee, Winifred D. *On the Move: American Women in the 1970s.* Boston: Twayne, 1988.

Watson, Mary Ann. *Defining Visions: Television and the American Experience Since 1945.* Belmont, Calif.: Thompson Wadsworth, 1998.

Weir, Margaret. *Politics and Jobs: The Boundaries of Employment Policy in the United States.* Princeton, N.J.: Princeton University Press, 1992.

Whitfield, Stephen J., ed. *A Companion to Twentieth-Century America.* New York: Blackwell, 2003.

Wildavsky, Aaron, and Naomi Caider. *The New Politics of the Budgetary Process.* 4th ed. Boston: Addison Wesley, 2000.

Wills, Garry. *Nixon Agonistes: The Crisis of the Self-Made Man.* Boston: Houghton Mifflin, 1970.

Witcover, Jules. *Marathon: The Pursuit of the Presidency, 1972–1976.* New York: Viking Press, 1977.

Wolfe, Tom, *Mauve Gloves and Madmen, Clutter and Vine.* New York: Farrar, Straus, and Giroux, 1976

Wuthnow, Robert. *The Restructuring of American Religion: Society and Faith Since World War II.* Princeton, N.J.: Princeton University Press, 1988.

Yergin, Daniel. *The Prize: The Epic Quest for Oil, Money, and Power.* New York: Simon and Schuster, 1991.

Zelizer, Julian E. *Taxing America: Wilbur D. Mills, Congress, and the State, 1945–1975.* New York: Cambridge University Press, 1998.

Acknowledgments

Many people helped me to write this book. Let me start with James Warren of Columbia University Press who commissioned this project and remained in touch as an advisor and sympathetic critic over the course of several years. I am grateful to him for his help and for his deep interest in the book.

Then there are the people who allowed me to test my ideas before academic audiences. Gareth Davies graciously invited me to England and took an active interest in the book. Anthony Badger introduced me to the delights of high table at Cambridge. Raymond Richards and Jan Pilditch facilitated my trip to New Zealand and showed me a wonderful time. Brendon O'Connor invited me to a conference in Brisbane; I thank him for his help and hospitality. I also gave a paper on the seventies at the History of Public Policy Conference. I am grateful to Meg Jacobs for arranging the session and to David Farber, Judith Stein, and Bruce Schulman for their participation and comments. David, in addition, was kind enough to send me an advanced copy of his edited book of essays on the seventies. Donald Critchlow, a longtime comrade in arms in the academic wars, organized this conference, talked with me about the seventies, and read preliminary drafts of this book. I appreciate his help on this project and on many others over the years. Closer to home, I want to thank Jennifer Brinkerhoff and Kathy Newcomer for letting me speak on the seventies at the Student Faculty Forum for Public Administration and Marcus Raskin for permitting me to drag the seventies into a seminar on the National Security State.

Nor do my debts end there. Julian Zelizer, whose career has inspired in me a faith that political history and policy history are viable fields, was kind enough to give me a draft copy of his book on congressional reform, which proved invaluable to me. Frances Kleeman generously shared materials related to the seventies from her personal collection. My department at George Washington University has always emphasized twentieth-century history, and I am grateful to each of my colleagues in this field, including Bill Becker and Ron Spector. Although I still do not know very much about foreign policy, it has helped to be in the same department as Jim Hershberg, Hope Harrison, and Gregg Brazinsky.

I owe very special thanks to Leo Ribuffo and Cynthia Harrison. Leo went out of his way to read and comment on an earlier draft. He also taught a novice at least a little about the history of religion. His perceptive comments, based on his own deep reading and research, have improved, if not perfected, this book. Having him in the office next to mine has raised my stature as a historian. Cynthia Harrison put her broad base of knowledge and superior editing skills to work on the manuscript and induced many improvements. She will still not be satisfied with the sections on women's history, but they are undoubtedly better as a result of her efforts. I thank her for her considerable efforts on my behalf.

Many others in academia have helped me as well, including Muriel Atkin, Kim McQuaid, Richard Stott, Robin Einhorn, Andrew Zimmerman, Horace Judson, Ed McCord, Shawn McHale, Brian Balogh, Howie Baum, and Larry DeWitt.

At home my family has been its usual supportive self. Sarah and Rebecca Berkowitz took particular interest in the sections of the book about the movies and television, even as they faced the existential dilemmas common to people their ages. Emily Frank has been a wonderful companion with whom to face the rigors of old age. I dedicate this book to my father, who, quite simply, is the inspiration for everything I do.

ABC (American Broadcasting Company), 108, 115, 139, 198; football on, 203–4; miniseries on, 211; news programming, 214, 221; situation comedies on, 210

abortion, 7, 9, 143, 159; Catholic Church's views on, 148; Hyde Amendment against, 147—148; legislation, 145–46, 148; right-to-life movement and, 148; Supreme Court rulings on, 146, 148

Abt Associates, 97

Abzug, Bella, 143, 145

Academy Awards, 182, 188, 195, 196

ACCD. *See* American Coalition of Citizens with Disabilities

Acheson, Dean, 34

Ackroyd, Dan, 213

Action News, 214

Administration Committee (House of Representatives), 101

advertising: for movies, 189, 197; television v. print, 216; women and, 138

affirmative action, 7, 159, 171–73; Civil Rights Act and, 4; labor force and, 173; Supreme Court on, 172–73

Afghanistan, 220–21, 231; Cold War and, 119–20; Soviet Union in, 119–20

AFL-CIO (American Federation of Labor–Congress of Industrial Organizations), 76, 87, 124

Africa, Cuba in, 116

African Americans. *See* blacks

Agnew, Spiro, 22–23, 48

agriculture, 66

Agriculture Committee (House of Representatives), 94

Air Force (movie, 1943), 182, 254n11

Airline Deregulation Act of 1978, 167

airline industry, deregulation of, 166–67

Alber, David, 194

Albert, Carl, 89

Albert, Eddie, 202

Ali, Mohammed, 190

All in the Family (television program), 199, 205–8, 211

Allen, Paul, 228

Allen, Woody, 194–97

Alsop, Joseph, 43

Altman, Robert, 181, 182, 197, 217

American Broadcasting Company. *See* ABC

American Coalition of Citizens with Disabilities (ACCD), 155

American Council of Education, 155

American Federation of Labor-Congress of Industrial Organizations. *See* AFL-CIO

American Graffiti (movie), 186

An American in Paris (movie), 196

American Independent Party, 15

American Law Institute, 145

American Public Transit Association, 155

Americans for Democratic Action, 90

Americans for SALT, 117

Anderson, Wendell, 114

Andrews, Julie, 179

Andy Griffith Show (television program), 210

Angola, 75

Annie Hall (movie), 195

Apple, R.W., Jr., 106

Archie Bunker. *See All in the Family*

The Argentine Firecracker. *See* Fox, Fanne

Armco Steel, 54

Armed Services Committee (House of Representatives), 94

Arms Control and Disarmament Agency, 116

Armstrong, William, 115

Arnaz, Desi, 202

Arthur, Beatrice, 208

"Ask President Carter" (radio program), 110

Asner, Ed, 211

Aspin, Les, 95

Associated Press, 111, 128

Astaire, Fred, 191

Atomic Energy Commission, 65

Avalon, Frankie, 191

Avildsen, John, 193

Babbit (fictional character), 207

baby boom, 68, 158; in labor force, 228

Badham, John, 193

Baker, Howard, 47

Bakke, Alan, 172

Bakker, Jim, 161

Ball, Lucille, 202

Ballad of the Green Berets (movie), 182

Baltimore, riots, 22

Bananas (movie), 195

Bancroft, Ann, 180

Bankhead, William, 113

Banking and Currency Committee (House of Representatives), 94

Barone, Michael, 1–6, 19

Battistella, Annabel. *See* Fox, Fanne

"battle of the sexes," 139

Beach Blanket Bingo (movie), 191

Beame, Abraham, 100

Beatles, 179

Beatty, Warren, 180

Bee Gees, 191

Bell, Daniel, 132

Belushi, John, 213

Benchley, Peter, 184

Bergman, Ingmar, 196

Berlin, 219

Bernstein, Carl, 21, 22, 29, 217

Bethlehem Steel, 121

The Beverly Hillbillies (television program), 202, 204, 205

Big Ten Athletic Conference, 135

Bilingual Education Act of 1968, 169

bilingual education, Supreme Court and, 170

Biskind, Peter, 188

blacks: civil rights of, 3, 7, 133, 137, 142, 150, 151, 157; as convention delegates, 18; in electoral process, 4; migration from South, 173; in movies, 190; political power of, 174; on television, 206, 208, 212

Blackmun, Harry, 146

Blue Hawaii (movie), 191

Bolshoi Ballet, 201

Bonnie and Clyde (movie), 180

Boston: busing protests in, 174–76; police strike, 23

Boston School Board, 175

Boston School Committee, 175, 176
Boston Women's Health Book
    Collective, 146
Bradley, Omar, 182
Brando, Marlon, 188, 190
Bremer, Arthur, 18
Brezhnev Doctrine, 40
Brezhnev, Leonid, 45, 46, 47, 48, 75, 120
Broder, David, 93
Brokaw, Tom, 29
Brookings Institution, 20, 96, 111, 123
Brooks, Albert, 213
Brown, Jerry, 107
Brown, Michael, 151
Brown v. Board of Education, 172
Bruce, Lenny, 195
Bryan, William Jennings, 162
Bryant, Anita, 152, 153, 160
Brzezinski, Zbigniew, 116, 117
Bureau of the Budget, 97
Burleson, Omar, 85
Burnett, Carol, 195
Burns, James McGregor, 90
Burns, Robert, 147
busing, 7, 159; black political power and,
    174; conflicts over, 174–76; against
    segregation, 4, 141
Butterfield, Alexander, 25

Caesar, Sid, 195, 213
Califano, Joseph, 10, 148, 155
Cambodia, 28, 35, 36; fall to Khmer
    Rouge, 49; Geneva Peace Accords
    and, 33; Mayaguez incident and, 80
Capra, Frank, 184
Carey, Hugh, 100
Carrie (movie, 1976), 186
Carroll, Peter, 6
Carson, Johnny, 212
Carter, Jimmy, 8, 10, 11, 83, 155, 160, 211,
    219, 227, 232; abortion views of, 148;
    airline deregulation efforts of, 167;
    China and, 43; Congress and, 112–14;
    detente under, 116–18, 120; domestic
policy of, 111–13; early career of,
    104–5; economy under, 120, 123–27;
    energy crisis under, 130–32; energy
    policy of, 127–28; foreign policy of,
    116–18, 220–23; inflation under, 124–
    27; Iran hostage crisis of, 220–22; at
    Kennedy Library, 118; O'Neill and,
    113, 114; Playboy interview of, 108; in
    presidential debates, 108–9; presiden-
    tial image of, 110, 222; in presiden-
    tial primaries, 106–7, 221–23; press
    and, 105–6, 115; rating in polls, 114;
    SALT and, 116–18; televised addresses
    of, 125, 127, 131, 224
Case, Clifford, 49
Case-Church bill, 49
Castro, Fidel, 51
Catholic Church: abortion views of, 148;
    homosexuality position of, 149–50
Caufield, John, 20
CBS (Columbia Broadcasting System),
    29, 37, 47, 108, 110, 142, 185, 203;
    documentaries, 216; News anchor, 215;
    president of, 205; radio reporters, 215;
    situation comedies on, 209; variety
    shows on, 201; WW II postwar pro-
    gramming, 198, 202
Central Intelligence Agency. See CIA
CETA. See Comprehensive and Employ-
    ment Training Act
Chamberlain, Neville, 37
Chancellor, John, 27, 106, 215
Chappaquidick, 20
Charley's Angels (television program),
    199, 210, 211
Chase, Chevy, 212, 213
"Checkers" speech, 14, 30
Chicago Tribune, 214
child birth, 8–9
China, 32, 33; Carter and, 43; Ford,
    Gerald, and, 43; Nixon policy
    towards, 39–43; U.S. foreign policy
    and, 39–44, 120, 231
The China Syndrome (movie, 1979), 129, 183

Chinatown (movie, 1974), 178, 183, 184, 197

Chisholm, Shirley, 16

Christian right: in politics, 160, 161; rights movement and, 162

Chrysler Corporation, 164

Church, Frank, 49, 51, 106, 107, 118, 223–24

Churchill, Winston, 37, 126

CIA (Central Intelligence Agency), 21, 118; Congress and, 32; Iran and, 220; oversight of, 50, 51

cinema. *See* movies

Citizen Kane (movie), 181

Citizen's Advisory Council on the Status of Women, 138

Civil Aeronautics Board, 167

civil rights: of blacks, 3, 7, 133, 137, 142, 150, 151, 157; Democratic Party and, 15; of disabled, 7, 8, 133, 137, 153–57, 232; of gays, 7, 133, 137, 150–53, 157, 232; legislation, 3, 4, 133, 134, 137, 140–42, 144; of women, 7, 133, 137–48, 157, 232

Civil Rights Act of 1964, 137, 140, 142; affirmative action and, 4; Title VI of, 155, 156, 170, 172; Title VII of, 173

Civil Rights Movement, in postwar era, 133, 151, 157

Clark, Dick, 114

Cleveland, Grover, 115

Coalition for Peace Through Strength, 117

Cold War, 2, 4, 32, 44, 51, 52, 77; Acheson and, 34; Afghanistan influence on, 119–20; Asian wars during, 6, 219; China and, 40, 42; detente and, 75, 120; end of, 231; under Reagan, 227

Coleman, John, 214

Colliers (magazine), 216

Collins, Robert, 168

Columbia Broadcasting System. *See* CBS

Columbo (television program), 185

Committee on Foreign Relations (Senate), 117

Committee on the Present Danger, 76, 117

communism, 52; containment of, 77, 120

Complete Book of Running (Fixx), 10

Comprehensive and Employment Training Act (CETA), 123–24

computer industry, economy and, 228–30

confidence: crisis of national, 2, 6, 131–32; in economy, 67; of WW II postwar era, 14, 140, 227

Congress, U.S.: abortion legislation in, 145–46, 148; budget control by, 97; bureaucracy in, 95–97; Carter and, 112–14; CIA and, 32; civil rights legislation in, 3, 4, 133, 134, 137, 140–41, 144; Democratic Party in, 16, 51, 60, 89, 93–95, 114, 123–24, 168; disabilities legislation in, 154, 155; energy crisis and, 65, 130; Ford, Gerald, and, 49, 74, 84, 96, 98; legislative process in, 3, 84, 86, 87–88, 90, 96, 97, 98, 99, 103, 147, 224–25; New York City and, 101; Nixon and, 16, 19, 23–24, 25, 28, 30, 36, 39, 97; post-Civil War, 98; post-Watergate, 93–97, 134; presidency and, 30, 80, 88, 96, 97, 98–99; reform of, 87, 90–92; Republican Party in, 13, 115, 223; scandals in, 88–89, 101–2; television and, 114; Watergate hearings in, 25–28. *See also* hearings, Congressional

Congressional Budget Office, 97, 99

Congressional Research Service (CRS), 97

Conners, Chuck, 47

conservatism, 1, 5, 76, 159, 168; resurgence of, 169, 177, 223

conservatives: cultural, 214; for deregulation, 166; tax cuts by, 167–68

Constitution, U.S.: fifteenth amendment of, 142; fourteenth amendment of, 142, 147

consumer price index, 126

convention(s): 1972 Democratic Party, 18; 1980 Democratic Party, 222; delegates, 18; television coverage of, 19, 216

Cook, Cardinal Terence, 147

Cooley, Harold, 94

Coolidge, Calvin, 22
Coppola, Francis Ford, 186, 187–88
corporate culture, 54
Cosell, Howard, 203
Council of Economic Advisors (CEA), 56, 57, 58, 60
Court, Margaret, 139
Cox, Archibald, 25, 27
Cronkite, Walter, 29, 46, 108, 110, 129, 215–16, 221
CRS. *See* Congressional Research Service
Crystal, Billy, 213
Cuba, 40; Africa and, 116; Soviet Union and, 117
Cuban Missile Crisis, 36
cultural conservatives: media and, 214
culture wars, 162
Curtin, Jane, 213
Czechoslovakia, 40

Daley, Richard, 18
Daly, Joel, 214
Damn Yankees (play), 204
Davidson, Sara, 67
Day at the Races (movie, 1937), 196
Day, Doris, 202, 203
De Palma, Brian, 186
Dean, James, 179
Dean, John, 24, 47; testimony of, 25, 26
Dean, Morton, 37
debates, presidential: Carter/Ford (1976), 107–9; Nixon/Kennedy (1960), 14
deflation, 59, 166, 231
Democratic Caucus, 93–94, 114
Democratic Congressional Campaign Committee, 101
Democratic National Committee, 3
Democratic National Headquarters, 21, 23
Democratic Party: 1980 defeat of, 223–24; civil rights and, 15; in Congress, 16, 51, 60, 89, 93–95, 114, 123–24, 168; conventions of, 18, 138; detente and, 44; House of Representatives and, 91, 93; 1974 Congressional gains of, 93;

presidential elections and, 15; Watergate and, 22, 30
demogrant, 19
Department of Health, Education, and Welfare, 141, 155, 156, 170
Department of Labor, 171
deregulation, 232; of airline industry, 166–67, 225; of brokerage industry, 225; conservatives and, 166; of energy policy, 225; under Reagan, 227
detente, 221; under Carter, 116–18, 120; challenges to, 46, 48, 75; China and, 39, 44; Democratic Party and, 44; under Ford, Gerald, 75–76; Jackson, Henry, and, 76–80; national security and, 45–46; opposition to, 76–80, 83; Soviet view of, 79
Dewey, Thomas, 37
DeWitt, Joyce, 199
diplomacy: after Vietnam, 52; in Arab-Israeli conflict, 64; U.S. foreign policy and, 39, 40–41, 44, 46–47, 48
disability rights, 7, 8, 133, 137, 150, 153–57, 232
disco, 191–92
divorce, 159–60
Dix, Dorothea, 144
Dobrynin, Anatoly F., 39, 44, 79
Dole, Robert, 36, 83
dollar: as international currency, 60; in international markets, 61
domestic policy: of Carter, 111–13; of Ford, Gerald, 84, 99–101; of Johnson, 84
The Doris Day Show (television program), 202
Douglas, Michael, 129
Dreiser, Theodore, 208
Dreyfuss, Julia-Louis, 213
Dreyfuss, Richard, 184
Duel (television movie, 1971), 185
Duke Law School, 12
Dulles, John Foster, 41
Dunaway, Faye, 180, 183
Dunne, Peter Finley, 207

Eagleton, Thomas, 18, 19

Easterlin, Richard, 68

economists, 1, 2, 6, 53; liberal v. conservative, 166; as policy advisors, 163, 225; in White House, 56

economy, 4, 8, 53; under Carter, 120, 123–27; computer industry and, 228–30; confidence in, 67; decline of, 1, 2, 7, 53, 55, 59, 66, 68, 69–70; under Ford, Gerald, 81–82; global, 5, 54, 163; government and, 53, 54, 57–58, 123–27; movies and, 184; Nixon and, 16, 56, 58, 60; presidential elections and, 126; productivity and, 66–67; under Reagan, 228; steel industry and, 54, 120–23

Ed Sullivan Show (television show), 195, 199, 201, 205, 212

Edison, Thomas, 228

education: bilingual, 7, 159, 169–70; women's rights in, 140–41, 230–31

Education Amendments of 1972, 140, 155

Education for all Handicapped Children Act of 1975, 154

EEOC. *See* Equal Employment Opportunity Commission

Egypt: war with Israel, 2, 48

Ehrlichman, John, 20, 24, 25

Eisenhower, Dwight, 13, 14, 76; Korean War and, 34; Nixon's relationship with, 23; Vietnam and, 33

Eizenstat, Stuart, 126, 130

elections, presidential: Carter/Ford (1976), 39, 82–83; Democratic party and, 15; economy and, 126; Johnson/Goldwater (1964), 14; Kennedy/Nixon (1960), 14, 17; Nixon/Humphrey (1968), 14–15; Nixon/McGovern (1972), 16–19; Reagan/Carter (1980), 223–24; Republican Party and, 4, 15, 19; South in, 15, 17, 19

elections, congressional, 91

electoral politics, 223; Watergate influence on, 12, 22

electoral process: African Americans in, 4; television in, 107–9

Elementary and Secondary Education Act of 1965, 4

Ellis, Albert, 150

Ellsberg, Daniel, 20, 25

energy crisis, 61–63, 64; under Carter, 130–32; Congress and, 65, 130; conservation and, 226; under Ford, Gerald, 82. *See also* oil crisis

environment, 65

Equal Employment Opportunity Commission (EEOC), 137, 138, 142

Equal Rights Amendment (ERA), 134, 141–45, 147, 148, 153, 159

ERA. *See* Equal Rights Amendment

Ervin, Sam, 24, 47

Evans, Robert, 43

Eyewitness News, 214

Faith, Michael, 176

Falk, Peter, 185

Falwell, Jerry, 161

Faulkner, William, 186, 254n11

Fawcett-Majors, Farrah, 210

FBI, 20, 24, 27; in Nixon administration, 20

Federal Reserve, 57, 58, 126, 228

The Feminine Mystique (Friedan), 149

feminists: abortion advocacy of, 9; medicine critique by, 8

films. *See* movies

First National Women's Conference, 144

Fitzgerald, F. Scott, 197

Flynn, Fahey, 214

Foley, Thomas, 94

folk medicine, 9

Fonda, Jane, 129

Ford, Betty, 217

Ford, Gerald, 2, 7, 11, 77, 79, 104, 154, 155, 212; China and, 43; CIA and, 51; Congress and, 49, 74, 84, 96, 98; domestic policy of, 84, 99–101; economy under, 81–82; energy crisis under, 82; foreign

policy of, 75, 78, 79, 80–81; in House of Representatives, 71–72, 87; Nixon pardon by, 73–74, 93; in presidential debates, 108–9; press and, 74; SALT and, 75–76; tax cuts under, 81
Ford, Henry, 130, 228, 229, 230
Ford, John, 186
foreign policy, U.S.: Afghanistan and, 119–20; of Carter, 116–18, 220–23; China and, 39–44, 120, 231; diplomacy and, 39, 40–41, 44, 46–47, 48; of Ford, Gerald, 75, 78, 79, 80–81; towards Iran, 220–22; Middle East and, 48, 219; of Nixon, 32, 35, 39–41, 44, 46; post war v. seventies, 219; Soviet Union and, 2, 44–46, 48, 219; towards Vietnam, 32–36, 38–39; Vietnam War influence on, 52, 227, 231
Forester, C.S., 222
Fox, Fanne, 89
Fox Studios, 179
France, Vietnam and, 33
Frankel, Max, 109
free market, 166
French Indochinese Union, 33
Friedan, Betty, 143, 145, 149
The Front Page (play), 214
Frum, David, 5

Gabor, Eva, 202
Galbraith, John Kenneth, 43
Gallup Poll, 43
GAO. See General Accounting Office
Garment, Len, 43
Garn, Jake, 117
Garrity, Arthur, 175, 176
Gates, Bill, 228–30
Gay Liberation Front, 151
gay rights: legislation for, 152–53; movement, 7, 8, 133, 137, 149–53, 157, 232
gays, 111, 136–37, 150; Catholic Church's position toward, 149–50; medical views on, 150, 153; polls on attitudes toward, 151; society's attitudes toward, 149, 151, 152, 153, 157, 232
General Accounting Office (GAO), 96–97, 99
Geneva Peace Accords, 33
George Washington Slept Here (movie and play), 202
Gershwin, George, 196
"The Ghost of Tom Joad" (Springstein), 123
Girl Scouts, 141
GNP. See gross national product
The Godfather (movie, 1972), 43, 178, 186–89, 197, 233
The Godfather (Puzo), 186, 187
gold standard, 61, 62
Goldberg, Bernard, 185
Goldwater, Barry, 14, 75, 81
Goodman, Benny, 191
Gore, Al, 125
Gorney, Karen, 192
government, U.S., 6, 165; branches of, 12; disability-rights movement and, 154–57; distrust of, 149, 224, 225; economy and, 53, 54, 57–58, 123–27; interventionist policy of, 2, 32, 78, 80–81, 227; leadership in, 98, 225; medicine and, 84; regulatory programs of, 166
The Graduate (movie, 1967), 180, 230
Graham, Billy, 43, 161
Graham, Hugh, 137
Grapes of Wrath (Steinbeck), 202
Gray, Patrick, 24
Great Society, 84, 85, 86, 90, 113, 156, 159, 169, 227
Greeley, Andrew, 111
Green Acres (television show), 202, 204
Green, Edith, 140
Griffith, Andy, 202
gross national product (GNP), 55, 81
The Gulag Archipelago (Solzhenitsyn), 139
Gunsmoke (radio and television program), 202, 203

Guttmacher, Dr. Alan, 147
Guys and Dolls (play), 193, 194

Hackett, Buddy, 195
Haiphong Harbor, 38
Halberstam, David, 29
Haldeman, H.R., 24, 27, 38, 41
Haley, Alex, 211
Halleck, Charles A., 72
handicapped. See disability rights
Happy Days (television program), 199,
    210, 211, 212
Happy Talk, news format, 214, 215
Harding, Warren, 73
Harris Poll, 6, 107, 151
Hart, Gary, 17, 18
Hartman, Robert T., 73
Hatcher, Richard, 226
Hawks, Howard, 182, 186, 254n11
Hawn, Goldie, 203
Hays, Wayne, 101–2
health: individual v. social responsibility
    for, 10; managed care in, 232
health insurance, 85–86. See also national
    health insurance
Health Insurance Association of America,
    85
health-maintenance organizations, 8
hearings, Congressional: on Watergate,
    25–28; women's rights and, 140
Hebert, F. Edward, 95
Helms, Jesse, 117
Hemingway, Ernest, 186
Hemingway, Mariel, 196
Henson, Jim, 213
Here's Lucy (television program), 202
Hersh, Seymour, 51
Hewitt, Don, 216
Hicks, Louise Day, 175
Hiss, Alger, 13
Hitchcock, Alfred, 186
Hitler, 76
Ho Chi Minh, 33
Hoey, Clyde, 24
Hoffman, Dustin, 180

Hofstadter, Richard, 5
Hogan, Lawrence, 147
Hollywood: directors, 180, 181, 182, 183,
    184, 185, 186, 187–88, 193, 232; movies
    and, 179–81; studios, 179, 180, 185, 188
homosexuality. See gay rights; gays
Hoover, Herbert, 83, 115, 118, 125, 223
Hope, Bob, 152, 195, 196
Horne, Lena, 201
House Education Committee, 140
House Foreign Affairs Committee, 72
House Judiciary Committee, 28, 29, 30
House of Mirth (Wharton), 208
House of Representatives, U.S.: commit-
    tees in, 91–92, 93–95; Democratic
    Party and, 91
House Ways and Means Committee, 79
housing, inflation and, 168
Houston Post, 215
Howard, Ron, 210
human rights, in Russia, 76, 78, 79
Humbard, Rex, 161
Humphrey, Hubert, 14–15, 16, 17, 18, 222
Huston, John, 183
Hyde Amendment, 147–48
Hyde, Henry, 147

I Love Lucy (television program), 202,
    203, 213
IBM, 229
Illinois Federation of Republican
    Women, 143
income, household, 55, 67, 168
Indochina war, 33
inflation, 53, 54, 228; under Carter, 124–
    27; of housing, 168; peaks in, 1, 55;
    social benefits linked to, 3, 60; unem-
    ployment and, 58, 59, 62, 70
Interiors (movie), 196
Iowa caucuses, 106
Iran, 125, 128, 219, 231; Carter and, 220–22;
    U.S. foreign policy towards, 220–22
Iraq, 219, 231
Isaacson, Walter, 32
Israel, 19, 219, 231; war with Egypt, 2, 48

Jackson, Henry, 16, 107, 116, 117; detente
and, 76–80
Jackson, Maynard, 174
Jackson-Vanik amendment, 78–79
Japan: automobiles from, 56; indus-
trial policy in, 164–65; MITI managed
economy in, 165; steel industry in,
121–22; Vietnam and, 33
Jarvis, Howard, 169
Javits, Jacob, 79, 155
Jaworski, Leon, 27, 28, 30
Jaws (Benchley), 184
Jaws (movie), 184, 188, 189, 197, 255*n*13
The Jeffersons (television program), 208
Jepsen, Roger, 115
Johnson, Lady Bird, 118
Johnson, Lyndon, 2, 13, 14, 15, 152, 169;
domestic policy of, 84; Great Society
program of, 84, 85, 86, 90, 113, 156, 159,
169, 227; McCormack and, 113, 114;
press and, 28; Vietnam War and, 20,
33, 34
Joint Chiefs of Staff, 75
Jong, Erica, 149
Jonkman, Bartel, 72
Jordan, Hamilton, 105, 108, 113
journalism, investigative, 29, 51, 129
Justice Department, 27

Kael, Pauline, 181, 182
Kahn, Alfred, 167
Kaiser aluminum, 121, 172–73
Kansas City Star, 215
Kaufman, George, 194
Keaton, Diane, 195, 196, 197
Kemp, Jack, 168, 223
Kennedy, Edward, 20, 106, 118; in 1980
Democratic primaries, 221–23; airline
deregulation and, 167; as Cold War dove,
116; health insurance plan of, 85, 86
Kennedy, Jackie, 118
Kennedy, John F., 4, 13, 14, 15, 20, 28, 36,
40, 56, 72, 74, 137, 227; assassination
of, 29; Vietnam and, 33
Kennedy Library, 118

Kennedy, Robert, 15, 17
Kent State University, 36–37
Keynes, John Maynard, 127
Khmer Rouge, 49
Khomeini, Ruhullah Masaui, 125, 220, 221
King, Billie Jean, 139, 140, 145
King, Coretta, 118, 143, 145
King, Martin Luther, 22, 34
King, Stephen, 186
Kirkland, Lane, 76
Kirkpatrick, Jeanne, 76
Kissinger, Henry, 36, 77, 78, 79, 188, 221;
China and, 39–43; Middle East war
and, 48; Pentagon Papers and, 20;
Vietnam War and, 35
Kleindienst, Richard, 24
Koch, Edward, 101
Korean War, 32, 33, 219; Eisenhower and,
34; *M*A*S*H* depiction of, 181, 182, 183
Kosygin, Alexey, 45
Kreps, Juanita, 116
Krol, Cardinal, 147
Kutler, Stanley, 20
Kuwait, 219

labor force: affirmative action and, 173;
baby boom in, 228; growth of, 225;
migration from farm to city, 66–67;
women in, 7, 67–68, 142, 232
labor, organized, national health insur-
ance and, 86
Lady's Home Journal (magazine), 138
laetrile, 9
LaFollette, Robert, 97
Laird, Melvin, 72
Laos, 33
Lasch, Christopher, 158, 159, 162, 163,
168, 173
Lassie (television show), 200, 217
Lau remedies, 170
Laugh In (television show), 212
Lawrence of Arabia (movie), 220
Leachman, Cloris, 209
League for the Independence of
Vietnam, 33

League of Nations, 98, 117
leaks, national security, 20, 51
Lee, Philip, 85
Legislative Reference Service (LRS), 97
Legislative Reorganization Act of 1946,
    90, 91
Legislative Reorganization Act of 1970,
    91, 97
Lerner, Max, 12
lesbianism, 149. *See also* gay rights; gays
Letterman, David, 201
Lev, Peter, 181
Lewis, Sinclair, 67, 207
liberalism, crisis of, 5, 227, 232
Library of Congress, 97
Liddy, G. Gordon, 23
Life (magazine), 216
Lindsay, John, 17, 37
Lodge, Cabot, 117
Look (magazine), 216
Loose Change (Davidson), 67
Los Angeles Times, 13
Love and Death (movie), 195, 196
LRS. *See* Legislative Reference Service
Lucas, George, 186
Lynd, Staughton, 123

Macy, John, 137
Magruder, Jeb, 24
Mahler, Gustav, 197
Mahoney, George P., 22
Mailer, Norman, 186
Main Street (Lewis), 67
The Maltese Falcon (movie), 183
Manhattan (movie), 193, 194, 196, 197
Manhattan Project, 65
Mansfield, Mike, 23
Mao Zedong, 41, 42
Marcus Welby, MD (television program), 185
marriage, institutional changes in, 232
Marshall, Garry, 212
Marx brothers, 195, 196
Marx, Groucho, 196
Mary Poppins (movie), 179

Mary Tyler Moore Show (television pro-
    gram), 199, 205, 208–9, 211
M*A*S*H (movie), 181, 182, 183
Maude (television program), 208
May, Elaine, 195
Mayaguez incident, 80–81, 221, 222
Mays, Willie, 140
McCarthy, Eugene, 160
McCarthy, Joseph, 51
McCord, James W., Jr., 23, 24
McCormack, John: Johnson and, 113, 114
McGill, William, 224
McGovern, George, 16–19, 233; polls
    during campaign of, 19
McLaine, Shirley, 43
McNamara, Robert, 50
McQueen, Steve, 9
"Me Decade," 5, 158, 177
"The Me Decade and the Third Great
    Awakening" (Wolfe), 159
Meader, Vaughn, 74
Mean Streets (movie), 193
Meany, George, 124
media: cultural conservatives and, 214;
    television dominance of, 214, 215, 216.
    See also movies; press; television
Medicare, 85, 86, 87, 88, 97, 99, 227
medicine, 6; folk, 9; government and, 84;
    homosexuality and, 150, 151, 153;
    malpractice of, 9; public policy and,
    8; self-help and, 10; women and, 8,
    145, 146
Medina, Ann, 139
Mental Health Law Project, 154
Meredith, Don, 204
Metro-Dade (county) Commission, 152
Michaels, Lorne, 212
Microsoft, 228, 229
Middle East, 2; civil wars in, 219, 231; oil
    in, 63, 64, 219; U.S. foreign policy and,
    48, 219; war, 48, 128
Milk, Harvey, 153
Mills v. Board of Education, 154

Mills, Wilbur, 16, 86, 103; fall of, 88–89; national health insurance and, 87–88
Mineta, Norman, 93
Miss America Pageant, 138
Mitchell, John, 24
MITI: Japanese economy influenced by, 165
Mondale, Walter, 114
Monday Night Football (television program), 203–4
Monty Python and the Holy Grail (movie), 115
Moore, Gary, 195
Moral Majority, 162
Morris, Garrett, 213
Moscone, Georgy, 153
movies: blacks in, 190; blockbuster, 188–89, 197, 232; current events and, 182, 183, 184, 187, 197; distribution of, 189; economy's influence on, 184; "film noir" genre of, 183; Hollywood, 179–81; about New York City, 193–94, 196; television's replacement of, 178–79; videotapes' influence on, 181
Moynihan, Daniel Patrick, 43, 76, 77
Mr. Blandings Builds His Dream House (movie), 202
Mr. Smith Goes to Washington (movie), 73
Ms. (magazine), 138–39
MS-DOS, 229
Mudd, Roger, 47, 115, 222
Municipal Assistance Corporation, 100
Murphy, Eddie, 213
Murray, Bill, 213
Murrow, Edward R., 29, 215
Muskie, Edmund, 17, 18, 21
My Lai Massacre, 34
Myers, Mike, 213

NAACP (National Association for the Advancement of Colored People), 175
Nader, Ralph, 101
narcissism, culture of, 69, 162, 165, 168
Nashville (movie), 181

National Academy of Sciences, 9
National Association for the Advancement of Colored People. *See* NAACP
National Broadcasting Company. *See* NBC
National Commission for the Human Life Amendment, 147
National Committee to Stop ERA, 144
National Conference of Catholic Bishops, 148
National Conference of Commissions on the Status of Women, 138
national health insurance, 3, 84; Clinton advocacy of, 232; Kennedy, Edward, plan for, 85, 86; Mills and, 87–88; organized labor and, 86
National Organization for Women (NOW), 138, 143, 149, 156, 162
national security, 52; detente and, 45–46; leaks and, 20, 51
National Security Council, 20, 48
Navy, U.S., 13, 142
NBC (National Broadcasting Company), 27, 29, 47, 74, 194, 201, 203; News anchor, 215; Saturday night programming, 212–13
NBC Comedy Hour (television program), 194
neo-conservative, 76
New Deal, 5, 84, 98, 112, 113, 225, 227; Republican Party and, 13
New Frontier, Republican Party and, 223
Newman, Katherine, 70
Newman, Lorraine, 213
news, television: Happy Talk format for, 214, 215; network, 215–16
New York Academy of Medicine, 149
New York City: bankruptcy of, 99–101; gay rights movement and, 149, 150–51; movies about, 193–94; television broadcasts from, 212, 213
New York Magazine, 191
New York Post, 194
New York Times, 20, 28, 29, 51, 101, 106, 150, 151

New Yorker, 181

Nichols, Mike, 180, 195

Nicholson, Jack, 183, 184

Nixon, Pat, 30

Nixon, Richard, 2, 3, 4, 78, 155, 169; China policy of, 39–43; Congress and, 16, 19, 23–24, 25, 28, 30, 36, 39, 97; domestic policy of, 85, 86; early life of, 12–13; economy and, 16, 56, 58, 60; Eisenhower's relationship with, 23; energy crisis and, 64–65; foreign policy of, 32, 35, 39–41, 44, 46; impeachment proceedings against, 2, 27, 28, 29, 30, 39; legacy of, 32, 48, 49; pardon of, 73, 93; personality of, 16, 26, 29, 35, 37, 110; presidential power of, 12, 20, 26, 27, 28, 46; resignation of, 30; self-perception, 13, 26, 30, 182; Soviet Union and, 44–46, 220; State of the Union address, 28; televised addresses of, 13–14, 24, 26, 27, 28, 30, 36, 41, 45; as Vice President, 13–14, 23; Vietnam War and, 32, 34–39; war on cancer, 9; Watergate cover-up by, 24, 25, 26–27

Nixon, Tricia, 20

North Vietnam, 2; offensives, 34, 35, 38, 49

Northwestern University, 135

Not Ready for Prime Time Players, 212

Novak, Michael, 187

NOW. *See* National Organization for Women

nuclear energy, 128–30, 225

Nunn, Sam, 117, 118

OFCC. *See* Office of Federal Contract Compliance

Office of Federal Contract Compliance (OFCC), 171, 172

Office of Price Administration, 13

Office of Strategic Services, 50

oil: in Alaska, 65; alternatives to, 225; domestic v. foreign production of, 62–63; embargo, 64; foreign, 2, 64; in

Middle East, 63, 64, 219; prices, 55, 61, 82, 126, 128, 130, 131; shortages, 64, 128

oil crisis, 1, 2, 3, 7, 126, 128, 231; Congress and, 65, 130

Olympics (1980), U.S. withdrawal from, 120

On the Waterfront (movie), 190, 191

O'Neill, Tip, 93, 94, 95, 96, 101; Carter and, 113, 114

OPEC (Organization of the Petroleum Exporting Countries), 82, 131

Organization of the Petroleum Exporting Countries. *See* OPEC

Oversey, Dr. Lionel, 151

Ozersky, Josh, 199

Pacino, Al, 188, 191

Panama Canal, 83

Paramount Studios, 188, 189

PARC v. Pennsylvania, 154

Parks, Rosa, 151

"Pastoral Plan for Pro-Life Activities," 147

Patman, Wright, 94

Patterson, James, 9

Patton (movie), 182, 183, 188

Peale, Norman Vincent, 14, 37

Pei, I.M., 118

Penn, Arthur, 180

Pentagon Papers, 20

People (magazine), 216

Perkins, Anthony, 186

Phillips curve, 58, 59

Phillips, Kevin, 15

Planned Parenthood, 147, 148

Playboy (magazine), 216; Carter interview in, 108

"the plumbers": arrest of, 21; bugging operations of, 20–21; sentencing of, 24

Poage, W. G., 94

Podgorny, Nikolay, 45

Podhoretz, Norman, 76

Polanski, Roman, 183

polio, 6

political intelligence, 20

political parties, coalitions in, 15. *See also* American Independent Party; Democratic Party; Republican Party

Pompidou, Georges, 46

Populist Era, 225

postwar era, 1, 2, 3, 8, 148; attitudes of, 162; civil rights movement of, 133; confidence of, 14, 140, 227; disability public policy during, 153–54; economic policy during, 225; religion in, 162; social structures of, 159–60; Supreme Court in, 172; television programming in, 198–202; transformation of, 224, 233; wars in Asia during, 6, 219

Powell, Adam Clayton, 148

Powell, Lewis, 172

presidency: career path to, 12; Congress and, 30, 80, 88, 96, 97, 98–99; image of, 2, 6, 28, 29, 31, 98, 108, 110, 231; misuse of, 12, 20–22; power of, 6, 53; press and, 20, 22, 28–29, 31, 47, 109; undermining of, 3, 28, 29, 30, 31; postwar, 16, 20, 28. *See also* Carter, Jimmy; Ford, Gerald; Nixon, Richard; Reagan, Ronald

President's Commission for a National Agenda for the Eighties, 132, 224, 231

President's Commission on the Status of Women, 137

Presley, Elvis, 179, 191

press: Carter and, 105–6, 115; Ford, Gerald, and, 74; liberal v. conservative, 168; post-Watergate, 88, 89, 90, 101–2; presidency and, 20, 22, 28–29, 31, 47, 109; Vietnam War and, 34; Watergate and, 20, 21, 22, 25, 27, 28; World War II and, 34

price and wage controls, 16, 60, 61, 63–64

Price, Melvin, 95

primaries, presidential: 1972, 16–18; 1976, 82; 1980, 221–23; Carter in, 106–7; Jewish voters and, 78

private enterprise, 6

productivity: economy and, 66–67, 225; workers and, 68

Progressive Era, 98, 110, 142

Project Apollo, 65

Project Independence, 65

Proposition 13, 169

Psycho (movie), 186

public policy: on disabilities, 153–57; economists and, 163, 225; medicine and, 8; post war v. seventies, 224

Puzo, Mario, 186–87

Rabbit Redux (Updike), 126

racial conflict, 3, 4, 22

racial quota, 171–72

Radner, Gilda, 213

Rafshoon, Gerald, 118

Rather, Dan, 21, 29, 217

Ray, Elizabeth, 102

Reagan, Ronald, 5, 8, 75, 160, 224, 226, 227; in 1976 primary, 83; in 1980 presidential campaign, 223; Cold War under, 227; Congress and, 103; deregulation under, 227; economy under, 228; welfare programs under, 227

Reasoner, Harry, 217

Rebozo, Bebe, 37

recession, 8, 55, 61; under Ford, Gerald, 81–82

Reconstruction, 98, 142

Rehabilitation Act of 1973, 155

Reiner, Carl, 212

religion: evangelical, 159, 160, 161; revival of, 160–62

Republican Party: in Congress, 13, 115, 223; New Deal view of, 13; New Frontier and, 223; presidential elections and, 4, 15, 19, 223; tax cuts and, 223, 227; Watergate and, 7, 30

Reston, James, 43

Restore Our Alienated Rights (ROAR), 175

retirement, personal savings accounts in, 232

Reuss, Henry, 94

Revenue Adjustment Act of 1975, 81

Reynolds, Frank, 115

Ribuffo, Leo, 161

Richardson, Elliot, 25, 27, 85

Riggs, Bobby, 139, 140, 145

rights revolution: Christian right and,
162; critics of, 158, 159; disability, 7, 8,
133, 137, 150, 153–57, 232; gay, 7, 8, 133,
137, 149–53, 157, 232; government and,
156; opposition to, 134; women's, 7,
133, 137–48, 157, 232

right-to-life movement, abortion and, 148

ROAR. See Restore Our Alienated Rights

Roberts, Oral, 161

Robertson, Pat, 161

Rock, Chris, 213

Rockefeller Commission, 51

Rockefeller, David, 221

Rockefeller, John D., 62, 63

Rockefeller, Nelson, 37, 43, 51, 159; as vice
president, 74–75

Rocky (movie), 189–90, 233

Roe v. Wade, 146

Rogers, Ginger, 191

Rogers, William, 41

Rolling Stones, 201

Rooney, Mickey, 186

Roosevelt, Franklin, 5, 28, 36, 98, 112, 113,
118; Soviet Union and, 43

Roosevelt, Teddy, 30, 166

Roots (Haley), 211

Roots (television program), 211–12

Rosen, Ruth, 5, 149

Rostenkowski, Daniel, 95

Roth, William, 168

Roundtree, Richard, 190

Rowan and Martin's Laugh-In (television
program), 203

Rumsfeld, Donald, 72, 74, 75

Runyon, Damon, 193

Russia. See Soviet Union

Rust Belt: cities, 208, 210; declining population in, 173

Rutgers, the state university, 135

Safer, Morley, 217

Sahl, Mort, 195

Saigon, 49–50

SALT. See Strategic Arms Limitations
Talks treaty

SALT II, 116, 117

Sandler, Adam, 213

Sarris, Andrew, 194

Saturday Evening Post (magazine), 216

Saturday Night Fever (movie), 191–93, 233

Saturday Night Live (television program),
212–13

Saudi Arabia, 64, 220

scandals: Congressional, 88–89, 101–2;
Grant, 24; Teapot Dome, 24. See also
Watergate

Scherer, Ray, 27

Schieffer, Bob, 38

Schlafly, Phyllis, 143, 144, 145, 150, 153

Schlesinger, Arthur, Jr., 5, 115

Schlesinger, James, 128

Schneider, Roy, 184

schools: desegregation of, 174–76; federal
funding for, 148; racial segregation in,
4, 148; sex discrimination in, 7, 135–36,
140–41, 230

Schuller, Robert, 161

Schulman, Bruce, 6

Schultz, Charles, 123, 124

Schweiker, Richard, 83

Scopes Trial, 162

Scorsese, Martin, 193, 197

Scott, George C., 182

Scott, Hugh, 29

segregation: in Boston schools, 174–76;
busing and, 4, 141; sexual, 7, 135–36; in
South, 133

Select Committee on Presidential
Campaign Activities, 24

self-help, medicine and, 10

Senate Armed Forces Committee, 118

Senate Intelligence Committee, 118

Senate Judiciary Committee, 23

Severeid, Eric, 108

Shaffer, Paul, 213

Shaft (movie), 190–91
Shanghai Communiqué, 42
Shaw, Robert, 184
Shire, Talia, 188
Shriver, Sargent, 19
Sid Caesar Show (television program), 212
Simon and Garfunkel, 180
Simon, Danny, 194
Simon, Neil, 194
The Simpsons (television program), 129
Singer sewing machine company, 69–70
Sino-Soviet relations, 40
Sirica, John, 24, 26, 27, 28
Sister Carrie (Dreiser), 208
Six Crises (Nixon), 42
Sixty Minutes (television program), 216–18
Skelton, Red, 199
Sklar, Robert, 211
Sleeper (movie), 195
social policy: great divide in, 232
Social Security, 3, 88, 99, 113, 144, 227
Somers, Suzanne, 199
The Sound of Music (movie), 179, 188
South: migration from, 173; in 1980 presidential election, 223; in presidential elections, 15, 17, 19, 109; racial tension in, 3; segregation in, 133; television portrayal of, 211; two-party system in, 4
South Vietnam, 2; civil war in, 33; fall of, 49; Thieu government of, 38
Soviet Union, 2, 32, 39, 49; Afghanistan and, 119–20; Cuba and, 117; emigration from, 78; expansion of, 33; grain purchases of, 61; human rights in, 76, 78, 79; most-favored-nation status of, 78–79; Nixon and, 44–46, 220; U.S. foreign policy and, 2, 44–46, 48, 219; U.S. trade with, 78–80
space exploration, 6
Spielberg, Steven, 185, 186, 194
Sports Illustrated (magazine), 216
sports, television, 203–4
Springsteen, Bruce, 123

stagflation, 1, 166, 231
Stallone, Sylvester, 189, 191
Stanton, Jim, 101
Star Wars (movie), 186, 197
State Department, U.S., 40, 51
"Stayin' Alive" (Bee Gees), 192
steel industry, 164, 165; Congress and, 122; economy and, 54, 120–23; in Japan, 121–22; in Youngstown, Ohio, 121–23
Steering and Policy Committee (House of Representatives), 94
Stein, Herbert, 61
Steinbeck, John, 12
Steiner, Gilbert, 111
Stennis, John, 27
Stevenson, Adlai, 159
Stonewall riots, 150, 151, 156
Strategic Arms Limitations Talks treaty (SALT), 45, 46, 120; Carter and, 116–18; under Ford, 75–76
Strauss, Robert, 124
Subcommittee Bill of Rights, 92
Sullivan, Ed, 199, 200, 201, 203, 205
summit meetings, U.S./Soviet: in Moscow, 45–46, 48, 75; in Washington, 47; Watergate and, 47
Sun Belt, 15
Sundquist, James, 95
supply-side economics, 167–68
Supreme Court, 7, 30, 147, 153; affirmative action and, 172–73; bilingual education and, 170; desegregation rulings of, 175; rulings on abortion, 146, 148; in WW II postwar era, 172
Swaggart, Jimmy, 161
Swann v. Charlotte-Mecklenberg, 175

Taft, Robert, 125
Taiwan, 42
Tamiment resort, 194
tax cuts, 56, 61, 167–69, 232; by conservatives, 167–68; under Ford, 81; Republican Party and, 223
Taylor, Elizabeth, 200

Taylor, Zachary, 16

television, 11, 233: advertising, 205; cable influence on, 181, 213, 233; China trip coverage by, 41; Congress and, 114; convention coverage, 19, 216; cultural function of, 218; in electoral process, 107–9; in House hearings, 91; mass appeal of, 199; media dominance by, 214, 215, 216; miniseries, 211; movies replaced by, 178–79; network anchors, 215; network programming, 198, 200; as news source, 29, 213–15; sports on, 203–4; U.S./Russia summits coverage by, 44–45, 49; Vietnam War coverage, 49, 50; Watergate hearings on, 25; women's movement and, 138, 139; World Series on, 211. *See also* news, television

Third World, 227

Thomas, Lewis, 9

Three Mile Island, 128–29

Three's Company (television program), 199

Thurow, Lester, 66, 158, 159, 163, 164, 168, 229

Time (magazine), 136, 217

Title IX of Education Amendments of 1972, 140, 141, 147, 155

Title VI of Civil Rights Act of 1964, 155

Title VII of Civil Rights Act of 1964, 173

Today Show (television program), 43

Tomlin, Lily, 203, 212

Tonight Show (television program), 195, 212

Toscanini, Arturo, 212

Townsend Plan, 169

trade deficits, 7, 55

Travolta, John, 191, 192, 196

Trilling, Lionel, 5

Truman, Harry S., 43, 98, 105

Turkey, 220

Twain, Mark, 207

Udall, Morris, 106

Ullman, Al, 90, 92

unemployment, 1, 55, 124, 231; inflation and, 58, 59, 62, 70; in steel industry, 120–23

United Artists Studio, 189

United Nations, 42, 144; Middle East war and, 48

United Press International, 215

United States Steel Corporation, 120, 121, 123

Universal Studios, 185, 189

University of California, Davis: racial quota system at, 171–72

University of Texas, 21

Updike, John, 126

urban policy, 226–27

USS *Seawolf*, 105

Van Dyke, Dick, 208

Vance, Cyrus, 116

Vanik, Charles, 79

vice president, U.S.: Agnew's resignation as, 1, 23, 48; Nixon as, 13–14, 23; Rockefeller as, 74–75; role of, 23

Viet Cong, 33

Vietnam: France and, 33; Geneva Peace Accords creation of, 33; Japan and, 33; U.S. foreign policy towards, 32–36, 38–39. *See also* North Vietnam; South Vietnam

Vietnam Memorial Wall, 81

Vietnam War, 1, 2, 3, 29, 219; costs of, 49; domestic effects of, 51, 52; Eisenhower and, 33; end of, 49; escalation of, 34, 35, 36, 38, 39; foreign policy influenced by, 52, 227, 231; France and, 33; Japan and, 33; Johnson and, 33, 34; Kennedy, John, and, 33; movies about, 182; Nixon and, 32; opposition to, 36–37, 138; origins of, 32–33; peace talks during, 35, 36, 38, 39, 42; Pentagon Papers and, 20; press and, 34; television coverage of, 49, 50

VisiCalc, 229

Vogel, Ezra, 165

Voting Rights Act, 3, 4

Wall Street Journal, 86, 168
Wallace, George C., 15, 17, 18, 107
Wallace, Mike, 217
Walt Disney Studios, 179, 201
Walters, Barbara, 43
Waniski, Jude, 168
Warnke, Paul, 116
Washington Post, 10, 21, 24, 27, 29, 86, 102, 115, 217, 226
Watergate, 2: Congressional hearings, 25–28; consequences of, 32, 86, 87, 88, 89, 90, 97–98, 103, 114; cover-up, 25–27; Democratic Party and, 22, 30; electoral politics affected by, 12; Middle East war and, 48; origins of, 20; press and, 20, 21, 22, 25, 27, 28; Republican Party and, 7, 30; Soviet/U.S. summit and, 47; special prosecutors, 25, 27; television coverage of hearings, 25. *See also* "the plumbers"
The Way the World Works (Waniski), 168
Wayne, John, 182
Ways and Means Committee, 87, 88
Weimar Germany, 56
welfare programs, 3; under Reagan, 227; reform of, 112, 224, 232
West Side Story (story), 191, 192
Wharton, Edith, 208
White House: economists in, 56; investigations unit, 20; reporters, 29; tapes, 26, 27, 28; transcripts, 28, 29; Watergate cover-up by, 21, 22, 24
Whittier College, 12
Wicker, Tom, 29
Wildavsky, Aaron, 57
Will, George, 224
Wills, Gary, 15
Wilson, Earl, 194
Wilson, Flip, 203
Wilson, Woodrow, 73, 98, 104, 166
Winkler, Henry, 210

Winters, Jonathan, 194
Wirth, Tim, 93
Wolfe, Tom, 5, 158, 159, 161, 163, 168, 232
women: advertising and, 138; as convention delegates, 18; divorce and, 160; education rights of, 140–41, 230–31; intercollegiate sports for, 135, 137, 141; in labor force, 7, 67–68, 142, 232; medicine and, 8, 145, 146; sexual liberation of, 149; social transformation and, 5, 68, 133, 138–39, 144. *See also* feminists; NOW
women's rights, 7, 133, 137–48, 157, 232. *See also* lesbianism
Wonderful World of Disney (television program), 201
Wood, Robert, 205
Woodruff, Judy, 106
Woods, Rose Mary, 27
Woodward, Bob, 21, 22, 29, 102, 217
World Series, 211
World Table Tennis Championships, 40
World War II, 1, 29, 33, 36; Japanese economy after, 164; movies about, 181; press and, 34. *See also* postwar era

Yergin, Daniel, 63
YMCA (Young Men's Christian Association), 141
Yorty, Sam, 17
Young Men's Christian Association. *See* YMCA
Young, Robert, 185
Youngman, Henny, 201
Youngstown, Ohio, steel industry in, 121–23, 164
Youngstown Sheet and Tube, 122, 123

zero-sum society, 163, 170, 173
Zhou Enlai, 40, 41
Zumwalt, Admiral Elmo, 76